ADVANCE
HOCKEY 365, Th

If hockey history and great stories are you. ...ommito's second volume of *Hockey 365* is most definitely for you.

— TSN's BOB MCKENZIE

What caught me was the blend of knowledge and history.... Whether you're a hockey lifer or a fringe fan, this book provides a great account of many of the games' defining moments and experiences.

DARREN DREGER, TSN's hockey insider

Hockey's version of an advent calendar, with a treat of a story for every day of the year.

— JAMES DUTHIE, TSN, and author of *Beauties*

An entertaining and captivating book that shares hockey stories from both the men's and women's game.

— CASSIE CAMPBELL-PASCALL, captain of two gold medal Olympic hockey teams and *Hockey Night in Canada* broadcaster

Hockey 365, The Second Period is like a daily supplement of hockey vitamins.... It rekindles old memories and uncovers forgotten folklore.

— CHRIS CUTHBERT, commentator, Sportsnet and *Hockey Night in Canada*

From events in hockey history that most fans remember to the moments that may have otherwise gone forgotten, Mike's book has something for everyone.

— TARA SLONE, co-host of *Rogers Hometown Hockey* and host of *Top Of [Her] Game*

Whether you've been studying the game since you were in the crease or you're just getting into the sport now, this book is bound to teach you some things and remind you why you love hockey.

— KELLY HRUDEY, former NHL goaltender and analyst for Sportsnet and *Hockey Night in Canada*

Hockey 365 is a hockey fan's treat. Mike Commito shares so many good stories that will grow your love for the game.

— DAVID AMBER, host of *Hockey Night in Canada*

Like a square on a quilt, each story can bring you back to moments of joy shared with those close to you. Whether it be family, friends, or the shared allegiance of fandom, like a quilt, this book will warm your heart.

— CRAIG BUTTON, TSN analyst and scout

The ultimate fan's daily inspirational devotional. Start each morning right with a quick, cool, or unusual hockey fact — it will set the path for a fantastic day, no matter what time of year.

— FRANK SERAVALLI, hockey insider

For the hockey fan in your life, *Hockey 365* has everything.... It was fun to relive so many hockey moments, a new one each day, some famous and some infamous. A thoroughly entertaining read.

— CHRISTINE SIMPSON, rinkside and features reporter
for Sportsnet and *Hockey Night in Canada*

Mike proves that the game never stops. You'll learn new stories and be brought back to familiar ones that made you fall in love with hockey in the first place.

— KEN REID, co-host of *Sportsnet Central* and bestselling author

Hockey 365, The Second Period is the perfect mix of storytelling and history of the game. Mike is a master of weaving them together, and every day I learn something new from him about the game we love.

— JAMIE MCLENNAN, former NHL goaltender, TSN hockey analyst,
and co-host of *OverDrive* on TSN 1050 Toronto

Evokes the best type of nostalgia for any hockey fan. It is an honour to have my "Bonino, Bonino, Bonino" call from *Hockey Night in Canada in Punjabi* represented amidst so many other great memories and stories of the game.

— HARNARAYAN SINGH, commentator for *Hockey Night in Canada in
Punjabi*, Sportsnet, and bestselling author of *One Game at a Time*

Endlessly fascinating. Despite how much I learned, I actually feel dumber for not knowing how much I didn't know.

— JUSTIN BOURNE, co-host of *Hockey Central* on
Sportsnet 590 The Fan and writer, Sportsnet

For those who read Mike's first book you are going to love this one just as much. For those who didn't, here is your opportunity to catch up. For hockey fans it is a fun read to see what each day brought historically in this great game.... A great, fun, enjoyable read for hockey fans of all ages.

— GORD STELLICK, former Toronto Maple Leafs GM and Sportsnet analyst

From recent stories to historical ones, a great trip through history to discuss daily with not only your hockey friends but all sports fans.

— MARTIN BIRON, former NHL goalie and Buffalo Sabres studio analyst

From the amazing to the embarrassing, tear-jerking to hilarious, noble to the bizarre, this game never stops serving up stories. And if you think you know them all, Mike Commito's *Hockey 365* series will remind you that there's always another tale to discover.

— SEAN MCINDOE, the Athletic

Chock full of fun and fascinating stories about hockey that informs and entertains readers. Whether it's a well-known fact or a piece of obscure trivia, Commito's prose brings the events of the past to life and makes you want to jump a day ahead to see what happened tomorrow.

— REAR ADMIRAL, co-host of the *Spittin' Chiclets* podcast and writer for Barstool Sports

A fun tour through hockey history. Well-researched, original, and filled with a ton of entertaining anecdotes — this book is a wonderful reminder of why we love this game.

— EMILY KAPLAN, National NHL reporter, ESPN

I loved Mike's book. It's perfect for random fact and trivia nerds like us. Pick it up for five minutes: you'll either learn ten new things or get a healthy dose of nostalgia, or both.

— ARDA ÖCAL, ESPN host and voice of the NHL Gaming World Championship

Mike Commito also could be nicknamed "Mike Committed," as his work has proven. His research is both impeccable and impressive.

— STAN FISCHLER, Emmy Award–winning hockey journalist and publisher and author of the *Fischler Report*

Mike's curiosity, superb research skills, and attention to the finest details highlight some of the great, well-known moments in hockey and some of the fascinating offbeat events, too.

— DAVE STUBBS, columnist, NHL.com

Once again, Mike Commito combines his vast knowledge and passion for hockey history in an unparalleled collection of the game's best stories.... An addictive read, filled with fascinating details about the moments and legends that captivate us.

— DAN ROBSON, senior enterprise writer for the Athletic and author of *Measuring Up*

Light and fun, but somehow still packed with trivia from every era of the game. A perfect one-a-day or in-one-sitting read. You won't even realize you're learning!

— RYAN LAMBERT, NHL columnist, EP Rinkside, and co-host of the *Puck Soup* podcast

Perfect as an introduction to sport if you're a new fan or an old-timer nostalgic for the old days, or simply into history ...Written as a story-a-day per page, it can be enjoyed over a few sittings, or over 365 days.

— KEVIN MCGRAN, sports reporter, *Toronto Star*

A friendly warning for hockey lovers — *Hockey 365, The Second Period* is seriously addictive. Once you start reading, the hardest part will be stopping.

— LISA DILLMAN, senior writer, the Athletic

The game of hockey is built on passion, not just the passion of its players and coaches but on the passion of people like Mike Commito, and that is revealed in every page in this fun and informative book.

— SCOTT BURNSIDE, national writer, the Athletic

Fun primer on hockey history, presented in 365 easy-to-digest nuggets; something that will appeal to hockey fans young and old, experienced or raw newcomers.

— ERIC DUHATSCHEK, senior writer, the Athletic

Mike Commito has done it again. The author pinballs through hockey history, scooping up the intriguing, easy-to-digest tales from both the ice and the boardrooms. Commito's rich knowledge of and deep love for the game seeps through in his daily flashbacks.

— LUKE FOX, NHL writer, Sportsnet

This book is a must-read for hockey history fans … so many facts and figures so well-researched and explained.

— SCOTTY BOWMAN, winningest coach in NHL history

This is such a great way to remember some amazing hockey history. Looking at the entry about my trade to the Leafs brought me right back to that exact moment.… A must read for anyone who loves hockey.

— DOUG GILMOUR, former NHL player and Hockey Hall of Fame inductee

Great read on hockey history that will spark your love of the game and the players who helped grow it.

— MANON RHÉAUME, first and only woman to play in the NHL

If you are a hockey fan, you have to read this book. I was blown away by all of the great stories, stats, and hockey news that I didn't know.… I've read a lot of hockey books and this one kept me engaged the whole time. Good for all ages!

— JOHN SCOTT, former NHL player and 2016 NHL All-Star Game MVP

This book is a must for hockey traditionalists and new fans alike. It is an interesting look at the game through the eyes of an experienced hockey historian, and his passion pays off in the writing. I read it twice … so far!

— TERRY RYAN, former NHL player and author of *Tales of a First-Round Nothing: My Life as an NHL Footnote*

A great framework here — the daily hockey story — for peculiar, dramatic, near-forgotten, outrageous, and heroic narratives that have sailed with the game's sea of history.

— DAVE BIDINI, Rheostatics, and author of *Tropic of Hockey*

Take a trip through the colourful history of the NHL with this thoroughly enjoyable book. Mike makes the journey a fun ride by presenting facts and figures in easily digestible bits. Highly recommended!

— MICK KERN, SiriusXM NHL Network Radio

The only thing better than *Hockey 365* is a follow-up edition called *Hockey 365, The Second Period*.… Commito gets full credit for this edition, in particular providing content about the contributions of black and women players.

— PERRY LEFKO, co-author of *Beating the Odds in Hockey and in Life* and *Undrafted*

HOCKEY 365, THE SECOND PERIOD

MIKE COMMITO

HOCKEY
365

THE SECOND PERIOD:
MORE DAILY STORIES FROM THE ICE

DUNDURN
PRESS

Publisher: Scott Fraser | Acquiring editor: Kathryn Lane | Editor: Michael Carroll
Cover designer: Ron Beltrame | Interior designer: Laura Boyle
Printer: Marquis Book Printing Inc.

Library and Archives Canada Cataloguing in Publication

Title: Hockey 365, the second period : more daily stories from the ice / Mike Commito.
Other titles: Hockey three sixty-five, the second period | Hockey three hundred sixty-five, the second period
Names: Commito, Mike, author.
Identifiers: Canadiana (print) 20210224460 | Canadiana (ebook) 20210224479 | ISBN 9781459748446 (softcover) | ISBN 9781459748453 (PDF) | ISBN 9781459748460 (EPUB)
Subjects: LCSH: National Hockey League—Anecdotes. | LCSH: Hockey players—Anecdotes. | LCSH: Hockey— Anecdotes. | LCSH: National Hockey League—Miscellanea. | LCSH: Hockey players—Miscellanea. | LCSH: Hockey—Miscellanea.
Classification: LCC GV847 C633 2021 | DDC 796.962/6402—dc23

We acknowledge the support of the Canada Council for the Arts and the Ontario Arts Council for our publishing program. We also acknowledge the financial support of the Government of Ontario, through the Ontario Book Publishing Tax Credit and Ontario Creates, and the Government of Canada.

Care has been taken to trace the ownership of copyright material used in this book. The author and the publisher welcome any information enabling them to rectify any references or credits in subsequent editions.

The publisher is not responsible for websites or their content unless they are owned by the publisher.

Printed and bound in Canada.

Dundurn Press
1382 Queen Street East
Toronto, Ontario, Canada M4L 1C9
dundurn.com, @dundurnpress 🐦 f 📷

For Zoe and Sophia

AUTHOR'S NOTE

Over the years, some National Hockey League teams have changed the way their names are stylized. Prior to the 1986–87 season, Chicago spelled Blackhawks as two words; before the 2006–07 campaign, the Anaheim Ducks were known as the Mighty Ducks of Anaheim, a homage to the Disney movie that inspired their name; and before the summer of 2014, the Arizona Coyotes were known as the Phoenix Coyotes. I've tried to reflect that in the stories throughout the book. So, in a 1960 story about Chicago, the team is referred to as the Black Hawks, but when writing about the club's Stanley Cup victory in 2015, they're the Blackhawks.

Of course, there are also plenty of examples of other clubs relocating to different cities and changing their names, such as when the Quebec Nordiques moved to Denver in 1995 and became the Colorado Avalanche. In those cases, when writing about where the franchise ended up, I've always tried to provide some context as to where the team originated.

You'll also discover that just like the first *Hockey 365*, there's no index in this book. I did that on purpose in the hope you'll read every page rather than hop to the moments involving your favourite team or player.

PRE-GAME SKATE

Hockey 365 started out as an idea on a beach in the Mayan Riviera in early 2017. A few months earlier I finally started getting paid gigs to write about hockey history for mainstream media outlets and had also committed to transitioning my Twitter account, which was gaining a modest following, into a daily emporium of hockey history facts and tidbits. I'd begun building up a neat little portfolio and wondered if I could take the formula that appeared to be working on social media and combine it with some of the writing I was already doing.

Although I'd always loved hockey, even though I never graduated beyond playing on our backyard rink, and had long been fascinated by history, I'd never thought about putting the two together. I knew hockey history existed as a field of study; I just never pictured myself in it. When I studied history, I ventured into the realm of environmental history, researching and writing about topics that included forest fires and black bear hunting, all the while seemingly oblivious that hockey history could be a viable pursuit for me.

Once I discovered I could take the skills I was developing as a burgeoning historian and apply them to the sport I loved, I dedicated every spare moment I had to carving out a place for myself in the hockey world. By the time I arrived on that lounging chair in Mexico, I'd been writing about hockey history for a couple of years on a variety of websites, often for free or sometimes in exchange for T-shirts, when I realized the next step in my evolution was to write a book. I was actually under contract at that time with a university press to publish my dissertation about the history of black bear hunting and management in Ontario, but after spending the better parts of five years researching that topic, I couldn't bring myself, no matter how hard I tried, to revise my thesis to get it manuscript-ready.

Instead, as I read through the pages of Val James's memoir, *Black Ice*, about his experience becoming the National Hockey League's first Black American player, I knew I wanted to write a hockey book and didn't want to wait until I finished the other project I had on the go.

As I stared out at the ocean, I took a swig of my *cerveza* and quickly realized what my hockey book would be about: 365 hockey history stories, one for every day of the year. It would be similar to a word-of-the-day calendar, but because it was a book, I'd have the opportunity to go into more detail.

On the flight home, I started putting together an outline. When I arrived back in Sudbury, I devoted myself to figuring out how I'd turn my book idea into reality. One of the first things I did was email the university press to let it know I could no longer continue with the book. The publisher was quite understanding and wished me well. I might still pursue that book one day, but then, all I could think about was hockey history.

After finding a literary agent, I eventually landed an agreement with Dundurn Press, and *Hockey 365* was born. Over the next six months, I hurriedly researched and wrote the manuscript. It was often difficult deciding on what milestone anniversaries to highlight, but I did the best I could to select the most historically significant moments from the game and not get bogged down in my own allegiances. While there was a lot I didn't include in the first book, truthfully, in the back of my mind, I always knew I'd write a second one, so I figured I could just include certain stories in another volume. It actually wasn't that long after *Hockey 365* came out that I stared emailing the publisher when we could get started on the next one. I told them I already had a great addition to the title: *The Second Period*.

Dundurn patiently told me everything sounded great, but we'd have to wait a few years to consider publishing another book. After all, the first one had just hit bookstore shelves and we needed to capitalize on that. The publisher had a point, and I'm obviously glad we waited. I was blown away by the response to the first book and couldn't believe that people I didn't even know were picking up my little hockey history book for themselves or as a gift for their loved ones.

People have often sheepishly told me that *Hockey 365* is the perfect bathroom book, as if that was a bad thing. I definitely had that thought in my mind when I wrote it. Each story is a page, and none of the stories link together explicitly, which makes it the ideal book to pick up and put down. I figured that as long as people were reading it and consuming hockey history, I didn't care where they were doing it. I was just thrilled someone was reading my words, even if it was on the toilet.

But the greatest response I received from the first book was when parents told me their kids loved hockey but weren't really much into reading, but after giving them a copy of my book, they read it cover to cover. That meant the world to me and made me reflect. When I initially went into the writing process, I hadn't really thought of young readers as part of my audience — I just wanted to write about hockey history — but then it struck me that since the stories were short and I tried to write them in a fun, accessible way, it made perfect sense that young readers would be drawn to the book. With that in mind, I take these stories as an opportunity to educate, but *Hockey 365* is by no means meant to be a comprehensive hockey history book. There's plenty I had to leave out, and I hope that reading these pages only spurs you to read more hockey history.

While I knew I'd eventually write this book, I hadn't necessarily planned on writing it when I did. When the Covid-19 pandemic turned the world upside down, I was contributing regularly for the Los Angeles Kings and was still in my role as team historian for the Sudbury Wolves, but with both clubs' seasons on hiatus, I realized I might not have this much time away from my regular hockey-writing commitments so I might as well get started on the next book. At first I didn't say anything to my wife, Chantal. I figured I'd write one page per day and see where that took me. If I was enjoying the process and it didn't seem too daunting, I'd bring her up to speed before I reached out to the publisher to make things official. I got her blessing, though she'll insist I went ahead with it, anyway, and then eventually signed another agreement with Dundurn to bring you *Hockey 365, The Second Period: More Daily Stories from the Ice.*

As challenging as it was sometimes to write a book while working from home, helping out around the house, and being a good father to our four-year-old, Zoe, and newborn, Sophia, who was born the day before things went into lockdown in Ontario, I had a lot of fun writing this book. If you read the first *Hockey 365*, you'll quickly recognize that this book includes 366 new hockey history moments. While a lot of your favourite players and teams are in this volume, I haven't focused on the same event or episode twice. So if you ask yourself, why didn't he include Wayne Gretzky scoring 50 goals in 39 games, it's because I covered that in the first book.

That being said, I've gone off the board quite a bit in this one. For me, hockey history is at its most interesting when we're revelling in some of the more bizarre and quirky episodes, so I've done my best to bring you more of those in this volume. I've also tried to include more stories about women's hockey and players of colour, but I'll acknowledge that as much as this book is called *Hockey 365*, the stories chiefly focus on incidents and players from the NHL, a men's league that has been and remains predominantly white.

When I wrote the first book, I kept myself out of the narrative as much as I could. There was one story, however, about Auston Matthews's four-goal debut in which I included myself because it was the first time my daughter, Zoe, and I watched a Toronto Maple Leafs game together. It was an important moment in hockey history, and for many Toronto fans, it's easy to think back and remember where you were and who you were with when it happened. As much as Ottawa Senators fans always like to remind me that the Maple Leafs didn't win that game, it honestly doesn't matter. Matthews did something unprecedented, and I got to experience that with my daughter, which is what makes hockey history special. So this time around, I've included myself in more of these stories because I know that when you're reading some of these moments, you're doing the exact same thing. You're thinking about where you were that night, who you watched the game with, and how it transports you back to that moment in your life.

My hope is that there's something in this book that speaks to you, whether it's about your beloved team or the favourite player of someone you care about, so sit down, yes, toilets included, and enjoy. *The Second Period* is about to begin.

JANUARY

JANUARY 1
FIRST WINTER CLASSIC, 2008

As snowflakes dusted the ice at Ralph Wilson Stadium, home of the Buffalo Bills, the National Hockey League (NHL) couldn't have scripted a better backdrop for the inaugural Winter Classic, the first regular-season outdoor game played in the United States. Following regulation and five minutes of overtime, the Pittsburgh Penguins and Buffalo Sabres were still deadlocked at 1–1. Despite the drop in temperature and blowing snow, the more than 70,000 people in the crowd were fixated on Sidney Crosby as he approached the puck at centre ice. Crosby, the league's rising superstar, had the opportunity to put the game away with his shootout attempt. In that moment, it was difficult, even for the most ardent cynic, not to be nostalgic about hockey. As the snow sprinkled down, it hearkened back to hockey's roots on frozen ponds where many players experienced the game for the first time. Penguins forward Colby Armstrong, who scored the first goal in the game, later told reporters that it reminded him of his childhood, a sentiment that undoubtedly resonated with fans alike.

Even Crosby, the league's best player, couldn't help but get caught up in the occasion. Growing up in Cole Harbour, Nova Scotia, Crosby played hockey outside a lot, sharpening his skills, and now, on the NHL's biggest stage, it was reminiscent of those childhood memories. As he skated in on Buffalo goaltender Ryan Miller, Crosby skillfully shovelled the puck through snow that had accumulated on the ice. In a last-ditch effort, Miller tried to poke-check him, but Crosby evaded him and put the puck between his pads. As Crosby skated back toward his teammates, he gleefully raised his arms in jubilant celebration. In the years that have passed, the Winter Classic, along with the Heritage Classic and Stadium Series games, has brought the NHL outside. While some have argued that the frequency of these spectacles has made it impossible to recapture the magic from that moment in Buffalo, it's difficult not to get caught up in those games and think back to your own memories of playing hockey on an outdoor rink.

JANUARY 2
LEAFS GET DOUG GILMOUR IN BLOCKBUSTER TRADE, 1992

No one could accuse Toronto Maple Leafs general manager Cliff Fletcher of taking New Year's Day off. The following day, January 2, 1992, Fletcher acquired centre Doug Gilmour from the Calgary Flames as part of a 10-player deal, one of the largest in NHL history. In addition to the playmaking pivot, who scored 91 points with the Flames two seasons earlier, Toronto also received goaltender Rick Wamsley, a pair of defencemen, Jamie Macoun and Ric Nattress, and prospect Kent Manderville. Meanwhile, Calgary got Gary Leeman, who scored 51 goals in the 1989–90 campaign, blueliners Michel Petit and Alexander Godynyuk, hard-nosed winger Craig Berube, and netminder Jeff Reese. While the blockbuster trade shocked the hockey world, it had been in the works for some time. After inking a three-year deal with the Flames in 1989–90, Gilmour became disgruntled with his contract and felt he was worth more than what he had initially signed for. Following arbitration in November 1991, which left neither side satisfied, the writing was on the wall.

Later that month, while on the road in a hotel room in San Jose, Gilmour later recounted in his book, *Killer*, that Flames GM Doug Risebrough, who was in the next room, exclaimed that he was trading him. For Gilmour, that was the moment he realized his time with the Flames was done. The day after Calgary's New Year's Eve game against the Montreal Canadiens, in which he scored a goal and assisted on Paul Ranheim's overtime winner, Gilmour made it clear to Risebrough that he wouldn't be returning to the Flames. Two days later, Gilmour made his Leafs debut, scoring a goal and adding an assist in a 6–4 loss in Detroit. In the final 40 games of the season, Gilmour scored 15 goals and 49 points. The following campaign, his first full season in Toronto, Gilmour scored 127 points, a franchise record that still stands, and began cementing his legacy as one of the greatest players ever to suit up for the Maple Leafs.

JANUARY 3
JAROMÍR JÁGR OLDEST PLAYER TO SCORE HAT TRICK, 2015

Jaromír Jágr scored his first NHL hat trick in a game against the Boston Bruins on February 2, 1991. The Czech rookie had gone nine games without a goal but broke out of his slump with a three-goal performance to power the Penguins to a 6–2 victory. Almost a quarter century later, Jágr, who was still in the NHL after returning in 2011–12 after a three-year sabbatical in the Kontinental Hockey League, scored his 15th career hat trick as a member of the New Jersey Devils. It was his first three-goal effort since he was with the New York Rangers in 2005–06. What made the milestone significant, however, was that Jágr was just over a month shy of his 43rd birthday, making him the oldest player in NHL history to score a hat trick. Jágr was almost a full year older than Gordie Howe, who scored three goals against the Penguins on November 2, 1969, as a 41-year-old. Howe played another season with Detroit before retiring. He hung up his skates for two years and then played in the rival World Hockey Association (WHA) for six years before returning to the NHL as a 51-year-old. Howe didn't score a hat trick that season, but he came close, recording two two-goal performances with the Hartford Whalers in his final campaign.

When Jágr was told after the game he had broken Howe's record, he was surprised and even a little dismayed. "Gordie Howe didn't do it? I was sure he did it," the grizzled veteran told reporters. Jágr divulged that while he was happy to have racked up three goals, bringing his season total up to nine, he didn't like the distinction of being the oldest player in league history to accomplish the feat. The following campaign, his first full season in a Florida Panthers uniform, the greying winger scored 27 goals, which included five two-goal performances, but he never scored another hat trick. Jágr played his final NHL game on December 31, 2017, as a member of the Calgary Flames, just a couple of months shy of his 46th birthday.

JANUARY 4
PUNCH-UP IN PIEŠŤANY, 1987

t was the final game of the 1987 World Juniors and Canada was squaring off in Piešťany, Czechoslovakia, against the Soviet Union, the most penalized team of the tournament that year. A win guaranteed Canada a silver medal, but if it defeated the Soviets by five goals or more, it would claim gold. With fewer than 14 minutes remaining in the second period, Canada was leading 4–2 and had the championship within its sights. But then all hell broke loose. After Everett Sanipass and Sergei Shesterikov collided, the two started fighting, and before long, everyone on the ice was battling. Steve Chiasson was tangled up with Andrei Smirnov, while blueliners Chris Joseph and Dmitri Tsygurov got into it. Elsewhere, Pavel Kostichkin grappled with Theo Fleury and Mike Keane with Valeri Zelepukin. While those skirmishes continued, suddenly a flurry of red and white sweaters came over the boards as the Canadians and Soviets emptied their benches to defend their teammates. The brawling went on for nearly 20 minutes.

Norwegian referee Hons Ronning, who many would argue was out of his depth, was unable to restore order. In a last-ditch effort, officials in the arena turned off the lights. When the fighting finally ended, the International Ice Hockey Federation (IIHF) convened an emergency meeting to determine what to do with both teams. The delegates voted 8–1 to eject both countries, with the lone dissenting voice coming from Canada's representative, Dennis McDonald. As a result, Canada was denied a rightful spot on the podium. When the team returned home, many Canadians believed that the Soviets initiated the brawl on purpose. Harold Ballard, the curmudgeonly owner of the Toronto Maple Leafs, had long been open about his dislike of the Soviet Union and suggested it had engineered the melee because "they've got a lousy team and were scared to go home, finishing in sixth place." Adamant that the Canadians deserved a medal for their efforts, Ballard had special gold medals commissioned for the members of the team.

JOEL QUENNEVILLE GETS FIRST HEAD-COACH GIG, 1997

After a tumultuous few seasons with Mike Keenan as GM and coach, the St. Louis Blues were looking for some stability behind the bench. After Keenan was dismissed from both duties on December 19, 1996, assistant Jimmy Roberts took over as interim head coach. While the club played hard for Roberts, according to star sniper Brett Hull, the players needed a guiding force. When the Blues named Joel Quenneville head coach a few weeks later, that's exactly what they got. Quenneville, a former defenceman who had logged more than 800 NHL games and been an assistant coach with the Colorado Avalanche for the past three seasons, winning the Stanley Cup in 1996, would bring structure to the Blues' game. "I want to see us on the puck," he later told reporters. "I want to see pressure. We need to be a smarter team with the puck and without the puck." Quenneville made his head-coaching debut two nights later at home, but the Edmonton Oilers spoiled the party, defeating St. Louis 5–2. Two nights later, on the road in San Jose, Quenneville picked up his first victory with the Blues. With just 25 seconds remaining in regulation time, centre Pierre Turgeon scored a goal on the power play to beat the Sharks 4–3. Following the game, Quenneville divulged that while he was still learning the personnel, it felt great to get that first win under his belt.

Over the next eight seasons, Quenneville became the stabilizing force behind the bench that the Blues needed. In 1999–2000, he guided the club to 51 victories, a franchise record, and its first Presidents' Trophy. After Quenneville's tenure in St. Louis ended in 2004, he returned to the Avalanche as head coach, but only stayed a few years before joining the Chicago Blackhawks as a pro scout in 2008. On October 18, 2009, he was promoted to head coach, and later that season, led the Blackhawks to their first Stanley Cup in nearly 50 years. Quenneville won two more championships in Chicago before becoming head coach of the Florida Panthers in 2019.

JANUARY 6

WAYNE GRETZKY RETURNS FROM INJURY, 1993

Wayne Gretzky hadn't played all season. When the superstar left training camp in September to be with his wife, Janet, for the birth of their third child, Trevor, it was discovered that he had a herniated thoracic disc. After going through a rigorous rehabilitation program, Gretzky was back on the ice in early December and was practising with the team later that month. His return couldn't have come at a better time. Despite beginning the 1992–93 campaign without their best player, the Los Angeles Kings managed to open the season 19–7–2 to sit atop the Smythe Division. By January, however, the team hadn't won since December 12 and was in the midst of a 1–7–3 skid. When it was announced that Gretzky would finally make his season debut on January 6, the Kings were abuzz with anticipation.

In his first game back, Gretzky centred wingers Mike Donnelly and Tony Granato. Speaking with reporters in advance of the Kings' game against the Tampa Bay Lightning, Granato said, "Could we use him? Come on, the guy's got over 50 NHL records." Donnelly was a little more blunt in his assessment: "To say that we are a better team without Wayne Gretzky is just plain stupid." As Gretzky skated out onto the ice at the Forum in Inglewood that night, he received a standing ovation from the crowd as they held up WELCOME BACK, WAYNE signs. Playing in his 1,000th career game and his first since April 28, 1992, Gretzky picked up two assists in a 6–3 loss to Tampa Bay. Despite the result, the Kings were much improved with the Great One back on the roster. Following the game, Luc Robitaille, who served as captain in Gretzky's absence, said, "Our team's better now. Wayne's the guy who will help us win the Stanley Cup." His words were almost prophetic. Later that year, Gretzky racked up 40 points in 24 playoff games, leading the Kings to the Stanley Cup Final for the first time in franchise history, but the team came up three wins short of a championship.

JANUARY 7
LUCKY LUC SCORES 500TH CAREER GOAL, 1999

When the Los Angeles Kings drafted Luc Robitaille in the ninth round of the 1984 draft, there was uncertainty about whether he would crack the NHL because of concerns about his skating ability. Robitaille, however, quickly dispelled those concerns when he made his NHL debut two years later, scoring 84 points and winning the Calder Trophy as the league's top rookie. Although the left winger became known as "Lucky Luc" throughout his career, luck had little to do with his success in the NHL. In his first eight campaigns with the Kings, he never scored fewer than 44 goals in a single season. By 1998–99, his second stint with Los Angeles, Robitaille had established himself as one of the best left wingers in league history.

Heading into a game against the Buffalo Sabres on January 7, 1999, Robitaille was just two goals shy of the 500-goal mark. Less than three minutes after the opening faceoff, Robitaille scored a power play goal to give the Kings the lead. As the clock ticked down, it looked as if Robitaille might have to wait for the team's next contest to reach the milestone, but then, with less than two minutes remaining, he took a pass from Pavel Rosa and chipped the puck up and over a sprawling Dwayne Roloson to notch his 500th career goal. Robitaille became the 27th player and just the sixth left winger in NHL history to accomplish the feat. As his teammates mobbed him, the Kings' faithful at the Forum rose to their feet to salute the veteran winger. Following the game, as reporters asked Robitaille and his teammates to reflect on his career, head coach Larry Robinson reiterated to those listening that Robitaille's accomplishment was the result of skill and nothing else. "You don't get 500 goals from being lucky," the bench boss explained. A few nights later, during the first intermission against the Edmonton Oilers, Robitaille received a special trophy from the NHL to commemorate the achievement, which was presented by Kings legend Marcel Dionne, who had assisted on Robitaille's first NHL goal more than a decade earlier.

HOWIE MEEKER SCORES FIVE IN A GAME, 1947

While serving in the Corps of Royal Canadian Engineers during the Second World War, Howie Meeker's legs were shattered when a grenade exploded during a training exercise in England. The blast, which Meeker remembers threw him 12 feet into the air, left him in the hospital for months. Doctors weren't sure if he'd walk again, but by the time he left the infirmary, Meeker was back on his feet and on the ice. Before enlisting, the Stratford, Ontario, native was quite the hockey player, and while stationed in London, he kept up his skating as much as he could. Once he was deployed to the front, just a year after leaving the hospital, Meeker was blown up again. While helping to construct a bridge across the Rhine River, Meeker and his fellow engineers were pinned down by enemy mortar fire. After a shell exploded near him, Meeker was tossed into the river. He was lucky to be alive.

Following his recovery, he returned to Stratford and began playing hockey again with his hometown team, the Indians, in the senior division of the Ontario Hockey Association (OHA). He suited up for seven games during that 1945–46 campaign, but it was enough to catch the eye of the Maple Leafs, who signed him later that year. In his rookie season with Toronto, the twice-wounded veteran turned heads on the ice. On January 8, 1947, he scored five goals in a 10–4 victory against Chicago. Although two of the goals were originally credited to Wally Stanowski, after a conference between players and officials, they were awarded to Meeker. He finished the season with 27 goals and took home the Calder Memorial Trophy as the league's top rookie. Following his hockey career, which included three straight Stanley Cups, Meeker became a Member of Parliament for Waterloo South. After politics, Meeker joined the *Hockey Night in Canada* broadcast, where he revolutionized the role of colour commentator by raising the bar for analysis, speaking his mind, and utilizing a telestrator to illustrate his points.

BRUINS RETIRE BOBBY ORR'S NUMBER, 1979

When the Boston Bruins retired Bobby Orr's number 4 on January 9, 1979, the eight-time Norris Trophy winner was just a few months away from his 31st birthday. Had he not suffered from chronic knee injuries over the course of his brilliant but short career, he might have still been playing hockey that evening when the Bruins took on the Soviet Wings in an exhibition game. When Orr made his debut for the Bruins in 1966, the young defenceman quickly redefined the role of blueliner with his dazzling end-to-end rushes, blistering speed, and nifty playmaking abilities. By his fourth season with the club, 1969–70, Orr rewrote the NHL's record books, racking up 120 points and capping that historic performance with a gravity-defying goal that gave the Bruins their first Stanley Cup in nearly three decades.

Despite Orr's meteoric rise, within five years his career was in jeopardy. With his knees scarred and battered from surgery after surgery, Orr managed just 10 games for the Bruins in the 1975–76 season. The following year, as a member of the Chicago Black Hawks, he suited up for 20 games, but after another procedure, missed the remainder of the season and the entire campaign the next year. Orr attempted a comeback in 1978–79, but his knees betrayed him once again and he was forced to hang up his skates for good after just six appearances. Later that year, he was inducted into the Hockey Hall of Fame, becoming the youngest player in NHL history to get the nod. So when Orr trotted onto the ice to watch his number ascend to the rafters at Boston Garden, becoming just the fifth player in team history to receive the honour, it was a bittersweet moment. He should have been out there with many of his former teammates. As the crowd rose to its feet to give him a standing ovation and a roaring chorus of cheers, Orr fought back tears. "I spent 10 years here in Boston, and they were the best 10 years of my life. I love you all so much." The feeling was mutual.

ALEX OVECHKIN SIGNS 13-YEAR DEAL, 2008

Standing at the podium in a black pinstriped suit, with messy hair and a toothless grin, Alex Ovechkin beamed as he fielded questions from reporters about his new deal with the Washington Capitals. Ovechkin, who scored 52 goals in his rookie season to win the Calder Trophy, had just signed a 13-year, $124-million extension. It wasn't the longest contract in league history — that distinction went to goaltender Rick DiPietro, who inked a 15-year pact with the Islanders two years earlier — but it was the NHL's first nine-digit deal. "Hockey is my life," Ovechkin told the media. "Money is money. If you think about money, you stop playing hockey." While Ovechkin acknowledged there would now be more pressure, he was up for the challenge. Ted Leonsis, the club's owner, admitted the deal wasn't without risk but believed there was no better player to make that type of long-term investment in: "Alex is the cornerstone of our franchise, and I fully believe that he will help us achieve our ultimate goal of being a Stanley Cup team."

Although the Russian sniper's new deal wouldn't begin until the following year, when the season ended a few months later, it already seemed like money well spent. Ovechkin finished the campaign with 65 goals, becoming just the 12th player in league history to score 65 goals or more in a season, and 112 points. For his efforts, Ovechkin was awarded the Ted Lindsay Award and the Art Ross, Rocket Richard, and Hart Trophies, becoming the first NHL player to win all four in a single season. With his contract expired as of this writing, Ovechkin has more than lived up to the lofty expectations. From the 2008–09 to 2020–21 seasons, he scored 567 goals, 128 more than the next closest player, won the Rocket Richard eight more times, and added two more Ted Lindsay Awards and Hart Trophies to his collection. Most importantly, in 2018, Ovechkin did what Leonsis hoped he would when he signed him to the mammoth contract 10 years earlier: led the Capitals to their first Stanley Cup in franchise history.

JANUARY 11
FLYERS DEFEAT SOVIET CENTRAL RED ARMY, 1976

The Soviets were incensed. Although they were only less than nine minutes into their exhibition game against the Philadelphia Flyers, they had acutely felt the brute force of the team that had come by its nickname "The Broad Street Bullies" quite honestly. After defenceman Ed Van Impe charged out of the penalty box, he skated toward Valeri Kharlamov and struck the Russian blueliner in the head. Kharlamov fell to the ice. Soviet head coach Konstantin Loktev was furious and called his players to the bench while he demanded a conference with the officials. After some deliberation, instead of giving the Soviets a power play for Van Impe's hit, referee Lloyd Gilmour actually handed the Red Army a bench minor penalty for delay of game. That was the last straw for Loktev. He ordered his team off the ice. As the Soviets retreated to the dressing room, announcer Bob Cole famously proclaimed, "They're going home!"

Discussing their concerns with NHL officials, the Soviets reportedly said they didn't want to be a part of a boxing match. They said they would continue playing hockey but argued that fighting wasn't part of the game. After nearly 15 minutes, the Soviets agreed to return and the game resumed. Less than a minute after the puck was dropped, Reggie Leach scored to give the Flyers a 1–0 lead. As the game wore on, Philadelphia limited the Soviets to just 13 shots while unleashing 49 shots on goaltender Vladislav Tretiak, who played brilliantly, to win the game 4–1. Following the game, Flyers winger Gary Dornhoefer praised Tretiak's play. "If it wasn't for Tretiak, I think we'd have hit double figures," he told reporters. Coach Loktev, on the other hand, had some choice words for the Flyers: "We never play such animal hockey." Captain Bobby Clarke offered a rebuttal to the Soviet bench boss: "We have been called a lot worse things. This wasn't one of our rough games."

JANUARY 12

MONTREAL TRADES CAMMALLERI IN MIDDLE OF GAME, 2012

Mike Cammalleri's days in Montreal were numbered, but most people figured he'd at least make it through his next game. Following a practice on January 11, 2012, the winger, who had grown increasingly dissatisfied with his cellar-dwelling Canadiens, made his frustrations clear when he spoke to reporters. "I can't accept that we will display a losing attitude as we're doing this year. We prepare for our games like losers. We play like losers. So it's no wonder why we lose." But the next day, in the middle of a game against the Boston Bruins, head coach Randy Cunneyworth pulled Cammalleri aside during the second intermission and informed him his services were no longer needed. The Canadiens had traded him, along with goaltender Karri Rämö and a 2012 fifth-round pick, to the Calgary Flames in exchange for Rene Bourque, prospect Patrick Holland, and a second-round pick the following year. While Cammalleri's former teammates continued in what would end up as a losing effort yet again, he had hopped into a cab and prepared to make his way out west to join his new club. After the game, Montreal general manager Pierre Gauthier said it was difficult to pull the disgruntled winger but that it was the right thing to do.

Although getting traded mid-game was a first for Cammalleri, Calgary was familiar territory. He had played for the Flames in the 2008–09 season, racking up 39 goals and 82 points, both career highs, before signing with the Canadiens in the off-season. In his first game back with Calgary, on January 14, Cammalleri scored his 10th goal of the season in a 4–1 loss to the Los Angeles Kings, the team that had drafted him 49th overall in 2001 before trading him to the Flames in 2008. Cammalleri finished the season in Calgary with 11 goals. The following year, in a lockout-shortened campaign, he scored 32 points in 44 games. After another season with the Flames, which saw Cammalleri reach the 500-point mark, he left for free agency, signing a five-year, $25-million deal with the New Jersey Devils in 2014.

JANUARY 13
TRIPLE CROWN LINE FORMED, 1979

They clicked right away. On January 13, 1979, in a game against the Detroit Red Wings, the Los Angeles Kings' Marcel Dionne, Dave Taylor, and Charlie Simmer played together on a line for the first time. Taylor, a two-way player skilled on both sides of the puck, had been flanking Dionne, the club's star centre, for more than a season, but Simmer had just been called up a couple of days earlier from the Kings' American Hockey League (AHL) affiliate, the Springfield Indians, where he'd been one of the team's leading scorers. In that game against Detroit, Dionne's former team, the diminutive pivot scored four goals, while Taylor potted one of his own and Simmer picked up an assist. Soon enough, the Kings trio became known, fittingly, as the Triple Crown Line, developing into one of the most prolific units in NHL history. During Los Angeles's final 38 games of the season, Simmer notched 48 points, Taylor picked up 42, and Dionne racked up an astonishing 69.

By the 1980–81 campaign, the Triple Crown Line was dominating the NHL and had combined for 328 points. At the end of that season, Simmer had 56 goals and 105 points, Taylor had 47 goals and 105 points, and Dionne had 58 goals and 135 points, marking the first time in league history that a line had each player score 100 points or more in a single season. Dionne was unquestionably the line's most talented player, but few players relished going into the corners more than Taylor, who would dig the puck out and get it to his star centre. While Taylor applied himself on the forecheck, Simmer drove to the net. As a big winger, Simmer was difficult to control in the crease and had a knack for getting his stick on pucks for deflections and rebounds, which earned him back-to-back 56-goal seasons. The Triple Crown Line stayed together, feasting on opponents across the league, until Simmer was traded to the Boston Bruins on October 24, 1984.

JANUARY 14

CLEGHORN BROTHERS EACH SCORE FOUR GOALS, 1922

After starting their professional careers with the Montreal Wanderers of the National Hockey Association, the Cleghorn brothers, Sprague and Odie, found themselves on opposite teams when they each made the jump to the NHL in 1918. For the next three seasons, older brother Sprague, who had a well-earned reputation as one of the dirtiest players in hockey, patrolled the blue line for the Ottawa Senators and Toronto St. Pats, while Odie played right wing for the Montreal Canadiens. Following the 1920–21 season, Sprague's rights were transferred to the Hamilton Tigers, but he refused to report to Steeltown. Instead, before ever suiting up in a game for the Tigers, he was traded to the Canadiens and was reunited with Odie.

On January 14, 1922, the brothers each had one of the best games of their careers. Four minutes into the matchup, Sprague opened the scoring against the team he'd spurned, and just over a minute later, Odie added a goal of his own, assisted by his older brother, to give the Canadiens a 2–0 lead over the Tigers. Less than a minute into the second period, Sprague found the back of the net, and five minutes later, he completed the hat trick. Before the frame came to a close, Odie picked up his second of the night. The Canadiens held a 7–3 lead heading into the final stanza, but the Cleghorn brothers weren't done yet. Sprague, who managed to remain penalty-free, scored again 30 seconds into the period. Less than seven minutes later, he set up Odie for his sixth career hat trick. After Joe Malone potted a goal to close the deficit to five for Hamilton, Odie lit the lamp again for his fourth of the game, marking the first time in NHL history that a pair of brothers on the same team each scored four goals in the same game. And they almost pulled it off again in their very next match. Odie scored four goals against Ottawa, but Sprague, who never scored another hat trick in the NHL, was held to two goals and an assist that night.

CAPITALS REPLACE HEAD COACH WITH HIS BROTHER, 1990

t surely made for an awkward conversation at the next family dinner. On January 15, 1990, the Washington Capitals fired head coach Bryan Murray, who had been behind the bench for more than eight years, and hired his younger brother, Terry, to take his place. "I've done a lot of pleasant things in my years with the Capitals," general manager David Poile told reporters. "This is not a very pleasant moment for me." Although Bryan was the only coach in the history of the franchise to guide it into the playoffs, the Capitals had never gotten past the second round. At the time of his dismissal, the team was sputtering. After a series of injuries to key players, Washington lost eight straight games and dropped to the bottom of the Patrick Division. Poile, however, said the firing had little to do with the skid. Rather, he believed the club needed a change because it didn't have the necessary consistency. He hoped Terry could provide that.

Terry had been an assistant coach with the Capitals for six years before becoming the head coach of the club's AHL affiliate, the Baltimore Skipjacks, in 1988. According to Poile, Terry was the only candidate he had considered. While it was a difficult situation for the brothers, Bryan couldn't help but feel happy for his brother, who was getting his first NHL head coaching job. With Terry behind the bench, the Capitals made it to the conference finals, the farthest the team had ever advanced, before coming up short to the Boston Bruins. Meanwhile, Bryan wasn't out of work for very long. In July 1990, the Detroit Red Wings moved GM Jim Devellano up into an executive position and dismissed head coach Jacques Demers, offering both positions to Bryan. Under Terry, the Capitals qualified for the post-season for the next three straight years, but he was dismissed partway through the 1993–94 campaign. In Detroit, Bryan stayed on as Red Wings GM until the end of the 1993–94 season. In 1998, as general manager of the Florida Panthers, Bryan named Terry as the club's new head coach.

ALEX OVECHKIN SCORES "THE GOAL," 2006

Whenever Alex Ovechkin decides to hang up his skates, he'll retire as the greatest goal scorer in NHL history. Even if he doesn't match Wayne Gretzky's record of 894 career goals, there has been no other player who has filled the back of the net quite like Ovechkin. While he's already scored more than 700 career goals, just the eighth player in league history to reach that milestone, there's one goal in that bunch that's been indelibly inked into the minds of hockey fans. On January 16, 2006, Ovechkin scored "The Goal" that has defined his career. With just over eight minutes remaining in a game against the Phoenix Coyotes, the Capitals were handily leading 5–1. Ovechkin, who was in his rookie season, picked up the puck at centre ice and was speeding toward the net down the right side with a full head of steam. As he cut to the middle and tried to toe-drag around Coyotes defenceman Paul Mara, Ovechkin fell down. Although he was sprawled on the ice, he still maintained control of the puck as he slid toward the net. Somehow, while rolling from his back to his chest, with his stick above his head, he managed to direct the puck into the net. Goaltender Brian Boucher, who had left his crease to initially stop Ovechkin's advance, was in disbelief.

Ovechkin got up from the end boards and celebrated the improbable goal, but it was still hard to make sense of what had just happened. As the replay was shown over the big screen in the arena, the players craned their necks to make sense of it. Wayne Gretzky, who was the Coyotes' head coach at the time, stared incredulously at the replay. Following the game, despite his club's 6–1 loss, Gretzky acknowledged that Ovechkin's goal was pretty sweet. In speaking with reporters, the Russian superstar was more definitive in his assessment: "The best goal I ever scored." Although it was just his 32nd goal in the NHL, it's the one everybody remembers. More than 15 years and over 700 goals later, Ovechkin's pronouncement still holds true.

JANUARY 17

ALEXANDRE DAIGLE TRADED TO FLYERS, 1998

Less than five years after infamously uttering, "I'm glad I got drafted first because no one remembers number two," Alexandre Daigle was with a new club. Drafted first overall by the Ottawa Senators in 1993, Daigle immediately signed a lucrative five-year, $12.25-million deal, making him one of the highest-paid players in the NHL. In his rookie year, Daigle scored a respectable 20 goals and 51 points, but by his second season, his production had dropped, and by his third year, an injury-shortened campaign, he scored just 17 points in 50 games. By the time he entered his fifth season, although he was just 22 years old, trade speculation was already swirling around Daigle. It was clear he wasn't going to develop into the franchise player the Senators had anticipated. After four and a half seasons and just 74 goals, Ottawa traded Daigle to the Philadelphia Flyers for Pat Falloon, another high draft pick who hadn't lived up to expectations, Václav Prospal, and a second-round pick in 1998.

Although Daigle had clearly underachieved in Ottawa, the Flyers believed they were getting a versatile and speedy forward who could help them break out of the zone. "Daigle is one of the best skaters in the league," Flyers GM Bobby Clarke told reporters after the trade. "Plus, he's young. He's got a tremendous upside." Early into his tenure in Philadelphia, playing on a line with Chris Gratton and John LeClair, Daigle got 14 points in his first 18 games. It looked as if Clarke's hunch was paying off. The following season, however, Daigle struggled again, and it became apparent he wouldn't be part of the Flyers' long-term plans. On January 29, 1999, Philadelphia worked out a three-way trade in which Daigle ended up with the Tampa Bay Lightning after the Flyers initially sent him to the Edmonton Oilers for Andrei Kovalenko. Following stopovers with the New York Rangers and Pittsburgh Penguins, along with a couple of stints in the minors, Daigle joined the Minnesota Wild for the 2003–04 season and recorded 20 goals and 51 points, his best performance since his rookie campaign in Ottawa.

WILLIE O'REE BECOMES NHL'S FIRST BLACK PLAYER, 1958

Willie O'Ree hardly slept on Friday night. That afternoon he had received a call from his coach, Joe Crozier, informing him he would be joining the Boston Bruins for a pair of weekend games against the Montreal Canadiens. O'Ree, who played for the Quebec Aces of the Quebec Hockey League, was getting called up as an emergency replacement for winger Leo Labine. When he skated onto the ice the next day, January 18, 1958, it was a historic moment. O'Ree became the first Black player to suit for an NHL hockey game. Originally from Fredericton, New Brunswick, O'Ree almost didn't make it to the NHL. During his junior hockey days in the Ontario Hockey Association, O'Ree sustained a serious injury that left him blind in one eye. As a result, he not only had to compensate for his limited vision but also had to keep it a secret if he hoped to crack the league's ranks. But now, here he was, on the game's biggest stage. "It was the greatest thrill of my life," O'Ree told reporters. "It's a day I'll never forget as long as I live."

Although O'Ree was a bundle of nerves when the game began, something his teammates unmistakably picked up on, as the matchup wore on, he settled in. In the third period, he nearly scored a goal. "I thought I had [Jacques] Plante beat pretty good but got hooked by defenceman Tom Johnson," O'Ree later explained. He eventually got on an NHL score sheet nearly three years later when he returned to the Bruins for 33 games, scoring a goal against the Montreal Canadiens on New Year's Day 1961. Although briefly in the NHL, O'Ree became an inspiration for other Black hockey players who followed. After hanging up his skates, he's been a tireless advocate for greater diversity and inclusion in the game, serving as the NHL's director of youth development and ambassador for NHL Diversity for more than two decades. On June 26, 2018, O'Ree received his long-overdue call to the Hockey Hall of Fame and was inducted the following November.

EVGENI NABOKOV GETS FIRST CAREER SHUTOUT, 2000

The Colorado Avalanche didn't have much of a scouting report on goaltender Evgeni Nabokov when they faced the San Jose Sharks on January 19, 2000. "I had never heard about him," Peter Forsberg would say after the game. Although the Kazakhstan native entered the contest with relative anonymity, at least among his opponents, they remembered his name by the time the final buzzer sounded. Nabokov, the Shark's ninth-round pick in the 1994 NHL Entry Draft, had been called up from the Cleveland Lumberjacks of the International Hockey League (IHL) a few weeks earlier. He had played in 52 minutes of relief appearances since being recalled but hadn't started a game yet.

In his first start, against the Avalanche, Nabokov was spectacular. Duelling with Patrick Roy at the other end of the ice, the Sharks' netminder turned aside all 39 shots he faced through regulation and overtime. Roy, who was tested less often than his counterpart, stopped all 15 shots he faced in a 0–0 tie, just the third scoreless game for the Sharks since entering the league in 1991. While the veteran earned his 47th career shutout, Nabokov notched his first. "I never could imagine that this was my first NHL game and I would get a shutout," Nabokov told reporters after the game. "I was hoping and guessing I could play in the NHL, so I guess my dream came true."

The following season, Nabokov received more opportunities. After San Jose starter Steve Shields was sidelined early in the campaign with an ankle injury, Nabokov took the reins. In his first 15 starts, he picked up 10 victories, turning aside 371 of the 399 shots he faced. Nabokov continued playing so well that even after Shields recovered from his injury, he couldn't crack the lineup and supplant the hot rookie. Nabokov finished the season with 66 appearances, racking up 32 wins and a .915 save percentage. For his efforts, Nabokov won the Calder Trophy as the league's top rookie, becoming the first goaltender to win the award since Martin Brodeur in 1994.

PATRICK ROY PLAYS 1,000TH
CAREER GAME, 2003

Patrick Roy was drawn to goaltending because of the equipment. As a youngster growing up in Quebec City, Roy fashioned makeshift pads by strapping pillows to his legs with belts and practising in the upstairs of his parents' house. Although he wasn't wearing the right equipment, in those moments, he imagined he was Rogie Vachon, one of his goaltending heroes. Eventually, Roy traded in his pillows for proper pads and continued daydreaming of a future in the NHL. Just over a decade after he first started turning away shots with cushions strapped tightly to his legs, Roy achieved his hockey dream. He made his debut with the Montreal Canadiens in 1985 and quickly established himself as one of the best goaltenders in the league, winning three Vezina Trophies, two Stanley Cups, and two Conn Smythe Trophies in Montreal.

After he was traded to the Avalanche in 1996, he continued his dominance in Colorado. By the 2002–03 campaign, his 18th in the NHL, Roy had added another two Stanley Cups and a third Conn Smythe to his trophy collection and was on the cusp of making league history. On January 20, 2003, Roy appeared in his 1,000th career game, becoming the first NHL goaltender to reach that milestone. In a pre-game ceremony, Roy received a silver stick from none other than his boyhood idol, Vachon, on behalf of the Avalanche. Even in his wildest dreams, Roy couldn't have scripted the moment any better. "At the beginning of my career, I never thought this would be possible," he acknowledged. Although he didn't get the win that night, Roy made 29 saves in a 1–1 tie against the Dallas Stars. He added another 29 regular-season appearances down the stretch before retiring in the off-season. When he hung up his goalie pads, Roy held league records for most victories (551) and games played (1,029) among goaltenders. Although these benchmarks were later surpassed by Martin Brodeur, Roy remains one of the greatest goaltenders in NHL history.

MARIO LEMIEUX SCORES FOUR IN ALL-STAR GAME, 1990

Just 21 seconds into the All-Star Game at Civic Arena in Pittsburgh, Mario Lemieux scored to give the Wales Conference a 1–0 lead. The Penguins' faithful who filled the rink gave their captain a roaring ovation. He scored another 13 minutes later after he blasted a shot through the legs of defenceman Al MacInnis and right past Campbell Conference goaltender Mike Vernon. With less than three minutes remaining in the opening frame, he completed a hat trick, recording the first-ever, first-period three-goal performance in All-Star Game history. As Lemieux skated toward the net, Campbell blueliner Al Iafrate attempted to cut him off, but the Penguins' superstar easily evaded the check and pulled the puck away while Iafrate fell to the ice. As Vernon charged out of his crease to halt the advance, Lemieux went around him, put the puck on his backhand, and flipped it into the net. After a quiet second period, Lemieux was back on the score sheet in the final frame. Just over a minute into the third, Lemieux stripped the puck from Jari Kurri deep in the Campbell zone and fooled netminder Kirk McLean, who had replaced Vernon in the second period, with an unsuspecting wrist shot. Lemieux's fourth tied Wayne Gretzky's record for most goals in an All-Star Game and gave the Wales a 10–4 lead, marking the first time in All-Star Game history that a team reached double-digit goals.

Following the game, which the Wales won 12–7, Lemieux was named most valuable player, becoming the first three-time All-Star MVP in league history, an impressive feat considering it was just his fifth appearance. In addition to bragging rights, Lemieux was given a Dodge Daytona. Vernon, making his case for the new wheels, laughed about how it was the second time Lemieux had scored a hat trick on him and won the MVP award. "So you'd think he'd throw something my way, you know?" he said, chuckling. Instead, Lemieux joked that since it was his third All-Star Game vehicle, he'd have his two brothers flip a coin for the keys to the Daytona.

JANUARY 22
ISLANDERS CLAIM EVGENI NABOKOV, 2011

B y now you should be familiar with Evgeni Nabokov, whose NHL debut was covered a few pages back. After a decade as San Jose's starting netminder, Nabokov was informed the Sharks wouldn't be extending his contract at the conclusion of the 2009–10 season. Instead, Nabokov signed a contract with SKA St. Petersburg and began the following year in the Kontinental Hockey League. Midway through the 2010–11 campaign, Nabokov had his sights on a return to the NHL. On January 20, 2011, he signed a one-year, $570,000 contract with the Stanley Cup–contending Red Wings. The only problem for Nabokov was that since he was playing in a professional league before signing the contract, he had to clear waivers before joining Detroit. As it turned out, two days later, the lowly New York Islanders claimed the veteran goaltender, thwarting his plans.

A disappointed Nabokov couldn't understand why the cellar-dwelling Islanders put in a claim for him. "It's just that I'm at the point in my career where I want to help a team win in the playoffs," he told Pierre Lebrun of ESPN. "I don't see how I could help the Islanders or what I could do for them. It doesn't make a lot of sense to me." As a result, Nabokov informed the Islanders that he had no intention of reporting and the club promptly suspended him. Nabokov sat out the remainder of the campaign but had a change of heart in the off-season. In May, he announced he would report to New York's training camp in September. On October 15, 2011, he made his debut for the Islanders, making 29 saves in a 4–2 win against the crosstown Rangers. In January, in a game against the Buffalo Sabres, Nabokov recorded his 300th career victory, becoming the 26th goaltender in NHL history to reach that milestone. Nabokov played three seasons for the Islanders, helping them earn a playoff berth in 2013 for the first time in five years before signing with the Tampa Bay Lightning as a free agent in 2014, where he played one more campaign before hanging up his goalie pads.

THE "TOILET BOWL," 1989

Hundreds of rolls of toilet paper streamed onto the ice at Le Colisée in Quebec City. Disgruntled with what they believed to be poor officiating, fans were throwing anything they could find to voice their displeasure. They dug into their pockets and hurled coins and cigarette lighters. Some reportedly even tossed their own winter boots. As the debris littered the ice, officials had to halt the game. There was less than 10 minutes remaining, and the Quebec Nordiques were trailing the Hartford Whalers 5–0. Kevin Dineen had just scored his second goal of the game. But what irked the home crowd was that it was the Whalers' third power play goal in 10 opportunities with the man advantage and they felt that referee Kerry Fraser was out to get them.

Nordiques fans had some history with Fraser. In 1987, during the fifth game of the Adams Division Final against the Montreal Canadiens, Fraser had disallowed a third-period goal by Alain Côté that would have given the Nordiques the lead. Instead, Montreal scored to win the game 4–3 and eventually took the series in seven games. Ever since then, Nordiques fans had it in for the referee. Two years later, believing their team was being unfairly penalized, they let him have it. By the time they cleared the ice, the game had been delayed for 20 minutes. Following the matchup, a few Whalers players had some choice words. Captain Ron Francis called it "an embarrassment to the NHL." Dineen, who was born in Quebec City, proclaimed that he renounced his hometown because of the antics. Other Whalers, however, happened to see the humour in the situation. Winger Scott Young, who assisted on Dineen's first goal, wanted to know where the fans were getting all the toilet paper from. "They must have been selling it at the concession stands," he theorized with reporters. Meanwhile, rookie goaltender Peter Sidorkiewicz, who made 27 saves for his second career shutout, was all smiles and joked that the game should have been called the "Toilet Bowl."

JANUARY 24
NEIL SHEEHY WEARS ZERO, 1988

As Neil Sheehy slipped his Hartford Whalers jersey over his head before the club's game on January 24, 1988, he was about to make NHL history. When the hard-nosed defenceman hit the ice for his Whalers debut, he became the first NHL skater to wear zero. Goaltender Paul Bibeault had donned it for the Montreal Canadiens in 1942, but since then it had been mothballed and hadn't been worn outside the crease. While it was a first for the NHL, the single oval digit wasn't anything new for Sheehy. He had actually worn it when he was playing for the Moncton Flames, the Calgary Flames' AHL affiliate, under head coach Terry Crisp. "It was a gimmick," Sheehy later told Michael Farber of the *Montreal Gazette*. "Crisp asked if I would wear it — he's always looking for ways to make the game more colourful — and I said sure."

But when Sheehy adopted zero again after he was acquired by the Whalers on January 3, 1988, he said he had a different motivation. "When my great-grandparents came from Ireland during the potato famine, the family name was O'Sheehy," he explained to Farber. "I was just trying to put the *O* back." While Sheehy got some jeers from opponents for sporting the unusual number, he also drew the ire of the NHL. The league's computers weren't programmed to account for the number. To fix the glitch, they had to spend $3,000 on a software upgrade, which led some of Sheehy's teammates to affectionately refer to him as "The $3,000 Man." Although Sheehy got on the score sheet in his first Whalers game, getting into a dustup with heavyweight Bob Probert, he made history again a few months later when he scored on Bruins goaltender Andy Moog, becoming the first and only player to score a goal with zero across his back. When Sheehy was traded to the Capitals the following off-season, he switched to 15, his old college number. No skater has worn 0 since. By the 1996–97 season, the NHL banned zero and double zero because they befuddled the league's database.

KENDALL COYNE SCHOFIELD MAKES ALL-STAR HISTORY, 2019

Kendall Coyne Schofield rocketed around the rink as if shot out of a cannon. It took her just 14.346 seconds to complete her lap. While her time was impressive, the significance of her circuit was that she was the first woman to compete at the NHL's All-Star Game skills competition. Coyne Schofield, a two-time U.S. Olympic medallist and member of the Minnesota Whitecaps of the National Women's Hockey League, was among a group of female players from American and Canadian teams who had been invited to attend the league's annual All-Star festivities and demonstrate some of the events. But when Colorado Avalanche forward Nathan MacKinnon had to withdraw from the fastest-skater competition due to injury, Coyne Schofield was asked to replace him. Although she was nervous about competing, Coyne Schofield knew how important her participation was and what it would mean for little girls watching from the crowd or at home. "I knew it was a moment that could break a lot of barriers and a moment that would change the perception of our game," she later said.

Coyne Schofield not only captivated the crowd but she also impressed her fellow competitors. Edmonton Oilers captain Connor McDavid, who clocked a time of 13.378 to win the event for the third straight year, was awestruck. "I thought she might have won the way she was moving," he told the media afterward. "She was a really good skater, and that was an amazing thing for the game to see her participate like that in an event like this." Although Coyne Schofield couldn't catch McDavid, she beat out the Arizona Coyotes' Clayton Keller, who finished eighth in the competition with a time of 14.526. "She's really fast," Keller acknowledged. "I was surprised. It was great to see that. It was a great experience for the NHL to have her do that event." The following year, at the 2020 All-Star Game in St. Louis, the NHL built on Coyne Schofield's appearance and showcased further the talent in the women's game by holding the Elite Women's three-on-three game, which featured some of the best players from Canada and the United States.

JANUARY 26
THE GREAT ONE'S BIRTHDAY

When I wrote the first *Hockey 365*, I didn't include birthdays. For me, they aren't necessarily significant. Sure, people grow up and do historic things but that doesn't make the day they were born any more important. So when I set out to write this book, my plan was to omit birthdays yet again. But then I remembered Wayne Gretzky. You could argue that his birthday is worthy of celebration because he grew up to become the greatest hockey player ever to lace up skates, but I decided to include it because he actually did a lot of impressive things on his birthdate.

Gretzky, of course, was born on January 26. When he turned 18 in 1979, he received quite the gift. Playing for the Edmonton Oilers of the WHA, Gretzky signed a 21-year personal services contract with team owner Peter Pocklington. Before a game against the Cincinnati Stingers, he inked the deal at centre ice with his family. The pact, reportedly worth $5 million, was set to make Gretzky an Oiler until 1999. "It looks like I'm here for life," Gretzky said after the game. Gretzky didn't even get halfway through that agreement, but we'll get into that later. Six years after that, on his 24th birthday, Gretzky hit the 50-goal mark in a 6–3 victory against the Pittsburgh Penguins, the third time he reached that milestone in fewer than 50 games. He also added two more goals to notch his 33rd career hat trick, giving him one more than Phil Esposito and Mike Bossy to set a new NHL record.

Another six years later, Gretzky celebrated his birthday with another hat trick. On January 26, 1991, as a member of the Los Angeles Kings, Gretzky recorded his 48th career three-goal performance, along with two assists, in a 5–4 victory against the Vancouver Canucks. Gretzky played four more birthday games in his NHL career. While he didn't record another birthday hat trick, the Great One continued to play well on his birthday. As a 38-year-old in his final birthday game in his last NHL season, he recorded three assists in a 4–1 win.

JANUARY 27

STEVE YZERMAN REACHES 100 POINTS FOR SECOND TIME, 1989

After scoring a goal and adding two assists in an 8–1 rout of the Toronto Maple Leafs to reach the 100-point plateau for the second straight season, Steve Yzerman was surprised to learn he had made Detroit Red Wings history by becoming the first player on the team to record two 100-point seasons. He could have sworn Gordie Howe had done that more than once during his illustrious tenure sporting the winged wheel. Although Howe had scored 95 points in 1952–53, his seventh season in the NHL, it took him another 16 years, during his 23rd campaign in Detroit, before he reached the century mark. He played two more seasons in the Motor City but didn't come close to hitting the milestone again.

Marcel Dionne should have been the first Red Wings player to record multiple 100-point seasons, but by the time he first accomplished the feat in 1974–75, in just his fourth season in Detroit, he had grown so frustrated with the club's losing that he found himself in a new uniform the following season. After landing in Los Angeles, Dionne recorded six 100-point seasons, including five straight, as the linchpin of the Kings' vaunted Triple Crown Line. Following Dionne's departure, winger John Ogrodnick notched 105 points in 1984–85, but after just two more seasons in Detroit, he was off to the Quebec Nordiques as part of a six-player deal.

Ogrodnick's centre that season happened to be Yzerman, who scored 89 points in just his second year with the club. Three years later, Yzerman notched 102 points. The following season, he was on pace to shatter his career high. After the 8–1 victory against Toronto on January 27, 1989, which brings us back to the story in question, he was sitting at 101 points with 30 games left to go. Yzerman didn't disappoint. He finished the campaign with 65 goals, 90 assists, and 155 points, establishing franchise records in all three categories, all of which still stand to this day.

JANUARY 28

WAYNE GRETZKY'S INCREDIBLE STREAK ENDS, 1984

Sixty-one goals and 153 points in 51 games — that's how many points Wayne Gretzky racked up in an incredible 51-game point streak that ended on January 28, 1984. The numbers are almost unfathomable. On their own, they would have made for an impressive season effort, but for Gretzky, who recorded the first 200-point season in NHL history a couple of years earlier, it was business as usual. Following the Edmonton Oilers' home opener against the Toronto Maple Leafs on October 5, 1983, in which Gretzky potted a short-handed goal and added an assist, he just scored game after game. As the streak continued, many wondered if Gretzky could keep it up across the entire 80-game season. It certainly wasn't out of the realm of possibility. After recording a 30-game point streak the previous season to eclipse Guy Lafleur's 28-game run from the 1976–77 campaign and establish a new league record for the longest streak, Gretzky felt there wasn't as much pressure to continue the streak this time around, so he just played loose and the points piled up.

When the Oilers hosted Los Angeles, Gretzky didn't have an answer for the Kings, the same team that had halted his streak the previous season. During the first period, Gretzky lured goaltender Markus Mattsson toward him and then slipped the puck over to defenceman Charlie Huddy on the opposite side. Despite having a wide-open net, Huddy sent the puck wide by a good 20 feet. When the team adjourned to the dressing room for intermission, Gretzky joked with Huddy that the miss might have been the end of the streak. While he was just kidding with his blueliner, it did prove to be Gretzky's best shot at extending his streak. He fired four shots on net but finished the game scoreless in a 4–2 loss to the Kings. After the contest, Gretzky acknowledged that he was disappointed it hadn't gone a little longer but looked forward to starting a new streak. The next season, Gretzky recorded 108 points over a 39-game streak, but even he couldn't break his own unbreakable record.

JANUARY 29
SABRES SNOWED IN, 1977

Although Buffalo was only hit with four inches of fresh snow, it was one of the worst winter storms in decades. Winds gusting up to 69 miles per hour thrashed previously fallen snow off Lake Erie and churned it into the city. Before work let out on Friday evening, the blizzard had already whipped up so much snow that it was impossible to drive, leaving thousands stranded downtown. The streets were dotted with abandoned cars while people sought refuge in office buildings, taverns, and anywhere else they could find shelter. Ben Colker, a National Weather Service meteorologist who had been stationed in Buffalo for nearly four decades, called it "the worst storm I have ever seen."

The following morning, the storm continued while the city dug itself out. Despite the conditions in Buffalo, the Sabres were scheduled to be in Montreal that evening to play the Canadiens. The match wasn't postponed, though several Sabres were snowbound in their homes. While Richard Martin, Jim Lorentz, Brian Spencer, and Lee Fogolin were buried under the avalanche of snow, their teammates trekked to Montreal. The Sabres had their work cut out for them. Not only were they winless in their past four games, scoring a measly six goals, but the Canadiens hadn't lost at home in 18 straight games.

Despite arriving at the Forum just before the puck dropped, and with only 15 players on their bench, the Sabres still managed to make a game of it. Although Montreal led for most of the game, Buffalo limited its opponents to just 19 shots on net. Trailing 3–2 eight minutes into the final frame, defenceman Jim Schoenfeld scored his fifth of the campaign, a career high, to tie the game for good. The club was scheduled to host the Los Angeles Kings the following day, but with Buffalo still snow-swept, the game was postponed. When the Sabres went back on the road a few days later, their snowed-in teammates rejoined them and made an immediate impact. Martin scored two goals and Spencer added a third-period tally in a loss to the New York Islanders.

JANUARY 30
HURRICANES LIMITED TO 10 SHOTS, 1999

"Sometimes a goalie has to win a game," Artūrs Irbe said after a game against the Montreal Canadiens. The Latvian netminder was certainly right about that. In a lopsided matchup against Montreal on January 30, 1999, the Carolina Hurricanes mustered just 10 shots on net while Irbe faced a 45-shot barrage. "The Canadiens were trying to smash us," Irbe told reporters. "It was really hard out there. I did what I could to keep the team in the game." Irbe was, in fact, the only reason the Hurricanes stayed in the game. In the first period, Carolina was outshot 14–2, and Irbe had to make several key saves, including a stop against centre Patrick Poulin who was on a short-handed breakaway, to keep his team afloat. After 40 minutes of regulation time, despite leading 3–0, the Hurricanes were still woefully outshot. Irbe, however, remained perfect until the third period before finally giving up a goal to Martin Rucinsky on a power play.

Meanwhile, the Hurricanes didn't even register a shot on net in the final frame, leaving Irbe to fend for himself. Nevertheless, he continued to play valiantly and stole the game for the Hurricanes, who picked up a 3–1 victory despite setting a franchise record for the fewest shots in a game. Although the Canadiens could only get one by Irbe, it was the first time in nearly 15 years that they denied the opposition a shot in a period. The last time it happened, coincidentally, they were playing the Hartford Whalers, a team that eventually relocated to North Carolina in 1997 to become the Hurricanes. Irbe's heroics were just another example of the resurgence he was having that season. After spending the 1997–98 campaign in Vancouver as a backup on a short leash, Irbe signed with Carolina just two days before training camp opened in September 1998. His one-year, $550,000 deal quickly proved to be a bargain. In his first 34 starts that season, the Latvian dynamo picked up 17 victories, including five shutouts, and usurped the starting job from Trevor Kidd.

JANUARY 31
ALL-STAR MVP JOHN SCOTT, 2016

I t started out as a gag on a popular hockey podcast. With the NHL set to debut a new three-on-three format at the 2016 NHL All-Star Game, Jeff Marek and Greg Wyshynski, hosts of the *Marek vs. Wyshynski* podcast, relished the thought of having veteran enforcer John Scott in the tournament. Scott, a lumbering six-foot-eight pugilist with five career NHL goals on his résumé, didn't exactly fit the bill for the speed and skill the league hoped to showcase in its revamped All-Star Game. It didn't take long before the idea made the rounds in the hockey world. When fan voting opened for the All-Star Game's division captains, fans stuffed the digital ballot boxes with Scott's name. By the time the voting closed, Scott had received more votes than any other player and was headed to the 2016 All-Star Game as the captain of the Pacific Division team. The NHL, however, wasn't pleased.

As Scott later recounted in his book, *A Guy Like Me*, the league tried to talk him out of going. But Scott, who never thought he'd have an opportunity to be an all-star, was adamant about participating. Even after the Arizona Coyotes conveniently traded him to the Montreal Canadiens, moving him out of the Pacific, where he was sent to the minors, Scott still had no plans to skip the game. When he finally arrived at Bridgestone Arena, Scott received the loudest ovation from the Nashville crowd. Although the league didn't want him there, Scott proved to be the highlight of the weekend. In the Pacific Division's semifinal game, he scored two goals, and when his team defeated the Atlantic 1–0 to win the All-Star Game, fans made him a write-in candidate for the most valuable player award. After it was announced that Scott had been named MVP, his teammates hoisted all 260 pounds of him onto their shoulders and lifted him above the ice in celebration. For a player who admittedly never thought in a million years he'd get into an All-Star Game, it was the perfect ending to an unlikely story.

FEBRUARY 1

"DON'T MESS AROUND WITH GORDIE," 1959

Lou Fontinato was one of the most fearsome players in the NHL, but even he learned the hard way that you don't mess with Gordie Howe. In the first period of a game between the New York Rangers and Detroit Red Wings on February 1, 1959, Fontinato, the first player in league history to rack up 200 penalty minutes in a season, felt Howe was picking on New York rookie Eddie Shack and challenged him to fight. Howe accepted, and the two exchanged punches for nearly a minute. Rangers coach Phil Watson called it the greatest fight he'd seen in two decades. Players on both benches were captivated by the ferocity of the tilt. One Red Wings player later likened Howe's punches connecting to the sound of someone chopping wood. When the skirmish mercifully concluded, Fontinato had clearly gotten the worst of it. He skated away bloodied and with a broken nose and dislocated jaw.

Although it was reportedly the fifth time in his hockey career that Fontinato had broken his beak, Howe had left an unmistakable mark on him. According to one report, Fontinato "looked like he ran the 100-yard dash in a 90-yard gym." Fontinato even stated that Howe "kinda rearranged my nose." Although Howe had a well-earned reputation as one of the league's toughest players, he didn't drop the gloves much. But with the way he unleashed his uppercuts, you couldn't tell he was less experienced than his opponent. Although he dislocated one of his fingers and sustained a gash under his left eye that required stitches to close, Howe came away from the battle in one piece. Not long after the brawl, *Life* immortalized it with a photo spread that included a shot of Fontinato's bandaged nose next to a menacing image of Howe. Below both pictures were the words: "Don't mess around with Gordie." With the damage to Fontinato's face laid bare for all to see on the pages of the popular magazine, it appears that NHL players took the message to heart. Howe only fought three more times over his next 13 seasons.

FEBRUARY 2
IAN TURNBULL SCORES FIVE, 1977

Toronto Maple Leafs blueliner Ian Turnbull was all smiles after a game against the Detroit Red Wings on February 2, 1977. Not only had his club thumped its Motor City rivals 9–1, but the 23-year-old rearguard, who was mired in a lengthy goalless drought a couple of weeks earlier, continued to break out of his slump in dynamic fashion. Turnbull lit the lamp five times, establishing a new NHL record for most goals in a game by a defenceman. Perhaps most impressive was that Turnbull needed just five shots to accomplish the feat. Following his milestone evening, Turnbull told reporters, "It was a long drought, although I had just as many chances in the last 30 games and nothing happened. When they go in, you smile. When they don't, you try again."

After a scoreless first period, Turnbull broke the deadlock less than two minutes into the second frame. Taking a pass from Lanny McDonald, he rifled the puck past Red Wings goaltender Eddie Giacomin. After the Maple Leafs added three more goals that period to make it 4–0, Turnbull notched his second of the night on a breakaway. When the game resumed for the final stanza, Giacomin, who had been shellacked for five goals, was replaced mercifully by Jim Rutherford. The change in net did little to alter the outcome of the game. Less than five minutes into the period, Turnbull completed the hat trick for the first time in his NHL career. But he wasn't done just yet. After McDonald made it 7–0 for Toronto, the Red Wings finally got on the board. But just over a minute later Turnbull scored his fourth of the night to restore the seven-goal lead. With less than two minutes remaining in the game, the young blueliner scored again. Not only had Turnbull broken the mark previously set by a defenceman, but that type of output from a defender hadn't been seen for nearly 50 years. The last time it had happened, former Maple Leafs blueliner Hap Day buried four goals in a losing cause against the Pittsburgh Pirates on November 19, 1929. Since Turnbull's heroics, no other NHL defenceman has matched his achievement.

FEBRUARY 3
ALEXANDER MOGILNY SCORES 50, 1993

As Alexander Mogilny arrived at John F. Kennedy International Airport on May 5, 1989, he stunned the hockey world. He was on his way to Buffalo, New York, to join the Sabres, the team that had selected him 89th overall in the 1988 Entry Draft, making him the first Soviet player to defect to North America. A week earlier the 20-year-old winger had helped the Soviet national team capture gold at the World Championship in Sweden. Following the tournament, Mogilny, accompanied by Sabres GM Gerry Meehan and director of amateur evaluation and development Don Luce, boarded a flight in Stockholm to begin his journey to the NHL. Although the Soviet Union was loosening some of its regulations and allowing certain players to pursue careers in North America, such as Sergei Priakin, who was granted permission to join the Calgary Flames in March 1989, a player as young and promising as Mogilny wouldn't have been able to make the jump to the NHL without defecting.

Less than four years after making that fateful decision, Mogilny made hockey history again. With just 28 seconds remaining in a game against the Hartford Whalers on February 3, 1993, Mogilny took a pass from Brad May to net his 50th of the season, becoming the first Russian player to score 50 goals in an NHL campaign. Following the contest, Mogilny was proud of his accomplishment but was already looking ahead to the next milestone. "I feel good about it," he told reporters. "[But] you can't just sit back.... It's time to go to the next level. Go for 60." A few weeks later he did exactly that, scoring his 60th in a game against the Detroit Red Wings. Then, on March 20, 1993, Mogilny potted his 70th of the season, becoming the seventh player in NHL history to accomplish that feat. He finished the season with 76 goals, a Sabres franchise record that still stands. Mogilny's decision to defect wasn't without risk, but it proved to be the right choice. The trailblazer finished his NHL career with 1,032 points in 990 games and should be in the Hall of Fame for his efforts on and off the ice.

FEBRUARY 4
DEVILS ACQUIRE ILYA KOVALCHUK, 2010

After months of negotiations, Ilya Kovalchuk turned down the Atlanta Thrashers' final offer. The Russian sniper, who was drafted first overall by Atlanta in 2001, was set to become an unrestricted free agent at the end of the season and was due for a major raise. Since scoring his first NHL goal in his second career game on October 6, 2001, Kovalchuk had racked up 328 goals with the Thrashers, the most in the league over that span. Hoping to retain their star goal scorer, Atlanta reportedly offered a 12-year contract worth over $100 million, but Kovalchuk declined. With the team unable to ink Kovalchuk to a long-term deal, it informed him he would be traded. The following day, February 4, 2010, Atlanta traded Kovalchuk, along with defenceman Anssi Salmela, to the New Jersey Devils for winger Niclas Bergfors, defenceman Johnny Oduya, centre Patrice Cormier, and a first-round pick in the 2010 Entry Draft. For the Devils, a stingy, defensively minded team not known for goal scoring, Kovalchuk was exactly the player they needed. "We felt Kovalchuk was a player who could come and fill the need that we felt we had for an explosive scorer and someone who could add a different dimension to our power play with that type of shot," New Jersey GM Lou Lamoriello said at a press conference.

In his first game with the Devils, Kovalchuk made an immediate impact. He picked up two assists in a 4–3 victory against the Toronto Maple Leafs, and a week later, recorded his first goal. In 27 games with New Jersey, Kovalchuk notched 10 goals to finish the season with 41, his sixth straight campaign with 40 or more goals. In the off-season, the Devils looked to lock him in. On July 19, 2010, Kovalchuk signed a 17-year, $102-million contract, but the league rejected the deal because it argued the structure circumvented the salary cap. After the NHL Players' Association filed a grievance, an arbitrator was brought in and the Devils and Kovalchuk settled on a revised 15-year deal worth $100 million.

FEBRUARY 5
DAVE TAYLOR SCORES 1,000 POINTS, 1991

The day after Dave Taylor found out the Los Angeles Kings had selected him 210th overall in the 1975 NHL Amateur Draft, he showed up for his next shift at a nickel mine as usual. Taylor, who was from the tiny community of Levack, Ontario, spent his summers working underground. Even while playing hockey for the Golden Knights at Clarkson University in Potsdam, New York, Taylor returned home each summer and took a job in the mine to make money to bring back to school. He was part of the blast crew. At the end of each shift, Taylor and his team were the last to leave the mine. They lit their fuses on the explosives they'd prepared and then carefully make their way to the surface to detonate. When Taylor arrived for work after being drafted, the shift boss asked him, "They didn't give you a wheelbarrow full of money to stay out of the mine?" Taylor replied, "No, I don't think they do that for 15th-round draft choices. I'll be here all summer."

But Taylor defied expectations and proved he wasn't just any 15th rounder. He took his hard-rock work ethic with him back to Clarkson and continued to improve his game. In his final season with the Golden Knights, Taylor really caught the Kings' attention, scoring 108 points in 34 games, a school record that still stands. After his record-setting season, Taylor went to his first NHL training camp in 1977. The team liked what it saw, and he made the regular-season roster out of camp. By January 1978, he was flanking superstar Marcel Dionne, and the following season, the pair formed the prolific Triple Crown Line with the addition of Charlie Simmer. The rest is history. Even after the trio's run of dominance ended, Taylor continued to be an integral part of the Kings. On February 5, 1991, playing in his 930th career game with the Kings, Taylor scored his 1,000th point, becoming the 29th player in league history to reach that milestone. Not bad for a 15th-round draft pick.

WAYNE GRETZKY'S 99 RETIRED LEAGUE-WIDE, 2000

Wilf Paiement was the last player other than Wayne Gretzky to wear 99 in the NHL. During parts of three seasons in Toronto, Paiement sported the number before he was traded to the Quebec Nordiques in 1982 when he switched to 27. Although Gretzky was just in his third NHL campaign, he had already proved he was in a class all his own. In the coming years, as he continued to rewrite the league's record books, Gretzky made the number iconic, and it became synonymous with his superstar hockey skills. When he retired in 1999, the league wanted to ensure that no other player on any team wore 99 again. On February 6, 2000, prior to the NHL All-Star Game at the Air Canada Centre in Toronto, the first since 1978 that didn't include Gretzky, the Great One's famous digits were raised to the rafters. While Gretzky didn't address the crowd during the ceremony, he did drop the puck for a ceremonial faceoff between the Pittsburgh Penguins' Jaromír Jágr and the Mighty Ducks of Anaheim's Paul Kariya.

A couple of days earlier, Gretzky was actually with Jágr and Kariya, along with Gordie Howe, Mario Lemieux, Eric Lindros, and Pavel Bure, to shoot a short promotional film in advance of the festivities. The video, which aired in the arena before the game and later on national television, featured Gretzky, Howe, and Lemieux, three of the game's greatest players, walking through the woods and reminiscing about their career highlights. As they continue their stroll, they arrive at a frozen pond among the pines where Jágr, Kariya, Lindros, and Bure are playing hockey. The younger players invite the legends out to join them, but as Gretzky contemplates the idea with a stick in his hand, he passes the puck back to them and simply says, "It's your turn now." As Kariya, Lindros, and Bure skate off, Jágr calls them back and initiates a stick tap for the three legends, saluting their accomplishments. It was a fitting tribute for the retirement ceremony: although the Gretzky era was over, the torch had been passed.

FEBRUARY 7

FINNISH FLASH BECOMES A MIGHTY DUCK, 1996

Teemu Selänne wanted to remain a Winnipeg Jet. Although the team was relocating from Winnipeg to Arizona at the end of the season, Selänne, who had scored 76 goals in his rookie campaign in 1992–93, had hoped to be a part of the club's future. Despite receiving assurances he would be accompanying the team to the desert, trade rumours continued to swirl. Finally, on February 7, 1996, Selänne, along with Marc Chouinard and a fourth-round pick, was traded to the Mighty Ducks of Anaheim in exchange for Chad Kilger, Oleg Tverdovsky, and a third-round pick. Selänne received word during practice and was so upset that he stormed off to the dressing room, tore off his nameplate from above his locker, and hurried out of the Winnipeg Arena without talking to any reporters. While the Finnish sniper was still reeling from the news, his new teammates in Anaheim were ecstatic. In Selänne's book *My Life*, Paul Kariya recalled how shocked everyone in the dressing room was. "We could not believe it, and our minds were blown," he told the authors.

Kariya was a star, but the acquisition of Selänne, one of the most prolific scorers in the league, added a new dimension to the club. The pair had instant chemistry and quickly became one of the most dynamic duos in the league. A few nights later, Selänne joined his teammates for the start of five games on the road and made his Mighty Ducks debut against the New York Islanders. Selänne scored the tying goal in the second period, but Anaheim lost 4–3. Following the road trip, in his second home game, Selänne scored a hat trick. It was just the second three-goal performance in Mighty Ducks franchise history; Terry Yake first accomplished the feat against the New York Rangers on October 19, 1993. In his first 15 games with his new squad, Selänne racked up 10 goals and 23 points. Before the trade, Anaheim was 13 games below .500, but with Selänne in the lineup, it went 9–5–1 and improved to four games above .500.

FEBRUARY 8
WOMEN'S HOCKEY MAKES
OLYMPIC DEBUT, 1998

The earliest known photograph of women playing hockey was taken around 1890. Captured on the Rideau Hall Rink in Ottawa, the picture features a group of women that includes Isobel Stanley, daughter of Governor General Lord Stanley, who later donated a hockey trophy that became the most iconic prize in all of sport. Despite the fact that women had been playing hockey since the sport's humble beginnings, support for the women's game proceeded at a snail's pace. It was only in 1990, nearly a century after Isobel Stanley was photographed playing hockey in an ankle-length white dress, that the International Ice Hockey Federation (IIHF) sanctioned the first women's championship. Two years later, as the sport continued to grow in popularity, the International Olympic Committee (IOC) voted to include women's hockey as a full-medal sport beginning in 2002. The IOC, however, gave the organizers of the 1994 Winter Olympics in Lillehammer, Norway, the chance to include it in their program, but they declined the opportunity. Four years later, when the games were in Nagano, Japan, the organizers agreed to put it on the docket. Women's hockey was going to finally make its Olympic debut.

On February 8, 1998, the first games were played. In the initial match on the schedule, Sari Krooks scored the first-ever women's Olympic hockey goal when she opened the scoring in Finland's 6–0 defeat of Sweden. Following that contest, the top-ranked Canadians trounced Japan 13–0, and to cap off the historic slate of games, the United States shut out China 5–0. Although Canada was favoured to win gold, it lost to the United States in the final, while Finland nabbed the bronze from the Chinese. On paper, it looked like just another tournament, but it was far more than that; it was a watershed moment for the sport and the growth of the game. For many watching from around the globe, it was the first time they'd seen women playing on the international stage. For the young girls tuning in, that meant something. Unlike previous generations, they now had their own hockey heroes to inspire them.

SENATORS ACQUIRE PHANEUF, 2016

t wasn't that Dion Phaneuf was a bad player; it was just that at 30 years old and with five years remaining on his deal at an annual cap hit of $7 million, he wasn't part of the Toronto Maple Leafs' long-term plans. Although the Leafs were ready to deal their captain, most assumed the club couldn't make the move without retaining some of his salary. But somehow they pulled it off. On February 9, 2016, Toronto traded Phaneuf to the Ottawa Senators as part of a nine-player deal and managed to avoid keeping any of his contract on the books. Along with Phaneuf, the Senators received Matt Frattin, Casey Bailey, Ryan Rupert, and Cody Donaghey. Going to the Leafs were Jared Cowen, Milan Michalek, Colin Greening, Tobias Lindberg, and a second-round pick in 2017. Although the Leafs took on more expenses in the short term by acquiring veteran players from Ottawa, the key part of the deal was shedding long-term salary.

Phaneuf had patrolled the Leafs' blue line admirably for the past six seasons, but he was miscast as a top pairing defenceman. Although he could still throw the bone-crunching hits that had earned him acclaim early in his career, he wasn't considered a number one defenceman, though he was thrust into that position in Toronto. By the 2015–16 campaign, just two years after the club signed Phaneuf to a seven-year, $49-million contract extension, the Leafs were in a rebuilding phase and his declining play continued to be a source of contention. Once in Ottawa, however, Phaneuf found himself in a much better position. He slotted in behind the top defensive pair of Marc Methot and Erik Karlsson. The following season, he was an integral part of the Senators' playoff run that came just one goal short of a berth in the Stanley Cup Final. Meanwhile, with Phaneuf out of the picture in Toronto, the team's blue line became even more porous, and the team finished at the bottom of the standings in 2015–16, earning the club the first overall pick, which they used to draft Auston Matthews.

FEBRUARY 10

BRETT HULL SCORES 700, 2003

B rett Hull thought he might never reach the 700-goal mark. After scoring his 699th career goal in a game against the Edmonton Oilers on January 22, he was held without a goal for the next seven contests. Even in a matchup against the Florida Panthers on January 30, in which he rifled 10 shots, Hull still couldn't find the back of the net. As his goal-scoring drought continued, he started thinking about all the things that could go wrong. He was turning 39 in the off-season and knew he had only so much hockey left in him. Hull was worried that he could get injured suddenly, might never play again, and would be stuck at 699. But given Hull's penchant for lighting the lamp, those concerns never materialized and it was only a matter of time before he potted the milestone goal. On February 10, 2003, in the second period of the Red Wings' game against the San Jose Sharks, Hull took a cross-ice pass from Pavel Datsyuk and wired a one-timer from the bottom of the left faceoff circle to beat goaltender Evgeni Nabokov. It was vintage Hull. He had broken his slump, and with it, etched his name in the NHL's record book by becoming just the sixth player in league history to score 700 career goals. Only Wayne Gretzky had accomplished the feat in fewer games.

While the faithful at Joe Louis Arena rose to their feet, the Red Wings hopped over the boards to congratulate him. "It was a special moment," said head coach Dave Lewis. "I'm glad all the fans here in Detroit got to see that." Following the game, Hull said: "It's a great feeling. And I'm proud to do it in this jersey. To have it here in front of Hockeytown was great." Hull added 16 goals more down the stretch to finish the season with 37, reaching the 30-goal mark for the 12th time in his career. When he retired two years later, after a brief stint with the Phoenix Coyotes, he had 741 career goals and now sits with the fourth most in league history.

CUNNEYWORTH SCORES FIRST GOAL FOR SABRES IN 17 YEARS, 1999

When Randy Cunneyworth scored his first goal for the Buffalo Sabres, on November 15, 1981, Cory Sarich was three years old and just learning how to skate. Nearly two decades later, Sarich was Cunneyworth's teammate on the Rochester Americans, Buffalo's AHL affiliate. In the years that had passed since scoring that goal, Cunneyworth went on to play for Pittsburgh, Winnipeg, Hartford, Chicago, and Ottawa in the NHL. In August 1998, he returned to the Sabres as a free agent. Cunneyworth, who had logged 852 career NHL games, started the season in the minors with the Americans, where he served as a player and assistant coach. In early February 1999, he and Sarich were recalled by the big club. Buffalo bench boss Lindy Ruff, Cunneyworth's linemate in 1981, looked forward to having them both back, particularly Cunneyworth.

In the second period of a game against the Montreal Canadiens, on February 11, 1999, Cunneyworth took a pass from Jason Woolley and scored a backhander to make it 5–0. While the goal didn't change the outcome of the game — the Sabres went on to win 5–2 — it was significant because it set an NHL record for the longest gap between goals with one team: 17 years, two months, and 27 days. When Cunneyworth was asked about the milestone after the game, he smirked and said, "Is that a slump or what?" Sarich, who was probably still in diapers when Cunneyworth scored his first goal for the club, was happy for his teammate. "You just see a love for the game out of Randy Cunneyworth," the 21-year-old defenceman said. "He plays with so much emotion and he's been a great leader all year in Rochester." Cunneyworth played six more games for the Sabres that season, scoring another goal, his last in the NHL, on February 28, 1999. The following season, he played exclusively with Rochester and continued his role as a player and assistant coach. Before the start of the 2000–01 campaign, Cunneyworth hung up his skates but kept his duties behind the bench, becoming the head coach of the Americans.

FEBRUARY 12
SAN JOSE SHARKS UNVEIL JERSEY, 1991

Gordie Howe was one of the best players to wear the San Jose Sharks' jersey. Although he had hung up his skates more than a decade earlier, following his final NHL season with the Hartford Whalers as a 51-year-old, he still looked as though he could have been the expansion team's first player. When he slipped the teal jersey over his head, he spotted the number 91 on the back, the year of the club's first season. Howe joked that at first glance he thought it was his old number 9 and that the team was about to announce it was signing him. Instead, on February 12, 1991, at the Ice Capades Chalet in Cupertino, California, Howe helped the club unveil its uniform. Along with team owner George Gund III, Howe skated onto the ice wearing the Sharks' jersey. Gund sported the white home jersey trimmed in teal, black, and grey, while Howe wore the teal road one.

Emblazoned on the crest of the sweaters was a ferocious hockey-stick-chomping shark emerging from a triangle, a nod to the triangle-shaped region off the coast of San Francisco known as "The Red Triangle" because of its shark-infested waters. The logo unmistakably signified that NHL hockey was back in the Bay Area. Fifteen years earlier, the California Golden Seals, part of the NHL's bold expansion in 1967, relocated to Cleveland, becoming the Barons. Gund and his brother, Gordon, were minority owners of the team and wanted to move the club back to their hometown. After just two seasons in Ohio, however, the Barons merged with the Minnesota North Stars. While the Gunds stayed on as owners, they eventually agreed to relinquish their controlling interest in the team in 1990 for the rights to an expansion team in the Bay Area. Not long after selling the North Stars to Howard Baldwin and Morris Belzberg in May 1990, the Gunds were given a new franchise. Less than a year later, the Sharks were born. But having the support of Howe, one of the game's most revered ambassadors, made it more than just another hockey-uniform unveiling.

FEBRUARY 13

DOUG GILMOUR HAS KILLER NIGHT, 1993

D oug Gilmour assisted on Mike Foligno's opening goal in a game against the Minnesota North Stars on February 13, 1993. Then he assisted on John Cullen's goal, on Dave Andreychuk's goal, on Glenn Anderson's goal, on another Andreychuk goal, and then, finally, on a goal by Dave Ellett. When the contest was in the books, the Toronto Maple Leafs had defeated Minnesota 6–1 and Gilmour had assisted on all six goals, tying a team record for the most helpers in a single game. The last time a Toronto player had earned six assists in a game was when defenceman Babe Pratt did it in a 12–3 rout of the Boston Bruins on January 8, 1944. Following the game, given the significance of the milestone, reporters asked Gilmour if he'd ever met Pratt. Looking in the direction of Foligno, who had just turned 34, Gilmour smiled and said, "I just remember Foligno playing with him."

When reporters made their way to Foligno, they explained Gilmour's joke to him. "The only thing that upsets me about [Gilmour] tying Pratt's record was that the guys were asking me how Pratt was to play against," Foligno said. "I'm happy for Doug, but I don't like the thought of people thinking I played that long ago." While everyone had a laugh at the expense of the Leafs' oldest player, Foligno added that Gilmour "has been the heart and soul of our team for the longest time. He's playing so well that it makes everybody else want to dig down and work a little harder." That was the hallmark of Gilmour's game. Despite being the team's unquestioned star, he still approached every game as if he were trying to earn his roster spot each and every night. In addition to his incredible playmaking skills, he had a dogged work ethic that rubbed off on his teammates and made them want to elevate their game. Gilmour continued to lead by example down the stretch, racking up 43 points in the club's final games to finish the season with 127 points, a franchise record that still stands to this day.

FEBRUARY 14
SERGEI FEDOROV HITS 1,000, 2004

Three minutes into the second period of a game against the Vancouver Canucks, on February 14, 2004, the Mighty Ducks of Anaheim's Sergei Fedorov made history. After cleanly winning a faceoff in Vancouver's zone, he sent the puck back to Keith Carney, who wired a one-timer to beat goaltender Johan Hedberg. With the assist, Fedorov notched his 1,000th NHL career point, becoming the first Russian-born player to reach that milestone. It wasn't the first time the smooth-skating centre had been a part of Russian hockey history. Less than a decade earlier, as a member of the Detroit Red Wings on October 27, 1995, Fedorov was part of an entire five-man unit made up of Russian players. While the league had featured plenty of Russian players by that point, a team had never deployed five of them at once. Along with Fedorov, Detroit sent out wingers Slava Kozlov and Igor Larionov, as well as blueliners Vladimir Konstantinov and Slava Fetisov, all of whom had played for CSKA Moscow, the famed Red Army team of the former Soviet Union. They came to be known as the "Russian Five" and were an integral part of the Red Wings' Stanley Cup win in 1997.

After winning two more championships in Detroit, Fedorov signed with the Mighty Ducks as a free agent on July 19, 2003. After assisting on Carey's goal, Fedorov also picked up a helper on the game-winner. Driving to the net in the third period, he flung the puck at Hedberg. The Canucks' goaltender made the save, but the puck bounced out to Petr Schastlivy, playing his second game since being acquired from the Ottawa Senators, who cashed in the rebound. Following the game, Fedorov was asked to comment on his milestone assist in the second frame. He told reporters it was nice, but the other assist was more important to him because it earned the team two points. Despite his modesty, in advance of the Mighty Ducks' next matchup at home on February 16, the team honoured Fedorov and showered him with gifts in a pre-game ceremony.

FEBRUARY 15

KINGS ACQUIRE "THE CAT," 2001

f the Los Angeles Kings hoped to make the playoffs, they needed help in net. Their netminding platoon of Jamie Storr, Steve Passmore, Stephane Fiset, and Travis Scott had a combined save percentage of .884, the worst in the league. After finishing an eight-game homestand with a record of 2–5–1, the club took action. On February 15, 2001, the Kings acquired goaltender Felix Potvin from the Vancouver Canucks for future considerations, which at the time of the deal were believed to be conditional draft picks based on how well he played. When the trade was announced, Kings GM Dave Taylor believed the acquisition of Potvin would bring stability to the team's goaltending and give the club the momentum it needed to make the playoffs.

Although Los Angeles was getting a proven NHL goaltender with playoff experience, Potvin had struggled during his time in Vancouver. His save percentage with the Canucks wasn't much better than what the Kings were getting out of their goaltenders, but the team felt that given his track record, a fresh start in Los Angeles might be just what he needed. Potvin agreed. "I'm still young and I think a change of scenery will be very good for me." Potvin knew the Kings weren't out of the playoff picture yet and was eager to help the club qualify for the post-season: "My goal is to play in the playoffs every year." Potvin made his first start with Los Angeles a week later on the road against the Edmonton Oilers, making 22 saves in a 5–0 loss. Two nights later, however, Potvin picked up his first victory and shutout. He made 19 saves in a 2–0 win over the Calgary Flames. Although he faced just eight shots through the first two periods, he made a few key saves in the final frames. Down the stretch, Potvin made the difference the Kings hoped he would. In 23 starts, he posted a 13–5–5 record, including five shutouts and a .919 save percentage. Bolstered by his sterling play, the Kings qualified for the Stanley Cup Playoffs.

THRASHERS UNVEIL THEIR NAME, 1998

The NHL had returned to Atlanta. After the Flames relocated to Calgary in 1980, Atlanta was granted another franchise in 1997, along with three other cities. Owned by the Turner Broadcasting System (TBS), the Atlanta club was set to hit the ice for the 1999–2000 season. Not long after the team was founded, however, it hit a snag when Ted Turner wanted to name his franchise the Thrashers after the Georgia state bird, the brown thrasher. But there was one problem. The San Francisco–based skateboard magazine *Thrasher*, which had a circulation of more than 150,000, wouldn't give the owners the right to use the name without compensation. After months of trying to reach an agreement, TBS filed a suit against the periodical. Litigation failed to resolve the issue, but eventually the parties negotiated an out-of-court settlement that gave the team the right to use the name. On February 16, 1998, TBS announced that its hockey team would officially be known as the Thrashers. Two months later, thousands filled the atrium of the CNN Center in Atlanta to get a glimpse of the crest the club would sport in its inaugural season.

While brown thrashers are small birds and might not seem as if they could strike fear into the hearts of opponents, they are aggressive and fiercely protective. Despite the thrasher's diminutive stature, the team looked to incorporate those behavioural elements into the club's emblem. Dave Maggard, vice-president of administration for Turner Sports, said, "We didn't want to have a silly comic book character or a weak-looking logo. The idea was to have a bird, yet at the same time a bird of prey." Emblazoned on a baby-blue background, the logo featured a menacing copper, bronze, and gold bird clutching a hockey stick with its wing. The Thrashers made their NHL debut on October 2, 1999, a 4–1 loss on the road against the New Jersey Devils. Although it was hoped the Thrashers would establish a long-term nest in Atlanta, they stuck around for just over a decade before they migrated to Winnipeg and became the new Jets.

JOE SCHAEFER GETS THE CALL, 1960

Ever since playing roller hockey on the streets of New York City as a youngster, Joe Schaefer dreamed of suiting up for the Rangers. While the prospect of turning pro eluded him, Schaefer eventually started playing amateur ice hockey as a goaltender in Brooklyn. After serving in the U.S. Navy during the Second World War, Schaefer returned home and continued playing in net for teams in Brooklyn, Long Island, and New Jersey. By 1952, word of Schaefer's netminding skills had reached the Rangers' brass and they brought him on as the club's emergency goaltender. Schaefer, who worked at a factory on Long Island, would get to take in all the Blueshirts' games at Madison Square Garden and be asked to take over in net if a goaltender was ever injured.

For the next seven years, Schaefer watched. And watched. But nothing happened. Then, on February 17, 1960, Schaefer was called into action. Early into the second period of a game against the Chicago Black Hawks, Rangers goaltender Lorne "Gump" Worsley suffered cut tendons on his right hand during a goalmouth scramble. While Worsley was taken to the hospital, the 35-year-old Schaefer left his familiar seat in the stands and changed into his uniform. When Schaefer entered the contest, the Rangers were leading 1–0. For the next 12 minutes, he valiantly turned aside all the shots he faced until Eric Nesterenko scored on a power play to tie the game. Less than two minutes later, Tod Sloan scored to give Chicago the lead. The Black Hawks added three more in the final frame to secure a 5–1 victory against the Rangers. Despite the score, Schaefer still made 17 saves in hockey's top league and got to live a childhood dream. "All my life, I dreamed of this night," he told reporters after the game. "Now I'm ready to quit." But Schaefer didn't hang up his pads. A year later, on March 18, 1961, he was called in to relieve Worsley again in a game against the Black Hawks. Schaefer made 27 saves in a 4–3 loss, his final NHL appearance.

FEBRUARY 18
THRASHERS ACQUIRE BLAKE WHEELER, 2011

Blake Wheeler might not have been part of the Boston Bruins' long-term plans, but he became an integral player on his new team. On February 18, 2011, to retool for a deep playoff run, Boston sent him, along with Mark Stuart, to the Atlanta Thrashers in exchange for Rich Peverley and Boris Valábik. Wheeler, originally drafted fifth overall by the Coyotes in 2004, signed with the Bruins in 2008 after failing to come to terms with Phoenix. In three campaigns with Boston, the six-foot-five winger had recorded 110 points and was set to become a restricted free agent by season's end. At the time of the trade, Wheeler had 27 points in 58 games, but in Atlanta he scored 17 points in his first 23 contests. In the off-season, while the Bruins celebrated the club's first Stanley Cup championship in nearly four decades, the Thrashers prepared to relocate to Winnipeg after the franchise was sold to True North Sports & Entertainment. Wheeler signed on for another two years with the rechristened Jets, scoring 64 points, a career high, and leading the team in scoring in his first season in Manitoba. Two years later, following a lockout-shortened campaign in which he racked up 41 points in 48 games, Wheeler signed a six-year extension worth $33.6 million.

In the first year of his new deal, he scored 28 goals and 69 points, new career highs in both categories. When the Thrashers original-ly acquired Wheeler, coach Craig Ramsay said he was getting a "big body with good puck skills," but Wheeler proved to be so much more. Since becoming a Jet, he has been a warrior for the team, missing just six games in his first full eight seasons in Winnipeg, and has con-tinued to find ways to elevate his play, even as he becomes one of the club's elder statesmen. In the 2017–18 season, Wheeler racked up 68 assists, a franchise record that he has since surpassed, and 91 points. Signing on as a Jet until the end of 2023–24, Wheeler will go down as one of the greatest players in franchise history.

FEBRUARY 19

FLAMES SIGN MARTIN ST. LOUIS, 1998

Despite scoring 50 points in 56 games with the Cleveland Lumberjacks of the IHL, Martin St. Louis was no closer to the big leagues. St. Louis, the University of Vermont's career leader in assists and points, couldn't get called up to the NHL because his rights weren't owned by any of the clubs. Although he was listed at five-foot-eight, small by hockey standards, St. Louis's skills more than made up for his perceived lack of size. It was rather fitting that on February 19, 1998, he signed with the Calgary Flames, a team that had enjoyed much success with Theo Fleury, an offensively gifted player deemed undersized, in the lineup. "I think I proved I can skate with the big guys," St. Louis said after inking his contract. Before getting an opportunity in Calgary, he was assigned to the Saint John Flames, the club's AHL affiliate in New Brunswick. In 25 games, St. Louis scored 26 points.

The following season, he started with Calgary, accompanying the team to Japan for a two-game series against the San Jose Sharks and making his NHL debut on October 9, 1998, in a 3–3 tie. After returning home, St. Louis notched his first goal on October 20. He picked up an assist in the following game but was sent back to Saint John in early December. The next year, St. Louis spent most of the 1999–2000 campaign in Calgary but was utilized chiefly in a fourth-line role. In the 2000 NHL Expansion Draft, the Flames left him exposed, but neither the Columbus Blue Jackets nor the Minnesota Wild selected him. Following the draft, the Flames bought out the final year of the contract, making him an unrestricted free agent. On July 31, 2000, St. Louis signed a two-year deal with the Lightning. In his first season in Tampa Bay, St. Louis scored 40 points in 78 games. Two years later, he played as if he had been struck by lightning. In 2003–04, St. Louis scored 94 points, winning the Art Ross Trophy and snagging the Hart Trophy as the league's most valuable player.

THE NHL'S "PERFECT" GAME, 1944

Less than two hours after dropping the puck, the game was over. On February 20, 1944, before 18,534 fans at Chicago Stadium, an NHL record, the Black Hawks and Toronto Maple Leafs duelled to a 0–0 draw. The lack of goals wasn't nearly as surprising as the fact that referee Bill Chadwick didn't even use his whistle once to call a penalty, making it the first scoreless, penalty-free game in league history. Although the score sheet indicated that no goals were scored in the defensive spectacle, that wasn't exactly the case. Less than half-way through the second period, Black Hawks winger Fido Purpur knocked the puck into the net past Leafs goaltender Paul Bibeault. Purpur, however, had connected with the puck in the air with his stick above his shoulders, which was prohibited in the rulebook. While the puck might have found the back of the twine, it was an illegal play, and Chadwick nullified the goal. And that was as close as the fans came to witnessing a goal that game.

Despite the fact the Leafs and Black Hawks were tied for third place and in the midst of a playoff race, neither team played with the kind of desperation that would break the deadlock. Other than Purpur's illegitimate attempt, Bibeault, along with his Chicago counterpart, Mike Karakas, kept the pucks out of the nets without breaking a sweat. The tie dropped the Black Hawks into a fourth-place stalemate with the Boston Bruins. Down the stretch of the regular season, Chicago picked up three more wins than Boston, qualifying for the playoffs as the last-place team. The Black Hawks won their semifinal series against the Detroit Red Wings before getting swept in four straight games by the Montreal Canadiens in the Stanley Cup Final. Although the Black Hawks and Leafs' scoreless, penalty-free draw was the first, and the last, in NHL history, there have been a few games since that have proceeded without infractions. The next one didn't occur for another two decades when the Bruins hosted the Canadiens on January 30, 1966.

FEBRUARY 21
CANADIAN WOMEN WIN GOLD, 2002

The rivalry between the Canadian and American women's national hockey teams reached a crescendo at the Winter Olympics in Salt Lake City, Utah. After the United States took the inaugural gold in women's hockey at the Winter Games in Nagano, Japan, in 1998, the Canadians were still bitter about the loss. Despite defeating the Americans in the final at the next three straight World Championships, they desperately wanted to add an Olympic title to their collection. Although they went 0–8 against the Americans in pre-tournament competition, the Canadian women were determined to pry the gold from the reigning champions. They might have also had some extra motivation in Salt Lake. There were whispers that the Americans had stomped on the Canadian flag in their dressing room, and it was rumoured that some American players had signed autographs over pictures of Canadian players' faces in the Olympic Village. So when the two teams squared off on February 21, 2002, for the final game of the tournament, Canada used those reports to fuel them further.

Less than two minutes into the first period of the championship game, Caroline Ouellette scored to give Canada a 1–0 lead. It was the first time in the tournament that the Americans trailed. Early in the second period, American Kathryn King tied the game on a power play, but a few minutes later, Hayley Wickenheiser knocked in Danielle Goyette's rebound, restoring the Canadian advantage. With just one second left in the frame, Jayna Hefford scored to give Canada a 3–1 lead. And that was it. Although Karyn Bye scored for the Americans with three minutes remaining in the game, it was too late. The Canadians were Olympic hockey champions. Following the game, Wickenheiser, who was named tournament MVP, addressed the report about the Americans walking on the Canadian flag in their dressing room. Looking defiantly into the camera, she exclaimed, "The Americans had our flag on their floor in the dressing room and now I want to know if they want us to sign it." It remains one of the most badass post-game remarks in hockey history.

MAPLE LEAFS' PRACTICE GOALIE BEATS
MAPLE LEAFS, 2020

David Ayres thought it was just going to be another night watching the Toronto Maple Leafs from his usual seat in the stands. Ayres, who was the operations manager at the Mattamy Athletic Centre, formerly Maple Leaf Gardens, and trained with the club as a practice goalie, was once again serving as the emergency backup goaltender for Toronto's home game against the Carolina Hurricanes on February 22, 2020. Although Ayres had been in that position before, he'd never been called into action. But just six minutes into the first period, Carolina goaltender James Reimer left the game after his defenceman, Jaccob Slavin, landed on top of him. Czech netminder Petr Mrázek came into the game in relief, but he, too, left the contest less than halfway through the second period after a collision with hard-nosed Toronto winger Kyle Clifford.

With the Hurricanes suddenly out of goaltenders, Ayres, who was watching from the crowd, was informed that he better get ready. After quickly putting on his gear, Ayres skated onto the ice to make his NHL debut. When he entered the game, Carolina had a 3–1 lead, but many expected he was going to get shelled. It certainly seemed that way after he allowed goals on the first two shots he faced. The Hurricanes, however, rallied around Ayres and clamped down. He stopped the next, and final, eight shots he faced to backstop the team to a 6–3 victory, becoming the first emergency backup goaltender in NHL history to win a game. Some commentators derided the league's system that allowed a 42-year-old practice goalie to step into an NHL game, and most of the headlines referred to him as a Zamboni driver, but for me, despite being a Leafs fan, it was a special moment. Ayres got to live his childhood dream. Following the game, Ayres became a household name, making an appearance on *The Late Show with Stephen Colbert*. Currently, he's working with Disney to bring his story to the silver screen.

FEBRUARY 23
LEMIEUX AND JÁGR EACH NET 50, 1996

Mario Lemieux and Jaromír Jágr made a friendly wager. Both players were approaching the 50-goal mark in the 1995–96 season and decided to put a nice bottle of champagne on the line to see who reached the milestone first. Heading into the Pittsburgh Penguins' game against the Hartford Whalers on February 23, 1996, the Penguins' dynamic duo were each two goals away from 50. While Lemieux had struck 50 four times already in his illustrious career, it was the first time Jágr was so close to the benchmark. Less than eight minutes into the game, Lemieux opened the scoring and was just one goal back from earning a bottle of bubbly. But five minutes after Lemieux assisted on Pittsburgh's tying goal early in the second period, Jágr scored his 49th of the campaign to draw even with his superstar teammate. Both players seemed poised to reach 50 that evening; it was just a matter of who made it there first. It wouldn't be the first time Lemieux made it to 50 in the same game as a teammate. Less than three years earlier, he and Kevin Stevens both did it in a matchup against the Edmonton Oilers, becoming the first pair of teammates in NHL history to accomplish the feat in the same game.

After the Whalers took a 4–3 lead early in the final frame, the Penguins went to work on a power play. Lemieux fired a shot past Whalers goaltender Sean Burke to tie the game and win the bet. Although Jágr lost the wager, which Lemieux was quick to point out when he returned to the bench, there was still plenty of time on the clock for the Czech to reach the milestone, as well. Less than four minutes later, he pulled it off. Although Jágr was down a bottle of champagne, he made history of his own by becoming the first Czech-born player to rack up 50 goals in an NHL season, and together, he and Lemieux became the second pair of teammates to reach the mark in the same game.

FEBRUARY 24

CANADA WINS GOLD ... AGAIN, 2002

Taking a page out of the Canadian women's hockey playbook, the men followed suit a few days after the former's gold-medal triumph over the United States and took home the gold. On February 24, 2002, Canada defeated the United States 5–2 at the Winter Games in Salt Lake City, Utah, to become men's hockey Olympic champions for the first time since 1952 when the Edmonton Mercurys, an amateur club representing Canada, claimed victory in Oslo, Norway.

On paper, it seemed like a foregone conclusion that the men's team would win gold. General manager Wayne Gretzky's squad featured 14 future Hall of Famers, arguably one of the best teams to hit the ice internationally for Canada. But despite all that talent, the men's team struggled through the group stage of the tournament. It lost its opening game 5–2 to Sweden, then squeaked out a 3–2 victory over Germany before finishing with a 3–3 tie against the Czech Republic. In the elimination round, Canada defeated Finland 2–1 and seemed on a collision course for a pivotal rematch against Sweden in the semi-finals. But Belarus stunned the hockey world, defeating Sweden 4–3 in the quarter-finals and knocking it out of the tournament. Canada then made short work of the Belarusians, trouncing them 7–1 before taking on the United States in the gold-medal game.

After Tony Amonte opened scoring for the Americans less than halfway through the first period, Chris Pronger sent the puck across the ice toward Mario Lemieux. But instead of accepting the pass, in a moment of brilliance that few other players could pull off, Lemieux deliberately let the puck go between his skates and onto the stick of an advancing Paul Kariya, who wired the tying goal past a diving Mike Richter. After Canada took the lead with a goal by Jarome Iginla, the United States tied the game 2–2 in the second period. But with less than two minutes remaining in the middle frame, Joe Sakic scored the go-ahead to put the game out of reach. Canada added two more to capture gold.

FEBRUARY 25
MAPLE LEAFS TRADE GILMOUR TO NEW JERSEY, 1997

At this point you're probably wondering why I'm writing about Doug Gilmour so much. The truth is he was my mom's favourite player, and since writers know they can always count on their mothers to read their work, you've got to play to your base. But this isn't a Gilmour story my mom would appreciate. She's a diehard Maple Leafs fan, and this tale is about his tenure coming to an end in Toronto.

On February 25, 1997, the Leafs sent Gilmour, their captain, along with Dave Ellett, to New Jersey for Steve Sullivan, Jason Smith, the rights to junior prospect Alyn McCauley, and a conditional draft pick. Gilmour realized the Leafs weren't going to re-sign him when his contract expired at the end of the following season, so he knew the trade was coming. Upon learning the news that he was going to the Devils, Gilmour was relieved. It ended months of speculation. Gilmour, sitting second in Leafs scoring with 60 points, instantly became the Devils' leading scorer. For a defensively minded and offensively starved team like New Jersey, the addition of Gilmour and his premier playmaking abilities strengthened its chance at a Stanley Cup.

In his first game with the Devils, Gilmour scored a goal and added three assists in a 5–3 victory against the New York Islanders. In New Jersey's final 20 regular-season games, Gilmour racked up 22 points as the club headed into the playoffs as the number one seed in the Eastern Conference. The Devils got through their first-round matchup but were then eliminated by the New York Rangers in five games. The following season, Gilmour was sidelined with an eye injury and only suited up for 63 games for the Devils. Nevertheless, he still racked up 53 points as New Jersey claimed the top spot in the Eastern Conference for the second year in a row. The playoffs, however, proved to be another disappointment. The Devils were upset by the lowly Ottawa Senators and made another early exit. In the off-season, Gilmour signed with the Chicago Blackhawks as a free agent.

FEBRUARY 26
HAVARD AND YALE FACE OFF, 1900

When Harvard and Yale Universities squared off in a two-mile rowing race on Lake Winnipesaukee in New Hampshire in 1852, it marked the first intercollegiate competition in the United States and the beginning of a fierce athletic rivalry between the two institutions that continues to this day. Following that first race, in which the Cambridge crew defeated their New Haven counterparts, the schools soon began competing in other sports. In 1875, they met on the football field for the first time, the start of an annual matchup that has simply became known as "The Game." By the turn of the century, Harvard and Yale had established rivalries on both the water and on the gridiron before taking the competition to the ice.

On February 26, 1900, they played the first hockey game between the schools at the St. Nicholas Rink in New York City. Two thousand spectators turned up that night to watch. Although supporters of both teams were in attendance, newspaper coverage suggested that the chants from the Yale boosters drowned out the chorus from the Crimson contingent. While Harvard scored the first goal of the game, the Yale squad, which reportedly skated circles around the Bulldogs club because of its superior physical conditioning, quickly took control of the game. After taking a 2–1 lead in the first half — they played two 20-minute halves that evening — Yale added three more goals and emerged with a 5–4 victory. Exactly 21 years later, the two teams faced off for the 37th time. After Harvard opened the scoring in the opening period, Yale knotted it up in the second frame only to allow its Cambridge rivals to rattle off 12 unanswered goals in a 13–1 rout, the largest margin of victory between the two teams, which still stands to this day. As Harvard and Yale began to meet with more regularity in the years since, the rivalry has only intensified. Following that first historic matchup, as of this writing, the two schools have met on the ice 261 times, with Harvard getting the better of its opponent with 146 wins.

FEBRUARY 27
BLUES ACQUIRE THE GREAT ONE, 1996

When Brett Hull played on a line with Wayne Gretzky at the 1992 NHL All-Star Game at the Spectrum in Philadelphia, St. Louis Blues fans couldn't help but daydream about the possibilities. A few years later it became a reality. On February 27, 1996, the Los Angeles Kings traded Gretzky to St. Louis for Roman Vopat, Craig Johnson, Patrice Tardif, and two future draft picks. It wasn't that long ago that Gretzky had brought the Kings to their first-ever Stanley Cup Final, and it had only been a couple of years since he scored his 802nd career goal on home ice to surpass his boyhood idol and establish a new NHL record, but it was a different time for hockey in Los Angeles. It seemed as though the magic had run out.

Following their historic playoff run, the Kings had gone through three ownership groups, entered bankruptcy proceedings in 1995, and missed the playoffs for two straight years. Gretzky was frustrated with the Kings' struggles on and off the ice, and it seemed unlikely he was going to re-sign with the club. Worried they would lose him for nothing, the Kings looked to trade him. Although the New York Rangers and Vancouver Canucks were both hoping to land the Great One, the Blues proved to be the most persistent. The trade was immediately heralded as a bad deal for Los Angeles. Meanwhile, in St. Louis, they were tickled pink. "Brett Hull can't keep the smile off his face," Blues president Jack Quinn told reporters following the move.

Despite the optimism in St. Louis, the chemistry between Hull and Gretzky never materialized the way many had expected. In fact, after Gretzky's arrival, GM and head coach Mike Keenan openly criticized his star winger, suggesting Hull had never played worse. Although St. Louis tried to retain Gretzky with an extension, Keenan reportedly lowered his offer during the playoffs when the Blues went down 0–2 in their series against the Detroit Red Wings. In the off-season, Gretzky bolted and signed with the New York Rangers, reuniting with long-time Edmonton Oilers teammate Mark Messier.

FEBRUARY 28
THE GOLDEN GOAL, 2010

would have been at work on time had it not been for Zach Parise. During graduate school, I had a part-time job at the Travelodge Hotel. On the day of the gold-medal game between Canada and the United States at the 2010 Winter Olympics, I was scheduled to work in the early evening. I tried to switch my shift to make sure I had enough time to watch the game, but I had no luck. Nevertheless, I figured I could watch most of the game and still make it into work, so I headed to a friend's house to catch the game with my buddies. Seven minutes into the second period, Canada took a 2–0 lead. Even after Ryan Kesler scored to get the United States on the board, everything still seemed to be going according to plan.

With less than a minute left in the game, Canada was still up by a goal, and it seemed as though it was going to win in regulation and I'd make my shift on time. But then, with 24.4 seconds remaining, Parise scored to tie the game. I was deflated. Work didn't even cross my mind. I was just thinking about how Canada might have blown its chance at winning on home soil. At that point, I probably could have made it to the hotel for the start of my shift, but knowing I wouldn't be able to catch the game at the front desk, I stayed put. I don't think I even called in to say I'd be late.

Less than eight minutes into overtime, Sidney Crosby called for a pass from Jarome Iginla and then scored "The Golden Goal." After a brief celebration with my friends, I hopped into my car and drove to work. I don't even remember how late I was by the time I arrived, but I know I didn't get into trouble. When my supervisor asked where I was, I told him I was watching the hockey game. On that day, no further explanation was required.

FEBRUARY 29
NICKLAS LIDSTRÖM HITS 1,000-GAME MARK, 2004

When Nicklas Lidström made his NHL debut as a 21-year-old in 1991–92, he never thought he'd play 1,000 career games. Even after seeing Detroit Red Wings teammate Brad Marsh reach the milestone that season, the young Swedish blueliner still doubted he'd have that sort of longevity. But Lidström only got better as he aged. In 2002, after winning his third Stanley Cup with the Red Wings, he won the Conn Smythe Trophy, becoming the first European to win that award. At the age of 31, after winning his first Norris Trophy as the league's top defenceman, he won the award for the next three straight years.

Heading into the 2003–04 campaign, Lidström had missed just 17 games since entering the league, an incredible feat, and was approaching 1,000 games played. On February 29, 2004, in a home game against the Flyers, Lidström played in his 1,000th career NHL game, becoming the first Red Wings defenceman in franchise history to reach that milestone and just the sixth Swedish player to do so. When Detroit's public-address man, Budd Lynch, made the announcement during the contest, the crowd rose to its feet to give Lidström a standing ovation. That was when it really hit him. He had done it. Following the game, reporters wanted to know if Lidström thought he could catch Scott Stevens's record of 1,635 games, since surpassed by Chris Chelios, the most played by a defenceman. "I still can't see myself playing at the age of 40. But I never thought I was going to reach 1,000 games, either," Lidström said.

Over the next seven seasons, Lidström won another Stanley Cup and picked up four more Norris Trophies, collecting his last as a 41-year-old. Although Lidström didn't match Stevens's mark, he did once again defy his own expectations. When he finally hung up his skates, he was 42 years old. Currently, as of this writing, he sits in sixth place for most all-time games played by a blueliner and will endure as one of the best defencemen ever to play the game.

MARCH 1

CAPITALS GET ADAM OATES, 1997

Adam Oates wanted out of the Boston Bruins. The disgruntled playmaker, in the first year of a three-year contract, felt he was underpaid. When the situation became untenable, the Bruins traded him, along with goaltender Bill Ranford and hardnosed winger Rick Tocchet, to the Washington Capitals on March 1, 1997, in exchange for netminder Jim Carey, forwards Jason Allison and Anson Carter, a third-round pick in 1997, and a second-round pick in 1998. Oates, however, refused to report to Washington. Although the ink was barely dry on the three-year deal he signed in Boston, he wanted it revised and went as far as saying he wouldn't play for another team unless he got what he wanted. The next day, Oates missed the Capitals' game against the New York Islanders. After some back-and-forth talks between his agent, Brian Cook, and Washington general manager, David Poile, over the next few days, Oates agreed to honour his existing contract with the hope of restructuring it in the off-season.

On March 4, Oates made his Capitals debut, scoring the game-winning goal in a 2–1 victory against the Calgary Flames. He scored 12 points in Washington's final 17 regular-season games with the expectation that his deal would be renegotiated in the summer. There was just one problem: in May 1997, the Capitals fired David Poile, leaving Oates and Cook to deal with the club's new general manager, George McPhee. Cook established a deadline of June 25 for when he expected a new deal for his client, but that day came and went. By late July, Oates's deal still hadn't been restructured, so he informed the club that he wouldn't be at training camp and demanded a trade. The saga was finally resolved on August 20, 1997, when Oates signed a new three-year deal with Washington that included an option for a fourth season and reportedly paid him $3 million per season, a considerable raise from his original deal. In his first full season with the Capitals, Oates dished out 58 assists and was second in team scoring behind Peter Bondra.

MARCH 2
MARIO LEMIEUX RETURNS TO LINEUP, 1993

After racking up 104 points in his first 40 games of the 1992–93 season, Mario Lemieux stunned the hockey world when he announced he'd been diagnosed with Hodgkin's lymphoma, forcing him to withdraw from the lineup. For the next month, he underwent difficult radiation treatments to fight the disease. On the morning of March 2, 1993, Lemieux finished his final round of radiation. Although he was weakened from the cancer-fighting regimen, he flew to Philadelphia to join his teammates for a game that evening. While the Pittsburgh Penguins never received a warm welcome by the Flyers' faithful at the Spectrum, this time it was different. The crowd gave Lemieux a standing ovation that lasted two minutes. As a WELCOME BACK sign flashed across the screens above the scoreboard, Lemieux acknowledged the heartwarming greeting by raising his stick above his head.

Despite being out of the lineup for nearly two months while he battled cancer, Lemieux seemingly hadn't lost a step. Early in the second period, he scored from the left faceoff circle and added an assist on a Kevin Stevens power play goal less than two minutes later. Although Pittsburgh lost 5–4 that night, Lemieux's triumphant return sparked his team. They went on a 17-game winning streak that culminated in the club earning its first-ever Presidents' Trophy.

During Lemieux's two-month absence, the Buffalo Sabres' Pat LaFontaine had taken the lead in the scoring race by 12 points. In the Penguins' final 20 regular-season games, Lemieux was simply magnificent. He scored 30 goals and 56 points to catch LaFontaine and win his fourth Art Ross Trophy by 12 points. Lemieux finished the campaign with 69 goals and 160 points in just 60 games. In the off-season, he received his second Hart Trophy and third Lester B. Pearson Award (now the Ted Lindsay Award). But perhaps most fittingly, Lemieux also won the Bill Masterton Memorial Trophy, awarded annually to the player who best exemplifies the qualities of perseverance, sportsmanship, and dedication to hockey.

MARCH 3
GORDIE HOWE NIGHT, 1959

As part of a special evening, the Detroit Red Wings honoured their star winger Gordie Howe on March 3, 1959. During "Gordie Howe Night" at the Olympia, he was showered with gifts. Among the presents Howe received were a diamond ring from his teammates, a three-week trip to Florida for the family, a colour TV set, golf clubs, and a lawn mower. The fans also contributed a 130-piece layette set for the Howes' third child, expected to arrive later that month. But one of the truly special gifts he received that evening was a 1959 Oldsmobile station wagon, which the club had wrapped in cellophane and affixed with a bow. Unbeknownst to Howe, when the car was driven onto the ice, the Red Wings had another surprise for him inside. As Howe approached the station wagon to unwrap it, he recognized some familiar faces sitting in the back seat: his parents, Albert and Katherine. The Red Wings had secretly flown them in earlier that day from Saskatoon, Saskatchewan.

Holding on to the door handle, it was clear Howe was overcome with emotion. He bowed his head and fought back tears. As Howe thanked the crowd and the team for the gifts, he proclaimed it was "the greatest day of my life since I came to this grand city of Detroit. It's a long way from Saskatoon ... don't mind the odd tear."

When Howe was still a hockey-crazed youngster growing up in Saskatoon, the Red Wings were in town for an exhibition game. Howe reportedly made his way to the hotel where the team was staying and asked Sid Abel, his boyhood hockey hero, if he could carry the centreman's skates to the rink. Two decades later, Abel was his coach and Howe was being recognized for his incredible contributions to the club, a 13-year tenure at that point, including four scoring titles, three Hart Trophies, and four Stanley Cups. Even in his wildest hockey dreams, there was no way Howe would have thought that one day as an NHL veteran he and his parents would be together celebrating "Gordie Howe Night."

MARCH 4
PENGUINS ACQUIRE RON FRANCIS, 1991

After he learned he was traded, the normally reserved Ron Francis had a few choice words for the Hartford Whalers, his former organization. "I'm not bitter, but I'm disappointed that they publicly demeaned me," he told reporters. "Every second day there were stories about the contract, the captaincy, the trades. If they wanted to trade me, it's their prerogative. But after 10 years of giving everything I had when I stepped on the ice, I feel they could have done it differently." On March 4, 1991, the Whalers traded Francis, along with Ulf Samuelsson and Grant Jennings, to the Pittsburgh Penguins for John Cullen, Zarley Zalapski, and Jeff Parker.

Francis, who had served as captain from February 1985 until he was unceremoniously stripped of the duties earlier in the season by head coach Rick Ley, had been with the Whalers his entire career. Selected fourth overall by Hartford in the 1981 NHL Entry Draft, Francis went on to record 264 goals and 821 points in 714 games with the Whalers to lead the franchise in virtually every offensive category. Although Francis's relationship with the club had become strained, the move still came as a disappointing blow. Two weeks earlier he said the team had contacted his agent and explained they were interested in reopening contract talks, so Francis thought he still might be a Whaler after the trade deadline.

While Francis was sad to leave Hartford, he was excited about the move to Pittsburgh where he'd slot in as the team's number two centre behind Mario Lemieux. After suiting up for just three games with the Penguins, Francis reportedly leaned over to Samuelsson, who had been with him for his entire career in Hartford, and said, "Ulfie, I think we can win the Stanley Cup." Francis's words proved prophetic. In the playoffs, Francis scored seven goals, including four game-winners, and 17 points as the Penguins went on to capture their first Stanley Cup in franchise history. The following season, after signing a five-year contract with Pittsburgh, Francis played an integral role yet again in helping the club win back-to-back Cups.

MARCH 5
KINGS ACQUIRE GÁBORÍK, 2014

When the NHL trade deadline rolled around in 2014, there were only three teams that had scored fewer goals than the Los Angeles Kings. So it was no surprise that one of the items on the club's shopping list was a goal scorer. Marián Gáboík, a three-time 40-goal scorer, seemed the perfect fit. After the Kings pried Jeff Carter from the Columbus Blue Jackets two years earlier, they acquired the Slovak sniper from the same team on March 5, 2014, in exchange for Matt Frattin and conditional draft picks. Missing 22 games that season due to a broken collarbone, Gáboík was eager for a fresh start to prove he still had his scoring touch.

Prior to being traded to the Blue Jackets on April 3, 2013, Gáboík had reached the 40-goal mark three times during his stints with the New York Rangers and Minnesota Wild. While some doubted Gáboík's style of play would fit with the Kings' more defensive-minded system, he quickly put those concerns to rest. Playing on the Kings' top line alongside centre Anže Kopitar and captain Dustin Brown, Gáboík scored five goals and 16 points in the club's last 19 regular-season games. In the 2014 Stanley Cup Playoffs, Gáboík scored critical goals in the Kings' playoff run, including the tying one in Game 7 of the Western Conference Final against the Chicago Blackhawks, along with a pair of tying goals in two games in the Stanley Cup Final against the New York Rangers, his former team. When the dust settled, Gáboík had scored 14 goals, the most that post-season, and helped the Kings secure their second Cup in three years.

With Gáboík in the lineup, the Kings went from one of the most offensively anemic teams in the regular season to the highest-scoring club in the playoffs. Following the Stanley Cup victory, Los Angeles rewarded the seven-time 30-goal scorer by signing him to a seven-year, $34-million contract. In his first full season with the Kings, Gáboík scored 27 goals and 47 points. He played the better part of three more seasons in Los Angeles before being traded to the Ottawa Senators.

RAY BOURQUE JOINS THE AVALANCHE, 2000

Ray Bourque wanted one more shot at the Stanley Cup. The 21-year veteran blueliner had been with Boston his entire career, guided the Bruins to the Stanley Cup Final in 1988 and 1990, and come up empty-handed at the hands of the Edmonton Oilers in both series. He remained hopeful that he would eventually get the opportunity to hoist the trophy in a Bruins sweater, but as the club's 1999–2000 season unfolded, that seemed unlikely. With Boston sputtering and poised to miss the playoffs for just the second time since 1967, Bourque, not knowing how much hockey he had left in him, requested a trade to a Stanley Cup contender. On March 6, 2000, the Bruins granted his wish and traded Bourque, their franchise leader in games played and career scoring, along with Dave Andreychuk, to the Colorado Avalanche for Brian Rolston, Martin Grenier, Samuel Påhlsson, and a first-round pick in either 2000 or 2001.

Prior to the trade, Colorado was 30–27–10 and sat seventh in the Western Conference. Although Bourque was no longer the superstar he was earlier in his career, with him in the lineup, the Avalanche won 12 of their last 15 regular-season games and captured the Northwest Division. In the post-season, Colorado advanced to the Western Conference Final to take on the defending champions, the Dallas Stars. In Game 7, after rallying back from a three-goal deficit, the Avalanche pulled to within one. With less than 10 seconds remaining, Bourque had the game-tying goal on his stick, but the puck bounced off the post.

In the off-season, the 39-year-old defenceman opted to forgo unrestricted free agency and signed a one-year, $5.5-million contract with the Avalanche on June 14, 2000. "I think there's some unfinished business in terms of getting back to the Stanley Cup Finals," Bourque told reporters after the deal was announced. It proved to be the right decision. After securing the Presidents' Trophy with 118 points, the Avalanche went on to defeat the New Jersey Devils and win a second championship. After 22 years, Bourque finally got his Stanley Cup.

CAM NEELY NOTCHES 50 GOALS ONCE MORE, 1994

As the 1993–94 campaign approached, the Boston Bruins' Cam Neely would have been happy if he took 50 shifts that season. For the past two years, the hard-hitting goal scorer had been limited to only 22 games due to recurring issues with his left knee. In fact, when the season began in October, Neely was actually contemplating retirement if the situation with his nagging joint didn't improve. So when he ended up scoring 50 goals that year, it was completely unexpected. Neely had recorded back-to-back 50-goal seasons three years earlier, but as he continued to struggle to stay in the line-up, it seemed doubtful he'd reach that goal-scoring milestone again.

Heading into the Bruins' game against the Washington Capitals on March 7, 1994, Neely was sitting at 48 goals. Six minutes into the contest, the hard-nosed winger scored on the power play. He was now only one goal away. Just over halfway through the third period, with Boston leading 5–3, blueliner David Shaw fired a shot on net. Neely redirected the puck through the pads of Washington goaltender Don Beaupre to trigger a shower of hats and a raucous ovation from the Boston faithful. "It was a great feeling," Neely said after the game. "I definitely didn't expect anything like this." Scoring his 50th goal in just his 44th game of the season, Neely tied Mario Lemieux to become the second-fastest player in NHL history to reach the 50-goal mark. The pair trailed Wayne Gretzky, who scored 50 goals in 39 games during 1981–82, a seemingly impossible feat, and then 50 goals in 42 games two years later.

Despite Neely's incredible accomplishment, he isn't officially recognized as a member of the NHL's "50 Goals in 50 Games Club" because while it was his 44th game of the season, it was actually Boston's 66th contest. If anything, Neely's achievement is even more impressive because he battled back from a knee injury that almost forced him to hang up his skates for good. Neely's return to scoring form, however, was short-lived. In 1996, at the age of 31, he announced his retirement due to a degenerative hip condition.

MARCH 8
DOMINIK HAŠEK PICKS UP FIRST WIN, 1991

With Ed Belfour out with a hamstring injury, the Chicago Blackhawks recalled Dominik Hašek from the Indianapolis Ice, Chicago's AHL affiliate. It would be Hašek's first start for the Blackhawks in nearly four months. Although he was a talented goaltender and had proved his mettle in international competition, there wasn't much room for him in Chicago. Belfour, who had already started 60 games before going down with his injury, was the club's undisputed goaltender. And in Indianapolis, Hašek shared the crease with highly touted prospect Jimmy Waite. While it was frustrating for Hašek, he was eager to make the most of his appearances. On March 8, 1991, he made his second start for the Blackhawks in a game against the Buffalo Sabres, making 29 saves to record his first career NHL victory. Following his performance, the next day in the *Chicago Tribune*, Mike Kiley wrote: "It may be the start of a great career for Hašek." Kiley was proven right. It just wouldn't be in Chicago.

Although Hašek made another start, a 25-save victory against the Pittsburgh Penguins, and two more appearances in relief that season, the net was unquestionably Belfour's. While Hašek earned more opportunities the following year, with Belfour still the top netminder and Waite waiting in the wings, Chicago's crease remained crowded. As a result, on August 7, 1992, the Blackhawks traded Hašek to the Buffalo Sabres, the team he picked up his first career victory against, in exchange for goalie Stephane Beauregard and Buffalo's fourth-round pick in the 1993 NHL Entry Draft, which Chicago used to select Eric Daze. During his first season in Buffalo, Hašek shared the net with veteran netminders Daren Puppa and Grant Fuhr, but the next year, after Fuhr suffered a knee injury in November, Hašek took the reins. In the 1993–94 campaign, Hašek posted 30 victories, including seven shutouts. For his efforts that year, he was awarded the Vezina Trophy as the league's best goaltender, a distinction he earned five more times in Buffalo.

THEO FLEURY SCORES THREE SHORTIES, 1991

E ven Theo Fleury couldn't explain what happened. "I've never had more than one short-handed goal before," he said. "I don't really know what happened." Heading into a game against the Calgary Flames on March 9, 1991, the St. Louis Blues had one of the most frustrating power plays in the league. Although they did well with a man advantage — there were just seven teams with a better conversion rate — they gave up the most short-handed goals in the NHL. Early into the first period, the Blues were on a power play when Fleury, the Flames' diminutive forward who played his heart out every night, fired a shot past goalie Vincent Riendeau. After a busy second period in which Calgary and St. Louis combined for five goals, Fleury was sent back onto the ice early into the third period to kill another penalty. With defenceman Scott Stevens draped all over him, Fleury managed to fight him off and release a shot from close range, picking up his second short-handed goal of the night and tying the league record. After the Flames and Blues continued to exchange goals, Calgary held a 7–4 lead in the final minutes of the game.

With less than four minutes on the clock, the Flames' František Musil drew an interference penalty. The Blues were once again on the power play. There was no way Fleury could score another short-handed goal, right? Wrong. Less than halfway through Musil's penalty, Fleury streaked down the ice and scored his third short-handed goal of the game, establishing a new NHL record. Following the game, Blues head coach Brian Sutter, while disgusted with his team's performance, praised Fleury's efforts. "I've never seen anything like it at any level," he told reporters. In the nearly three decades that have followed, no other NHL player has matched Fleury's incredible performance against the Blues. Fifty-six different players have notched two short-handed goals in a single game since Fleury's feat through to the end of the 2020–21 campaign, but no one else has racked up a short-handed hat trick.

GOALIE EVGENI NABOKOV SCORES, 2002

t doesn't matter which team you cheer for — everyone can appreciate a goalie goal. Unless, of course, you're rooting for the team that just got scored on by a goalie. They're rare occurrences, but when they do happen, it's special. On November 28, 1979, Billy Smith was the first NHL goaltender credited with a goal as the last New York Islanders player to touch the puck before the Colorado Rockies' Rob Ramage scored on his own net, but on December 8, 1987, the Philadelphia Flyers' Ron Hextall was the first to actually score. Just over a year later, Hextall did it again, but this time in the Stanley Cup Playoffs, becoming the first NHL goaltender to record a goal in the post-season. In the years that followed, three other goaltenders — Chris Osgood, Martin Brodeur, and José Théodore — recorded goals by shooting the puck into the net. On March 10, 2002, Evgeni Nabokov joined the club. With 47.2 seconds left in a game against the Canucks, Nabokov capped off a 7–4 San Jose Sharks victory with an empty-net goal. Nabokov was actually planning to pass the puck to blueliner Brad Stuart, but then decided to go for it. While he had practised scoring hundreds of times, he had never come close to making it at the NHL level.

After collecting the puck at the top of his crease, Nabokov flipped the puck up and down the length of the ice. It landed just before the Vancouver blue line and then slid into the right corner of the net. As his teammates on the ice mobbed him in celebration, the Sharks' bench was all smiles. "I was just laughing, it was great," said Owen Nolan, who had a goal and four assists in the contest. While Nabokov's goal didn't change the outcome of the game, he was thrilled to have pulled it off and add it to his list of accomplishments. Following Nabokov's feat, it was more than a decade before another NHL goaltender scored a goal. On October 19, 2013, Mike Smith scored, and more recently, Pekka Rinne did it on January 9, 2020.

MARCH 11
FINAL GAME AT THE FORUM, 1996

t wasn't just the last game at an arena. It was the final matchup at one of hockey's most revered cathedrals. For 72 years, the Montreal Canadiens had called the Forum home. Nestled on the corner of Atwater Avenue and Sainte-Catherine Street, the building had hosted some of the franchise's most glorious moments. Among the Canadiens' two dozen Stanley Cups, 12 of them were clinched before the Montreal faithful at the Forum. So when the team was set to move into the Molson Centre, a $230-million, state-of-the-art facility, the final game felt like something more than the termination of an occupancy that had stretched beyond seven decades. It was the end of an important era in hockey history.

On March 11, 1996, the Canadiens played their last contest at the Forum. While the club defeated the Dallas Stars 4–1, the victory was merely a footnote in an evening that celebrated the club's rich history and venerated some of its greatest players. Before the game began, Jean Béliveau, Maurice Richard, and Guy Lafleur participated in a ceremonial faceoff at centre ice, but the highlight of the night was undoubtedly the closing ceremonies. Even before the final buzzer sounded, the fans rose to their feet in anticipation of what was to follow. In the dressing room, Émile Bouchard, the franchise's oldest living captain, lit a torch and proceeded onto the ice. In an emotional ceremony, Bouchard passed the torch to some of the captains who had followed in his footsteps. When it made its way to Richard, the crowd gave the fiery goal scorer the longest ovation, which lasted more than seven minutes. Finally, in a literal passing of the torch, it was given to Pierre Turgeon, the club's current captain. Acknowledging the history in his hands, Turgeon dutifully skated around the ice. Five nights later, when the Canadiens christened their new building, Turgeon emerged onto the ice holding high the lit torch — a new chapter was about to begin.

MARCH 12
OVECHKIN SCORES 600, 2018

Nastya Ovechkin had a feeling her husband was going to score his 600th career goal. She had just returned home from Moscow in time for the Washington Capitals hosting of the Winnipeg Jets on March 12, 2018. Although Alex Ovechkin was still a couple of goals away from reaching the milestone, a wife perhaps knew. Early in the first period, Ovechkin scored on a five-on-three power play to move closer to the mark. Less than four minutes into the second frame, it looked as if Nastya's intuition was right. With the Capitals scrambling around Connor Hellebuyck's crease, Ovechkin fired the puck up and over the sprawling Winnipeg netminder to notch his 600th career goal, becoming the 20th player in league history to accomplish that feat. Only Wayne Gretzky, Mario Lemieux, and Brett Hull had reached the milestone faster than he had. In addition to etching his name into the record books, Ovechkin's two-goal performance moved him past Jets winger Patrik Laine for sole possession of the goal-scoring lead that season.

Heading into the contest, Laine, who idolized Ovechkin growing up, and the Russian sharpshooter were tied at 40 goals apiece. Although Laine added one of his own five minutes into the third period, Ovechkin was once again on pace to win the NHL's goal-scoring title for the seventh time. The Russian sniper picked up seven more goals that campaign to finish with 49 and take home his seventh Rocket Richard Trophy. But Ovechkin saved his best for the playoffs that year. In the post-season, he racked up 15 goals, including the game-winning goal in Game 7 of the Eastern Conference Final against the Tampa Bay Lightning and three in the Stanley Cup Final as he led the Capitals to their first Cup in franchise history. The following season, Ovechkin continued to make his case as the greatest goal scorer in NHL history when he notched 51 goals to reach the 50-goal mark for the eighth time in his career. Had the 2019–20 season not been halted by the Covid-19 pandemic, it's likely Ovechkin would have hit 50 again.

MARCH 13
LONGEST HOCKEY GAME ENDS, 2017

Admittedly, I'm cheating a bit on this story. When the puck dropped for Game 5 of the playoff series between the Storhamar Dragons and the Sparta Warriors of the GET-ligaen, Norway's premier hockey league, it was March 12, 2017. But when the game finally ended, more than eight and a half hours later, it was the early morning of March 13. After 60 minutes of regulation, the two teams were tied 1–1. The first overtime period solved nothing. The second overtime period solved nothing. The third overtime period solved nothing. The fourth overtime period solved nothing. The fifth overtime period solved nothing. The sixth overtime period solved nothing. If you're tired of reading that over and over, just imagine how the players must have felt. In the seventh overtime period, Storhamar was awarded a penalty shot, but Warriors goaltender Samuel Ward made the save and the clubs remained deadlocked.

In between periods, in order to keep their energy levels up, players were scarfing down pizza, pasta, and peanut butter sandwiches. Finally, with time winding down in the eight overtime period, the Dragons' Joakim Jensen wired a slap shot from the faceoff circle to beat Ward and mercifully end the game. For some of the players, it felt as though it was never going to be over. "It just seemed like every time you would look up at the clock there would be one minute left in another overtime and another overtime," said Dragons forward Joey Tenute following the game. The contest endured for 217 minutes and 14 seconds of play, easily surpassing the 176 minutes and 30 seconds of play that the Detroit Red Wings and Montreal Wanderers battled through in 1936, making it the longest recorded game in hockey history. Despite the gruelling matchup, it was the playoffs and the exhausted players were back at it again less than two nights later. Although Storhamar held a 3–2 series lead following the 2–1 marathon overtime victory, Sparta won the next two games to take the series.

MARCH 14
JOE MULLEN GETS 500, 1997

J oe Mullen didn't want to talk about it. For about a month, he'd been stuck at 499 goals. Five years earlier, he'd scored his 400th career goal in a game against the Edmonton Oilers, becoming the first U.S.-born player to reach that mark, but as he approached the next milestone, the gritty winger was tight-lipped. Although Mullen was the highest-scoring American player at the time, he never pictured racking up 500 career goals in the NHL. A native New Yorker, Mullen had grown up playing roller hockey on the streets of Hell's Kitchen. After playing for Boston College, he went undrafted and was signed as a free agent by the Blues. Following five seasons in St. Louis, Mullen was traded to the Calgary Flames, where he won a Stanley Cup in 1989. The next season, he was dealt to the Pittsburgh Penguins, where he was a part of back-to-back Stanley Cup wins and established new benchmarks for U.S.-born players.

After a brief stint with the Boston Bruins, Mullen returned to the Penguins as a free agent for the 1996–97 season. But Mullen, who was turning 40 that year, struggled early into the campaign. He spent much of October and November in the press box as a scratch. Mullen's first goal of the season didn't come until December 30. He recorded his fourth, the 499th of his career, on February 18 and then was stalled. While Mullen didn't want to talk about when he'd reach the plateau, he was sure it would happen. He had to be. Before a Penguins' road game against the Avalanche on March 14, 1997, Mullen was approached by Colorado's equipment manager, Steve Latin, asking if he'd sign a pair of Michel Goulet jerseys. Goulet, who was the Avalanche's director of player personnel and a member of the NHL's 500-goal club, had been collecting signatures from the league's other 500-goal scorers. Still sitting at 499 goals, Mullen was reluctant to autograph the pair of jerseys but obliged the request. That night Mullen not only signed, he delivered. Late in the second period, he scored his 500th goal.

MARCH 15
CRAIG SIMPSON SCORES 50, 1988

n his first two seasons in Pittsburgh, Craig Simpson scored 37 goals. Drafted second overall by the Penguins in 1985, he was poised for a breakout year in 1987–88. Through his first 21 games of the season, Simpson had scored 13 goals. But then, on November 24, 1987, he, along with Dave Hannan, Chris Joseph, and Moe Mantha, was traded to the Oilers in exchange for Paul Coffey, Wayne Van Dorp, and Dave Hunter. Arriving in Edmonton, the 21-year-old winger found himself on a line with Mark Messier and Glenn Anderson and picked up right where he'd left off. As Simpson found chemistry with his new linemates, he shattered his career high in goals and seemed likely to approach the vaunted 50-goal mark.

Heading into a matchup against the Winnipeg Jets on March 7, 1988, after racking up 31 goals with the Oilers, Simpson sat at 47. He picked up two goals that game but figures he should have recorded a hat trick to reach the milestone. As Simpson recalls, he was on a two-on-one with Wayne Gretzky. Anticipating Gretzky might not get the puck to him on the far side, Simpson switched his approach. By the time he made his move, Gretzky had already threaded the needle, sending the puck through the defenceman's skates over to where Simpson should have been. That was the last time he moved out of position while on a rush with the Great One. Although Simpson was kicking himself, he wasn't stuck at 49 for long. Just over a week later, on March 15, 1988, he caught a pass from Messier at the edge of the goal crease and slipped it by Buffalo Sabres goaltender Jacques Cloutier to record his 50th. Simpson not only became the third-youngest 50-goal scorer behind only Gretzky and Pierre Larouche, he also became the first player in NHL history to score 50 goals in a season while splitting time with two teams. Simpson finished the season with 56 and added 13 more in the playoffs as the Oilers went on to win their fourth Stanley Cup.

MARCH 16
CLARENCE CAMPBELL SUSPENDS THE ROCKET, 1955

Montreal Canadiens fans held their collective breath as they waited for NHL President Clarence Campbell to make his ruling. Three days earlier, in a game against the Boston Bruins, Montreal winger Maurice "Rocket" Richard got into a dust-up with Hal Laycoe. During the altercation, however, Richard landed a punch on linesman Cliff Thompson. With blood streaming down his face, the Rocket was assessed a match penalty, a punishment that carried an indefinite suspension, a $100 fine, and investigation by the league president. It wasn't the first time Richard was in hot water with Campbell. A few months earlier, during a contest against the Toronto Maple Leafs, Richard had struck linesman George Hayes, for which he received a $250 fine, which some viewed as too lenient. Given his track record, and the severity of the infraction, many expected Campbell to throw the book at Richard once and for all.

On March 16, 1955, after a three-hour meeting and a 1,200-word assessment, Campbell determined that Richard would sit out Montreal's final three games and the entire post-season. The Rocket was devastated. In the wake of the decision, he reportedly contemplated retirement. Montreal was beside itself, too. Many believed that Campbell treated francophone players more harshly than their English counterparts, and the suspension of Richard, who was on his way to winning the scoring title — a distinction that had eluded his grasp since he'd joined the NHL in 1942 — was the last straw. In the ensuing days, Campbell received death threats, a few threatening to blow up the league's office, the historic Sun Life Building on Metcalfe Street in Montreal. With tensions running high and against advice, Campbell attended the Canadiens' next game on St. Patrick's Day. Things turned ugly in the arena, and a riot spilled onto the streets. By the time police had things under control, hundreds of thousands of dollars' worth of damage had been done and at least 60 people had been arrested.

MARCH 17
MARTIN BRODEUR BECOMES WINNINGEST GOALIE, 2009

Martin Brodeur couldn't have scripted it any better. On March 14, 2009, with his friends and family in the stands in his hometown of Montreal, Brodeur made 22 saves to record his 551st career victory, tying Patrick Roy for the most wins by a goaltender in NHL history. Before the game, the New Jersey Devils' netminder met with Roy at his hotel. Roy, who had tended goal for the Montreal Canadiens from 1985 to 1996, just wanted to wish him good luck. For Brodeur, that meant a lot. He had grown up idolizing Roy and then had the opportunity to play with him internationally and against him in the NHL. After matching Roy, Brodeur's next opportunity to surpass him was on St. Patrick's Day, no less. Given his stellar career, which included four Stanley Cups, three Conn Smythe Trophies, and three Vezina Trophies, Roy had come by the nickname "St. Patrick" quite honestly.

Three nights after the victory in Montreal, the Devils hosted the Chicago Blackhawks. With history on the line, New Jersey gave its goaltender an early lead. Just 38 seconds into the game, captain Jamie Langenbrunner scored to make it 1–0. Brodeur, doing his part, made 14 saves in the first period, and the Devils went into intermission with a two-goal lead. After New Jersey extended its lead late in the second period, the Blackhawks responded with a power play goal less than a minute later. When Brodeur stepped onto the ice for the final frame, he was 20 minutes away from making history. But with just over three minutes remaining, Dustin Byfuglien scored to cut the deficit to one. Although the victory was still within his sights, Brodeur needed to remain sharp until the final buzzer. With only three seconds left on the clock, Troy Brouwer nearly tied the game, but Brodeur made the save to secure the win and his name in the record books. As Brodeur skated around the ice, the crowd chanted his name. He was the winningest goaltender in NHL history.

MARCH 18

GORDIE HOWE MAKES COACHING DEBUT, 1967

P acing back and forth behind the bench in a suit and tie, Gordie Howe looked out of place. The hard-nosed winger should have been on the ice with his teammates, but a bruised right shoulder had forced him out of the game. Since the 1949–50 season, his fourth campaign in the NHL, Howe had only missed 18 games. He was incredibly durable and regarded as one of the toughest and most skilled players in the game. Despite having a sore shoulder, Howe had tried to stay in the lineup. Before the Detroit Red Wings' game against the Boston Bruins on March 18, 1967, Howe had taken a warm-up with the team and desperately wanted to play. There was just one problem. His shoulder was so sore that he couldn't shoot. Even though a limited Gordie Howe was better than no Gordie Howe, head coach Sid Abel vetoed the idea. So with his star winger sidelined, Abel took the opportunity to watch the game from the press box and give Howe some coaching experience. Although Howe had actually coached a few Red Wings exhibition games, he had never been behind the bench for a regular-season match.

Things didn't start off the way Howe would have drawn it up. Less than two minutes into the game, the Red Wings went down 1–0. Making matters worse, Detroit winger Paul Henderson reinjured his groin early in the contest and sat out the rest of the way. Howe didn't end up doing much juggling with his lines, and his team tried to earn him the victory. The Red Wings tied the game late in the first period, and after the Bruins regained the lead in the second frame, Detroit answered back to tie the match 2–2 before the final frame. But after the Red Wings tied the contest for the third time in the third period, the Bruins scored two goals in less than a minute to put the game out of reach. While Howe's first time behind the bench didn't go exactly as planned, it was short-lived. He was back on the ice the next night for Detroit's game against the Toronto Maple Leafs. His shoulder must have been feeling much better — he scored two goals and picked up an assist.

MARCH 19

SABRES SCORE NINE IN A PERIOD, 1981

There wasn't much action in the first period. Although the Buffalo Sabres' Jon Van Boxmeer scored six minutes in to give the Sabres a 1–0 lead over the Toronto Maple Leafs, it seemed like just another game at the Auditorium. But when the teams took to the ice in the second period, everything changed. In the first half of the second frame, the Sabres scored four unanswered goals, taking a 5–0 lead, and the barrage continued. After Gilbert Perreault scored Buffalo's fifth of the match, Darryl Sittler connected 11 seconds later to get the Leafs on the board. Thirty seconds later, Terry Martin scored and Toronto closed the gap. But less than two minutes after that, Craig Ramsay notched one and Buffalo once again had a four-goal lead. Forty-two seconds further on, Sittler scored his second of the game to make it 6–3. Less than two minutes later, André Savard, who had already assisted on two of Buffalo's goals, scored his 25th of the season. As time wound down in the second period, the scoring remained relentless. With just over three minutes left, the Sabres added three more to make it 10–3.

It was a record-setting period. The Sabres' nine-goal period outburst erased the previous mark of eight. After the Red Wings scored eight goals in the third period as part of a 15–0 shellacking of the New York Rangers on January 23, 1944, five other teams, including the Sabres, had racked up eight in a period. In addition to that benchmark, the combined 12 goals and 31 points between the two teams set NHL records for the most goals and points in a single period. But it didn't stop there. The barnstorming continued in the third period. The Leafs mercifully pulled Michel "Bunny" Larocque, who had given up 10 goals, and replaced him with Jiří Crha, who didn't fare much better. Although Toronto opened the scoring first in the final frame, the Sabres followed up with four more goals to win 14–4. Savard, who finished with three goals and three assists, called it a "great, beautiful night." For Buffalo, anyway.

MARCH 20
PENGUINS TRADE MARKUS NÄSLUND, 1996

I t looked as though Markus Näslund was finally living up to his billing. Drafted 16th overall by the Penguins in 1991, the Swedish left winger had faced his share of early struggles in Pittsburgh. In his rookie campaign, 1993–94, he recorded 11 points in 71 games. The following season, he split time with the Penguins and the Cleveland Lumberjacks, the club's International Hockey League affiliate. Frustrated with the situation, Näslund requested a trade. But by the 1995–96 season, Näslund found himself on the Penguins' top lines, playing with Jaromír Jágr and Ron Francis and then alongside Mario Lemieux and Tomas Sandström. In his first 21 games of the season, Näslund racked up 23 points, including his first career hat trick on November 28, 1995, against the Ottawa Senators. As the season continued, Näslund's torrid pace dropped off and he occasionally found himself in the press box as a scratch. Despite his improved play, he was in the last year of his contract and continued to be the subject of trade rumours.

On March 20, 1996, the Penguins traded him to the Vancouver Canucks for Alek Stojanov, a hard-nosed winger taken eight spots ahead of Näslund in the 1991 draft. It turned out to be one of the most lopsided deals in NHL history. Stojanov suited up for just 45 games for the Penguins, scoring six points, while Näslund went on to play 884 games in Vancouver and become one of the greatest players in franchise history. Although Näslund had initially wanted out of Vancouver after finding himself at loggerheads with head coach Mike Keenan, he eventually earned more opportunities and established himself with the Canucks. By the 2000–01 campaign, he was team captain and scored 41 goals before breaking his leg with 10 games remaining on the schedule. In 2001–02, playing on a line with Todd Bertuzzi and Brendan Morrison, dubbed The West Coast Express, Näslund racked up 90 points. The next season, he recorded 104 points and was named a finalist for the Hart Trophy.

MARCH 21
SOUTH KOREA TROUNCES THAILAND, 1998

By the first intermission, South Korea had already fired 71 shots on net. Pramote Saeheng, the goalkeeper for Thailand, who was making its international hockey debut at the 1998 Asia-Oceania U18 Championship, made a valiant effort, but South Korea held a 36–0 lead. Things didn't get any better for Saeheng and Thailand in the second period. South Korea outshot their opponents 50–1 and added another 24 goals. Leading 60–0 heading into the final frame, the South Koreans didn't let up. They scored 32 more goals to win 92–0, the most lopsided defeat in international hockey history. When the dust settled, the scorekeepers had to fill out a five-page game report just to record all those goals, of which 33 belonged to sniper Song Dong-hwan. The South Koreans ended up winning the championship, while their Thai counterparts went 0–5 with a minus 214 goal differential.

Less than a month later, at the European juniors, Kazakhstan inflicted similar damage on its opponents. It was actually Kazakhstan's first entry in the European U18 tournament, since it would have previously matched up in the Asian Oceania competition, where South Korea had recently dominated. The Kazakhs opened the competition by thrashing Iceland 63–0 and then defeating Luxembourg 39–0. They went on to win their division, guided by the incredible performance of future NHLer Nik Antropov, who recorded 23 goals and 54 points in only five games.

Although South Korea still holds the record for inflicting the biggest loss on the international stage, and probably will for quite some time, Slovakia's women's team came close in 2008. During the Olympic qualifying competition, the Slovaks trounced Bulgaria 82–0 in what would be the largest margin of victory in an international women's game. Dobromir Krastev, chair of the Bulgarian Hockey Federation, called it "an insulting mockery."

NHL EXPERIMENTS WITH RED LINE, 1932

n the final game of the 1931–32 season, the NHL tried to shake things up. In a matchup between the Boston Bruins and the New York Americans, on March 22, 1932, the league included a red line at centre ice in an effort to generate scoring opportunities. The idea was put forth by Boston coach Art Ross, who was always trying to improve the game. While the NHL had adopted forward passing within all three zones in advance of the 1929–30 season, it was only permitted if players were in the same zone. A pass couldn't cross either of the two blue lines, otherwise the play would be ruled offside. Ross hoped that a centre red line would add more excitement and skill to the game because it would allow teams to break out of the defensive zone by passing up to players in the neutral zone before crossing the red line.

Although Ross had been advocating for the change all season, introducing it in a meaningless game between the cellar-dwelling Bruins and Americans, with nothing at stake, was the wrong move. New York's *Daily News* referred to it as "one of the dullest games played here in years." Despite Boston supposedly having an advantage since the rule change was Ross's idea, they lost 8–6. Coverage of the game concluded that the Americans were more adept at passing up and through the neutral zone than their counterparts. There was also some confusion among the officials, who continued to call offsides even though players were permitted to make passes across the blue lines. And so, despite the high-scoring affair and Ross's insistence that it would open up a team's attacking tactics, the red line didn't stick around. Although the league didn't immediately adopt it, Ross, as with many of his hockey innovations, was on the right track. Prior to the 1943–44 season, more than a decade after Ross's experiment, the NHL finally adopted the red line, leading to the emergence of the modern hockey era.

MARCH 23

THE GREAT ONE BECOMES THE GREATEST GOAL SCORER, 1994

L ate in the second period in a game against the Vancouver Canucks on March 23, 1994, Marty McSorley dished the puck to Wayne Gretzky, who easily found the back of the net. As Gretzky jubilantly raised his arms into the air and skated away from the net, the faithful crowd at the Great Western Forum erupted into a raucous ovation. Gretzky had just scored his 802nd career goal, vaulting him ahead of his boyhood idol, Gordie Howe, for the most goals in NHL history. The Great One was now the greatest goal scorer.

Had Gretzky not scored that night in Los Angeles, his next opportunity would have been on the road against the Oilers, which would have set the stage for him to make history yet again in Edmonton. Five years earlier, when he was chasing down Howe's points record, he rewrote the record book against the Oilers. It couldn't have happened in a more fitting place. Gretzky had begun his NHL career with the Oilers, shattering league records and winning four Stanley Cups before he was dealt to the Los Angeles Kings in August 1988. While Gretzky had the game against Edmonton circled on his calendar when he was zeroing in on the points record, a potential matchup against his former team didn't really cross his mind this time around. "I was just hoping I could do it as fast as I could and let my mom and dad go home," Gretzky once told me. But time was of the essence. Gretzky's father, Walter, who had suffered a brain aneurysm in 1991, was running short on his medication while he and wife, Phyllis, followed their son on the record-breaking tour. Not wanting his dad to miss out on the milestone, Gretzky had some extra motivation to topple the record in Los Angeles. Following the goal, Gretzky's family joined him on the ice where the NHL acknowledged the accomplishment and presented him with a book that included the score sheet from every game that he scored a goal in. Just some light reading.

MARCH 24
MIKE LEGG'S LACROSSE GOAL, 1996

Mike Legg never played lacrosse. And yet the right winger, who was drafted by the New Jersey Devils in 1993, is probably best known for scoring a lacrosse-style goal. On March 24, 1996, with a berth to the National Collegiate Athletic Association (NCAA) Frozen Four on the line, the University of Michigan Wolverines were trailing 2–1 to the University of Minnesota Gophers in the second period. While the Wolverines were on a power play, Legg was behind the Gophers' goal when he scooped the puck up off the ice and onto his blade. Carefully balancing the disk on his stick, Legg put it into the corner of the net behind goaltender Steve DeBus. Although Legg had practised the move plenty of times, he was still surprised when it went in. "It has to be just right," Legg told reporters. "I have to be all alone behind the goal. I have to get down and get my stick real flat on the ice, then use gravity to get the puck on its edge. Then you take a step and put it in the top corner." Teammate Bill Muckalt, who actually spent some time on a lacrosse field, was astounded. "We were all in awe seeing him do that," he said after the game.

Following Legg's game-tying heroics, the teams traded goals before Muckalt notched the game-winner with two minutes remaining. After defeating Boston University in the semifinals, Michigan advanced to the championship game against Colorado College. Legg once again scored the tying goal, and Michigan won in overtime to secure its first NCAA title. But it was Legg's goal against the Gophers that has been immortalized in hockey lore. For some, it is known as a lacrosse goal, while others simply call it "The Michigan." After Carolina Hurricanes winger Andrei Svechnikov became the first NHL player to pull it off on October 29, 2019, in a game against the Calgary Flames, and then again just over a month later, there's a case to be made that perhaps, moving forward, it should be known as "The Svech."

MARCH 25

PIERRE LAROUCHE SCORES 50 GOALS FOR TWO TEAMS, 1980

With time winding down, the Chicago Black Hawks pulled their goaltender in an effort to tie the game against the Montreal Canadiens, who were up 6–4. But after Montreal defenceman Rod Langway scored with 43 seconds left to extend the lead, the Black Hawks sent Tony Esposito back into his net. It was just as well for Pierre Larouche, who was approaching his 50th goal of the season. The 24-year-old centre notched his 49th goal late in the second period but didn't want to score his milestone marker on an empty net. With Esposito back in his crease, Larouche scored again. "I wouldn't want to tell my children there was nobody in the net when I got my 50th, " he told reporters after the game. Larouche had a better story he could tell his kids. With that goal, he became the first player in NHL history to score 50 goals for two different teams.

Four years earlier, as a member of the Pittsburgh Penguins, Larouche reached the 50-goal mark for the first time in his career in a game against the Washington Capitals on April 3, 1976. Larouche, who had torched the Quebec Major Junior Hockey League for 94 goals and 251 points in the 1973–74 season, was drafted eighth overall by the Penguins later that year. After scoring 31 goals in his rookie campaign in Pittsburgh, the 20-year-old Larouche hit the 50-goal mark the next season, becoming the youngest player in NHL history to score 50 or more goals in a season, a mark surpassed four years later when Wayne Gretzky entered the league. But after finishing that season with 53 goals, Larouche dropped off to 29 the following season. Despite his talents, he wasn't a fit in Pittsburgh, and on November 29, 1977, Larouche was traded to the Canadiens, along with future considerations, for Pete Mahovlich and Peter Lee. By his second full season in Montreal, 1979–80, Larouche, flanked by wingers Guy Lafleur and Steve Shutt, picked up where he left off in Pittsburgh and reached the 50-goal mark for the second time in his career, making NHL history again.

MARCH 26

FIGHT NIGHT AT THE JOE, 1997

There had been bad blood brewing between the Detroit Red Wings and Colorado Avalanche for quite some time. During their 1996 Western Conference Final series, Colorado's Claude Lemieux cross-checked Detroit's Kris Draper from behind, sending him face first into the boards. Draper suffered a broken jaw, a shattered cheek and orbital bone, and sustained a concussion. When the two teams met in Detroit for the first time the following season, Lemieux wasn't in the lineup. It was a rough game, but not the powder keg many expected it to be. That game came down the stretch as both clubs geared up for the playoffs.

On March 26, 1997, the Red Wings hosted the Avalanche in a game that became known as "Fight Night at the Joe." Following a few quick dust-ups early into the first period, the Avalanche's Peter Forsberg collided with the Red Wings' Igor Larionov. While the two wrestled along the boards, Detroit's Darren McCarty decked Lemieux, who was making his first appearance at Joe Louis Arena since the Draper incident. As McCarty got his shots in on Lemieux, goaltender Patrick Roy charged out of his crease to defend his teammate. But before he could intervene, Detroit's Brendan Shanahan leaped toward him, tackling him to the ice. As Adam Foote attempted to pull Shanahan away from his goaltender, Mike Vernon joined the fracas. After Roy dragged Vernon out of the skirmish, the pair got into a spirited bout that left the Avalanche goaltender bloodied.

Following the first-period melee, the second frame was punctuated by six goals and even more fights. Although trailing by two goals in the third period, the Red Wings overcame the deficit and won in overtime. After the victory, Vernon said it was a game that brought the team together: "Whether it was the first-period fighting or the overtime goal, a game like this only helps give you confidence going into the playoffs." The Red Wings went on to win the Stanley Cup that year, but that game at the Joe ignited one of hockey's greatest rivalries.

MARCH 27

SHERRY ROSS FIRST WOMAN TO DO NHL PLAY-BY-PLAY, 1993

After covering the New Jersey Devils for more than a decade as a writer, Sherry Ross received an offer she couldn't refuse. In December 1991, while she was between gigs, the Devils' president and general manager, Lou Lamoriello, approached her about becoming a broadcaster for the club. Ross accepted and began a six-game tryout doing colour commentary for New Jersey's radio broadcasts. Her first game was on December 21, 1991, when the Devils hosted the Chicago Blackhawks. According to Ross, it didn't go well. The game ended in a 1–1 tie, and she felt that with so little action on the ice, she didn't contribute much throughout the broadcast. But as Ross continued working as an analyst, her confidence grew and she earned the job, becoming the first full-time female broadcaster on radio or television in the NHL. Ross relished her new role. In a story with the *Daily Record*'s Sandy Seegers, Ross talked about how much she loved radio. "I'm not looking to go back to writing," she said. "I'd be a happy camper if this works out for me. I could see myself staying with the Devils forever."

Just over a year later, Ross got another opportunity when the Devils hosted the Washington Capitals on March 27, 1993. Gary Thorne, who had been serving as the Devils' play-by-play voice since 1987, was late arriving to the game after calling a contest in Winnipeg for ESPN. In his absence, Ross put on her headset and called the first period, becoming the first woman to do play-by-play of an NHL game. As Ross continued to establish her bona fides as a radio analyst, she blazed a trail for women in the industry. In 1994, she became the first woman to serve as an analyst during the Stanley Cup Final. And nearly two decades after filling in for Thorne, Ross made history again when she became the first English-speaking female broadcaster to provide play-by-play for an entire NHL game when the Devils hosted the Ottawa Senators on November 25, 2009. Ross replaced Matt Loughlin, who missed the contest following the death of his father-in-law.

MARCH 28

CAPITALS WIN FIRST ROAD VICTORY, 1975

t was just a road victory, but for the Washington Capitals it felt like something more. Playing in their first NHL season, Washington endured a dreadful campaign. The club lost 37 consecutive games on the road and racked up 64 losses. Through 75 games, they had just six victories. When they arrived in Oakland to take on the California Golden Seals on March 28, 1975, the Capitals were mired in a 17-game losing streak, and most people expected it would continue. But three minutes into the first period, Washington captain Doug Mohns scored on a pass from former Seals player Tommy Williams to go up 1–0. Less than a minute later, Ron Anderson extended the lead. The Seals got on the board with just over four minutes remaining in the first frame, but Gord Smith responded less than a minute later to restore Washington's two-goal lead.

After the intermission, the two teams combined for just nine shots in a dreary second period, but rookie Charlie Simmer converted on one of them to make it 3–2. Early into the third period, the Seals' Butch Williams sprung Dave Gardner on a breakaway, who made it 3–3. Shortly after giving up the tying goal, Washington's Nelson Pyatt tallied his fourth of the season to take the lead for good. With the Seals' net vacant, Pyatt added an empty-netter in the final 16 seconds to secure a 5–3 victory.

The Capitals had snapped their skid and won their first game on the road. In the dressing room following the game, Tommy Williams picked up a garbage can and hoisted it as if it were a trophy. Although there's still some debate over whether it was a metal trash can or Rubbermaid pail, either way, after so many losses, it felt like the Stanley Cup. Williams even took it out onto the ice and skated around as if they had, in fact, won the championship. When he returned to the dressing room, everyone signed it. It might not have been hockey's ultimate prize, but for Washington, the "Stanley Can" was a close second.

FAN GETS UP CLOSE AND PERSONAL WITH TIE DOMI, 2001

A s the Toronto Maple Leafs' Tie Domi sat in the penalty box in the third period at the First Union Center in Philadelphia, he heard something from the Flyers' fans. Never one to back down from taunting, the hard-nosed forward turned and sprayed his water bottle into the crowd. After a couple of squirts, a Havertown concrete worker, Chris Falcone, got out of his seat and made his way toward the penalty box. From the second row, Falcone leaped onto the glass in an attempt to snatch the water bottle from Domi. As the attendant tried to get him to back off, Falcone leaned on the glass, trying to snag the bottle or land a punch. Suddenly, the glass panel collapsed and Falcone tumbled into the penalty box. With the two now nose to nose in the confined space, colour commentator Harry Neale warned, "Watch the lawsuit, Tie." Falcone lunged toward Domi, but the Leafs winger got hold of him and pulled his jacket over his head. Then Domi got in a few quick shots before the officials separated them.

Following the game, Domi joked to reporters: "Hey, that's old-time hockey, it was perfect. Hey, he comes into my territory, that's what happens." But Domi should have heeded Neale's legal advice. About two years later, Falcone filed a lawsuit against Domi, seeking up to $50,000 in damages. Although Domi kept winning the court cases, Falcone, represented by a relative, continued to appeal the decisions. By 2004, Domi was still embroiled in the situation and racking up legal bills. With his lawyers unable to resolve the matter, Domi took the case into his own hands. He figured if he could talk to Falcone himself, he could get the man to drop the lawsuit. In his book, *Shift Work*, Domi recounts how he asked Falcone to meet him in the visitors' dressing room after a game in Philadelphia. Domi told Falcone that he would fly him and his family up to Toronto for two playoff games and install them in the Royal York Hotel if he dropped the lawsuit. Falcone agreed, and that was that.

MARCH 30
VICTORIA COUGARS WIN STANLEY CUP, 1925

The Montreal Canadiens were simply outmatched. Although they had taken the third game of the Stanley Cup Final against the Victoria Cougars of the Western Canada Hockey League (WCHL) to avoid getting swept, it was clear they couldn't match the speed and skill of their western counterparts. When the puck dropped for the fourth and potentially deciding game on March 30, 1925, the Cougars continued their dominance. Playing under West Coast rules, which included the use of six skaters and a limited forward pass, Victoria skated circles around Montreal.

After Frank Frederickson got the Cougars on the board five minutes into the game, the Canadiens simply couldn't muster a response. According to newspaper coverage of the day, there were often five Montreal players behind the blue line simply waiting for the Cougars' attack, which proved costly. While the Canadiens added a tally in the second period, Victoria got three more goals that frame to put the game out of reach. In the third period, the Cougars fired 21 shots on goal while limiting Montreal to just six. After adding two more goals to take the game and the series, Victoria was awarded the Stanley Cup.

While it wasn't the first time a West Coast club had wrestled the trophy away from its eastern counterparts, the true significance of the Cougars' victory wouldn't be understood for several years. The following season, after the Regina Capitals relocated to Portland, Oregon, becoming the Rosebuds, the WCHL became the Western Hockey League (WHL). The Cougars emerged as the league's top team and took on the Canadiens in Montreal in a battle for the championship. This time around, however, the Canadiens got the better of their opponents and the Stanley Cup remained in the East. But there would be no rematch the next year. The WHL, which had been enduring financial problems, folded after selling its top players and teams to the NHL. In 1947, the NHL formally took control of the Stanley Cup, and the 1925 Victoria Cougars became the last non-NHL team to hoist Lord Stanley's mug.

MARCH 31

GOLDEN KNIGHTS CLINCH PACIFIC DIVISION, 2018

The Vegas Golden Knights defied expectations all season. Playing in their inaugural NHL campaign, the team, comprised largely of castoffs from the league's other teams, wasn't expected to be very competitive. Although history has shown that expansion teams don't fare well initially, Vegas proved to be the exception. Embracing the perception that they were a team of misfits, they banded together and proved their detractors wrong. As the season unfolded, they racked up victory after victory and rewrote the NHL's record book. In their 50th game of the season on February 1, 2018, they recorded their 34th win, establishing a new benchmark for most wins in a debut season. A few weeks later on February 21, 2018, following a 7–3 rout of the Calgary Flames, Vegas notched its 84th point, setting a record for most points by an expansion team in its opening season. And just over a month after that, it clinched a playoff spot, becoming the first NHL team in nearly four decades to earn a trip to the post-season in only its first campaign.

When the Golden Knights hosted the San Jose Sharks on March 31, 2018, the Pacific Division title was on the line. With the game tied 2–2 in the third period, William Karlsson, who had been a revelation for the Golden Knights that season, scored his niftiest goal of the year, going between his legs on a short-handed breakaway to beat Sharks goaltender Martin Jones top shelf. It held up as the game-winner as Vegas defeated San Jose 3–2 to claim the Pacific title, becoming the first modern expansion team from any of the four major North American leagues to win its division in its first season. The Golden Knights picked up another win a few nights later to notch their 51st and final victory of the season, extending their record for the most wins by a first-year expansion NHL team. By the time this book comes out, the Seattle Kraken will be gearing up for their inaugural campaign and will have their work cut out for them if they hope to match Vegas's accomplishments.

APRIL 1

REGGIE LEACH SCORES 60, 1976

Reggie Leach came by his nickname "The Riverton Rifle" quite honestly. He was from Riverton, Manitoba, and had one of the most lethal shots in the NHL. After racking up 255 goals in junior hockey with the Flin Flon Bombers, including one season in which he sniped 87, Leach was drafted third overall by the Bruins in 1970. He only spent parts of two seasons in Boston, however, before he was traded to the Golden Seals. Following two years with California, Leach was acquired by the Philadelphia Flyers on May 24, 1974, in exchange for Larry Wright, Al MacAdam, and a first-round draft pick. In Philadelphia, Leach was reunited with former Bomber teammate and friend Bobby Clarke. Along with Bill Barber, they formed the fearsome LCB Line. After scoring just 60 goals in his first four NHL seasons, Leach regained his scoring touch flanking Clarke and Barber. In his first season with the Flyers, Leach scored 45 goals and helped the club win its second straight Stanley Cup. Following his breakout campaign, Leach, and The LCB Line, continued to light the lamp.

Heading into a game against the lowly Washington Capitals on April 1, 1976, Leach was sitting at 58 goals. In an 11–2 rout of Washington, Leach found the back of the twine twice to reach the 60-goal mark, becoming only the second player in NHL history to accomplish that milestone. In addition to Leach's landmark achievement, Clarke picked up five assists, a club record, and Barber recorded a hat trick. The performance gave The LCB Line 140 goals for the season, tying the league record for most goals in a campaign by one line. Two nights later in a game against the Buffalo Sabres, the unit combined for another goal, breaking the record set by the Boston Bruins' line of Phil Esposito, Ken Hodge, and Wayne Cashman in the 1970–71 season. In the playoffs, Leach continued filling the back of the net. He scored 19 goals in 16 games, winning the Conn Smythe Trophy in a losing effort to the Montreal Canadiens in the Stanley Cup Final.

APRIL 2

PAUL COFFEY BEATS BOBBY ORR'S GOAL RECORD, 1986

Paul Coffey thought it would be impossible to surpass one of Bobby Orr's records. Although the smooth-skating defence-man's end-to-end rushes were reminiscent of how Orr played the game, the Boston superstar's 46 goals and 139 points in a season seemed out of reach for any blueliner coming after him. In his fourth season with the Edmonton Oilers, Coffey came close. He scored 40 goals in the 1983–84 campaign, becoming just the second defence-man in NHL history to attain the 40-goal mark, but he was still six goals short of equalling Orr's mark. Two years later, Coffey was poised to rewrite the record books.

Heading into a game against the Vancouver Canucks, on April 2, 1986, Coffey was sitting at 45 goals. With less than 30 seconds remaining in the first period, Coffey tried to make a pass from the right faceoff circle, but it deflected off the skate of Vancouver de-fenceman Doug Lidster and past goaltender Wendell Young. It wasn't a typical Coffey goal, but it tied Orr's record nonetheless. Early in the second period, Coffey broke out of his zone with the puck. As he skated up the ice, he blew by centre Craig Coxe and entered the Canucks' end with relative ease. Splitting defencemen Doug Halward and Rick Lanz and getting around forward Gary Lupul, Coffey then slid the puck under a sprawling Young. When Coffey returned to the bench, his teammates mobbed him in celebration. They knew how special it was that he'd just broken one of Bobby Orr's records. Orr couldn't be at the game because he was at a charity golf tournament in Palm Springs, California, but he sent a congratulatory telegram. In Edmonton's final two games, Coffey picked up another goal and assist to finish with 48 goals and 138 points, finishing just one point shy of Orr's single-season benchmark. In the years since Coffey's historic campaign, no other NHL blueliner has reached the 40-goal mark. In fact, over that span, only two other defencemen, Kevin Hatcher and Mike Green, have notched more than 30.

APRIL 3
MARIO LEMIEUX SCORES 70, 1988

With 34 seconds remaining in a game against the Hartford Whalers, Mario Lemieux deposited the puck into the empty net for his 70th goal of the season, becoming just the fourth player in NHL history to accomplish that feat. The goal put him in some illustrious company, but more importantly, it capped off an incredible ascension that year. Even before the 1987–88 campaign began, all eyes were on Lemieux at the Canada Cup. Playing alongside Wayne Gretzky, Lemieux scored a tournament-leading 11 goals, including four game-winners. His most significant goal, of course, came in the deciding third game against the Soviets on September 15, 1987. With time winding down, Canada and the Soviet Union were tied 5–5. As Gretzky entered the zone with Larry Murphy on an odd-man rush, he passed it back to Lemieux, who shot it over the glove of goaltender Sergei Mylnikov to take the lead, and ultimately, the championship.

Lemieux took his game to new heights that tournament, and though he'd scored 141 points in just his second season in the league, it felt as if the start of something special was on the horizon. Despite missing three games in November with injuries to his shoulder and back, Lemieux went on to rack up 69 goals and 166 points before the Pittsburgh Penguins' last contest against Hartford on April 3, 1988. By that point in the season, Lemieux had already locked up the Art Ross Trophy as the league's leading scorer, and the final game would just add to his Hart Trophy candidacy. In addition to his empty-net milestone marker, Lemieux added an assist to finish the campaign with 168 points. Despite his MVP-calibre performance that season, the Penguins missed the playoffs by a single point and Lemieux became the first non-playoff player to win a scoring title since Roy Conacher did it with the Chicago Black Hawks in 1948–49. A few months later, the NHL Awards confirmed what many already knew: Lemieux was the league's most valuable player. In winning his first Hart, the Pittsburgh captain broke Gretzky's eight-year reign as MVP.

APRIL 4

PHIL ESPOSITO SCORES 76, 1971

After scoring two goals on the road in a game against the Los Angeles Kings on March 11, 1971, Phil Esposito said he felt relieved. His first goal that contest, a net-front deflection in the first period, gave him 59 goals on the season, breaking Bobby Hull's record set two years earlier for most tallies in a campaign. With less than five minutes remaining in the second period, Esposito scored again to become the first player in NHL history to reach the 60-goal mark. After the game, while fielding questions from reporters, Esposito reflected on how many more times he could light the lamp that season: "I'll be happy with 65, maybe 70."

Less than a month later, Esposito was suiting up for the Boston Bruins' final game of the season. He had already surpassed his expectations and went into the matchup against the Canadiens with 73 goals. In the second period, with the game tied 1–1, Esposito scored to break the deadlock. With less than five minutes remaining in the frame, the burly Bruins centre cashed in a Bobby Orr rebound to reach the 75-goal and 150-point marks. The Boston faithful rose to their feet at the Garden and applauded Esposito's efforts. While he tried to shrug it off, he hesitantly acknowledged the crowd. Early into the third period, he scored again to complete the hat trick to record his seventh three-goal performance that season, another NHL record. Esposito added an assist on the Bruins' final goal of the game to bring his season totals up to 76 goals and 152 points, both league records.

Following the game, he was at a loss for words. "Overwhelming," he told reporters. "Just overwhelming. I can't think of any other way to put it." Both of Esposito's records stood until Wayne Gretzky entered the league. After Gretzky established a new points benchmark in 1980–81 with 164, he overtook Esposito's goal-scoring record the next year, potting his 77th on February 24, 1982. Gretzky finished the campaign with 92, a record that will never be broken.

APRIL 5

SEDINS PLAY FINAL HOME GAME, 2018

You couldn't have scripted a better ending for their final home game. With the contest knotted 3–3 in overtime, Daniel and Henrik Sedin were back on the ice. The crowd acknowledged their return with another boisterous cheer. Throughout much of the third period, the fans at Rogers Arena had been on their feet, saluting the brothers with standing ovations and chants of "Hall of Fame." It had been an emotional week. On April 2, 2018, the 37-year-old identical twins from Örnsköldsvik, Sweden, had announced they were retiring after playing 17 seasons with the Vancouver Canucks.

Taken second and third overall, respectively, at the 1999 NHL Entry Draft, Daniel and Henrik went on to become the best players in franchise history. When they were on the ice together, they had an uncanny, almost telepathic ability to find each other. No better example of this was in a game against the Calgary Flames on April 10, 2010. After Canucks defenceman Christian Ehrhoff fired the puck from the blue line, Henrik, who had his back to the net but still knew exactly where his brother was, made a no-look tip pass to Daniel, who then scored a nifty between-the-legs goal for a hat trick. The play seemed supernatural, but for the Sedin twins, it was just another day at the office.

By the time the pair decided it was time to hang up their skates, they were atop every category in the Canucks' record book. Daniel had the most goals, while Henrik had the most assists, points, and games played. The brothers also had a pretty stocked trophy case. After Henrik won the Art Ross and Hart Trophies following a 112-point campaign in 2009–10, Daniel followed up by snagging the Art Ross Trophy and Ted Lindsay Award the very next season. With time winding down in overtime against the Arizona Coyotes on April 5, 2018, you knew how it would end. After passing back and forth to each other, Daniel fired the puck from the point to win the game — the perfect way for the brothers to close their magical chapter in Vancouver.

APRIL 6

JOHNNY BOWER OLDEST GOALIE IN PLAYOFFS, 1969

After relieving Bruce Gamble three times, Johnny Bower got the nod for Game 4 of the Toronto Maple Leafs' 1969 first-round playoff series against the Boston Bruins. With the Leafs on the verge of elimination, coach Punch Imlach looked to his stalwart goaltender to keep the team alive. As Bower skated to his crease for the pivotal matchup on April 6, 1969, he was 44 years, four months, and 28 days old, making him the oldest netminder ever to play in an NHL playoff game. Although he made 27 saves in a valiant effort, Toronto lost 3–2 and was swept out of the post-season. Following the game, the storyline should have been Bower's age-defying milestone, but when reporters made their way to the dressing room, a bigger headline had emerged. Almost immediately after the defeat, club president Stafford Smythe had fired Imlach. When Bower, one of the coach's staunchest supporters, learned the news, he was dismayed. He told the press corps he'd have to let the front office know he'd just played his last game with the team. Bower felt he owed Imlach a great deal for his time in Toronto, which included two Vezina Trophies and four Stanley Cups. So if Punch was out, he was, too.

Throughout the summer, Bower remained adamant that he wasn't returning, but Leafs captain George Armstrong lured him back just before the start of the 1969–70 campaign. After turning 45 in November, Bower was actually old enough to collect his NHL pension. When he inquired about where he could pick up his cheques, he was told he wasn't eligible yet because he was still playing. Bower made his first appearance that season on December 10, 1969. He let in five goals in what proved to be his final NHL game. A couple of weeks later, he tore the ligaments in his right knee during practice and was put in a cast from ankle to thigh. Bower retired for good on March 19, 1970, but stayed with the Leafs as a scout and goalie coach, remaining a beloved ambassador of the team until his death in 2017.

APRIL 7

ANDY BROWN IS LAST UNMASKED GOALIE, 1974

Almost 15 years after Jacques Plante first started wearing a mask full-time in the NHL and revolutionized the goalie position, Andy Brown still wasn't wearing facial protection in the crease. Even as the game got faster and players' shots became more lethal, Brown still refused to don a mask. By the 1973–74 season, he was just one of two goaltenders in the NHL still unmasked. The other was the Minnesota North Stars' grizzled veteran Gump Worsley, who was playing in his 21st campaign and was set to retire soon. Brown, on the other hand, was a career minor leaguer and had just entered the NHL a couple of years earlier with the Detroit Red Wings before he was traded to the Penguins. Playing in Pittsburgh, Brown kept two masks, one white, one blue, above his locker in his Civic Arena dressing room. Although he was clearly prepared to wear a mask at home or on the road, they were only ever used in practice. Brown maintained that he simply never got used to wearing a mask during games.

Five days after Worsley made what would be his last NHL start, Brown got the nod for the Penguins' final game of the season, on the road against the Atlanta Flames on April 7, 1974. Tied 3–3 in the third period, Atlanta's Keith McCreary cashed in a rebound less than five minutes into the frame to take the lead. The Flames added two more goals to defeat the Penguins 6–3. In the off-season, Brown tried to re-sign with Pittsburgh, but management was unwilling to meet his reported five-year contract demand. Having reached an impasse with the Penguins, Brown looked to the rival World Hockey Association. He signed with the Indianapolis Racers, which was fitting because he raced sprint cars with the United States Auto Club circuit in the offseason. Although he had to wear a helmet behind the wheel, he continued to tend goal in Indianapolis without a mask. Brown never returned to the big leagues, making his final appearance for the Penguins the last time an NHL goalie played without a mask.

APRIL 8
AUSTON MATTHEWS SCORES 40, 2017

After his electrifying four-goal first game, which established a modern league record for most goals in a debut by a rookie, Auston Matthews seemed destined to rewrite the Toronto Maple Leafs' record book. Following that performance, some Toronto fans joked that he was on pace for 328 goals. They could be forgiven for letting their imaginations run wild. It was the first time, at least in most Leafs fans' lifetimes, that the team had such a dynamic and offensively gifted player on its roster. Certainly, the 19-year-old looked as if he'd score 40 goals, a feat that hadn't been accomplished by a Toronto player since Mats Sundin did it in the 2001–02 season, and it didn't seem outside the realm of possibility that he might push for 50.

Of course, Matthews didn't maintain the torrid pace from his first game, but he did continue to light the lamp and establish new club benchmarks along the way. On March 28, 2017, in a game against the Florida Panthers, Matthews scored his 35th goal of the campaign, surpassing Wendel Clark's rookie goal-scoring record. A few games after that, he recorded his 39th goal and 67th point, breaking another franchise record for most points in a season by a rookie and eclipsing the mark set by Slovak centre Peter Ihnačák in 1982–83. But after being held off the score sheet in his next two games, there were just two contests left on the calendar. Matthews was running out of opportunities to reach the 40-goal mark. With a playoff berth on the line in the team's penultimate regular-season game on April 8, 2017, Matthews, who wears number 34, fittingly fired the puck into an empty net with just 3.4 seconds left to seal the victory and notch his 40th goal of the season, becoming just the sixth teenager in NHL history to reach that milestone, joining Wayne Gretzky, Sylvain Turgeon, Mario Lemieux, Dale Hawerchuk, and Rick Nash. Matthews finished the campaign with 69 points and won the Calder Trophy, making him the first Leafs player to take home the rookie award since Brit Selby in 1966.

APRIL 9

NATHAN HORTON GETS GOAL WITHOUT PLAYING, 2014

Nathan Horton had the first goal in the game. The veteran winger, however, didn't even suit up for the contest. Despite being out with a lower-body injury, Horton was credited with a goal in a game he didn't even play. The antecedent to the score sheet quirk actually dated back to a frightening incident when the Dallas Stars hosted the Columbus Blue Jackets on March 10, 2014. After Horton scored early in the first period to give Columbus the lead, Dallas forward Rich Peverley collapsed on the Stars' bench. Peverley, who had been acquired by Dallas in July 13 as part of the Tyler Seguin trade, had been diagnosed with an irregular heartbeat during a training camp physical and ended up missing the club's pre-season schedule and home opener after undergoing treatment. Peverley made his Stars debut on October 5, 2013, and went on to record seven goals and 30 points in his first 62 games with the team.

But on that night it was clear something wasn't right. As his teammates frantically tried to alert the medical staff and officials, play was halted and Peverley was quickly carried off the bench and taken to hospital. Following the emergency, the Stars were, rightfully, not up for continuing the game. They had more pressing things on their minds than hockey. As a result, the contest was postponed to a later date. Just over a week after the incident, Peverley had successful surgery to correct his abnormal heart rhythm. While Peverley recuperated, the game was eventually replayed on April 9, 2014. All of the statistics were wiped with the exception of the lone goal. Horton, who had been injured the night before in a matchup against the Phoenix Coyotes, didn't play, forever making him the answer to one of the ultimate hockey trivia questions. The Blue Jackets ended up adding two more goals that game to defeat the Stars 3–1. Although Peverley recovered, he missed the entire 2014–15 campaign and then retired in September 2015. After hanging up his skates, he joined the Stars' player development department.

APRIL 10

JONATHAN CHEECHOO SCORES 50, 2006

When Jonathan Cheechoo was 12 years old, he had to write a letter describing what he thought he'd be doing in 10 years. In his younger days, he might have written that he'd become a trapper like his grandfather, but as he began developing his skills as a hockey player, Cheechoo set his sights on something else. Instead, he wrote that he'd be playing in the NHL for the San Jose Sharks. While his plan might have seemed lofty at the time, within a decade, the young Cheechoo turned his dream into a reality. Growing up in Moose Factory at the mouth of the Moose River at the southern end of James Bay in Northern Ontario, Cheechoo, a member of the Moose Cree First Nation, left home at an early age to pursue hockey. In 1998, when he was selected 29th overall by San Jose, no less, at the NHL Entry Draft, more than 100 friends and family made the journey from the small community to Buffalo to watch him fulfill his destiny.

After starting his pro hockey career with the Cleveland Barons, the Sharks' AHL affiliate, Cheechoo became a full-time NHLer in 2003–04, scoring 28 goals that season. Following the 2004–05 lock-out, Cheechoo had a slower start to the 2005–06 campaign, picking up just seven goals through the first 24 games. Cheechoo's season, however, took off after the Sharks acquired Joe Thornton from the Boston Bruins on November 30, 2005. Flanking the playmaking centre, Cheechoo began racking up goals. In his next 53 games, he potted 42, with Thornton assisting on all but 10 of them. Heading into a game against the Phoenix Coyotes, on April 10, 2006, Cheechoo was sitting at 49 goals. No Sharks player had ever reached the 50-goal milestone. In the second period, with San Jose on a power play, Cheechoo deposited a Thornton rebound into the back of the net to reach the vaunted benchmark. Cheechoo finished the season with 56 goals, a franchise record, becoming the first Sharks player to win the goal-scoring title and take home the Rocket Richard Trophy.

APRIL 11

ISLANDERS WIN FIRST PLAYOFF SERIES, 1975

M any expected the New York Rangers to make short work of the New York Islanders. Although the upstart Long Island team had improved significantly from the previous season, recording 33 wins and qualifying for the post-season for the first time, it still seemed overmatched against its crosstown rivals in the opening-round, best-of-three series. In the first game, the Islanders stunned the Rangers, rallying from a two-goal deficit in the third period and scoring three straight goals to take the first match 3–2. After the Blueshirts evened the series handily with an 8–3 victory in the second game, the deciding contest was set for April 11, 1975.

For Islanders general manager Bill Torrey, who had been working diligently to transform the team from expansionist fodder to competitor, it proved to be a showcase of the talent he'd been assembling. With time winding down in the first period, Clark Gillies, a hard-nosed winger selected fourth overall in the 1974 Amateur Draft, scored the opening goal with an assist from Bob Bourne, acquired from the Kansas City Scouts on September 10, 1974. The next two Islanders goals came from defenceman Denis Potvin, who was taken first overall in 1973. The Montreal Canadiens had tried to swing a deal with the Islanders for the rights to Potvin, but Torrey had resisted and opted to pluck the blueliner with the first pick, a move that paid dividends for the franchise. Heading into the final frame, the Islanders were up 3–0 and poised to take the series. The Rangers, however, scored three unanswered goals to force overtime. But just 11 seconds into the extra frame, one of Torrey's moves paid off again. J.P. Parise and Jude Drouin, both acquired in a landmark trade with the Minnesota North Stars on January 5, 1975, connected to give the Islanders their first playoff series victory in club history. The Islanders then went on an improbable run, overcoming a 3–0 deficit in the quarter-finals against the Pittsburgh Penguins before coming up short in the semifinals against the Philadelphia Flyers, who went on to repeat as Stanley Cup champions that year.

APRIL 12

FINAL WINNIPEG JETS HOME GAME, 1996

t was the end of an era. The Winnipeg Jets were playing their final home game. The club, which had been hemorrhaging cash for years, was moving to Phoenix, Arizona, the next season where they would become the Coyotes. But before the Jets took off, there was still hockey to be played. With a playoff berth on the line, Winnipeg hosted the Los Angeles Kings on April 12, 1996. Although Robert Lang quieted the sellout crowd of 15,567 less than two minutes into the game, Craig Janney scored two straight goals in the first period to give the Jets the lead. As play continued, the contest was punctuated by outbursts from the boisterous crowd often shouting "Phoenix sucks!" After Ray Ferraro tied the game early in the second period, Norm Maciver and Shane Doan added goals that frame to give the Jets the lead for good. With only one second remaining in the third period, captain Keith Tkachuk fired the puck into the empty net to record his 50th goal of the season and secure the victory, clinching a playoff spot.

Despite drawing the powerhouse Detroit Red Wings, who had won the Presidents' Trophy with a record-setting 62 wins, Winnipeg was thrilled to give its team one final send-off in the post-season. While many expected the Wings to down the Jets four straight, Winnipeg made a series of it, chiefly because of Nikolai Khabibulin's brilliant play in net. After losing the first pair of games, the Jets won the third contest 4–1 when the series shifted to Winnipeg. Although the Jets lost the fourth game, after being woefully outshot again, Khabibulin turned in his best performance for Game 5 in Detroit. The Russian netminder made 51 saves in a 3–1 victory to stave off elimination. When the Jets returned home for the pivotal sixth game, the Winnipeg Arena was abuzz. Their legion of white-clad fans literally shook the walls of the building. But despite the undying support, the Jets finally ran out of runway. Following the game, the crowd stayed on their feet while the team took one last skate around the ice.

MIKE ALLISON'S GLOVELESS GOAL, 1989

After getting hemmed into the boards behind the Edmonton Oilers' goal line, Mike Allison made his way to the far side of the net despite having defenceman Randy Gregg draped over him like an ill-fitting shirt. While the Oilers' blueliner continued to maul him, Allison lost his left glove but continued his drive to the net. As the pair got tangled up farther to the right of goalie Grant Fuhr, they started to fall. Just before Allison crashed to the ice, he got the puck off his stick and beat Fuhr five-hole. It was an incredible effort, but Allison scoring while falling was actually one of the least impressive parts of the play. He managed to navigate his way, and the puck, to the net with one gloveless hand practically tied behind his back, all the while dragging a relentless Gregg with him. What resonates most for Allison, however, is what it meant for the Kings. Facing elimination on the road and trailing 1–0 with mere minutes to go before the second intermission, it was the spark the club needed.

The series, of course, wasn't just any regular matchup. Wayne Gretzky, who was traded from the Oilers to Los Angeles less than a year earlier, was facing his former team. After setting the all-time points record in Edmonton during the regular season, all eyes were on Gretzky yet again. This time, though, there was far more at stake. Heading into Game 6 in Edmonton, Los Angeles was down 3–2 in the series, and while some might have thought the Kings would come up short, that was the farthest thing from anyone's mind in the dressing room. "We weren't going to lose that series," Allison once told me. Following Allison's goal, the Kings scored three unanswered ones in the third period to win 4–1 and force Game 7 back in Los Angeles. In the decisive game, Gretzky opened the scoring less than a minute into the contest and closed it with a short-handed empty-netter. The Kings handily won 6–3 and advanced to take on the Calgary Flames.

APRIL 14

CANADIENS WIN FIFTH STRAIGHT CUP, 1960

I t was an unprecedented run likely never to be repeated in the NHL. On April 14, 1960, the Montreal Canadiens won their fifth straight Stanley Cup. After sweeping past the Chicago Black Hawks in the semifinals, Montreal took on the Toronto Maple Leafs for the chance to make history. The Canadiens won the first three games and were on the verge of another sweep, something that hadn't been done in the same playoff run since the Detroit Red Wings first did it in 1952. Just over eight minutes into the first period, captain Jean Béliveau fired a shot from the blue line, beating Johnny Bower. The Leafs' goaltender had been preoccupied with moving Bernie "Boom Boom" Geoffrion out of the way, and the puck slipped by him. Less than 30 seconds later, defenceman Doug Harvey unleashed a cannonading shot to make it 2–0. Although the Leafs threw everything they had at the Canadiens, the defending champions thwarted them at every turn. With less than four minutes remaining in the second period, Dickie Moore and Maurice Richard connected to find Henri Richard, who put the puck in the back of the net to give the Canadiens a three-goal lead. While the Leafs desperately tried to rally early in the third frame, Béliveau took the wind out of their sails when he scored his second goal of the game to make it 4–0.

When the final buzzer sounded, the Canadiens became the first team in NHL history to win five consecutive championships. Counting their last two victories over the Leafs in the Stanley Cup Final in 1959, the Canadiens had won 10 straight playoff games and had been finalists every year since 1951. Despite the incredible run and the crowning achievement that evening, the celebrations after the game were subdued. Many of the players had been there before. Coach Toe Blake, though, was already thinking ahead: "I like odd numbers. And after six comes seven." While it took longer than he would have liked, Blake got his sixth in 1965, his seventh in 1966, and then retired after his eighth as a coach in 1968.

APRIL 15

RED WINGS GO BACK-TO-BACK, 1937

A string of improbable injuries made it unlikely that the Detroit Red Wings would repeat as Stanley Cup champions. Less than halfway through the 1936–37 campaign, the club lost its captain, Doug Young, to a broken leg. Young's replacement, Rolly Roulston, then fractured his leg not long after that. And to top it off, with just a few games remaining in the regular-season schedule, Larry Aurie, an All-Star right winger who was leading the NHL in goals, broke his leg in a game against the New York Rangers. Aurie still finished atop the league in goals but didn't play again that year. Despite the absences in the lineup, Detroit seemed poised to make short work of the Montreal Canadiens, taking the first two match-ups in the best-of-five series. But early into the third game, Vezina-winning goalie Normie Smith injured his arm and ceded the crease to rookie netminder Earl Robertson, who had spent most of the season with the Wings' minor-league affiliate in Pittsburgh. Montreal wound up winning that night and took the next game to even the series as Smith recuperated.

With Detroit on the verge of elimination, Smith returned to the net. Despite battling through soreness, he was brilliant and back-stopped the club to a 2–1 triple-overtime victory to advance. It was a fitting performance for Smith, who had stopped a record-setting 92 shots through regulation and six overtime periods, the longest game in NHL history, to take the first game of a playoff series against the Montreal Maroons the previous year. After his superb return to close out the Canadiens, Smith started the first game of the Stanley Cup Final against the New York Rangers. But after taking a blistering shot from Lynn Patrick in the arm in the first period, Smith was forced to leave the game. Robertson proved exceptional in relief. He went on to record two consecutive shutouts against the Rangers to clinch the Stanley Cup on April 15, 1937, giving the Wings the distinction of becoming the first U.S. club to win the trophy in back-to-back years.

APRIL 16

BLUE JACKETS SWEEP THE LIGHTNING, 2019

The hockey world was stunned. The Tampa Bay Lightning, winners of the Presidents' Trophy with a record-tying 62 victories, was swept out of the playoffs in the first round by the Columbus Blue Jackets. It was a result no one had expected. Although Columbus had bolstered its odds in the post-season by acquiring Matt Duchene and Ryan Dzingel and retaining impending free agents such as Artemi Panarin and Sergei Bobrovsky, neither of whom were expected to return, the team still didn't clinch a playoff spot, the second wild card, until its penultimate game of the season. On paper, it looked like a lopsided matchup. After its incredible season, perennial contender Tampa was expected to make short work of its opponent.

In the first game of the series, the Lightning led 3–1 heading into the third period. Sam Blazer, a writer for the *1st Ohio Battery*, a Blue Jackets blog, tweeted that if Columbus came back to win the game, he'd get the website's emblem tattooed on his behind. Nearly eight minutes into the final frame, it looked as though Blazer wouldn't find himself lying on a tattoo chair anytime soon. But after blueliner David Savard scored to bring the Blue Jackets within one, Josh Anderson notched a short-handed goal to tie the game. Just over two minutes later, with Alex Killorn in the penalty box, Seth Jones wired a shot on a power play to take the lead. There were still six minutes left in regulation time, but Tampa wasn't able to muster a response, and the Blue Jackets took the first game. While the Lightning searched for answers, Blazer, true to his word, booked an appointment to get inked. Although it would have been easy to dismiss the result as a one-off, the Blue Jackets continued to outplay the Lightning with suffocating forechecking as well as stellar goaltending from Bobrovsky. After taking the next two games, Columbus completed the sweep on April 16, 2019, winning its first post-season series in franchise history and pulling off one of the greatest playoff upsets of all time.

APRIL 17

MARTIN BRODEUR SCORES IN PLAYOFFS, 1997

Martin Brodeur always tried to emulate Ron Hextall's puck-handling abilities. When Brodeur was young, his father, Denis, a photographer for the Montreal Canadiens, told him how the Philadelphia Flyers goaltender was practically a third defenceman the way he adroitly handled the puck. That resonated with the young Brodeur, and as he developed his skills as a goalie, he modelled his game after Hextall's. By the time Brodeur made his NHL debut with the New Jersey Devils in 1992, he was lauded for his dexterity with the puck around the net. It wasn't long before Brodeur redefined the goaltending position.

Although Hextall was one of the first goalies to perfect the practice of clearing the puck out of the defensive zone by chipping it up the ice to his teammates or caroming it off the glass, Brodeur built on that approach and began playing the puck seamlessly with his teammates to initiate a breakout. While Brodeur surpassed Hextall by truly becoming that third defenceman his father described to him when he was younger, lighting the lamp still eluded him. Hextall, of course, was the first goaltender in NHL history to score a goal by shooting the puck into the net, a feat he first accomplished in the regular season on December 8, 1987, and then again two years later in the post-season. But given how well Brodeur handled the puck, it was only a matter of time before he etched himself into the record book alongside Hextall.

With less than a minute remaining in the first game of New Jersey's opening-round playoff series against the Canadiens on April 17, 1997, Brodeur saw an opportunity. The Devils were leading 4–2, so Montreal pulled goaltender Jocelyn Thibault for an extra attacker. As Brodeur collected the puck behind his net, he flipped the puck up and out of the zone. It landed just beyond the Devils' emblem at centre ice and slid into the empty net. Brodeur tapped his stick on the ice in celebration; he was just the second NHL netminder to score a goal in the playoffs.

APRIL 18

FRENZY ON FIGUEROA, 2001

The Los Angeles Kings were trailing the Detroit Red Wings 3–0, so it looked as if the Kings were going to lose and find themselves in a 3–1 series deficit against Detroit, a powerhouse team that boasted seven future Hall of Famers and had finished the season with 111 points. It was expected the Red Wings would make short work of the Kings in Game 5 and that would be that. After losing the first two games at Joe Louis Arena, the Kings took Game 3 at home with a 2–1 victory, but to have a fighting chance, they needed to steal Game 4.

Early in the second period, however, Los Angeles was down 3–0. Despite a significant deficit in a pivotal game, the Kings didn't give up. They outshot the Red Wings 12–9 that frame and went into the final period with steely determination to get back in the game. With just over six minutes to go, Detroit's Martin Lapointe took a slashing penalty, and the Kings went to work on a power play. Ten seconds later, Scott Thomas, only in the lineup that night because Steve Kelly was down with the flu, scored to give the Kings life. Less than four minutes later, after another undisciplined play by Lapointe, the Kings scored again on a power play. The Kings kept pushing to tie the game, but time wasn't on their side. They still trailed with less than a minute remaining. With 53 seconds left, Bryan Smolinski tied the game and the STAPLES Center erupted. Then, less than three minutes into overtime, rookie Éric Bélanger cashed in an Ian Laperrière rebound to win the game. With the series now tied 2–2 following such an unlikely win, forever known as the "Frenzy on Figueroa," the Kings started to believe they could vanquish the Red Wings. Three nights later, they defeated Detroit on the road, and then, on April 23, they eliminated the Red Wings from the playoffs with a 3–2 overtime victory at home, picking up their first playoff series victory since 1993.

APRIL 19

STEVE YZERMAN COMES HOME, 2019

H e was coming home. After months of speculation, it was confirmed that Steve Yzerman was returning to Detroit. On April 19, 2019, Yzerman was named general manager of the Red Wings. Drafted fourth overall by the club in 1983, Yzerman went on to play his entire 22-season NHL career with Detroit. After becoming the youngest captain in franchise history in 1986, Yzerman went on to score 65 goals, 90 assists, and 155 points in the 1988–89 season, establishing club records in all three categories. As Yzerman continued to establish himself as one of the league's best players, his game evolved, and under the direction of head coach Scotty Bowman, he began to focus on the defensive side of the puck, becoming a fearsome two-way player. In 1997, he led the Red Wings to their first Stanley Cup in more than four decades. The next year, Detroit repeated as champions, with Yzerman winning the Conn Smythe Trophy as MVP of the playoffs. He added another Cup in 2002 before retiring in 2006 as the longest-tenured captain for one team in NHL history.

After hanging up his skates, Yzerman remained with the Red Wings as vice-president and alternate governor. While he honed his skills in the front office, he also began assembling rosters for Hockey Canada, winning the World Championship in 2007 and Olympic gold in 2010. In May 2010, Yzerman became general manager and vice-president of Tampa Bay, where he built the Lightning into a perennial contender. Over the next eight seasons, the Bolts advanced to the conference final three times and the Stanley Cup Final in 2015. Although things were going well in Tampa, Yzerman was commuting from Detroit, which put a strain on his family. Before the start of the 2018–19 campaign, he announced he was stepping down from his roles to spend more time at home. After taking the season to determine his future, Yzerman returned to Detroit to a hero's welcome, ready to start the next chapter in his storied hockey career.

APRIL 20
PENGUINS DEFEAT DEVILS 7–0, 1993

t could have been a truck. It could have been a train. There was a bit of a discrepancy in the coverage regarding what New Jersey Devils head coach Herb Brooks actually said before he fielded questions from reporters. In any case, he was asking if anyone had seen what had struck his team. It was pretty apparent. The Devils were run over by Pittsburgh in a 7–0 blowout, a victory that gave the defending Stanley Cup champion Penguins a 2–0 lead in the series. It was a dominating performance. Although it was fairly tight through the first period, with the Penguins only up by two goals at intermission, they blew the doors off in the middle frame. Rick Tocchet scored early in the second period and then Pittsburgh added three more goals in a span of just over four minutes to take a 6–0 lead. When the Devils returned for the third period, Brooks had mercifully replaced goaltender Chris Terreri with Craig Billington, who made three saves before conceding the seventh goal to Joe Mullen. Even the Penguins' netminder, Tom Barrasso, who made 36 saves in his third career playoff shutout, got in on the offence, picking up two assists, which gave him as many points as Scott Stevens and Scott Niedermayer, New Jersey's leading scorers in the series.

Besides giving Pittsburgh a distinct advantage in the series, the victory, the club's 13th straight playoff win dating back to the previous year, established a new NHL record for most consecutive post-season victories, surpassing the mark of 12 set by the Edmonton Oilers from 1984 to 1985. Perhaps more impressive was that the 7–0 defeat capped a 20-game undefeated streak going back to March 9, 1993. The Penguins had won a league-record 17 games in a row before tying their final regular-season game against New Jersey, no less. Pittsburgh extended that streak with another win in Game 3 but lost its first game in nearly two months as the Devils avoided the sweep. New Jersey's victory, however, was short-lived. It was eliminated the next day.

APRIL 21

RED WINGS AND CANADIENS
TAKE EUROPE, 1938

The Detroit Red Wings and Montreal Canadiens were Europe-bound. After sorting out details with the British Ice Hockey Association and the French Hockey Federation in late March 1938, it was announced the two clubs would embark on a barnstorming campaign through England and Paris to play the first NHL games outside North America. The league had tried to set up a European tour three years earlier with the Canadiens and another team, but it fell through. With everything set this time around, and the Duke of Windsor even reportedly donating a trophy for the occasion, the NHL was keen to bring its brand of hockey abroad and grow the game. Following a series of exhibition contests in Sydney and Halifax, Nova Scotia, the Canadiens and Red Wings set sail for England.

The first game was played on April 21, 1938, at Earl's Court in London. Montreal goaltender Wilf Cude, a Wales native, was given a warm welcome from the 8,000 fans and received a horseshoe-shaped wreath made of leeks. Although newspaper coverage described the ice as soft, the crowd was treated to a fast, offensive spectacle. Following regulation time, the clubs were deadlocked at four goals apiece. In overtime, Toe Blake netted the game-winner to give the Canadiens a 5–4 victory and take the first game of the series. The teams then travelled south to Brighton for another high-flying game, a 5–5 draw punctuated by two fights. Following the first two contests, Detroit and Montreal crossed the English Channel for a few games in Paris. At the first matchup at the Palais des Sports, the Canadiens rallied and scored five goals in the third period to win 10–8. After they split the remaining two contests in Paris, they returned to England to close out the circuit with four more contests. Canadiens head coach Cecil Hart believed the teams had put on a wonderful display and really showcased the game to British and French fans, but it would be more than two decades before the NHL returned to Europe.

ANDREW BRUNETTE NETS GAME 7 WINNER, 2003

t was the first time the Minnesota Wild had made the playoffs. Squaring off against the Colorado Avalanche, a team that had won the Stanley Cup two years earlier and hadn't lost a first-round series since 1998, Minnesota had its work cut out. After taking the first game of the series, the Wild lost the next three straight contests and found itself mired in a 3–1 deficit. Minnesota, however, battled back from elimination, winning on the road in Denver and then forcing a decisive Game 7 after winning at home in overtime.

Following a scoreless first period in the final game of the series on April 22, 2003, Peter Forsberg got the Avalanche on the board early in the second period, but the Wild's Pascal Dupuis answered back less than a minute later. The game remained knotted through the rest of the frame and well into the third period. With less than seven minutes remaining in regulation time, Colorado captain Joe Sakic one-timed a pass from Alex Tanguay on the man advantage to give the Avalanche a 2–1 lead. After Rob Blake took a charging penalty with only five minutes to go, the Wild went to work on the power play. Marián Gáborík, who had just recorded his second straight 30-goal season, knocked in a rebound after Patrick Roy denied Andrew Brunette. Although there was still plenty of time on the clock, neither team could break the deadlock and the game went to overtime.

Three minutes into sudden death, Minnesota's Sergei Zholtok entered the Colorado zone and made a drop pass to Brunette. Exercising patience with the puck, Brunette went wide and then skated toward the net, where he switched to his backhand and beat Roy. The Wild had won its first playoff series in franchise history. After getting bumped in the crease by Derek Morris, Brunette left his stick in the net and skated toward his teammates, arms raised in exuberance. The Valley East, Ontario, native ended up being the last NHL player to score on Roy. A month later, the three-time Conn Smythe Trophy winner announced his retirement.

SHARKS STUN VEGAS IN GAME 7 COMEBACK, 2019

With the Vegas Golden Knights leading 3–0 in Game 7 with 10:54 remaining, the San Jose Sharks appeared to be dead in the water. The tide, however, turned quickly. After Joe Pavelski won an offensive zone faceoff, he was crosschecked by Cody Eakin. As the San Jose captain lost his balance, he collided with Paul Stastny, who shoved him. Dropping to the ice, Pavelski hit his head. As he lay there motionless, blood dripping from his helmet, officials halted play. While teammates and medical staff attended to Pavelski, Eakin was sent to the penalty box to await his punishment. It seemed as though he'd be assessed a double minor, but instead he was given a five-minute major and a game misconduct. The Sharks went to work. Just six seconds into their power play, Logan Couture scored to put San Jose on the board.

As he celebrated the goal with this teammates, Couture exclaimed, "That's one!" With nearly five minutes left on the man advantage, the Sharks still had plenty of time to recover. Less than a minute after Couture's tally and rallying cry, Tomáš Hertl tipped in a shot from Erik Karlsson to pull the Sharks within one. That's two. Nearly three minutes later, Couture fired a shot to tie the game. That's three. With things spinning out of control and San Jose still on the power play for more than a minute, the Golden Knights called a timeout. Gerard Gallant's attempt to calm the waters, however, was too little, too late. Only 30 seconds after play resumed, Kevin Labanc, who assisted on the three previous goals, scored to give the Sharks the lead. In just over four minutes, they had scored four power play goals, marking just the second time in NHL history that a team had scored four goals on one major power play in a playoff game. Despite the demoralizing turn of events, the Golden Knights regrouped and tied the game with 47 seconds remaining to force overtime. But early in the extra frame, the Sharks' Barclay Goodrow scored to complete one of the most incredible playoff comebacks of all time.

APRIL 24
PENGUINS WIN IN QUADRUPLE OVERTIME, 1996

Centreman Ron Francis said it was about four hours past his bedtime. The Pittsburgh Penguins had just defeated the Washington Capitals in quadruple overtime. By the time Francis left the ice, it was 2:15 a.m. and the game was the longest NHL match in six decades. The only games that had gone longer were played in 1933 and 1936. It was a test of both teams' perseverance, but it was particularly challenging for the Penguins, who lost two critical players for most of the game. Following the first period, goaltender Tom Barrasso left the game with back spasms and was replaced by backup Ken Wregget. While Wregget played exceptionally in relief, setting a franchise record for most saves in a game, Pittsburgh was forced to play the final 100 minutes of the contest without its superstar centre Mario Lemieux, who was given a game misconduct with 36 seconds remaining in the second period for uncharacteristically instigating a fight against Todd Krygier.

After the Penguins' Petr Nedvěd tied the game 2–2 in the third period, the game went into sudden death. The first overtime solved nothing. Late in the second overtime, however, the Capitals had an incredible opportunity to put the game away. Chris Tamer was called for intentionally knocking Pittsburgh's net off its moorings to prevent a goal, and Washington was given a penalty shot. It was the first time in Stanley Cup Playoffs history that a penalty shot was awarded in overtime. Joe Juneau took the shot for the Capitals. Skating in with a full head of steam, he shot the puck right at Wregget, who easily made the save. The game remained deadlocked through the third extra frame and most of the fourth, and it appeared as though the teams would head into quintuple overtime. But with 45 seconds remaining in the fourth overtime, Nedvěd scored on a power play to give the Penguins a hard-fought 3–2 victory and even the series at two games apiece. As of this writing, that game remains the sixth longest in NHL history. The Penguins went on to win the series 4–2.

APRIL 25
JOEL WARD NETS GAME 7 WINNER, 2012

After scoring seven goals and 13 points in 12 playoff games with the Nashville Predators in 2012, Joel Ward was a sought-after free agent. It was the first time the rugged winger found himself in that position. Following four seasons of junior hockey, the Scarborough native went undrafted to the NHL, and after an unsuccessful tryout with the Detroit Red Wings, he enrolled at the University of Prince Edward Island and continued playing hockey. Although he graduated with a degree in sociology, Ward still dreamed of making the NHL. After turning pro with the Houston Aeros of the AHL in 2005–06, Ward signed with the Minnesota Wild on September 27, 2006, and made his NHL debut on December 16, two weeks after turning 26 years old. Ward, however, spent most of the season with the Aeros, Minnesota's AHL affiliate. Following another campaign in the minors, he signed with the Predators in 2008 and established himself as a full-time NHLer, scoring 17 goals and 35 points in his first season in Nashville. After turning heads in the 2012 post-season, Ward signed a four-year deal with the Capitals. But Ward struggled in his first season in Washington. He scored a career-low six goals and spent some time in the press box as a healthy scratch.

In the playoffs, though, Ward reminded the Capitals why they had signed him. Squaring off against the Boston Bruins, the defending Stanley Cup champions, Ward came up big in Game 7 on April 25, 2012. Early into overtime, he entered the zone with Mike Knuble. After Knuble shovelled the puck into Tim Thomas's pads, the rebound came right out to Ward and he backhanded it into the net. It was the first time the Capitals had won a Game 7 on the road. Ward's overtime heroics, however, were marred by racist remarks on social media from Bruins fans. Although Ward, one of the few Black players in the NHL, said he was unfazed by the comments, it was another ugly reminder that hockey still had a long way to go to truly become an inclusive sport.

APRIL 26

CANUCKS SLAY THE DRAGON, 2011

After taking a 3–0 series lead against the Chicago Blackhawks, it looked as though the Vancouver Canucks were finally going to exorcise their demons after being tormented by Chicago for the past two post-seasons. This time around, however, things might be different. Vancouver was coming off a league-leading 54 victories in the regular season to earn the Presidents' Trophy for the first time in franchise history. Although the Blackhawks were the reigning Stanley Cup champions, the Canucks had a stranglehold on the series and seemed poised to avenge their past post-season departures. But a team as talented and determined as Chicago wasn't going to go down without a fight. Facing elimination, the Blackhawks made a statement in Game 4, chasing Robert Luongo from his net and winning 7–2 to extend the series. After shutting out the Canucks 5–0 in the next game, the Blackhawks won the subsequent match at home in overtime to send the series back to Vancouver for a decisive Game 7.

Canucks fans collectively held their breath. It couldn't end like this. Not after the season they had. Not to Chicago. Again. It felt like if they could just get past the Blackhawks, it would be the galvanizing moment the team needed. Less than three minutes after the puck was dropped, Alex Burrows scored to give the Canucks a 1–0 advantage. Following a scoreless second period, Burrows had an opportunity to extend the lead with a penalty shot early in the final frame, but he was stopped by Corey Crawford. As time wound down, the Blackhawks continued to push. With less than two minutes remaining on the clock, captain Jonathan Toews scored short-handed to send the game into overtime. Early in the extra frame, Luongo made a superb save against Patrick Sharp to keep the Canucks alive. Five minutes later, an eternity in overtime, Burrows took advantage of a Chris Campoli turnover in the defensive zone and wired a shot past Crawford. Rogers Arena erupted. The Canucks had finally slain the dragon and eventually advanced to the Stanley Cup Final.

COYOTES WIN IN OVERTIME, 2012

Being a Phoenix Coyotes fan in 2012 wasn't for the faint of heart. After winning a division title for the first time since the franchise relocated to Arizona in 1996, the Coyotes squared off against the contending Chicago Blackhawks, who were just two years removed from a championship, in the opening round of the playoffs. Once the series began, as many predicted, the Coyotes were outmatched by their opponents. Despite being woefully outshot, goaltender Mike Smith played brilliantly and kept his team in the series. The first five games all went to overtime, marking just the second time in NHL history that a series opened with that many contests decided in sudden death. Guided by their netminder's stellar performances, which included a 43-save effort to take Game 1, the Coyotes clawed their way through those nail-biting contests, picking up three victories to lead the series. After shutting out the Blackhawks 4–0 in the sixth game, the Coyotes advanced to the semifinals for the first time since 1987, back when they were still the Winnipeg Jets.

In the next round, the Coyotes took on the Nashville Predators, who finished the regular season with the third-most points in the Western Conference. They would have their work cut out for them once again. After Phoenix took the lead in the first period of the opening game on April 27, 2012, the two teams traded goals to finish regulation time tied 3–3. The Coyotes needed extra time yet again, making them the first team in NHL history to have six of its first seven playoff games go to overtime. While Smith continued to be the difference-maker, Ray Whitney proved to be the overtime hero. Approaching his 40th birthday in just over a week, Whitney, who was known as "The Wizard" for his superb playmaking abilities, scored the game-winner 14 minutes into the extra frame to record his first overtime playoff goal in nearly 17 years. Despite their nerve-wracking start to the playoffs, the Coyotes wouldn't play another overtime game until they were eliminated by the Los Angeles Kings in the conference finals.

APRIL 28

HURRICANES STUN DEVILS, 2009

You couldn't have asked for a more exciting Game 7, unless, of course, you were a New Jersey Devils fan. Just over a minute into the contest, the Carolina Hurricanes struck first. The lead, however, was short-lived. Less than two minutes later, Zach Parise threw the puck in front to Jamie Langenbrunner, who put it in the back of the net to tie the game for the Devils. New Jersey added another goal before the period came to a close to head into intermission holding a 2–1 lead. Early in the second frame, Ray Whitney knotted up the match for Carolina. But just over five minutes later, with a man advantage, Brian Rolston rifled a shot from above the faceoff circle to restore the Devils' lead. Later in the period, with the Hurricanes on a five-on-three power play, Martin Brodeur made some critical saves as Carolina attempted to tie the game. The Hurricanes, however, couldn't solve Brodeur and went into the third period down by a goal. Still trailing for most of the frame, it appeared as though the Devils were going to advance.

As the clock ticked down, Carolina made a final push. Down in New Jersey's end with a minute and 20 seconds left to play, defenceman Tim Gleason sprawled to keep the puck in the zone, and then from his knees, got the disk to Joni Pitkänen, who passed it across the ice to Jussi Jokinen, who wired it past Brodeur to tie the game. Jokinen, of course, was no stranger to late-game heroics. A week earlier, he had scored with 0.2 seconds remaining to snatch Game 4 from the Devils. This time around, the Hurricanes had even more time to work with. They hopped over the boards steeled to get another one. Less than a minute later, Eric Staal rushed up the ice and fired a shot to give the Hurricanes the lead with 31.7 seconds to go. Brodeur stared straight ahead, then dropped his head in disbelief. The Devils were so close to advancing, but instead, Carolina pulled off one of the greatest last-minute comebacks in NHL history.

APRIL 29

MIGHTY DUCKS WIN FIRST PLAYOFF SERIES, 1997

After four seasons in the NHL, the Mighty Ducks of Anaheim were going to the Stanley Cup Playoffs. Although the club got off to a sluggish start in the 1996–97 campaign, with Paul Kariya sidelined with an injury until November, they bounded up the standings as the season progressed. While Teemu Selänne, who was playing his first full season with the Mighty Ducks after being acquired from the Winnipeg Jets, had little difficulty finding the back of the net in Kariya's absence, his scoring only picked up after the dynamic duo were reunited. Selänne finished with 51 goals and 109 points, the second most in the league in both categories, while Kariya recorded 99 points in 69 games, for the third most in the NHL that season. Their potent offence was matched by the superb play of Guy Hebert, who continued to be one of the league's top netminders. During the team's 12-game undefeated streak from February 22 to March 19, Hebert started every game and posted a sterling .946 save percentage in those contests. After closing out the final seven games of the regular season with another unbeaten streak, Anaheim went into the playoffs, for the first time in franchise history, with home ice advantage.

Taking on the Phoenix Coyotes, making their first post-season appearance since relocating from Winnipeg, the Ducks won the first two games of the series but then lost the next three. Facing elimination on the road in the sixth game, Kariya scored the overtime winner to send the series back to Anaheim for a decisive Game 7. Early in the game, Dave Karpa fired a 60-foot shot through traffic that fooled Nikolai Khabibulin to put the Ducks on the board. Holding the lead, Hebert played brilliantly, making critical saves, including a poke check against Keith Tkachuk, who was all alone on a breakaway. Anaheim added two more goals in the second period, and Hebert stopped every shot he faced to secure the victory. The Ducks' luck ran out in the next round, though, as they were swept by the Detroit Red Wings, who went on to win their first Stanley Cup in more than four decades.

STEVE SMITH SCORES ON OWN NET, 1986

t wasn't how Steve Smith imagined his birthday would go. With just over five minutes remaining in Game 7 between the Edmonton Oilers and Calgary Flames, the game was tied at two goals apiece. Retrieving the puck behind his net, Smith attempted a routine cross-ice clearing pass to Paul Coffey. Instead of hitting his intended target, however, Smith accidentally shot the puck into the back of Grant Fuhr's leg and saw the disk bounce into the net. As Calgary's Lanny McDonald, who was bearing down on him from the opposite side of the crease, raised his arms in celebration, Smith collapsed to the ice. The rookie defenceman was distraught. Although there was still plenty of time left to tie the game, it proved to be the last goal on the score sheet. Edmonton, the defending Stanley Cup champions and searching for its third straight title, was eliminated from the playoffs, while the Flames advanced to the Clarence Campbell Final.

Following the game, a bleary-eyed Smith faced the media and valiantly fielded questions. The 23-year-old acknowledged his error and said he would just have to find a way to live with it. If Smith found solace in anything, it was that he had the support of his teammates. Wayne Gretzky told reporters that the Flames beat them fair and square and the loss didn't rest on the young blueliner's shoulders. If anything, Smith's blunder overshadowed a number of defensive errors in the contest. It also didn't help that Jari Kurri, who led the team in regular-season goals with 68, was in a scoring slump in the post-season and actually played that final game after a piece of shattered stick was lodged in his right index finger during warmup. Although it probably felt like an eternity, Smith got his redemption a year later. In Game 7 of the Stanley Cup Final against the Philadelphia Flyers, head coach Glen Sather decided to dress eight defencemen, so Smith returned to the lineup after a four-game absence. The Oilers ended up winning 3–1 to claim their third championship in four years.

MAPLE LEAFS WIN GAME 7, 1993

After fracturing the orbital bone beneath his right eye in the first game of the Toronto Maple Leafs' playoff series against the Detroit Red Wings, it looked as if Nikolai Borschevsky would be out for the rest of the round. The Russian winger, who had scored a team-leading 34 goals during the regular season, was an integral part of Toronto's offence. Although the Leafs won three straight games after dropping the first two contests in the series, they could have used his scoring touch. With the series set to be decided in a do-or-die Game 7 on May 1, 1993, Borschevsky returned to the lineup. Shaking up his lines, head coach Pat Burns paired him with Wendel Clark and Doug Gilmour, a bit of manoeuvring that proved quite fortuitous for the Leafs.

After 40 minutes of regulation time, the Leafs trailed 3–2 heading into the final period. Toronto appeared to have caught a break halfway through the third when the game's first penalty was called on Jim Hiller, but the Leafs couldn't capitalize on the power play, failing to get a single shot off. With time winding down, Gilmour was all alone in front of the net. He fired a shot glove-side and tied the game with less than three minutes remaining. Although Peter Zezel nearly won the game in regulation time on a wraparound attempt, the Leafs needed sudden death. It was the first time Detroit and Toronto were going to overtime to decide a best-of-seven series since 1950 when the Red Wings defeated the Leafs 1–0 to win the semifinals that year. Early in the extra frame, Gilmour passed the puck to a streaking Bob Rouse, who one-timed a shot at the net. Standing in front of the crease, Borschevsky tipped the puck past a sprawling Tim Cheveldae to win the game. As the team poured off the bench onto the ice, equipment manager Brian Papineau jubilantly sprayed water up and down as if uncorking a bottle of champagne. However, Borschevsky's overtime heroics weren't the most enduring memory; it was Papineau's celebration.

MAY 2

NORDIQUES TOP CANADIENS IN GAME 7, 1985

Ever since the NHL's realignment in 1981, which brought the Quebec Nordiques into the Adams Division with the Montreal Canadiens, the Battle of Quebec intensified. The provincial rivalry was often fuelled by political and ideological differences, and even which beer each team's fan base consumed — the Canadiens and Nordiques were at one time owned by rival breweries. But it was always what happened on the ice that mattered most. After meeting in the post-season for the first time in 1982, with the Nordiques coming out on top, the two teams faced off again in the playoffs two years later. In the final game of that series, held on the Friday before Easter, chaos erupted. Toward the end of the second period, a skirmish led to a bench-clearing brawl in which 252 penalty minutes were handed out. Another flare-up ensued after the ejected players, perhaps feeling they had nothing else to lose, went at it again before retiring to their respective dressing rooms for the evening. The officials eventually cleared the ice a second time and dispatched both teams for an additional cooling-off period before the final frame began. When play resumed, the Canadiens scored five unanswered goals to take the contest, and ultimately, the series, but the incredible comeback was overshadowed by the mayhem in what has become known infamously as the "Good Friday Massacre."

The next year, when the Nordiques and Canadiens met again, it was another bitterly fought series, but for the first time in their playoff encounters, a Game 7 was required. After Quebec jumped out to a 2–0 lead in the decisive game on May 2, 1985, Montreal rallied to even the score late in the second period. Following a scoreless final frame, the teams proceeded to overtime. Just over two minutes into sudden death, Peter Šťastný won an offensive zone faceoff and got the puck to Pierre Price, who fired it at the net. The rebound came back to Šťastný, and after missing his first attempt, he put the puck in the net to claim the latest Battle of Quebec.

MAY 3

WINNIPEG JETS SIGN PAIR OF SWEDISH STARS, 1974

T wo years after the WHA lured Bobby Hull away from the NHL with a lucrative 10-year contract, the Winnipeg Jets made headlines again when they announced on May 3, 1974, that they had signed Swedish stars Anders Hedberg and Ulf Nilsson. While the two Swedes had been courted by a number of NHL clubs, they decided on the Jets because they felt that club gave them the best opportunity to play together. Although they had never played together in Sweden, outside of appearances on the national team, they were a perfect match. Hedberg possessed blinding speed with a powerful shot and was never afraid to go to the net, while Nilsson had the vision and creativity to set up plays. After arriving in Winnipeg, the duo made an immediate impact. In their first regular-season game, Hedberg scored two goals, with Nilsson assisting on both, as the Jets outpaced the Quebec Nordiques to a 5–3 victory.

The pair also clicked playing with Hull, forming what became known as "The Hot Line," a name they came by honestly with their blistering performances on the ice. Hedberg finished the 1974–75 season with 53 goals and 100 points and was awarded the Lou Kaplan Trophy as the WHA's top rookie, while Nilsson racked up 94 assists dishing to his linemates. Hull, who turned 36 that season, scored 77 goals and felt he'd found a new lease on life playing alongside the Swedes. "I was ready to call it quits, then I finally found a couple of kids who could play the game the way I wanted to play it," he later said. The next season, the potent combination of Hull, Nilsson, and Hedberg continued to tear up the WHA, and The Hot Line finished top three in league scoring. In the playoffs, Nilsson scored 26 points and Hedberg racked up 13 goals as the Jets picked up their first Avco Cup. Hedberg and Nilsson led the Jets to another championship two years later before making the jump to the NHL and signing contracts with the New York Rangers on June 5, 1978.

DUELLING HAT TRICKS, 2009

Expectations were high for the second-round playoff series between the Pittsburgh Penguins and Washington Capitals in 2009. Two of the game's brightest stars, Sidney Crosby and Alex Ovechkin, would finally go head-to-head in the post-season. Selected first overall in their respective draft classes, Crosby and Ovechkin had been rivals on the ice since breaking into the NHL in 2005–06. In some respects, they were complete opposites. Crosby was an elite playmaker who carried himself with quiet confidence, while Ovechkin was a boisterous and charismatic goal scorer. As they continued to establish themselves as two of the league's top players, their rivalry only intensified. The playoffs were expected to be a decisive chapter in the Crosby-versus-Ovechkin saga. It didn't disappoint.

In the second game of the series on May 4, 2009, Crosby struck first to give the Penguins a 1–0 lead. Early in the second period, Ovechkin answered back. He rifled a one-timer from the left faceoff circle to knot it up. Later in the frame, Crosby responded, scoring his second of the game and restoring the Penguins' lead. After the Capitals evened the score with less than five minutes remaining in the second period, they went into the final frame tied 2–2. With Washington on a power play, Mike Green dished it to Ovechkin, who fired another one-timer to take the lead. Less than three minutes later, Ovechkin skated in all alone against defenceman Sergei Gonchar. Getting the better of his Russian counterpart, Ovechkin beat goalie Marc-André Fleury to record his first career playoff hat trick. As Ovechkin launched himself against the glass in celebration, the fans at Verizon Center erupted and hats rained onto the ice. Crosby, however, wouldn't be outdone. With just 30 seconds remaining, he whacked at the puck several times in the crease before finally batting it out of mid-air and into the net. While Crosby had matched Ovechkin's feat, the Penguins lost 4–3. The Russian might have won the battle, but Crosby triumphed in the war that post-season. Pittsburgh eventually eliminated the Capitals and went on to win the Stanley Cup.

MAY 5
ROGER CROZIER WINS CONN SMYTHE, 1966

After the Montreal Canadiens won their second straight Stanley Cup just over two minutes into overtime on a goal by Henri Richard, Detroit Red Wings goaltender Roger Crozier was presented with the Conn Smythe Trophy. It wasn't the Cup, but it provided a sliver of consolation for Crozier. The Conn Smythe, which recognizes the most valuable player of the playoffs, was first awarded in 1965 to the Canadiens' Jean Béliveau. Although Detroit lost the final, despite insisting that the game-winning goal shouldn't have counted because Richard pushed the puck into the net with his hand, the NHL's Board of Governors voted Crozier the MVP, making him the first goaltender to win the award and the first player to win it as a member of the losing team. Crozier was disconsolately removing his gear in the Red Wings' dressing room when he learned he'd won the trophy. He changed quickly and went out to accept the Conn Smythe in his street clothes. In a brief speech, Crozier said the award took some of the sting out of the disappointment he felt. In addition to getting his name engraved on the hardware, Crozier received a cheque for $1,000 and a gold-coloured Ford Mustang.

Although Crozier played valiantly in the championship series, battling back from an injury he sustained in the fourth game, many felt he was a curious pick for the Conn Smythe. There were stronger cases to be made for Canadiens goaltender Gump Worsley and Detroit's Norm Ullman, who had led the playoffs in scoring with 15 points. Crozier, however, had played brilliantly in the Red Wings' semifinal series against the Chicago Black Hawks, stopping 143 of the 153 shots he faced. In the Stanley Cup Final against the Canadiens, his play dropped off, but he still performed admirably. After returning from his injury, Crozier surrendered five goals in the fifth game, and Montreal took a 3–2 series lead. Since Crozier was awarded the Conn Smythe in 1966, just four other players — goaltenders Glenn Hall, Ron Hextall, and Jean-Sébastien Giguère, and forward Reggie Leach — have earned the trophy in a losing effort.

MAY 6

FIRST AVCO CUP BECOMES A NO-SHOW, 1973

Just weeks before the first championship was to be decided in
the World Hockey Association, the upstart league announced
it had sold the naming rights to the trophy to Avco Financial
Services, a company headquartered in Newport Beach, California.
The prize, known as the Avco World Trophy, wasn't all that dissimilar
from the Stanley Cup. It featured a silver bowl atop a globe encased
in crystal, which was mounted on a black cylindrical base. The key
difference was that, unlike the NHL's prize, the WHA's trophy was
sponsored by a private corporation, something detractors of the rival
league were quick to criticize. But this was the WHA, a league that
experimented with blue pucks — it was supposed to be different.
And so the New England Whalers and Winnipeg Jets, competing for
the WHA's first title, would also be battling it out for the right to the
Avco Cup.

There was just one problem; the trophy wasn't ready yet. With
the Whalers holding a 3–1 series lead and poised to win the first
championship, team president Howard Baldwin didn't want to leave
his players empty-handed. Instead, Baldwin reportedly sent one of
his staffers out to buy the biggest trophy they could find, which
would have to do. When the Whalers drubbed the Jets 9–6 on May
6, 1973, they celebrated with the stand-in trophy. Captain Teddy
Green, who had won the Stanley Cup twice with the Boston Bruins,
attempted to skate it around the ice but was forced to abandon
his plan after he was mobbed by adoring fans. It was just as well.
Green retired to the dressing room to continue the celebrations,
sipping champagne from the trophy and then pouring the rest over
his head. Following the victory, Baldwin had already set his sights
on another trophy. In an attempt to recapture the original spirit of
the Stanley Cup, he challenged the NHL to permit the Whalers to
take on either the Montreal Canadiens or the Chicago Black Hawks,
who were competing in the final, in a one-game duel for the historic
mug. The challenge wasn't accepted.

MAY 7

PATRICK MAROON SENDS BLUES TO CONFERENCE FINAL, 2019

Patrick Maroon had never scored a bigger goal. Early in the second overtime of Game 7 against the Dallas Stars, the St. Louis Blues' Tyler Bozak won a faceoff deep in the Stars' zone and shovelled the puck over to Maroon. The burly winger then passed it to Robert Thomas, who started driving toward the net. After Thomas fired a shot that hit the post and bounced off the back of goaltender Ben Bishop and into the crease, Maroon, following closely, found the loose puck and put it in the back of the net to send the Blues to the Western Conference Final for the second time in four years. As the goal horn sounded, the Blues surged off the bench and mobbed Maroon at centre ice. He was the perfect overtime hero. A St. Louis native, Maroon had signed a one-year deal with the Blues on July 10, 2018, for the chance to play for his hometown team and be closer to his family. After celebrating the goal with his teammates, Maroon scanned the stands for his 10-year-old son, Anthony. While the Enterprise Center was still erupting, Maroon spotted his son and pointed at him. Anthony was overcome with emotion and had tears streaming down his cheeks. It was a touching moment, reminiscent of one Maroon had experienced in that building a few years earlier as a member of the visiting team.

When Maroon was with the Edmonton Oilers, he scored a goal against the Blues on December 19, 2016. Anthony was in the crowd that night, too, wearing an Edmonton jersey, one of the few in the St. Louis arena vehemently celebrating his father's goal. Following the game, Maroon was interviewed by Sportsnet's Gene Principe. After some typical questions about the game, Principe replayed the reaction of Maroon's son to the goal and asked him what he thought about it. Fighting back tears, Maroon said it was emotional for him because he didn't get to see Anthony very much. Less than two years later, Maroon came home when he signed with the Blues and shared a season with his son they would never forget.

MAPLE LEAFS GET JUST SIX SHOTS IN ENTIRE GAME, 2000

F acing elimination against the New Jersey Devils in Game 6 of the Eastern Conference semifinals, things didn't start off well for the Toronto Maple Leafs. Just 18 seconds into the game, Petr Sýkora scored to give New Jersey the lead. Toronto didn't exactly mount a determined response. It took more than seven minutes for the team to register its first shot on goal, a backhand attempt by Igor Korolev that Martin Brodeur swatted away. The Leafs got just two more shots that frame, tying a franchise record for the fewest shots in a period, not the kind of milestone you wanted to achieve in an elimination game. After Jason Arnott extended the Devils' lead 25 seconds into the second frame, Toronto's struggles persisted. New Jersey continued to smother the Leafs, limiting them to only two shots on Brodeur that period, a new benchmark in futility. In the final 20 minutes, Toronto still couldn't get close. Even when the Leafs did get out of their own end, the Devils clogged up the neutral zone, and any shot Toronto had was from practically outside the red line. With its season on the line, Toronto mustered just one shot against in the final frame. New Jersey centre John Madden mercifully put the Leafs out of their misery when he scored with six seconds remaining to all but end the game.

It didn't take too long to fill out the official score sheet after the buzzer sounded in the 3–0 defeat. Toronto finished the contest with just six shots, a modern-day NHL record for the fewest in any game. It was a new low for the Leafs. The Philadelphia Flyers had limited the club to 13 shots during a playoff game on April 15, 1975, but at least the club reached the double-digit mark that night. If the Leafs' fans could find any consolation in their team's ineffectiveness, it was that it had lost to the eventual Stanley Cup champions. The Devils went on to defeat the Flyers in the conference final in seven games before clinching the title in double overtime against the Dallas Stars.

MAY 9
NORTH STARS SALE APPROVED, 1990

The Gund brothers longed to bring the NHL back to the Bay Area in California. After buying the Minnesota North Stars in 1978 following the team's merger with the Cleveland Barons, the failed relocation of the California Golden Seals, the brothers always had an eye westward. By 1990, the team was struggling financially, and after the city of Bloomington decided against millions of dollars of improvements to the Met Center, where the North Stars played, the Gunds announced in January that they would ask for permission to move the club to San Francisco. The proposal didn't sit well with the NHL, which already had plans for expansion into the Bay Area. If the Gunds relocated the team, the league would miss out on a lucrative $50-million expansion fee. Instead, a compromise was reached and the brothers sold the North Stars to Howard Baldwin, former team president of the New England Whalers and a key architect of the WHA's merger with the NHL in 1979, and Morris Belzberg, a retired rental-car executive, for $31 million for the rights to an expansion team in the Bay Area. On May 9, 1990, the NHL's Board of Governors approved the deal.

Although the Gunds' new club, which became the San Jose Sharks, wouldn't hit the ice until 1991, they absconded with the North Stars' entire front office, including general manager Jack Ferreira and assistant GM Dean Lombardi. As part of the deal, the following off-season, the Sharks also stocked their team with 16 players from Minnesota, before both clubs took part in the expansion draft, a strange quirk considering the North Stars had been around for more than two decades. Things only got weirder from there. After making an improbable run to the Stanley Cup Final in 1991, the North Stars found themselves plucking players at the expansion draft just five days after losing to the Pittsburgh Penguins. Despite the ownership change in Minnesota, the team relocated to Dallas two years later.

MAY 10

KASPARAITIS WINS SERIES IN OVERTIME, 2001

After racing toward centre ice, Darius Kasparaitis dived and began sliding in the direction of the Pittsburgh Penguins' blue line. Kicking his feet as if he'd just jumped into a swimming pool, he continued gliding down the rink as his teammates leaped on top of him. As more Penguins piled on, they picked up momentum and kept on sliding. By the time they came to a stop, you couldn't even see Kasparaitis. It was just a mass of hockey players. At the bottom of the heap, Kasparaitis was undoubtedly still processing what had just happened. The Pittsburgh blueliner had scored the overtime winner in Game 7 to give the Penguins a 3–2 victory over the Buffalo Sabres to advance to the Eastern Conference Final. Kasparaitis wasn't known for his scoring touch. He'd potted three goals during the regular season and it was just his second career playoff goal. It almost looked as though the Penguins weren't going to make it until overtime. Halfway through the third period, they were trailing 2–1 with their season on the line. Two nights earlier, Pittsburgh was down by a goal and on the verge of elimination before Mario Lemieux, the Penguins' co-owner turned player, scored with 1:18 remaining to send the game into overtime. In the extra frame, Martin Straka netted the game-winner to force Game 7.

With time winding down in the decisive contest on May 10, 2001, Robert Lang scored to keep the Penguins' post-season dream alive. Late in overtime, Lang carried the puck into the Buffalo zone on the right wing and sent the puck over to a trailing Kasparaitis, who fired a shot that went over Dominik Hašek's glove and into the net, becoming the first Penguins defenceman to score an overtime goal in the playoffs. Following the game, he still couldn't believe he'd scored the Game 7 overtime winner. "I've dreamed about this goal for nine years," he told reporters, and added that he didn't think he'd ever do it again. As far as the playoffs went, his words were prophetic; he never scored again in the post-season.

MAY 11

GARY SHUCHUK WINS IN DOUBLE OVERTIME, 1993

Barry Melrose had a good feeling about Gary Shuchuk. Although the Kings' coach hadn't used the rookie yet in Los Angeles's Smythe Division Final series against the Vancouver Canucks, he knew his game well. Prior to becoming the Kings' bench boss for the 1992–93 season, Melrose had been the coach of the Adirondack Red Wings, Detroit's AHL affiliate, where he first coached Shuchuk. Taken by the Red Wings in the NHL's 1988 supplemental draft, Shuchuk played four years of collegiate hockey at the University of Wisconsin, winning an NCAA championship in 1990 before turning pro the following season. Shuchuk played six games for Detroit in 1990–91 but spent most of his time in the minors under the tutelage of Melrose. The following campaign, Shuchuk scored 32 goals and 80 points in Adirondack and was an integral part of the club's Calder Cup that year. After the championship season, Melrose was named head coach of the Kings, while Shuchuk continued to develop in the AHL.

On January 29, 1993, Shuchuk was traded to the Kings, along with Jimmy Carson, in exchange for Paul Coffey, Sylvain Couturier, and Jim Hiller. Shuchuk, who hadn't played an NHL game that season yet, played out the regular season in Los Angeles. While Shuchuk didn't get many opportunities in Detroit, Melrose believed in him and always figured he'd become an NHL player. Although he spent some time in the press box as a scratch to start the playoffs, Melrose tried to find room for him. After sitting out the first four games of the Kings' series against Vancouver, Shuchuk dressed for the fifth matchup on May 11, 1993. Melrose had a feeling Shuchuk would have a positive influence on the game, and his hunch paid off. Six minutes into double overtime, the longest game in Kings' history to that point, Shuchuk took a pass from Luc Robitaille at the side of the net and put it past Kirk McLean to give Los Angeles a 3–2 series lead. The Kings closed it out the next game and eventually made it all the way to the Stanley Cup Final.

CLARK GILLIES REDEEMS HIMSELF BIG-TIME, 1984

t was no secret that Clark Gillies had a rough season. The hard-nosed winger, who had reached the 30-goal mark in six of the past nine seasons with the New York Islanders, had registered just a dozen goals in 76 regular-season games. Toward the end of the campaign, the Islanders scratched him for two games, so Gillies sat down with general manager Bill Torrey to figure out how he could get back to the level he was known for. Selected fourth overall in the 1974 NHL Amateur Draft, Gillies had an immediate impact on Long Island. While he brought a physical presence to the lineup, Gillies could also put the puck into the back of the net. As a member of the Islanders' Trio Grande Line with Mike Bossy and Bryan Trottier, Gillies scored four straight 30-goal seasons and was an integral part of four consecutive championships. By 1983–84, however, Gillies's play had dropped off and he was relegated to the fourth line. After talking with Torrey about what was going on, they agreed he needed to work on his conditioning. With the playoffs just around the corner and the Islanders eyeing their fifth straight Stanley Cup, Gillies made a concerted effort to improve his game.

His hard work paid off: through the first three rounds of the playoffs, he racked up seven goals. When the Islanders advanced to the Stanley Cup Final to take on the Edmonton Oilers, Gillies truly elevated his game. Although he was held off the score sheet in the first contest of the series, in the second game, Gillies's redemption tour continued. After Trottier opened the scoring 53 seconds into the game, Gillies recorded a hat trick to power the Islanders to a 6–1 victory and even the series at a game apiece. He added two more in the next game to finish the post-season with 12 goals, behind only Jari Kurri and Wayne Gretzky. Although the Islanders failed to secure a fifth straight Stanley Cup, Gillies proved he could still be the player who had long captured the imaginations of fans at Nassau Coliseum.

DOUG WILSON MAKES GM IN SAN JOSE, 2003

When the San Jose Sharks acquired Doug Wilson from the Chicago Blackhawks in 1991, he brought instant credibility to the newly minted franchise. Wilson, who had spent his entire NHL career in Chicago, had been one of the league's top defenceman, winning the Norris Trophy in 1982 and then being named as a finalist for the award again in 1990. His skills on the blue line and experience were invaluable to the fledgling Sharks. In two seasons in San Jose, Wilson served as the club's inaugural captain and was the team's first representative at the All-Star Game in 1992. After hanging up his skates in 1993, Wilson worked as a consultant for Canada's national junior team, winning four consecutive gold medals, before he returned to the Sharks in 1997 as the organization's director of professional development.

Wilson served in that role for more than five years until May 13, 2003, when the Sharks promoted him to general manager, the fourth in franchise history. As of this writing, Wilson has been GM for the better part of two decades. During his time in San Jose, Wilson has established himself as one of the league's shrewdest general managers and has never shied from pulling off bold moves. Early in his tenure, on November 30, 2005, he acquired Joe Thornton from the Boston Bruins in a seismic trade. Thornton went on to win the Art Ross and Hart Trophies that year, and though he's currently a Toronto Maple Leaf, he'll eventually retire as one of the best players in Sharks history. In 2011, Wilson sent Devon Setoguchi, Charlie Coyle, and a second-round pick to the Minnesota Wild for Brent Burns, who, after racking up 76 points in 2016–17, became the first Sharks defenceman to win the Norris Trophy. Wilson also acquired Dan Boyle, Evander Kane, and Erik Karlsson, and drafted and developed Joe Pavelski, Marc-Édouard Vlasic, Logan Couture, and Tomáš Hertl. Had Wilson not been inducted into the Hockey Hall of Fame in 2019 as a player, he was working toward a solid case in the builder category for everything he's engineered in San Jose.

ISLANDERS DAVID VOLEK SLAYS PENGUINS, 1993

The Pittsburgh Penguins' shot at a three-peat was slipping away. The two-time defending Stanley Cup champions, who finished the regular season with an 18-game undefeated streak and won the Presidents' Trophy after racking up 119 points, were on the verge of being upset by the plucky New York Islanders. After failing to close out the Patrick Division Final two days earlier, the Penguins found themselves in a do-or-die Game 7 on May 14, 1993. Pittsburgh opened the scoring less than eight minutes into the game, but the Islanders knotted it up just before the first intermission. Following a scoreless second period, the teams headed into the final frame tied 1–1. Six minutes into the third, David Volek, who had defected from Czechoslovakia in 1988, scored to give the Islanders the lead. Less than three minutes later, from nearly 60 feet out, Benoît Hogue fired a shot that clipped the stick of Penguins defenceman Larry Murphy before striking goaltender Tom Barrasso in the arm and bouncing into the net.

Although Pittsburgh was down by a pair of goals, this was a club that boasted four future Hall of Famers and was eyeing its third straight championship; they weren't going down without a fight. Seven minutes after Hogue's ugly goal, Ron Francis scored to give the Penguins life. As time ticked down, Pittsburgh searched desperately for the equalizer. With the Penguins' net empty, Rick Tocchet deflected a shot past Islanders goalie Glenn Healy, who had made 39 saves up to that point, to tie the game with only a minute remaining. The fans at Civic Arena were on their feet. Pittsburgh's postseason dream, however, was dashed not long into the extra frame. Just over five minutes into overtime, Ray Ferraro entered the Penguins' zone on a two-on-one with Volek. He passed the puck to the wide-open Volek, who one-timed it past Barrasso to give the Islanders a 4–3 victory. Volek scored just eight goals during the regular season but will be remembered forever as the unlikely overtime hero who vanquished the Penguins.

STANLEY CUP AWARDED FOR FIRST TIME, 1893

After taking in his first hockey game at the Montreal Winter Carnival in 1889, Frederick Arthur Stanley was hooked. It was unlike anything he'd ever seen. Stanley had arrived in Canada six months earlier to begin his posting as the fledgling nation's sixth governor general. Hockey quickly become an important part of his life during his stay in Canada. Since his children were also drawn to the sport, Stanley found ways to support and grow the game. He had a rink constructed at his residence, Rideau Hall, where in 1891 his daughter, Isobel, took part in one of the first recorded games of women's hockey. Stanley was also a booster of the Ottawa Hockey Club, while his son, Arthur, helped found the Ontario Hockey Association (now the OHL) in 1890. The governor general's most significant contribution, however, was the donation of a trophy. On March 18, 1892, at the Rideau Club, Stanley's aide, Frederic Lambert, read a message that outlined the governor general's intention to donate a challenge cup, "which should be held from year to year by the champion hockey team in the Dominion of Canada."

Following the announcement, Stanley entrusted Captain Charles Colville, who had previously served as his secretary, to purchase the trophy. Colville commissioned a decorative bowl from a silversmith in London for ten guineas and had "Dominion Hockey Challenge Cup" engraved on one side of the mug and "From Stanley of Preston," along with the family's crest, on the other side. The trophy was presented for the first time a year later, on May 15, 1893, at the annual meeting of the Montreal Amateur Athletic Association. On behalf of Stanley, who was preparing to return to England to take on new duties as the Earl of Derby, Dr. John Sweetland, one of the trophy's first trustees, presented the cup to J.A. Taylor, president of the association, in recognition of the Montreal Hockey Club finishing atop the standings of the Amateur Hockey Association of Canada. It wasn't long before the trophy became known simply as the Stanley Cup and was regarded as the ultimate prize in all of hockey.

MAY 16

YZERMAN'S BULLET WINS IN DOUBLE OVERTIME, 1996

Early into the second overtime of Game 7 between the Detroit Red Wings and St. Louis Blues, Detroit's Vladimir Konstantinov made an errant pass that was picked up by none other than Wayne Gretzky. Attempting to gain control of the puck with just one hand on his stick, Gretzky lost it between his skates before it was picked up by Steve Yzerman. Although it was an uncharacteristic play for the Great One, it seemed rather innocuous. Yzerman hadn't yet crossed the red line, and the Blues had several defending players as the Red Wings' captain advanced toward their zone. What St. Louis didn't expect was that just as the puck made its way over the blue line, Yzerman would unleash an absolute bomb from 60 feet out. It rifled past goaltender Jon Casey, hit the crossbar, and bounced into the net. It was one of the most dramatic finishes to a Game 7 in NHL history. In fact, it was only the second time that one was scoreless heading into overtime, let alone double overtime. The previous occasion was in 1950 when the Red Wings defeated the Toronto Maple Leafs 1–0.

While the excitement of Yzerman's bullet eventually subsided, it has persisted in hockey lore and is remembered as one of the most iconic goals in playoff history. Now you probably have the urge to put this book down and watch the clip on YouTube. If so, did you watch the replays, too? You had to, because that's what probably makes this goal so memorable. Whenever I think about the goal, I think of one angle in particular. From behind the net, you can see Yzerman wind up and blast it. As the puck begins its supersonic journey toward the net, the camera zooms out and you can see it rise up and over Casey's blocker before clanging off the crossbar and into the back of the net. After the game, Yzerman said he was surprised the puck went in because he didn't shoot a lot from the blue line, but with a shot like that, maybe he should have tried it more often.

MAY 17
LEAFS TOP KINGS IN GAME 1, 1993

The 1993 Clarence Campbell Conference Final started off with a bang. It was the first time the Toronto Maple Leafs and Los Angeles Kings had squared off in the playoffs since 1978, and expectations were sky-high. The much-anticipated matchup featured two of the league's best players going head-to-head: Wayne Gretzky and Doug Gilmour. After Gilmour opened the scoring late in the first period, Gretzky assisted on a Pat Conacher goal with five minutes remaining in the second period to tie the game. It was a battle through 40 minutes of regulation time, but the clubs took things up a notch in the final frame. Just before the halfway mark of the third, Gilmour levelled the Kings' Alexei Zhitnik with a big open-ice hit. After Zhitnik released a pass at his own blue line, Gilmour went low and nailed him, sending the defenceman head over heels. The Kings were incensed and felt Gilmour should have been given a kneeing penalty for going so low on Zhitnik, but it was deemed a clean hit.

Not long after, Gilmour was pinned against the boards by Darryl Sydor but got the puck out in front of the Kings' net to Glenn Anderson, who beat Kelly Hrudey to give the Leafs the lead. Just over a minute later, Gilmour scored his second of the evening. But Gilmour wasn't done yet. He assisted on another goal to wrap up a four-point performance and take the playoff scoring lead from Gretzky. Despite Gilmour's incredible effort that night, the game is best remembered for what happened next. With just over two minutes remaining, Gilmour cut across the offensive zone and was hammered by Marty McSorley. As Gilmour lay on the ice, captain Wendel Clark immediately came to his defence, dropping his gloves and taking on McSorley in a spirited tilt. Although Clark was at a size disadvantage, he got the better of McSorley, opening up a cut under his right eye that required stitches. The Leafs took the game 4–1, but ended up losing the series in seven games, missing out on a trip to the Stanley Cup Final.

CANADIENS WIN STANLEY CUP IN GAME 7, 1971

The Chicago Black Hawks were hungry for their first championship in a decade, while the Montreal Canadiens hoped to nab their tenth in the past 15 years. On May 18, 1971, Chicago and Montreal duelled for the Stanley Cup, just the seventh time in NHL history that the rights to the trophy were decided in Game 7. The previous time it had happened was six years earlier when the Canadiens and Black Hawks last met in the final. Just 14 seconds after the opening faceoff back then, captain Jean Béliveau opened the scoring to record the fastest goal to start a Game 7 in the Stanley Cup Final. Before the first period came to a close, the Canadiens added three more to take a 4–0 lead, and ultimately, put the game out of reach. The Black Hawks couldn't solve goalie Gump Worsley, and Montreal picked up its 13th Cup. Béliveau, who racked up 10 points in the seven-game series, was named the inaugural winner of the Conn Smythe Trophy as the most valuable player of the playoffs.

Six years later, the Black Hawks wanted revenge. Although the Hawks didn't get off to as hot a start as the Canadiens had the last time they'd squared off for the Cup, they did open the scoring late in the first period. Danny O'Shea added to their lead in the second frame, but the Canadiens answered back when Jacques Lemaire netted a shot from 65 feet out to put Montreal on the board. With less than two minutes remaining in the second period, Henri Richard scored to tie the game. Five nights earlier, Canadiens coach Al MacNeil had benched Richard toward the end of the fifth game with the club trailing 2–0. Following the loss, an irate Richard told reporters that MacNeil was incompetent. The coach wouldn't make the same mistake again in Game 7. Early in the third period, Richard scored to give Montreal the lead, which it held on to, winning the Cup yet again. Although MacNeil and Richard embraced after clinching the championship, it was the former's final game behind the Canadiens' bench.

WHALERS FIRE PIERRE MCGUIRE, 1994

When the news broke that the Hartford Whalers had fired head coach Pierre McGuire, captain Pat Verbeek didn't mince words, calling it "the best thing that could happen to this hockey team right now." It was the end of a tumultuous tenure behind the bench. On May 19, 1994, McGuire was dismissed after previously serving as the club's assistant general manager and taking over as coach in November when GM Paul Holmgren stepped aside to focus on his general manager's duties. Under McGuire's direction, the Whalers went 23–37–7 and missed the playoffs for the second straight year. While his record on the ice left much to be desired, it was McGuire's dealings with his players that ultimately led to his dismissal.

Although he had some experience behind the bench, acting as an assistant coach at Babson College, St. Lawrence University, and the Pittsburgh Penguins, where he won a Stanley Cup in 1992, he reportedly didn't earn the respect of his players. As the season went on, McGuire increasingly found himself at odds with his players, who felt he was more concerned with himself. The situation came to a head in March when six players and assistant coach Kevin McCarthy were arrested after a brawl with bouncers at a nightclub in Buffalo. Following the incident, McGuire didn't back his players up and got into a dispute with Verbeek over whether there was a curfew that night. The Whalers' captain was incensed with how McGuire handled the situation, and it was apparent to everyone in the dressing room that the coach chose to cover for himself while hanging his players out to dry. "I think there's certain times when you can find out how much a coach is behind his players," Verbeek later told reporters. At the end of the season, Holmgren hauled McGuire into his office and told him he needed to patch things up with his players. When McGuire reportedly only reached out to goaltender Sean Burke, Holmgren wasn't left with much choice and sent his head coach packing.

MAY 20

GOLDEN KNIGHTS ADVANCE TO STANLEY CUP FINAL, 2018

When the Vegas Golden Knights made their improbable run to the Stanley Cup Final in 2018, I was in the middle of proofing the first *Hockey 365*. All of the stories had been locked in and we were just doing a final check before the book went into layout, and ultimately, publication. As I scanned through the pages and the stories, I couldn't help worrying that I'd made an oversight by not including something about the Golden Knights' inaugural season. And then once they advanced to the Stanley Cup Final, I thought if they somehow won a championship in their first year, it would be a shame not to capture it in a book meant to highlight some of the most notable anniversaries in hockey. Even if Vegas didn't hoist the Cup, what the club was doing was still unprecedented.

Once the Golden Knights advanced to the Stanley Cup Final on May 20, 2018, some, even the NHL, suggested this was the third time in league history that a team had advanced to the Stanley Cup Final in its first season, but that didn't sit right with me. The Toronto Arenas played one round of the playoffs before taking on the Vancouver Millionaires for the right to Lord Stanley's mug in 1918, and the St. Louis Blues' post-season run to the final in 1968 went through their fellow expansionists. The format that year was set up deliberately so that an expansion team would earn a berth to the Stanley Cup Final. For me, the Golden Knights' run was significantly more impressive. They swept the Los Angeles Kings, took out the San Jose Sharks, and then downed the Winnipeg Jets, one of the favourites that year, to advance to the final. It was hard not to root for Vegas, a team comprised of castoffs from the NHL's other 30 clubs. The Knights affectionately referred to themselves as the "golden misfits" and were out to prove everyone wrong. So I couldn't help but smile when they defied expectations yet again by grabbing the Clarence Campbell Bowl, a practice that another team might have superstitiously shied away from.

MAY 21

PENGUINS ACQUIRE JEAN PRONOVOST, 1968

When the Pittsburgh Penguins acquired Jean Pronovost and John Arbour from the Boston Bruins in exchange for cash and a player to be named later, they said the acquisition of the two young players would give the club "skate and muscle." But with Pronovost, they got so much more. The younger brother of future Hall of Fame defenceman Marcel Pronovost, Jean had spent the past two seasons playing with the Oklahoma City Blazers of the Central Hockey League before joining the Penguins. In his first season in Pittsburgh, Pronovost notched 16 goals and 41 points in 76 games. The following campaign, 1969–70, he racked up 20 goals and was voted the Penguins' MVP along with Dean Prentice.

While the fledgling Penguins, who had joined the league as part of the NHL's ambitious expansion in 1967–68, struggled on the ice, Pronovost flourished. In 1973–74, head coach Ken Schinkel put Pronovost on a line with centre Syl Apps, Jr., and left winger Lowell MacDonald. They immediately clicked. While Pronovost finished the season with 40 goals, the trio collectively racked up 100 goals and was soon known as "The Century Line." As Pronovost and his linemates continued to light the lamp, they also earned the moniker The Bicentennial Line because between the three of them they were piling up more than 200 points in a season. Following back-to-back 40-goal campaigns, Pronovost had a breakout year in 1975–76, scoring 52 goals and 104 points. On March 24, 1976, in a game against the Boston Bruins, Pronovost put a rebound past Gilles Gilbert to become the first Penguins' player to score 50 goals in a season. That also happened to be the same game that Pittsburgh centre Pierre Larouche became the youngest player to break the 100-point mark. By the end of the 1975–76 season, Pronovost had played 595 games with the Penguins and had scored 243 goals, the most in franchise history by a country mile. He played two more years in Pittsburgh before he was traded to the Atlanta Flames.

KINGS ADVANCE TO STANLEY CUP
FINAL, 2012

The Los Angeles Kings had been veritable road warriors in the 2011–12 post-season, having never lost a game away from the STAPLES Center. When they took on the Phoenix Coyotes for the fifth game of the Western Conference Final, they were looking to extend their road winning streak to an NHL-record eight straight games. After Phoenix jumped out to an early lead in the first period, the Kings responded with a short-handed goal halfway through the frame. In the second period, the two teams traded pairs of goals and went into the final stanza tied 3–3. As time wound down in the third period, neither club had broken the deadlock and overtime loomed.

Late in the extra frame, Jeff Carter fired the Kings' 50th shot on Mike Smith, but the Coyotes' goaltender turned it away. As the puck bounced out of the crease, Dustin Penner, who had a disappointing regular season, gathered it up and put it through Smith's pads with just over two minutes left to play. While the Kings celebrated, the Coyotes were livid. Moments before the goal, Los Angeles captain Dustin Brown took Michal Rozsíval out of the game when he collided with him at the blue line. As Rozsíval lay on the ice, a scrum ensued. The Coyotes felt it was a late hit and that Brown had caught the defenceman with his knee. Rozsíval had to be helped off the ice, and Phoenix lost a key part of its back end at the most critical moment of the season. Just 12 seconds later, Penner scored the overtime winner. As the two teams gathered for the handshake line, Phoenix's Martin Hanzal and captain Shane Doan each had some choice words for Brown. Although the Coyotes were bitter at how their season had finished, they still made an incredible run that year. They won their division for the first time in franchise history, and despite never having advanced past the first round of the playoffs since relocating to the desert, came within three wins of playing for the Stanley Cup.

MAY 23

BLACKHAWKS WIN IN DOUBLE OVERTIME, 2015

When Antoine Vermette was scratched for the third game of the Chicago Blackhawks' Western Conference Final against the Anaheim Ducks, he was disappointed. Acquired from the Phoenix Coyotes for Klas Dahlbeck and a first-round pick, Vermette had been benched for the first two games of Chicago's opening-round series against the Nashville Predators but had been in the lineup ever since. Although he had no points in his past five games, he felt he'd still played well and provided the Blackhawks with depth down the middle. But coach Joel Quenneville's shakeup of the lines didn't work as anticipated. Chicago lost 2–1 and now trailed the Ducks two games to one in the series. Looking ahead, Vermette hoped to get back on the ice: "My job is to be ready whenever I have a chance to be in the lineup."

With the Blackhawks eager to do better in the pivotal fourth match-up on May 23, 2015, Quenneville reunited Vermette with Patrick Sharp and Teuvo Teräväinen on the third line. In a wild third period, the two teams combined for six goals, including three by Anaheim in 37 seconds, the second-fastest three playoff goals scored by one team in NHL history, leaving them tied 4–4 after regulation time. The Ducks fell short of the record held by the Toronto Maple Leafs, who three times in a span of 23 seconds had scored against the Atlanta Flames on April 12, 1979. It just so happened that Quenneville, who was patrolling Toronto's blue line at the time, had assisted on the final goal in that offensive flurry.

The extra frame between Anaheim and Chicago solved nothing, and double overtime loomed. Just over five minutes into the second overtime, after goaltender Frederik Andersen denied a shot by Vermette, the veteran centre stayed with the play and converted his own rebound to give the Blackhawks a 5–4 victory and knot up the series. With Vermette remaining in the lineup for the rest of the playoffs, Chicago defeated Anaheim in seven games, went on to vanquish the Tampa Bay Lightning, and captured its third Stanley Cup in six years.

ISLANDERS WIN FIRST CUP, 1980

The Islanders were keen to bring the Stanley Cup back to New York for the first time in four decades. After making short work of most of their opponents in the preceding rounds, they took on the Flyers in the Stanley Cup Final. Following a tough loss in Philadelphia in Game 5, the series shifted back to Nassau Coliseum on May 24, 1980, giving the Islanders the opportunity to clinch the championship on home ice. Although the Flyers struck first with a goal by Reggie Leach seven minutes into the opening period, the Islanders answered back a few minutes later to knot it up. Two minutes after that, Clark Gillies entered Philadelphia's zone and made a drop pass to Butch Goring, but Goring hadn't crossed the blue line yet and was well offside. The infraction was undetected by the officials, and Goring was able to get the puck to Duane Sutter, who fired it into the top corner of the net to give the Islanders the lead. The Flyers were in an uproar. They argued that the goal shouldn't have counted. Although Philadelphia tied the game with just over a minute remaining in the first period, it was demoralized by the missed call.

The Islanders controlled play in the second period, adding two more goals to head into the final frame with a 4–2 lead. The Cup was within their grasp. But less than two minutes into the third, the Flyers' Bob Dailey wired a slapshot from 55 feet out to start the comeback. Just over four minutes later, rookie John Paddock, who had scored only three goals in the regular season, notched the equalizer to give the Flyers a fighting chance to force a Game 7. Neither team scored again in regulation time, and the Islanders went into the extra frame with the chance to become the 12th team in NHL history to win the Stanley Cup in overtime. They didn't disappoint. Seven minutes in, Bob Nystrom took a pass from John Tonelli and put the puck through the pads of Pete Peeters to clinch the first of four straight championships.

SENATORS FALL GOAL SHORT OF STANLEY CUP FINAL, 2017

t was Game 7 of the Eastern Conference Final, and the Ottawa Senators were a goal away from advancing to play for the Stanley Cup. After tying the game with just over five minutes left in the third period, they forced overtime. Squaring up against the Pittsburgh Penguins, who were trying to become the first team in nearly two decades to win back-to-back titles, the Senators aimed to cap off their improbable playoff run and return to the Cup final for the first time since 2007. The first overtime period solved nothing, and the two teams steeled themselves for double overtime. Five minutes into the extra frame, Chris Kunitz, relegated mostly to the Penguins' fourth line since returning from an injury in the previous round, caught a pass from his former superstar centre, Sidney Crosby, and wired it past Craig Anderson to keep Pittsburgh's dream of a repeat alive. While the Penguins celebrated, Anderson, who made 39 saves that evening, merely stared straight ahead. They had come so close.

The Penguins indeed went on to win the Stanley Cup for the second straight year, while the Senators embarked on a process that within three years stripped away everyone from the team that had fallen a goal short of the Stanley Cup Final. By the next season, changes were already under way. Ottawa traded Marc Methot to the Dallas Stars, and early in the campaign, Kyle Turris was dealt to the Nashville Predators as part of a three-way transaction with the Colorado Avalanche. As the trade deadline approached in February 2018, Dion Phaneuf was shipped to the Los Angeles Kings and Derick Brassard was moved to Pittsburgh. The biggest changes, however, occurred before the 2018–19 season began when Mike Hoffman was traded acrimoniously to the San Jose Sharks, then quickly flipped to the Florida Panthers, while captain Erik Karlsson was dispatched to San Jose. More shifts followed, and finally, on September 25, 2020, Bobby Ryan, who had just won the Bill Masterton Trophy and was the last remaining player from the 2017 playoff run, was placed on waivers for the purpose of a buyout.

MAY 26
ALAIN VIGNEAULT NAMED COACH OF THE CANADIENS, 1997

Alain Vigneault was set to join the New York Islanders' bench as an assistant coach for the 1997–98 season but then received an offer he couldn't refuse. On May 26, 1997, he was named head coach of the Montreal Canadiens. Vigneault, who was drafted 167th overall by the St. Louis Blues in 1981, played parts of two seasons with them before finishing his career in the minors. Not long after hanging up his skates, Vigneault began coaching at the age of 25. He got his start in the Quebec Major Junior Hockey League (QMJHL), coaching for the Trois-Rivières Draveurs and eventually the Hull Olympiques, two clubs he played for when he was younger. In his first season behind the bench in Hull, Vigneault guided the team to a league championship. After four more seasons with the Olympiques, Vigneault made the jump to the NHL when he was named as an assistant coach for the newly minted Ottawa Senators. He served in that role under Rick Bowness for the better part of four seasons until the entire coaching staff was fired during the 1995–96 campaign.

After his dismissal, Vigneault returned to junior, where he became the head coach of the Beauport Harfangs, leading them to the QMJHL finals. While Bowness found a job as an associate coach with the Islanders for the 1996–97 campaign, Vigneault stayed in Beauport. By the end of the season, Bowness had become the head coach in New York and wanted Vigneault back in the fold. The two had a verbal agreement for Vigneault to become an assistant coach on Long Island, but after Mario Tremblay resigned as head coach of the Canadiens, it wasn't long before Vigneault was named as his replacement. Bowness didn't begrudge his former protege; he knew it was a dream job Vigneault couldn't pass up. In his first season behind the bench in Montreal, Vigneault recorded 37 victories, and the club advanced to the second round of the playoffs for the first time since 1993.

MAY 27
ROCKIES SOLD TO JOHN MCMULLEN, 1982

The Scouts didn't last long in Kansas City. After two money-losing seasons, the team was sold to sportscaster Bud Palmer and oil tycoon Jack Vickers, who relocated the club to Denver, where they became the Colorado Rockies. Despite the change in venue and name, things didn't improve much for the Rockies. After qualifying for the playoffs in 1978 for the first time in franchise history, the Rockies found themselves under new ownership. In July 1978, the team was sold to Arthur Imperatore, Jr., president of a trucking firm in New Jersey. From the outset, Imperatore was upfront about his intentions to relocate the team to his home state once construction of the arena in the Meadowlands Sports Complex was completed. Until then, the Rockies would remain in Denver. Although Imperatore became the club's longest-tenured owner, it was still hamstrung by instability. By the beginning of the 1980–81 season, the Rockies were on their fifth coach in just five years.

Having failed to bring the team to New Jersey, Imperatore sold the Rockies to Peter Gilbert, a cable television magnate from Buffalo, in February 1981. At his introductory press conference, Gilbert acknowledged that he was the club's third owner since moving to Denver but said it would be different this time. "Welcome to Rocky III," he told reporters. Gilbert said he would do everything in his power to make the team a winner and keep it in Colorado. But less than a year later, as the Rockies continued to struggle financially, Gilbert explored the possibility of moving the club to Ottawa after he spent a weekend there in January 1982, touring the city with Mayor Marion Dewar. By May 1982, there were even rumours swirling that George Steinbrenner, owner of the New York Yankees, was interested in buying the troubled franchise. Instead, Gilbert sold the Rockies to a New Jersey group headed by shipbuilder John McMullen. On May 27, 1982, the NHL Board of Governors approved the sale, and the Rockies finally moved to New Jersey, where a few months later they were rebranded as the Devils.

KINGS AND HAWKS CLASH IN DOUBLE-OVERTIME THRILLER, 2014

t was one of the greatest playoff games in NHL history. With the Chicago Blackhawks, the defending Stanley Cup champions, facing elimination against the Los Angeles Kings in Game 5 of the Western Conference Final, the two clubs duelled through a double-overtime epic. The game has entered hockey lore because of the frenetic first overtime, but it was a breathtaking affair as soon as the puck was dropped. After Drew Doughty took a tripping call against Chicago captain Jonathan Toews just 30 seconds into the contest, Brent Seabrook blasted a shot from the blue line to give the Blackhawks the lead. Less than three minutes later, Johnny Oduya buried a Patrick Kane rebound to extend the lead. Although the Kings cut the deficit just before the 10-minute mark, Chicago quickly answered back to restore its two-goal lead. A little over two minutes later, Marián Gáborík scored his league-leading 11th goal of the playoffs to make it 3–2 and cap off an exhilarating five-goal first period. In the second frame, the Kings scored a quick pair of goals to take the lead. The Blackhawks trailed for the rest of the period, but early into the third, Ben Smith drove to the net and knocked in a rebound to tie the game. Chicago had an incredible opportunity late in the match on the man advantage, but Jonathan Quick made some critical saves to keep the game tied and send it into overtime.

There were nearly eight minutes of continuous play without stoppage in the extra frame. The two teams went end to end, back and forth, exchanging numerous dangerous scoring chances. Kings right winger Justin Williams said his fellow players weren't even sitting on the bench because they were so on edge, and Blackhawks coach Joel Quenneville later referred to the game as quite possibly the greatest overtime he'd ever seen. Both goaltenders stopped everything that came their way, making double overtime necessary. Just over two minutes into the second overtime period, Michal Handzuš backhanded the puck into the net to stave off elimination and conclude one of the most thrilling playoff games ever.

MAY 29
IGGY VERSUS LECAVALIER, 2004

I t was one of the most enduring scenes from the 2004 Stanley Cup Final. Just over six minutes into the first period in the third game of the series, the Calgary Flames' Jarome Iginla and the Tampa Bay Lightning's Vinny Lecavalier were battling behind the net. As the intensity increased and shoving turned to missed punches, the two captains dropped their gloves and a bout ensued. It was a rare match-up between two star players, but it was even more unique because fights are usually few and far between in the playoffs, let alone in the Stanley Cup Final. Although Lecavalier was outmatched by Iginla, whose mix of skill and strength made him one of the most lethal power forwards in the league, the Lightning captain held his own as the two went at it.

While Iginla later insisted he wasn't spoiling for a fight to spark his team, the scrap seemed to be a turning point for the Flames and they carried that intensity with them through the rest of the game. More than halfway through the second period, the Calgary captain set up Chris Simon on a power play to put the Flames on the board. A couple of minutes later, Iginla rang a shot off the post as the Flames put Tampa on its heels. As the Flames continued to press, they caught a break when Lecavalier tried a centring pass from behind the Calgary net that was picked up near the blue line by Shean Donovan, who took off down the ice with Chuck Kobasew. As the pair drove toward the Tampa net, defenceman Darryl Sydor blocked any opportunity for a cross-ice pass, so Donovan, skating on his off wing, released a shot that beat Nikolai Khabibulin to make it 2–0. With time winding down in the third period, Iginla continued to be the difference-maker. After Robyn Regehr made a pass toward him, Iginla tipped it into the net, putting the finishing touch on a victory many of his teammates believed he inspired with his physical play and leadership in the first period.

MAY 30
BONINO, BONINO, BONINO! 2016

Sometimes the call is more memorable than the goal. Think of Rick Jeanneret's call when Brad May scored in overtime to give the Buffalo Sabres a sweep over the Boston Bruins in the 1993 playoffs, or Howie Rose's soliloquy after Stéphane Matteau scored in double overtime to send the New York Rangers to the Stanley Cup Final in 1994. Even if you didn't watch those games live, chances are those colourful calls still resonate with you. Just listening to them transports you back to that moment in hockey history all over again, and sometimes it feels as if you're experiencing it for the first time. I'm no Sabres fan, but I've heard Jeanneret's "May Day" call countless times over the years, and it still makes my hair stand on end each and every single time.

If you're like me, that might be how you feel about the first game of the Stanley Cup Final between the Pittsburgh Penguins and San Jose Sharks on May 30, 2016. With just over two minutes remaining in the game, Nick Bonino scored to give Pittsburgh a 3–2 lead. It was a significant goal in the sense that it held up as the game-winner to give the Penguins a 1–0 series lead, but I wouldn't even pretend to tell you that I have any clue about how the play-by-play announcer summed it up on the broadcast I was watching. Instead, the goal sticks out for me, and probably for you, because of how Harnarayan Singh, the play-by-play announcer for *Hockey Night in Canada in Punjabi*, which is the Punjabi broadcast of *Hockey Night in Canada*, called it. Right after the puck went in the net, Singh took a deep breath and exclaimed, "Bonino, Bonino, Bonino, Bonino, Bonino, Bonino, Bonino, Bonino, Bonino! Nick *Boninooooooooooooo*!" Singh's impassioned call went viral and was soon shared across the globe. When the Penguins won the Stanley Cup nearly two weeks later, Singh was invited by the team to be a part of the celebrations in Pittsburgh, where he did the call again in front of thousands of cheering fans.

TRUE NORTH BUYS THRASHERS, 2011

Thousands of hockey fans clad in Jets gear gathered in downtown Winnipeg to celebrate the return of the NHL to the city. It was a moment they had been waiting for since their beloved Jets had relocated to Phoenix in 1996. Although Winnipeg had been home to the Manitoba Moose, a minor league club, since the Jets took off, it wasn't the same. The fans longed for the return of NHL hockey. On May 31, 2011, it was announced that True North Sports & Entertainment had purchased the Atlanta Thrashers from the Atlanta Spirit and planned to move the team to Winnipeg. Although the sale and proposed relocation still needed approval by the NHL's Board of Governors the next month, Manitoba hockey fans were ecstatic. The NHL was finally returning to Winnipeg.

Following the announcement, speculation immediately turned to what the team would be called. For many, the only real option seemed to be the Jets. Bringing an NHL team back to Winnipeg and calling it anything else would have been sacrilegious. Although it was arguably the most fitting choice, True North was considering other options such as the Whiteout, a nod to the playoff tradition in which fans decked themselves out in white in response to the Calgary Flames' "C of Red," and the Falcons, a homage to Winnipeg's senior hockey team that represented Canada in the 1920 Olympics and won gold. By the time the NHL Entry Draft rolled around the next month in Saint Paul, Minnesota, the club hadn't decided yet on a new name and it seemed as though the first pick would be made without a moniker. But as the franchise took to the stage to make its first selection at seventh overall, True North chairman Mark Chipman unassumingly said that general manager Kevin Cheveldayoff would make "our first pick on behalf of the Winnipeg Jets." Fans watching back home at the MTS Centre rejoiced. The Jets would fly again.

KINGS ADVANCE TO STANLEY CUP FINAL, 2014

After coughing up a 3–1 series lead in the Western Conference Final against the Chicago Blackhawks, the Los Angeles Kings found themselves in Game 7 with a berth in the Stanley Cup Final on the line. The Kings, however, were no strangers to staring down elimination during a playoff run. In their opening-round series against the San Jose Sharks, they battled back from a 3–0 deficit, becoming the fourth team in NHL history to win a best-of-seven series after being down three games to none. After winning the opening two games of their next series against the Anaheim Ducks, the Kings dropped three straight and were on the brink yet again. They fought off elimination twice and won their second Game 7 of the playoffs. By the time they found themselves on the ropes against the defending champions, the Kings were 6–0 in elimination games that post-season.

Although the Chicago Blackhawks jumped out to a 2–0 lead, the Kings' Justin Williams, undefeated in career Game 7s, tied the game. But just 12 seconds after Los Angeles knotted it up, Chicago scored again to cap off an exciting first period. In the second frame, Tyler Toffoli tied the game again, but Patrick Sharp scored his second of the night to restore the Blackhawks' lead. With less than eight minutes remaining in regulation time, Marián Gáborík scored his league-leading 12th goal to tie the game 4–4 and force overtime. Just under six minutes into the extra frame, Williams set up defenceman Alec Martinez, who fired a shot from the point. The puck went through traffic and glanced off Nick Leddy and into the back of the net. The Kings won their third Game 7 of the playoffs and were off to the Stanley Cup Final for the second time in three seasons. By the time the Kings took on the New York Rangers for the right to Lord Stanley's mug, their resolve was steeled and the Cup was theirs to lose. Sure enough, less than two weeks later, Martinez played the overtime hero again, scoring the championship-clinching goal.

JUNE 2

SABRES ANNOUNCE DRAFT OF TARO TSUJIMOTO, 1974

When Buffalo Sabres fans opened their newspapers on the morning of June 2, 1974, they learned how their team fared at the amateur draft held a few days earlier. Unlike previous years, the NHL held the draft in secret by telephone so that its rivals, the WHA, wouldn't get wind of the proceedings. One name certainly raised some eyebrows. With the 183rd overall pick, Buffalo took Taro Tsujimoto, a young Japanese player from the Tokyo Katanas. While Sabres fans were intrigued by the selection, there was just one problem. Tsujimoto didn't exist.

Sabres general manager Punch Imlach had grown frustrated with how long the draft was taking, and by the second day, he'd had enough. Wanting to have some fun at the league's expense, Imlach told his colleagues they should take someone unknown to everyone. Pushing that a step further, one of the Sabres' executives suggested they pick a player who didn't even exist. Imlach jumped all over the idea. Paul Wieland, Buffalo's director of communications, proposed that the team make the player Japanese and say his last name was Tsujimoto, the moniker of an Asian grocery store just outside Buffalo that Wieland used to drive by as a college student. To put together a credible player profile, Wieland called the store's owner and asked for some background information, such as the Japanese word for *sabre*, which is *katana*.

So when NHL president Clarence Campbell rang up the Sabres to find out who they were taking in the 11th round, they said Taro Tsujimoto of the Tokyo Katanas. Campbell accepted the pick but was reportedly unhappy about having to call the league's other general managers and spell out Tsujimoto 17 times. Following the draft, Imlach and the Sabres remained committed to the gag. As training camp approached, they were unwavering. Tsujimoto was listed on the roster, and the team even went as far as preparing a stall for him in the dressing room. When the Japanese phenom never reported to camp, Imlach eventually confessed and the NHL removed the selection from its records.

JUNE 3
RED WINGS TRADE TERRY SAWCHUK
TO BRUINS, 1955

The news caught Terry Sawchuk by surprise. The netminder first heard a rumour that he was on the trading block over the radio and then received a telephone call from the Boston Bruins. They were calling to tell him they had acquired him from the Detroit Red Wings as part of a nine-player deal. On June 3, 1955, Sawchuk, along with Vic Stasiuk, Marcel Bonin, and Lorne Davis, was sent to Boston in exchange for Ed Sanford, Réal Chevrefils, Norm Corcoran, Gilles Boisvert, and Warren Godfrey.

Although Sawchuk started off his hockey career on defence, following the tragic death of older brother, Mike, a goaltender, he was reportedly urged by Red Wings scout Bob Kinnear, who oversaw the outdoor league in Winnipeg the brothers played in, to consider going between the pipes. Sawchuk acquiesced, donned his sibling's equipment, and picked up the position rather quickly. In 1947, he turned pro with the Omaha Knights of the United States Hockey League, where he recorded 30 victories and was named the most outstanding rookie. The next season, he was promoted to the Indianapolis Capitals, the Red Wings' AHL affiliate, where he continued to turn heads. He racked up 38 wins and took home the league's top rookie award. After playing a handful of games for Detroit in 1950, Sawchuk became a full-time NHL goaltender the following season, where he won the Calder Trophy, capturing rookie of the year honours yet again. Over the next four seasons in Detroit, Sawchuk won the Vezina Trophy three times as the league's best goaltender and backstopped the club to three Stanley Cup victories.

Sawchuk returned to Detroit in 1957 as part of a trade for Johnny Bucyk, backstopping the Red Wings for another seven years before capping off his career with a championship in Toronto and sojourns in Los Angeles, the Motor City again, and New York. Not long after his final appearance with the Rangers, Sawchuk died in 1970 under mysterious circumstances after some roughhousing with teammate Ron Stewart went wrong.

JUNE 4
RANGERS HIRE HERB BROOKS, 1981

After Herb Brooks guided the Americans to an improbable gold-medal victory at the 1980 Winter Olympics in Lake Placid, the New York Rangers wanted to see if he could perform another miracle. This time it would be on Broadway to lead the Blueshirts to their first Stanley Cup in more than four decades. On June 4, 1981, in the Hall of Fame lounge of Madison Square Garden, Brooks was introduced as the next head coach of the Rangers. General manager Craig Patrick, who had been Brooks's assistant coach at the Olympics, told reporters that nobody else had been considered for the job. Following a rough start to the 1980–81 campaign, Rangers GM and coach Fred Shero had resigned from the organization, and Patrick, the club's director of operations, had taken over his duties. Although it was an interim post, Patrick became the fourth member of his legendary family to step behind the Rangers' bench, following in the footsteps of his grandfather, Lester; uncle, Muzz; and father, Lynn. From the very beginning, the expectation was that the vacancy would eventually be filled by Brooks. They just had to wait.

At the time, Brooks was just beginning his tenure as head coach of HC Davos in Switzerland. After six months, however, Brooks resigned and returned to the United States. Although Brooks said he had no immediate plans to coach in the NHL, this was largely because he was still under contract with the Swiss league club. Instead, he said he was returning to Minneapolis–St. Paul to start a hockey school. By end of May 1981 and free of his contractual obligations, Brooks entered into talks with the Rangers to take over as bench boss. He inked a deal on June 1 and was officially introduced a few days later. After coaching the underdog U.S. Olympic team to the top of the podium, Brooks was up for the challenge of ending New York's 41-year Stanley Cup drought. But it wasn't meant to be. Brooks lasted just three full seasons behind the bench and never made it beyond the second round of the playoffs.

JUNE 5
HURRICANES MOUNT COMEBACK, 2006

t was one of the easiest goals Rod Brind'Amour ever scored. With just 31.1 seconds remaining in Game 1 of the Stanley Cup Final between the Edmonton Oilers and Carolina Hurricanes, the match was tied 4–4, and it looked as though they were headed to overtime. But as goaltender Ty Conklin, who had replaced Dwayne Roloson in the final six minutes, went behind the net to play the puck, he didn't realize that his defenceman, Jason Smith, was right behind him. When Conklin passed the puck back, it bounced off the blueliner's stick and was picked up by Brind'Amour, who swooped around the net. The Carolina captain handily backhanded it into the empty goal to give the Hurricanes a 5–4 victory in regulation time. It was a dramatic ending but probably wasn't even the most absurd thing that happened in that contest.

For starters, halfway through the second period, following a scramble in front of the Hurricanes' net, referee Mick McGeogh called Niclas Wallin for covering the puck with his glove in the crease and awarded the Oilers a penalty shot. Stalwart defenceman Chris Pronger made the attempt and beat Cam Ward to become the first player to score a penalty shot goal in the Stanley Cup Final. Edmonton scored again less than six minutes later to take a 3–0 lead. After Brind'Amour scored just before the second intermission, the Hurricanes opened the third period with two quick goals by Ray Whitney to tie the game. Halfway through the final fame, with the Oilers on a power play, defenceman Steve Staios lost the puck at the blue line. It was scooped up by Justin Williams, who raced down the ice and scored on a short-handed breakaway to give Carolina a 4–3 lead. The Oilers tied it up three minutes later, but their celebration was short-lived when Marc-André Bergeron checked Andrew Ladd into Roloson. The netminder, who had been Edmonton's most valuable player, left the game and was done for the playoffs. Although the way the game ended for the Oilers was heartbreaking, losing Roloson was much worse.

JUNE 6

NHL CHANGES MINOR PENALTY RULES, 1956

Frank Selke was overruled. During the NHL's Board of Governors meeting in 1956, the league, along with representatives from other professional circuits, adopted a new rule that allowed a player serving a minor penalty to return to the ice once the opposing team scored. Under the previous system, a player had to serve his entire minor penalty regardless of how many goals were scored on a power play. Selke, manager of the Montreal Canadiens, couldn't help but think the change was directed at his club and its voracious power play unit. While he protested that the Canadiens had only scored multiple goals more than eight times in the past season while their opponents were short-handed, there was one instance that many believed was the impetus for the rule change. On November 5, 1955, with Montreal on a power play and the Boston Bruins attempting to kill the penalty, head coach Toe Blake deployed his top unit, which consisted of five future Hall of Famers: Jean Béliveau, Maurice Richard, Bert Olmstead, and defencemen Doug Harvey and Tom Johnson. In a span of only 44 seconds, Béliveau scored a hat trick.

When the league met the following off-season to review the rules, it had Montreal in its crosshairs. Selke, the lone voice of dissent, argued that it unfairly penalized the Canadiens, mentioning that, years earlier, there had been no talk of changes when Detroit had a dominant power play. Despite his attempts to persuade his colleagues, Selke was outvoted. Following the decision, Selke had some choice words for his peers and reportedly barked, "Go get a power play of your own!" When asked by reporters about the result, Selke said he felt bad for the fans who would miss out on some extra excitement.

I couldn't agree more with Selke's sentiment. With the NHL always trying to increase scoring across the league, I've always felt that a surefire way to do that would be to go back to the old rule. Forget making the nets bigger or reducing the size of goalie equipment, let the players serve out their entire minor penalties.

JUNE 7
CAPITALS WIN STANLEY CUP, 2018

When Alex Ovechkin grabbed the Stanley Cup from NHL commissioner Gary Bettman and started screaming before he even raised the trophy above his head, I'll admit I got a little caught up in the moment. I'm not a Capitals fan, and I've certainly never experienced my own team win a championship, but watching Ovechkin get to the top of the mountain made me beam. Ever since he entered the league in 2005, he's been one of my favourite players, and I always hoped he'd get the opportunity to hoist the Cup. I've seen the look of disappointment on his face when he couldn't get past Sidney Crosby and the Pittsburgh Penguins in the playoffs, and for many years, it seemed plenty of people were prepared to write him off in the post-season. And despite being arguably the greatest goal scorer in NHL history, rightly or wrongly, his career would be defined by winning a championship or not. He could break Wayne Gretzky's improbable goal-scoring record, but without a Stanley Cup to his name, for some, all of his other achievements would pale in comparison. So while I wanted Ovechkin to win the Cup for the sake of winning, more than anything else I wanted it for him so that when he eventually gets inducted into the Hockey Hall of Fame, nothing will detract from his legacy on the ice.

So, on June 7, 2018, I was a Capitals fan briefly. But the only thing better than watching Ovechkin accept the Stanley Cup that evening was the celebrations that followed. Two nights later, after he tossed out the first pitch at a Washington Nationals baseball game, Ovechkin did a keg stand — a handstand on a keg while guzzling beer from the tap — on the Cup. It was supposedly the first time that stunt had been attempted with the trophy, and as the Capitals continued their revelry throughout the summer, the practice caught on, much to the chagrin of the Hockey Hall of Fame. Although Lord Stanley's mug has been subjected to some wild parties over the years, a "Cup stand" was certainly one for the books.

STARS WIN FOURTH-LONGEST GAME IN STANLEY CUP FINAL HISTORY, 2000

Following the first game of the Stanley Cup Final between the Dallas Stars and Buffalo Sabres on June 8, 1999, Dallas captain Mike Modano was dejected. His team had dropped the first game 3–2, and despite firing 37 shots on goaltender Dominik Hašek, the Stars rarely got a rebound. A year later to the day, Modano and his team wouldn't make the same mistake twice. On June 8, 2000, the Stars were back in the Stanley Cup Final for the second straight year, but after winning a year earlier against Buffalo, they found themselves on the verge of elimination. Heading into the fifth game of the series, Dallas was trailing 3–1 and its shot at repeating as champions was slipping away.

The previous year they had to contend with Hašek; this time it wasn't any easier with Martin Brodeur and the New Jersey Devils. Aside from a three-goal effort in the first game and a two-goal victory in the second contest, the Stars were stymied by Brodeur. The trend continued for most of the pivotal fifth game. After the game ended in a scoreless tie, they went to overtime for the first time that series, but nothing was solved in the first two extra periods. Six minutes into the third frame, though, Brett Hull threw the Stars' 40th shot of the game on net from along the right-wing boards. Modano, who hadn't scored a goal yet in the final, picked up the rebound and put it through Brodeur's pads, ending the fourth-longest game in the history of the Stanley Cup Final and the longest before a goal was scored. Although the Stars had forced a sixth game back home in Dallas, they still had their work cut out for them. Only one team, the 1942 Toronto Maple Leafs, had recovered from a 3–1 series deficit in the final to go on and win the championship. While the Stars hoped to add their name to that list, it wasn't meant to be. The Devils won the Stanley Cup in double overtime two nights later.

JUNE 9
TOM GLAVINE GETS DRAFTED BY THE KINGS, 1984

t's not out of the realm of possibility to think that two-time National League Cy Young–winning pitcher Tom Glavine could have wound up in the Hockey Hall of Fame. After all, he was drafted higher than Brett Hull and Luc Robitaille, and we know how their careers turned out. On June 9, 1984, just four days after being selected by the Atlanta Braves in the second round of the Major League Baseball (MLB) Draft, Glavine was taken 69th overall by the Los Angeles Kings in the NHL Entry Draft. Glavine, who had scored 44 goals and 85 points in 23 games in his final season of high school hockey, went 48 spots ahead of Hull and 102 in front of Robitaille. A native of Billerica, Massachusetts, located a half-hour north of Boston, Glavine played both hockey and baseball while growing up. When it was time to think about college, Glavine wanted a school where he could pursue both sports. After careful consideration, he ultimately decided to attend the University of Lowell (now University of Massachusetts Lowell), just seven miles from his home, because it had solid programs in both sports. But less than a month after committing to Lowell, Glavine's college plans were thrown for a loop.

After the Braves and Kings both drafted him, he had a difficult decision to make. Instead of going to college to pursue hockey or baseball, Glavine ended up signing a contract with the Atlanta Braves and became a professional baseball player. Although he loved hockey, Glavine felt it was the right choice for his future. It hurt to give up his hockey dream, but Glavine's success on the mound certainly helped take away some of the sting. After making his MLB debut in August 1987, Glavine went on to win his first National League Cy Young Award in 1991 before winning the World Series in 1995 and another Cy Young in 1998. We'll never know if Glavine would have joined Hull and Robitaille in hockey's pantheon, but one thing's certain, he's a Hall of Famer either way. In 2014, he entered Cooperstown as a first-ballot inductee.

JUNE 10

COLORADO AVALANCHE WIN THE STANLEY CUP, 1996

With less than a minute in regulation time, Florida Panthers right winger Ray Sheppard shot a rebound at the side of the net that nearly beat Patrick Roy. To some of the fans at Miami Arena, it looked as though he'd scored, so they started tossing plastic rats onto the ice. Earlier in the season, Florida forward Scott Mellanby had killed a rat in the team's dressing room with his stick before going out and scoring two goals in a game. It wasn't long before word of Mellanby's "rat trick" inspired fans to toss fake rats onto the ice after every home goal. It became so popular that the club actually brought on Orkin, a pest control company, as a sponsor and started referring to its ice crews, who were responsible for clearing the playing surface of the replica vermin, as exterminators. Although the practice had been a thorn in the side of NHL commissioner Gary Bettman all season long, the league grudgingly tolerated the tradition during the Panthers' improbable playoff run because it had already promised it would introduce delay-of-game penalties the following season.

When the first-ever Stanley Cup Final game was played in Florida, the game had to be halted several times so that the "exterminators" could carry out their work. Despite the fans' exuberance, the Panthers lost 3–2 and the Avalanche took a 3–0 series stranglehold. Two nights later, on June 10, 1996, with the game tied 0–0 and overtime looming, a few rats rained down after Sheppard's near-goal. As play was halted to clear the ice, the rest of the Panthers' faithful held on to their toy plastic rats. They would have to wait for another opportunity. After two extra frames solved nothing, the fans continued to clutch their rats tightly. But early into the third overtime, Colorado's Uwe Krupp fired the puck past goaltender John Vanbiesbrouck to clinch the Stanley Cup for the Avalanche. Although it wasn't the result the Panthers' fans had hoped for, they nonetheless capped off their memorable season by letting their rats fly one last time.

JUNE 11

BLACK HAWKS ACQUIRE TONY ESPOSITO, 1969

Two years after the Chicago Black Hawks traded Phil Esposito in what became one of the most lopsided deals in NHL history, they acquired his younger brother, Tony, from the Montreal Canadiens. On June 11, 1969, in the league's annual intraleague draft, Chicago plucked Esposito, who had made his NHL debut that season with Montreal. Although Esposito didn't get many opportunities playing behind Rogie Vachon and Gump Worsley, he did get plenty of chances in Chicago. The Black Hawks had finished at the bottom of their division for the first time in more than a decade and had given up the fifth-most goals in the league, behind only the porous upstart expansion teams. After making 43 saves in a 7–2 loss to the St. Louis Blues in his debut with the Black Hawks, Esposito picked up his first victory in his third start, stopping all 30 shots he faced against his former team, the Canadiens. Through his first 10 games in Chicago, Esposito recorded six straight wins and three shutouts and established himself as the Black Hawks' starting goaltender.

Although his athletic style of play was unconventional at the time, with many crediting him as being one of the early pioneers of the butterfly position that caught on decades later, he was practically unflappable in net. As he continued to rack up shutouts, Esposito earned the nickname "Tony O" for turning away everything his opponents threw his way, finishing the campaign with 15 shutouts, a record in the modern era. With Esposito between the pipes, the Black Hawks had a turnaround season and finished atop their division. For his efforts, Esposito was awarded the Calder and Vezina Trophies, making him the first rookie goaltender to win both awards since the Boston Bruins' Frank Brimsek in 1939. Esposito went on to establish a Hall of Fame career in Chicago, winning the Vezina two more times, and although the Black Hawks missed the mark with Phil, they hit the bull's eye with Tony.

JUNE 12

BLUES PLAY "GLORIA" ALL THE WAY TO THE CUP, 2019

When the St. Louis Blues woke up on New Year's morning in 2019, they had the worst record in the NHL. A few months later, however, they were one victory away from hoisting the Stanley Cup. After rattling off 30 wins in their last 45 regular-season games, St. Louis qualified for the post-season. Then, after defeating the Winnipeg Jets, Dallas Stars, and San Jose Sharks, they advanced to the Stanley Cup Final for the first time in nearly five decades. Although most people expected the Blues would make the post-season and maybe even push for a deep playoff run before the 2018–19 campaign began, it was almost unfathomable that they would achieve the turnaround they did. Following the dismissal of head coach Mike Yeo in November 2018, Craig Berube took over behind the bench, but the team continued to sputter. Before the holiday break, tempers flared in practice, and teammates Zach Sanford and Robert Bortuzzo came to blows. Things weren't going well in St. Louis. And yet, in the new year, the Blues started performing like the team many anticipated they could be before the regular season began.

One of the things that seemingly brought the club together came from an unlikely source. Prior to a game one evening in Philadelphia, the team was at a nightclub where a patron reportedly told the DJ to keep playing the late Laura Branigan's song "Gloria." As the 1982 smash hit continued over the sound system, the Blues decided then and there to make it their victory song. The next night, they defeated the Flyers 3–0 and "Gloria" became the theme song for the Blues' improbable run. By the time they made it to the playoffs, "Gloria" was everywhere in the hockey world. In St. Louis, radio stations broadcast the song on repeat following each of the team's playoff series victories, and finally, when the Blues defeated the Boston Bruins in Game 7 on June 12, 2019, to win the Stanley Cup for the first time in franchise history, it was Laura Branigan who echoed through the champagne-soaked dressing room.

JUNE 13
SCOTTY BOWMAN ANNOUNCES RETIREMENT, 2002

t was a bittersweet moment for Scotty Bowman. Even before the Detroit Red Wings accepted the Stanley Cup, their third title in six seasons, the head coach spread the word that he was retiring. Pulling aside stalwart blueliner Nicklas Lidström, who was about to become the first European-born player to win the Conn Smythe Trophy, Bowman told him he had coached his last game. It was a fitting end for Bowman, who had just won his ninth Stanley Cup as a coach, surpassing the mark held by his former mentor and legendary Montreal Canadiens bench boss Toe Blake. Although Blake had also announced his retirement on the night he won his final championship with Montreal back in 1968, it wasn't a spur-of-the-moment decision for Bowman and certainly one that didn't hinge on whether the Red Wings won again or not. He had made up his mind months earlier during the Olympic break in February but kept the news to his inner circle. Not even his wife knew. He broke the news to her following the victory before speaking with reporters.

For Bowman, who was turning 69 that September, it was time to step away from the bench. He had won his first Stanley Cup nearly three decades earlier with the Canadiens and then went on to win four straight with the club before winning another in Pittsburgh and three more in Detroit. As the confetti rained onto the ice at Joe Louis Arena, Bowman emerged from the bench wearing his skates, ready for one last victory lap. After captain Steve Yzerman accepted the Stanley Cup from commissioner Gary Bettman, he motioned for his coach to be the first to hoist it. As Bowman glided around the ice with the trophy held high above his head, he received a raucous ovation from the hometown crowd. Although Bowman was done with coaching, he wasn't ready to walk away from the game yet. He stayed on as a consultant with the Red Wings before joining his son, Stan, GM of the Chicago Blackhawks, where he won three more Stanley Cups in an advisory role.

RANGERS FINALLY WIN THE CUP AGAIN, 1994

The curse had been lifted. After 54 long years, the New York Rangers were finally Stanley Cup champions again. Some of the Blueshirts' players were so excited they jumped off the bench prematurely to celebrate only to realize there was still 1.6 seconds left on the clock, enough time for the Vancouver Canucks to make one last-ditch effort to force overtime. Vancouver took one final faceoff but were unable to put the puck in the back of the net. As fireworks exploded in the rafters of Madison Square Garden, the Broadway faithful started chanting "1940!" More than five decades of futility had been vanquished, and for some, it truly felt like a curse had actually been broken.

The origin of the Rangers' supposed anathema can be traced back to when the Brooklyn Americans suspended operations following the 1941–42 season. Red Dutton, former player and owner of the team, had plans to formally relocate the club, which still continued to share Madison Square Garden with the Rangers, to Brooklyn and had already lined up financing for a new arena in the borough. But those plans were shelved until after the conclusion of the Second World War. When NHL president Frank Calder died suddenly in 1943, the league asked Dutton to take up his post. He reluctantly agreed to do so on the condition that he would have the opportunity to re-establish the Americans after the war ended. The league agreed, and Dutton dutifully accepted the role. By 1946, Dutton was eager to get his team back on the ice and was prepared to resign the presidency to make it happen. The league, however, decided not to honour the deal it had made with Dutton and informed him there would be no NHL franchise in Brooklyn. Believing the Rangers were behind the scheme, Dutton reportedly vowed the team would never win another Stanley Cup for as long as he lived. It was only seven years after Dutton passed away in 1987 that the Rangers finally hoisted the trophy again.

JUNE 15

CHICAGO WINS THE STANLEY CUP, 2015

As the clock ticked down, the Chicago Blackhawks' faithful rose to their feet. The Hawks were Stanley Cup champions for the third time in six years. After Duncan Keith scored the opening goal late in the second period, the Blackhawks added another in the third to defeat the Lightning 2–0 and close out the series in six games. Keith, who had been indefatigable throughout the entire run, was the unanimous choice for the Conn Smythe Trophy, awarded to the most valuable player of the playoffs. He had played like a machine, racking up 21 points and logging heavy minutes game after game without showing any signs of fatigue. After Keith accepted the Conn Smythe and skated back to his teammates, the Stanley Cup was carefully brought out onto the ice. Although it was their third championship since 2010, it was the first time since 1938 that the Blackhawks had clinched it at home, and the fans at the United Center rejoiced at the sight of the glimmering trophy.

Before presenting the Cup to captain Jonathan Toews, commissioner Gary Bettman addressed the crowd. "Well, Chicago," he said. "That's three Cups in six seasons. I'd say you have a dynasty." It was hard to argue with his words. The last time an NHL team won three championships in six seasons was when the Detroit Red Wings accomplished the feat from 1997 to 2002, and there are few who wouldn't consider those Detroit squads to be worthy of dynasty consideration. But for some people, *dynasty* is a term in hockey that should only be reserved for the Montreal Canadiens, who won five consecutive championships from 1956 to 1960, or the New York Islanders, who claimed four straight in the 1980s. Although Chicago didn't even record back-to-back titles during its run, it won three times in six years in a 30-team league while playing under the constraints of the salary-cap era, an incredibly difficult accomplishment yet to be matched. And while some might disagree, I think Bettman got it right that night.

JUNE 16

SABRES ACQUIRE DALE HAWERCHUK, 1990

D ale Hawerchuk was looking for a change of scenery. After nine seasons with the Winnipeg Jets, the former first overall pick and Calder Trophy winner asked to be traded following the 1989–90 season. Ever since Hawerchuk made his NHL debut as an 18-year-old in 1981, he had been the Jets' franchise player, racking up 379 goals and 929 points over that span. But by the 1988–89 campaign, the star centre was unhappy in Winnipeg. The struggling Jets lost 42 games that year and missed the playoffs for the first time during Hawerchuk's tenure. In the off-season, the club hired head coach Bob Murdoch to turn things around, and Hawerchuk seemed optimistic the move would help. Although the Jets' fortunes improved under Murdoch, Hawerchuk's production dropped as the new bench boss curtailed his minutes in favour of a four-line system.

After Hawerchuk requested a trade at the end of the season, the Jets had no shortage of suitors for the former Hart Trophy finalist. There were six or seven teams interested in the Hawerchuk sweep-stakes, but it was the Buffalo Sabres' offer that rose to the top of the heap. On June 16, 1990, Buffalo sent all-star defenceman Phil Housley, Scott Arniel, and Jeff Parker to Winnipeg in exchange for Hawerchuk and a swap of first-round picks that year. Over the next four seasons, Hawerchuk recorded no fewer than 86 points with the Sabres. Following the lockout-shortened 1994–95 campaign, which saw Hawerchuk limited to 23 games due to injuries, he signed with the St. Louis Blues, one of the teams that had been in the mix for him five years earlier, as a free agent. Meanwhile, Housley patrolled Winnipeg's blue line for the three seasons, including a career-best 97-point campaign in 1992–93. It was the swapping of first-round picks, however, that had the most long-lasting impact on both teams. Buffalo used the 14th overall pick to select Brad May, who went on to score one of the biggest goals in Sabres' history, while, five spots later, the Jets took Keith Tkachuk, who recorded back-to-back 50-goal seasons with the franchise.

WHALERS DRAFT BOBBY HOLÍK 10TH OVERALL, 1989

Bobby Holík wasn't there when the Hartford Whalers called his name at the 1989 NHL Entry Draft in Bloomington, Minnesota. The highly touted centre was still in Czechoslovakia and had two years to serve in the military. Instead, his sister, Andrea Holíková, accepted on his behalf. Three years earlier, Holíková, a rising tennis star, had defected to the United States to join her boyfriend, František Musil, who had also fled from Czechoslovakia to begin his NHL career with the Minnesota North Stars. At the time, Czechoslovakia didn't have an agreement in place with the league for the release of its players, so defection was the only option. It was a dangerous proposition, and even after players successfully made it out, there were serious consequences for family members left behind. After Holík's sister departed, their father, Jaroslav, who was the head coach of Dukla Jihlava, was demoted to assistant coaching duties. If Holík were to defect, as well, his father would likely face further repercussions. Before the draft, there were rumours that Holík had already defected and that the North Stars were hiding him until they announced him as their seventh overall pick.

Despite not knowing when Holík would be able to join the Whalers, the club was willing to take the risk because they believed he was the top eligible player available. General manager Eddie Johnston felt he was even better than Mats Sundin, who went first overall to the Quebec Nordiques, becoming the first European player to be taken with the top spot in the draft. But Hartford was optimistic that it would be able to get Holík to join the team after he completed his military service, and following the draft, Czech tennis superstar Ivan Lendl, who served on the club's board of directors, had already started negotiations to secure his release. Less than a year later, Holík signed a four-year contract with the Whalers and was granted permission to leave Czechoslovakia. In his debut season in Hartford, Holík scored 21 goals and 43 points.

OILERS HIRE KEVIN LOWE AS HEAD COACH, 1999

T wenty years after becoming the Edmonton Oilers' first NHL draft pick and scoring the club's first goal in the league, Kevin Lowe was hired as head coach. Lowe had patrolled the Edmonton blue line for the first 13 seasons of his career and was an integral part of five championships. Following a trade to the New York Rangers in December 1992, Lowe spent four seasons with the Blueshirts, with whom he won another Stanley Cup before returning to the Oilers in 1996 as a free agent. During the 1996–97 season, Lowe played his 1,000th career game with the club, becoming the first player in franchise history to reach that milestone. The next year, he returned to the Oilers for what many expected to be his final NHL season, but not long into the campaign, Lowe was diagnosed with viral labyrinthitis, an inner-ear infection, that left him unable to skate. After being limited to just seven games that season while he battled the illness, Lowe decided to finally hang up his skates.

Although the 39-year-old's playing days were behind him, he wasn't ready to walk away from the game just yet, so he remained with the Oilers as an assistant coach. Even before Lowe stepped behind the bench for his first game, there was already speculation that he was being groomed for a head-coaching gig with the club. Ron Low, who had been Edmonton's bench boss since 1995, was reportedly falling out of favour with the club's top brass. At the end of the 1998–99 season, the Oilers tabled Low a contract to return for another season, but he declined. Then, on June 18, 1999, Lowe was named as his replacement. After just one season, however, Lowe resigned from his coaching duties not long after long-time Oilers general manager Glen Sather stepped down to go to New York to become president and GM of the Rangers. Two days after Lowe's resignation, he was announced as Edmonton's new general manager. Lowe served in the role for eight seasons and was the architect of the team's run to the Stanley Cup Final in 2006.

JUNE 19

HURRICANES WIN STANLEY CUP, 2006

When Peter Karmanos announced that the Hartford Whalers would be moving to Raleigh in 1997, there were doubts about whether hockey would work in North Carolina. The team, rebranded as the Carolina Hurricanes, didn't even play in Raleigh for the first two seasons. While they waited for the Raleigh Entertainment & Sports Arena to be completed, they played 80 miles away at the Greensboro Coliseum. There were so few fans who turned up in those early years that portions of the upper deck were curtained off to hide all the empty seats. Despite the poor attendance, the Hurricanes won the newly minted Southeast Division in 1999 and qualified for the playoffs for the first time since relocating. The following season, with the team's new arena completed, the Hurricanes moved to Raleigh. Midway through the campaign, the team made a franchise-altering deal, sending Keith Primeau and a fifth-round pick to the Philadelphia Flyers for Rod Brind'Amour, Jean-Marc Pelletier, and a second-round pick. Although the Hurricanes missed the playoffs that year, the trade soon paid dividends.

Two years later, the team made an improbable run to the Stanley Cup Final, the deepest one in franchise history, since the Whalers had never advanced beyond the second round during their nearly two decades in Hartford. While the Hurricanes came up short against the powerhouse Detroit Red Wings, the odds-on favourites to win the Cup that year, the run put any doubts to rest that hockey couldn't work in North Carolina. The atmosphere was unparalleled. Drawing from football traditions, the fans brought tailgating to the hockey world, and inside the arena they made it the loudest building in the playoffs. Following two years of missing the post-season and the 2004–05 lockout, Carolina returned to the Stanley Cup Final. On June 19, 2006, in Game 7 at RBC Center in Raleigh, the Hurricanes defeated the Oilers 3–1 to win the Stanley Cup. Karmanos's dream of hockey succeeding in North Carolina had finally come true.

JUNE 20
JOSÉ THÉODORE WINS HART TROPHY, 2002

After finishing the 2001–02 campaign with a league-leading 52 goals and 96 points, Jarome Iginla had already bagged the Rocket Richard and Art Ross Trophies. Heading into the NHL's annual awards ceremony on June 20, 2002, it seemed likely that the Calgary Flames captain would add two more prizes to his collection. He appeared to be a lock to win the Lester B. Pearson (now Ted Lindsay) Award, bestowed annually to the "most outstanding player" as voted on by his peers. With goal scoring down across the board that season, Iginla still managed to get 52, 11 more than the next closest player, a feat certainly noticed throughout the league. Iginla was also a finalist for the Hart Trophy, awarded annually to the "player judged most valuable by his team," as determined by the Professional Hockey Writers Association. For that award, Iginla was up against Patrick Roy, who put together a sterling campaign as a 36-year-old, and Montreal Canadiens netminder José Théodore, who had the best save percentage in the NHL that year. While you could make solid cases for both goaltenders, it was hard to argue that anyone was more valuable to his team that season than Iginla. Calgary finished in the bottom half of the league in scoring with 201 goals, which meant his 52 goals accounted for more than a quarter of the team's offensive production. Although the Flames missed the post-season, without Iginla in the lineup, they would have finished at the bottom of the standings.

At the awards ceremony in Toronto, Iginla took home the Pearson but ended up losing the Hart to Théodore. They both finished with the same amount of points from the voters, but because the Canadiens' goalie had more first-place votes, the trophy went to him. Many in the hockey world felt as though Iginla was robbed, and as it turned out, he kind of was. The story goes that a Montreal writer left him off of his ballot. If Iginla was on the list, which he absolutely should have been, he would have walked away with the Hart.

JUNE 21
ONE OF THE GREATEST NHL
DRAFTS EVER, 2003

M y NHL draft year was 2003. As you might have guessed, I was passed over in every round and am still waiting for my call to this day. Even if I had a modicum of skill on the ice, I still haven't quite mastered skating backward and wouldn't have stood a chance. The 2003 Entry Draft was arguably the deepest in league history. Some will say the 1979 draft, loaded with talent because of the NHL's merger with the WHA, was better, and they'd have a strong case. That draft featured seven future Hall of Famers in Mike Gartner, Ray Bourque, Michel Goulet, Kevin Lowe, Guy Carbonneau, Mark Messier, and Glenn Anderson, not to mention more than a dozen other All-Star players.

Although we don't know yet how many players from the 2003 class will be inducted into the Hall of Fame, it has already proven to be one of the most bountiful drafts. Of the 292 players taken, 130 went on to suit up for at least one NHL game. The first round proved to be a veritable gold mine that changed the fortunes of many clubs. Marc-André Fleury, who was taken first overall by the Penguins, went on to backstop Pittsburgh to a Stanley Cup in 2009 and was an integral part of back-to-back championships in 2017. The Hurricanes took Eric Staal second overall. Three years later, he led the playoffs in scoring as Carolina won its first Cup in franchise history. Elsewhere in the first round, the Mighty Ducks grabbed both Ryan Getzlaf and Corey Perry. Anaheim won the Stanley Cup four years later with those two in the lineup. Meanwhile, Philadelphia snagged Jeff Carter and Mike Richards. While both players were key to the Flyers' Cup run in 2010, they ended up in Los Angeles, where they joined another 2003 first-round pick, Dustin Brown, and won two Stanley Cups with the Kings. Even beyond the first round, there were still plenty of gems, but perhaps none better than Patrice Bergeron, who went 45th overall to the Boston Bruins, with whom he established himself as one of the best players in franchise history.

JUNE 22
NORDIQUES DRAFT ERIC LINDROS FIRST OVERALL, 1991

When Quebec Nordiques owner Marcel Aubut handed Eric Lindros a jersey after the club selected him first overall at the NHL Entry Draft on June 22, 1991, the skillful power forward passed on the usual draft-day rite of passage. Instead of donning the new sweater, he draped it across his left arm as he shook hands with the club's top brass. The move wasn't surprising. In the months leading up to the draft, Lindros, the consensus first-overall pick, made it clear that if he was chosen by Quebec, he wouldn't play for the team. At the time, Lindros and his parents felt that Quebec City was too small a market and had misgivings about the province's precarious political situation.

Although the Nordiques hoped to persuade him otherwise, by August 1991, they still hadn't begun negotiations. When discussions did start later that month, Lindros sought $3 million in salary, an unprecedented amount for a rookie that many believed was a ploy to force the Nordiques to trade him. In early September, however, when Lindros was in Montreal to play in the Canada Cup tournament, it was clear that no amount of money would change his mind about the Nordiques. At a press conference the night before Canada's final round-robin game, he reiterated that he didn't want to play for Quebec. Although he said it was a business decision and had nothing to do with culture or language, it was clear Lindros would never suit up for the Nordiques. Hoping to force a trade, Lindros told the club he would go back to junior hockey for two more years until he was eligible to re-enter the draft. By October 1991, it was reported that he and his parents had even provided Quebec with a list of players the Nordiques could fetch if they dealt him to another team. Meanwhile, Aubut, who continued to reject Lindros's trade demands, filed a complaint with the NHL, accusing as many as six teams of tampering with Lindros. It would take a year before the saga finally came to an end when Lindros was dealt to the Philadelphia Flyers, but we'll get to that.

FLYERS TRADE JEFF CARTER AND MIKE RICHARDS, 2011

J eff Carter seemed as if he'd be a Philadelphia Flyer for a long time. After leading the team in goal scoring for the past two seasons, including a 46-goal campaign in 2008–09, Carter signed an 11-year, $58-million contract extension on November 13, 2010. Carter, who was slated to become a restricted free agent, appeared likely to be in Philadelphia for more than a decade. By the time his new deal kicked in, however, he was gone. After reaching the 30-goal mark for the third straight year with the Flyers, he was traded to the Columbus Blue Jackets on June 23, 2011, for Jakub Voráček and first- and third-round picks in the 2011 NHL Entry Draft. But Carter wasn't the only Flyer shipped out that day. The team also dispatched captain Mike Richards, along with Rob Bordson, to the Los Angeles Kings for Brayden Schenn, Wayne Simmonds, and a 2012 second-round pick. Much like Carter, Richards expected to be in Philadelphia for a while. He still had nine years remaining on a 12-year contract extension he'd signed in December 2007.

By clearing out both Carter and Richards, who had been drafted by the Flyers in the first-round of the 2003 draft and had become close friends during their time together in Philadelphia, the club freed up more than $100 million in salary to pursue netminder Ilya Bryzgalov and ink him to a long-term deal. Keen to shore up their goaltending, the Flyers signed Bryzgalov to a nine-year, $51-million contract that same day. While Carter was reportedly unhappy about going to Columbus, he wasn't there long. Just four days before the NHL's trade deadline, on February 23, 2012, he was acquired by the Kings in exchange for defenceman Jack Johnson and a conditional first-round pick. Reunited with Richards in Los Angeles, Carter was rejuvenated. In his first 16 games with the team, he scored six goals, and in the playoffs, added eight more to tie for the most in the post-season. On June 11, 2012, Carter scored a pair, including the Stanley Cup–clinching goal, securing the Kings' first championship in franchise history.

JUNE 24

LEAFS TRADE TUUKKA RASK TO THE BRUINS, 2006

When the Toronto Maple Leafs selected Tuukka Rask 21st overall in 2005, the Finnish goaltender wasn't expected to make the team for a few more seasons. Following the draft, he returned to Ilves Tampere of the Finnish Elite League, where he finished the 2005–06 campaign with a sterling .926 save percentage. But before even getting an opportunity to suit up for the Leafs, Rask was traded suddenly to the Boston Bruins on June 24, 2006, in exchange for fellow netminder Andrew Raycroft, who had won the Calder Trophy in 2004 as the league's top rookie. The move wasn't totally unexpected. Toronto wasn't going to re-sign veteran goaltender Ed Belfour, and with Justin Pogge, who had recently backstopped Canada to a gold medal at the World Juniors, still developing, the Leafs needed to shore up the crease and felt Rask was expendable. Although Raycroft had a poor start to the 2005–06 season and was hampered by a right knee injury, the team believed he was a bona fide starter who would have a resurgence in Toronto.

While the move paid off in the first season — Raycroft racked up 37 victories to tie a club record — it turned out to be one of the most lopsided deals in franchise history. Following his stellar debut, Raycroft struggled in his second campaign with the Leafs. He lost the starting job early in 2007–08 and finished with only two wins in 16 starts. At the end of the year, Toronto bought out his contract. After stints in Colorado, Vancouver, and Dallas, Raycroft was out of the league by 2011. Meanwhile, Rask made his NHL debut on November 20, 2007. Squaring off against his former team, he made 30 saves in a 4–2 victory against the Leafs. He spent the next two seasons in the AHL but became an NHL regular during the 2009–10 season. After serving chiefly as Tim Thomas's backup, Rask took the reins in 2013–14, recording 36 victories and winning the Vezina Trophy. Over the next seven years in Boston, Rask established himself as one of the league's top goaltenders.

JUNE 25
SENATORS ACQUIRE DAVID RUNDBLAD, 2010

The Ottawa Senators were searching for another high-end blue-liner to complement their smooth-skating defenceman, Erik Karlsson. David Rundblad appeared to be the perfect fit. Originally drafted 17th overall by the St. Louis Blues in 2009, he had represented Team Sweden at the World Juniors in past years and had even skated alongside Karlsson at the 2009 tournament. Although Rundblad was expected to continue playing in the Swedish Hockey League for at least another season, the Senators were confident he'd be ready to make the jump to the NHL for the 2011–12 campaign. On June 25, 2010, from the floor of the NHL Entry Draft, the Senators sent the 16th overall selection to the St. Louis Blues in exchange for Rundblad. After using their own pick to take centre Jaden Schwartz at number 14, the Blues used Ottawa's choice to take right winger Vladimir Tarasenko two spots later. Tarasenko, a native of Yaroslavl, Russia, had just finished his second season in the Kontinental Hockey League (KHL), where he had recorded 13 goals and 24 points in 42 games. Although he was still a couple of years away from joining the NHL, the Blues were eager to bring his scoring touch to their lineup.

Following another year in Sweden, Rundblad did, in fact, join the Senators for the start of the 2011–12 campaign. His time in Ottawa, however, was short-lived. After scoring his first NHL goal on November 27, 2011, Rundblad, along with a second-round pick, was sent to the Phoenix Coyotes less than a month later in exchange for centre Kyle Turris.

While the trade didn't work out as planned for Ottawa, it was a shrewd move for the Blues. Following two more seasons in the KHL, Tarasenko joined St. Louis for the lockout-shortened campaign in 2012–13. After scoring 29 goals in his first two NHL seasons, Tarasenko racked up 37 goals in 2014–15 and followed that up by reaching the 40-goal mark the next year. He went on to record five straight 30-goal seasons in St. Louis and was an integral part of its Stanley Cup victory in 2019.

OILERS GET GRIFFIN REINHART FOR FIRST-ROUND PICK, 2015

At the 2015 NHL Entry Draft, Peter Chiarelli sent the Edmonton Oilers' 16th overall pick and the club's second-round pick to the New York Islanders in exchange for defenceman Griffin Reinhart. Although shoring up the blue line was a top priority in Edmonton, it was a move that could come back to haunt Chiarelli. Originally taken fourth overall by the Islanders in 2012, Reinhart had established himself as one of the top defensive prospects after guiding the Edmonton Oil Kings to two Western Hockey League championships in three years and a Memorial Cup victory in 2013. Following junior hockey, Reinhart made the Islanders' roster out of camp to start the 2014–15 campaign, but after just a few games, he was sent down to the club's AHL affiliate. He was called up for a handful of contests but spent most of the year in Bridgeport. He suited up for one game for the Islanders in the playoffs that year but looked out of place in a 5–1 loss to the Washington Capitals. After leaving New York, Reinhart began the 2015–16 season with the Oilers, but was sent to the minors in November. Although he returned to the big club for 17 more games, he couldn't stay in the NHL and spent the next season in the AHL. Following one postseason appearance for the Oilers in 2017, the club left Reinhart exposed in the 2017 expansion draft. He was plucked by the Vegas Golden Knights but never played another NHL game.

Meanwhile, on Long Island, New York used the 16th overall pick to select playmaking centre Mathew Barzal and then packaged Edmonton's second-round pick and a third-rounder to acquire the 28th overall pick from the Tampa Bay Lightning, which they used to take Anthony Beauvillier. In his first full season with the Islanders, Barzal racked up 85 points and won the Calder Trophy as the league's top rookie. Following the departure of John Tavares in 2018, Barzal has become the club's top centre and appears to be a player the franchise can build around for years to come.

KINGS SIGN JOHN TONELLI, 1988

The Calgary Flames felt John Tonelli's best days were behind him. Although the 31-year-old was just coming off a 58-point campaign, his best since leaving the New York Islanders, Calgary offered him an NHL termination contract in order to cut bait. Head coach Terry Crisp believed Tonelli had lost a step and could no longer compete in back-to-back games. Although the Flames only had nine back-to-back contests during the regular season, Crisp thought it was a problem during the rigorous schedule of the playoffs and ended up benching Tonelli for a third of the team's post-season games. While Tonelli was only a year older than Joe Mullen, who had just recorded his second straight 40-goal campaign, Crisp knew Tonelli played a hard-working, grinding game which would be hard for him to keep doing. After accepting the Flames' termination contract, Tonelli was eager to prove them wrong and keen to sign a new deal with another team.

Despite being traded to the Flames from the Islanders just two years earlier, New York was interested in bringing Tonelli back once he became a free agent. Although it was enticing to consider returning to the club where he'd won four consecutive Stanley Cups, Tonelli considered the Los Angeles Kings a better fit for him. So, on June 27, 1988, he agreed to a one-year deal with the Kings. Los Angeles had a younger roster, so Tonelli liked the look of it out west. Tonelli's decision to join the Kings seemed even better just over a month later when they added the greatest player in the game to their lineup — Wayne Gretzky. Aside from a handful of games in the 1984 Canada Cup tournament, Tonelli had spent most of his career battling Gretzky, so the prospect of playing with him rather than against him was an added bonus. In his first season in Los Angeles, Tonelli proved his critics wrong. He scored 31 goals and 64 points, recording his most productive campaign since 1985. Tonelli returned to the Kings the following season and racked up 31 goals for the second straight year.

JUNE 28
LIGHTNING NAB BRAYDEN POINT, 2014

Every NHL team passed on Brayden Point at least once in the 2014 Entry Draft. The Buffalo Sabres actually had six opportunities to take him in the first three rounds but passed on him each and every time. Although Point was coming off a 91-point campaign with the Moose Jaw Warriors of the Western Hockey League, clubs were reluctant to take the high-scoring centre because they believed he was undersized. Despite the fact that the game was increasingly becoming faster and more skilled, many NHL executives continued to place a premium on size. Point, who was five foot ten, might have been diminutive by hockey standards, but his talent more than made up for his perceived lack of size. As more names were called, Point sat patiently with his family in the stands of the Wells Fargo Center in Philadelphia. As the third round got under way, the Tampa Bay Lightning traded the 80th overall pick and a seventh-round pick in 2015, previously acquired in a trade with the Vancouver Canucks, to the Minnesota Wild in exchange for the 79th overall selection. Moving up one spot, the Lightning finally called Point's name.

At the time, it wasn't necessarily heralded as the steal of the draft, but in the coming years it would be regarded as one of the shrewdest moves made that day. Following another season of junior hockey in which he recorded 87 points and won gold with Canada at the World Juniors tournament, Point made the Lightning for the 2016–17 campaign. After scoring 40 points as a rookie, Point registered a 32-goal season the next year. During the 2018–19 season, he scored 92 points, the 12th most in the league that year. But during the 2020 Stanley Cup Playoffs, teams really started to kick themselves for not snagging Point when they had the chance. In 22 post-season games, he got 14 goals and 33 points, including the game-winner against the Columbus Blue Jackets in the fourth-longest match in NHL history, narrowly losing the Conn Smythe Trophy to teammate Victor Hedman in Tampa's championship victory.

HOCKEY WORLD ROCKED BY
THREE MOVES, 2016

n less than half an hour, the hockey world was turned upside down. I was sitting in the office of the think tank where I worked when I checked Twitter and gasped. The Edmonton Oilers had dealt talented winger Taylor Hall to the New Jersey Devils for defenceman Adam Larsson. The trade was one-for-one. Edmonton had been trying to improve its back end for years, but I hadn't expected Hall to be the casualty in that pursuit. Two years earlier, he'd scored 80 points, and with the Oilers winning the Connor McDavid sweepstakes in 2015, Hall was the type of skilled winger you'd want to keep to play with your franchise centre. I tried explaining the gravity of the situation to my office mates, but they were unmoved. There was still an hour of work left, and they were busy combing through census data while I tried to make sense of it. Getting nowhere with them, I texted my buddy Blair, who was the only real Oilers fan I knew.

By the time I heard back from him, an even bigger trade came across the wire. The Montreal Canadiens traded P.K. Subban, who had won the Norris Trophy a few years earlier as the league's top defenceman, to the Nashville Predators in exchange for Shea Weber. It was another blockbuster — and just 20 minutes after the first trade broke. Although Weber had been the backbone of Nashville's blue line for years and had a cannonading shot feared throughout the league, it seemed Montreal was giving up the more talented player in the swap. But once again, my colleagues were uninterested in my litigation of the transaction. As they turned back to their screens, three minutes later, Lightning captain Steve Stamkos, slated to become a free agent in two days, re-signed with the club for eight years, ending months of speculation he was going to join his hometown Toronto Maple Leafs. On any other day, Stamkos staying put would have been headline news, but with everything that had already happened, it simply capped off some of the wildest 23 minutes in hockey history.

JUNE 30
LINDROS GOES TO ARBITRATION, 1992

After a year-long standoff, the Eric Lindros saga was final-ly over, or so it seemed. On June 20, 1992, the Quebec Nordiques traded the disgruntled centre to the Philadelphia Flyers for Peter Forsberg, Steve Duchesne, Kerry Huffman, Mike Ricci, Ron Hextall, a first-round pick in 1993, $15 million, and fu-ture considerations. The only problem was that the New York Rangers also thought they had acquired Lindros that same day. After reaching a tentative deal in a hotel suite in Philadelphia, Flyers president Jay Snider asked Nordiques president Marcel Aubut for permission to call Lindros to confirm that, before they paid a king's ransom for him, he actually wanted to play for the team.

Not long after Snider finished his conversation with Lindros and family, Aubut reportedly said that after bringing the deal back to his side, the Nordiques wanted the Flyers to drop the condition that Lindros had to sign a contract immediately. Snider returned to his suite to discuss it with his staff when Aubut abruptly entered the room and said the deal was off and that he was accepting a trade from the Rangers that reportedly included Sergei Nemchinov, Tony Amonte, Alexei Kovalev, James Patrick, either goaltender John Vanbiesbrouck or Mike Richter, a first-round pick, and $20 million in cash. Snider was incensed. He felt that the Flyers and Nordiques had already reached an agreement.

With both clubs believing they had struck a deal to land the highly touted prospect, the matter went to arbitration. Following five days of testimony, arbitrator Larry Bertuzzi made his decision. On June 30, 1992, he ruled in favour of the Flyers. After assessing all the in-formation, Bertuzzi found that the Nordiques had reached their ten-tative agreement to send Lindros to Philadelphia an hour before the Rangers had tabled their offer. When Lindros learned the news, he was relieved. "I'm just happy to get out of there," he said. Lindros made his Flyers debut the next season, scoring 41 goals and 75 points as a rookie.

JULY 1
JOHN TAVARES SIGNS WITH
MAPLE LEAFS, 2018

John Tavares was coming home. Following months of speculation that he would sign with his hometown Toronto Maple Leafs, Tavares made it official on July 1, 2018, when he signed a seven-year, $77-million contract with Toronto. Tavares, who had been drafted first overall by the New York Islanders in 2009, had been the face of that franchise since breaking into the league. In nearly a decade on Long Island, Tavares established himself as one of the top centres in the NHL, and when he became an impending free agent, he drew interest from around the league. Although he had considered staying in New York, Tavares also assessed offers from the San Jose Sharks, Dallas Stars, Tampa Bay Lightning, Boston Bruins, and, of course, Toronto.

While Tavares was drawn to the Leafs because of the chance to play with a talented young core that included Auston Matthews and Mitch Marner, he simply couldn't pass up the once-in-a-lifetime opportunity to suit up for the team he rooted for as a child. He captured that sentiment perfectly when shortly after it was announced he was coming to Toronto, he tweeted a picture of himself as a young boy sleeping in his bed, nestled among Leafs blankets and pillowcases. Along with the photo, Tavares also included the caption "Not every day you can live a childhood dream." The image quickly went viral. As someone who had that exact same bedspread when I was younger, it struck a chord. While I never realized my dream of suiting up for the Leafs, chiefly because I was bad at hockey and didn't really start playing until I was 29 years old, it was hard not to get caught up in the moment. Unless, of course, you were an Islanders fan. But I think what made it special, regardless of allegiance, is that so few of us actually get to realize our childhood dreams, and seeing Tavares do exactly that really made it feel as if it was so much more than just another free-agent signing. It was a homecoming, and the start of a new era in Toronto.

JULY 2
MARIÁN HOSSA SIGNS WITH
RED WINGS, 2008

After coming up just two victories shy of a Stanley Cup with the Pittsburgh Penguins, Marián Hossa had a difficult decision to make. Traded to Pittsburgh in advance of the deadline in 2008, Hossa was slated to become a free agent and desperately wanted to win a championship. Although he had found a good fit with the Penguins in the post-season, racking up 26 points in 20 games before falling short to the Detroit Red Wings in the final, he turned down the club's reported offer of a five-year contract worth $7 million per season. Instead, the Slovak winger looked to the Red Wings. When he initially entered into negotiations with the club, it had also offered him a long-term deal, but the annual salary was well below some of the other bids he was assessing. While Detroit was keen to add Hossa to its roster in order to repeat as champions, it had to re-sign Henrik Zetterberg and Johan Franzén the next year and didn't have the flexibility to offer Hossa the kind of contract he might otherwise fetch on the open market.

Although Hossa could have gotten more money elsewhere, he felt the Red Wings gave him the best chance to hoist the Stanley Cup. And so after careful consideration, on July 2, 2008, he signed a discounted one-year, $7.45-million deal with Detroit. After the signing, Hossa acknowledged it was tough to choose between the Penguins and Red Wings but believed he "would have a little better of a chance to win the Cup in Detroit." Those words came back to haunt him a year later. On June 12, 2009, the Red Wings and Penguins squared off in Game 7 in their rematch for the right to Lord Stanley's mug. This time, however, Pittsburgh came out on top, leaving Hossa to skate off the ice in defeat once again. A few weeks after that heartbreaking loss, Hossa signed a 12-year, $62.8-million deal with the Chicago Blackhawks. In 2010, he advanced to the Stanley Cup Final again for the third straight year, but this time he didn't leave empty-handed.

JULY 3

BRETT HULL SIGNS WITH STARS, 1998

B rett Hull said the Dallas Stars would have no chance against the Detroit Red Wings in the 1998 Western Conference Final. Although the Stars pushed the series to six games, they were knocked out by the Red Wings, just as Hull had predicted. Not long after casting doubt on Dallas's Stanley Cup chances, Hull left the Blues as a free agent and joined the Stars. On July 3, 1998, the winger signed a three-year, $17-million deal to become a Star. Earlier in the season, Hull rejected a three-year, $15-million contract offer to remain with the Blues because it only had a partial no-trade provision and he was seeking a full one. As a free agent, he had to field offers from the New York Rangers and the Chicago Blackhawks, where his father, Bobby, had played, but he ultimately decided on the Stars because he felt they gave him the best chance to win a Stanley Cup. With Dallas, Hull also received the full no-trade clause he desired, becoming the only player on the team with that privilege. Even Mike Modano didn't have that.

But by bringing in Hull, the Stars added more scoring to the lineup. During his time in St. Louis, Hull had recorded five 50-goal seasons, including a blistering 86-goal campaign in 1990–91. Playing in the same division as the Blues, Dallas was acutely aware of Hull's offensive capabilities. He scored more goals and points against the Stars franchise than any other team in the NHL. Of his 554 career goals, the 15th most in league history at the time, 62 of them found their way into the back of the Stars' net. In his first season in Dallas, Hull scored 32 goals despite wrestling with a pair of groin injuries limiting him to 60 games that year. In the playoffs, Hull and the Stars knocked off his former team in the semifinals before advancing to the Stanley Cup Final against the Buffalo Sabres, where he scored a controversial goal in triple overtime of Game 6 to clinch the first championship in franchise history.

JULY 4

WILD SIGN PARISE AND SUTER TO MATCHING DEALS, 2012

Zach Parise and Ryan Suter had often talked about playing on the same team. Although they had both represented the United States internationally from the World Juniors to the Olympics, outside of those tournaments, they had never really had the opportunity to play together. Even before they got to the NHL, they had squared off in college, with Parise at the University of North Dakota and Suter attending the University of Wisconsin. In 2003, they were both selected at the NHL Entry Draft. Suter went seventh overall to the Nashville Predators, and the New Jersey Devils took Parise at 17th. After turning pro, they continued to cross paths when they played together for the United States, but in the NHL, with Parise and Suter playing in opposite conferences, their meetings were few and far between. During the 2011–12 campaign, however, as they both approached unrestricted free agency in the off-season, they started talking about the possibility of joining forces. They revisited the idea when free agency opened on July 1, discussing potential landing spots that would work for both of them.

As the two most sought-after free agents that year, Parise and Suter were in the driver's seat. Parise, who had scored 45 goals and 94 points with the Devils three years earlier, was considering deals from New Jersey and the Pittsburgh Penguins, while Suter, who had been an integral part of Nashville's blue line for the past seven years, drew significant interest from the Detroit Red Wings. The Minnesota Wild, however, quickly became the preferred destination. Parise had grown up in Minneapolis, and his father, J.P., had played for the Minnesota North Stars for nearly a decade. Suter was raised not too far from there in Madison, Wisconsin, but his wife, Becky, was from Bloomington, a stone's throw from the Twin Cities. It seemed like the perfect fit for them on and off the ice. On July 4, 2012, the Wild inked both Parise and Suter to matching 13-year, $98-million deals. It was a significant investment, but the club hoped the signings would usher in a new era of Wild hockey.

JULY 5
MAPLE LEAFS SIGN DAVID CLARKSON, 2013

n the eyes of the Toronto Maple Leafs' top brass, David Clarkson seemed like a perfect fit. He was a local guy who had grown up rooting for the team in the Mimico neighbourhood of the city. His boyhood hero was Wendel Clark, and just like his idol, he was a former 30-goal scorer who threw big hits and wasn't afraid to drop the gloves. Clarkson was the pugnacious type of player that management wanted to add to the lineup. Following the 2012–13 lockout-shortened season, Clarkson led the New Jersey Devils in goals with 15, and given his connections to the Leafs, he seemed destined to wind up in Toronto. When free agency opened on July 5, 2013, the club signed him to a whopping seven-year, $36.75-million contract. The next day, the *Toronto Sun* lauded the signing, putting Clarkson on the front page with a superimposed mullet and handlebar moustache, part of Clark's signature look in Toronto, along with the headline "Wendel Clarkson."

While the newspaper couldn't resist drawing comparisons to Clark, many Leafs fans, myself included, weren't as enamoured with the signing. Clarkson had just turned 29, and seven years was a lot of term for an aging player who had reached the 30-goal mark, on an unsustainably high shooting percentage, just once in his career. In addressing some of the criticisms about the contract, general manager Dave Nonis infamously said, "I'm not worried about [year] six or seven right now. I'm worried about year one, and year one, I know we're going to have a very good player." Nonis was right to be worried about year one, but not for the reasons he thought. During a pre-season game against the Buffalo Sabres, Clarkson jumped into a brawl to defend a teammate and earned an automatic 10-game suspension for leaving the bench. After missing nearly the first month of the season, Clarkson finished the campaign with an abysmal five goals and 11 points in 60 games. He played just 58 more games for the Leafs before he was traded to the Columbus Blue Jackets in exchange for the injured Nathan Horton.

JULY 6

OILERS SIGN THOMAS VANEK TO OFFER SHEET, 2007

t didn't take the Buffalo Sabres long to match the Edmonton Oilers' offer sheet to Thomas Vanek. Although they had seven days to decide to match the seven-year, $50-million contract the Oilers had signed their star winger to, it only took them about seven minutes, according to Vanek's agent, Stephen Bartlett. There wasn't much to think about. The high-scoring Austrian winger was just coming off a 43-goal regular-season campaign and six goals in the club's playoff run to the Eastern Conference Final. Even before free agency opened, Sabres general manager Darcy Regier told teams not to bother trying to pry Vanek out of Buffalo. There was no point. They were prepared to match whatever money was tabled to keep him.

The Oilers, however, were eager to shore up their left wing after trading Ryan Smyth before the NHL trade deadline. Following unsuccessful attempts at signing free agents Paul Kariya and Michael Nylander, Edmonton set its sights on Vanek. While the Sabres had already issued him a qualifying offer to retain his rights while they negotiated a new contract, he was classified as what was known as a Group 2 free agent, which meant that in the meantime he could still consider offers from other clubs. Had the Sabres not matched the offer sheet, Edmonton would have had to compensate them by surrendering four first-round draft picks. But in the end, there was no question that the Sabres weren't going to match. They had already lost Chris Drury and Daniel Brière to free agency and were going to do everything in their power not to lose Vanek, who they believed was the future of the franchise. In his first season under the new contract, Vanek led the Sabres in goal scoring for the second straight year with 36 tallies. The following season, Vanek reached the 40-goal mark again and was among just eight players in the league to reach the milestone that year. After a dip in production over the next few seasons, Vanek, who was in the final year of his contract, was traded to the New York Islanders on October 27, 2013.

HURRICANES MATCH OFFER SHEET FOR SEBASTIAN AHO, 2019

As the NHL's free agency period approached in 2019, there was speculation among many in the hockey world that, unlike previous years, general managers would utilize offer sheets to pry restricted free agents from other teams. The crop of talented restricted free agents that off-season was bountiful and included the likes of Mikko Rantanen, Mitch Marner, Brayden Point, and Sebastian Aho. General managers, however, tend to shy away from offer sheets to avoid antagonizing their colleagues and potentially facing retribution down the road. In 2007, after the Ducks decided not to match the offer sheet Dustin Penner had signed with the Edmonton Oilers, Anaheim GM Brian Burke infamously challenged Kevin Lowe, Edmonton's GM, to a fistfight in a barn after Lowe called him out in a radio interview. Although offer sheets didn't typically end in barn brawls, they still remained rare. The last time the league had seen an offer sheet was when the Calgary Flames tabled one to the Colorado Avalanche's Ryan O'Reilly in 2013.

Despite the dynamic group of restricted free agents in 2019, it still seemed unlikely that anyone would issue an offer sheet. But when free agency opened on July 1, the Montreal Canadiens signed the Carolina Hurricanes' Sebastian Aho to a five-year, $42.27-million offer contract. Drafted 35th overall by the Hurricanes in 2015, Aho, who was turning 22 later that month, had led the team in scoring the previous season with 30 goals and 83 points. In an effort to dissuade Carolina from matching, Montreal heavily loaded the contract with signing bonuses that would pay the star Finnish forward $21 million in the first year of the deal. Although the Hurricanes had seven days to make a decision, they quickly said they'd match the offer for Aho. Six days later, on July 7, 2019, they made it official. The new deal paid off quickly for Carolina. Before the 2019–20 season was halted by the Covid-19 pandemic, Aho was well on pace to reach the 40-goal mark and would have become the first Hurricane to reach that milestone in nearly a decade.

JULY 8
STARS DRAFT JAROME IGINLA, 1995

When Joe Nieuwendyk learned he was being traded to the Dallas Stars for Jarome Iginla and Corey Millen, he reportedly asked, "Who's Jarome Iginla?" While the former Calgary Flames captain meant no disrespect with his remark, he and the rest of the league learned pretty quickly who Jarome Iginla was. Although Iginla was drafted 11th overall by the Stars in the NHL Entry Draft on July 8, 1995, he wasn't in Dallas very long. Less than six months later, the skilled power forward was traded to the Flames as part of the deal for the disgruntled Nieuwendyk, who was in the midst of a contract holdout with Calgary. Although the Stars were reluctant to part with Iginla, who they believed was the best prospect outside the NHL, the Flames were adamant about him being included in the return. They saw their future in Iginla.

Al Coates, interim general manager for the Flames, believed Iginla could be in Calgary as early as the next season and would be a major part of the club for the coming decade. "The most important thing ... was where we're going with the future of our team and our organization for this city ... and we're going where Jarome Iginla goes," he said. Coates's words proved prophetic. At the time of the trade, Iginla had already scored 68 points with the Western Hockey League's Kamloops Blazers that season, nearly matching his offensive production from the previous year, and finished the campaign with 63 goals and a whopping 136 points. After Kamloops was eliminated from the post-season, Iginla flew to Calgary for the team's playoff series against the Chicago Blackhawks. An hour after signing his first contract, Iginla made his NHL debut, picking up an assist in a 7–5 loss. In the next game, Iginla opened the scoring, but the Flames lost in triple overtime and were knocked out of the playoffs. Iginla's two-game debut was just a preview of things to come. He surpassed Coates's expectations, becoming the heart and soul of the franchise for nearly two decades and one of the best players in NHL history.

JULY 9

RANGERS SIGN BRENDAN SHANAHAN, 2006

After nine seasons with the Detroit Red Wings, Brendan Shanahan believed it was time to move on. Although Detroit had offered him a one-year contract to stay, he still felt there wasn't much of a fit for him with the organization anymore. After playing an integral part in three Stanley Cup championships, Shanahan thought he was more associated with the Red Wings' glorious past and not necessarily part of the club's future. He talked it over with long-time captain Steve Yzerman, who announced his retirement a week earlier after 22 seasons with Detroit, and after careful consideration, Shanahan respectfully declined the team's offer. The club had even offered him a multi-year deal at a lower annual salary, but for Shanahan the term and the dollars didn't matter; it was time to go. Instead, the veteran power forward signed a one-year, $4-million contract with the New York Rangers on July 9, 2006. While he could have fetched more money with the Montreal Canadiens, who reportedly offered him $5 million for one season, Shanahan decided on New York because he felt it was building something special. Although Shanahan was 37 years old, he still believed he could contribute to a championship. In his final season in Detroit, he had racked up 40 goals and was third in team scoring, behind only Pavel Datsyuk and Henrik Zetterberg.

Shanahan couldn't have scripted a better opening with the Blueshirts. Heading into his 19th season in the NHL, he was sitting at 598 career goals. After scoring his first goal as a Ranger late in the second period in a game against the Washington Capitals on October 5, 2006, Shanahan scored his 600th early into the final frame, becoming just the 15th player in league history to reach that milestone. He finished his first season in New York with 29 goals and 62 points, and after adding five more tallies in the playoffs, he re-signed with the club. Following one more campaign with the Rangers, Shanahan returned for a final season with the New Jersey Devils, with whom his career had begun more than two decades earlier.

JULY 10
OILERS ACQUIRE DAVID PERRON, 2013

After taking a call from Doug Armstrong, the St. Louis Blues' general manager, David Perron learned he'd been traded to the Edmonton Oilers. Drafted 26th overall in 2007, Perron had scored 198 points in 340 games over the past six seasons in St. Louis. Following his first 20-goal campaign with the Blues in 2009–10, Perron had a hot start the next season, scoring five goals in his first 10 games, until he sustained a concussion from Joe Thornton in a contest against the San Jose Sharks, which kept him off the ice for the next 13 months. Once he recovered, Perron returned to the lineup on December 3, 2011, and scored a goal in his first game back, finishing the season with 21 goals, a career high, and 42 points in 57 games. Following the 2012–13 shortened lockout season, however, the Blues had a difficult decision to make. Although the team valued Perron's dynamic skill and scoring touch, he still had three years left on his deal and it needed to free up salary to sign restricted free agent Alex Pietrangelo.

And so on July 10, 2013, he was traded to the Oilers, along with a third-round pick, in exchange for Magnus Pääjärvi and a pair of draft picks. But Perron wasn't done with St. Louis. After a pair of seasons in Edmonton and some time with the Pittsburgh Penguins and Anaheim Ducks, Perron returned to the Blues as a free agent, signing a two-year, $7.5-million contract on July 1, 2016. He scored 18 goals and 46 points in his first season back but was left unprotected heading into the 2017 NHL Expansion Draft and was plucked by the Vegas Golden Knights. Following a season in Las Vegas, in which he established a career high in points with 66, Perron signed a four-year, $16-million deal to return to St. Louis a third time. Although he was limited to 57 games due to an upper-body injury in 2018–19, Perron played a critical role in helping the Blues qualify for the playoffs and eventually win the Stanley Cup for the first time in franchise history.

MAPLE LEAFS TRADE YANIC PERREAULT TO KINGS, 1994

espite scoring 51 goals and 114 points in his second season with the Trois-Rivières Draveurs of the Quebec Major Junior Hockey League (QMJHL), Yanic Perreault went undrafted by the NHL. Although there was no denying his offensive abilities, Perreault, who was considered diminutive by hockey standards, was passed over because of concerns about his skating and play in his own end. The following season, however, Perreault made it difficult for teams to overlook him a second time despite the perceived knocks on his game. By the time the QMJHL and the Ontario Hockey League squared off in the sixth annual Molson-Chrysler All-Star Challenge on January 30, 1991, Perreault had already racked up 61 goals and 142 points in just 47 games. While Eric Lindros, projected to be the undisputed first overall pick that spring, was expected to be the main draw at the challenge, which featured the top players from each league, Perreault ended up stealing the show. He recorded a hat trick and added an assist in an 11–7 victory over the Ontario squad. Following the showcase, which only improved his draft stock, Perreault continued his torrid scoring pace and finished the regular season with 87 goals and 185 points. A few months later at the NHL Entry Draft, Perreault was taken 47th overall by the Toronto Maple Leafs.

Perreault, however, spent much of the next three seasons with the Leafs' AHL affiliate in St. John's, Newfoundland, until he was dealt to the Los Angeles Kings for a fourth-round pick on July 11, 1994. At the time of the trade, Perreault had suited up for just 13 NHL games. Following the 1994–95 lockout-shortened season in which he played 26 games for Los Angeles, Perreault started the 1995–96 campaign in the NHL for the first time in his career. Finding a fit on a line with Rick Tocchet and Tony Granato, Perreault scored 25 goals in his first full season with the Kings. After establishing himself as an NHL regular over the next three seasons, Perreault was reacquired by the Leafs on March 23, 1999.

JULY 12

OILERS TRADE ANDREW COGLIANO TO DUCKS, 2011

Andrew Cogliano never missed a day of work with the Oilers. After Edmonton took him 25th overall in the 2005 Entry Draft, Cogliano made his NHL debut on October 4, 2007, then appeared in 328 straight regular-season games with the club. Following his rookie campaign in which he scored 18 goals and 45 points, Cogliano developed his skills on the other side of the puck to become a burgeoning two-way player. By the 2011 off-season, however, it looked as if there might not be a fit for Cogliano with the Oilers. Despite everything he brought to the lineup, he needed a new contract, and with the team recently signing veteran centre Éric Bélanger and looking to make room for newcomer Anton Lander, Cogliano seemed like the odd man out. A week after filing for salary arbitration on July 12, 2011, he was traded to the Anaheim Ducks in exchange for a second-round pick in 2013. While Cogliano might not have been part of Edmonton's long-term plans, Anaheim had been eyeing him for a while. Ducks general manager Bob Murray said the team had been trying to acquire him for over a year. Two days before his scheduled salary arbitration hearing, Cogliano and Anaheim agreed to a three-year deal.

With the Ducks, Cogliano continued his "iron-man" streak. On New Year's Eve 2013, he played in his 500th consecutive game, becoming the 20th player in NHL history to reach that milestone. A few years later, on March 22, 2017, he played in his 777th straight game, surpassing Craig Ramsay for the fourth-longest streak in league history. By his seventh season in Anaheim, Cogliano had reached the 800th consecutive game and seemed poised to vault ahead of Steve Larmer, who had suited up for 884 straight games for third on the all-time list. But after a game against the Los Angeles Kings on January 13, 2018, Cogliano faced supplemental discipline from the Department of Player Safety for an interference penalty against Adrian Kempe. He was subsequently suspended for two contests, bringing his streak to a halt at 830 consecutive games.

VEGAS NAMES GEORGE MCPHEE GM, 2016

T he NHL's Las Vegas franchise didn't have a name yet, but it had found its general manager. Following an exhaustive hiring search, on July 13, 2016, owner Bill Foley named George McPhee as the club's inaugural GM. Foley selected McPhee out of seven candidates because of his experience and notable history of drafting and developing players. Prior to joining the New York Islanders in 2015 as a special adviser to general manager Garth Snow, McPhee had spent 16 seasons as the GM of the Washington Capitals, with whom he oversaw the rebuilding of the team and the rise of superstar Alex Ovechkin. Although Vegas was still a year from hitting the ice, McPhee planned to spend the next season surveying the league in preparation.

Heading into the 2017 NHL Expansion Draft, the rest of the league's teams had to submit a limited list of protected players who couldn't be plucked by Vegas, now known as the Golden Knights, who had to take one player from each of the NHL's 30 teams. Since most clubs couldn't protect every player they hoped to retain, Vegas was able to leverage its position and make side deals with teams that found themselves in a sticky wicket. One of McPhee's shrewdest moves at the expansion draft was acquiring Reilly Smith from the Florida Panthers in exchange for a fourth-round pick and a guarantee that the Golden Knights would select Jonathan Marchessault from Florida's list of available players. Another astute step was acquiring Shea Theodore from Anaheim in exchange for taking Clayton Stoner from the Ducks. While the outcome of the expansion draft didn't necessarily make Vegas look like a contender at the time, the gambits have since paid off. Smith and Marchessault both had career years in their first season in the desert, and Theodore looks to be the type of player the Golden Knights can build their blue line around. After Vegas advanced to the Stanley Cup Final in its inaugural season, McPhee was unquestionably named the winner of the NHL's Jim Gregory General Manager of the Year Award.

JULY 14

GUY LAFLEUR SIGNS WITH NORDIQUES, 1989

G uy Lafleur wanted to go back to where it all began. Nearly two decades after he was selected first overall by the Montreal Canadiens, he wanted to finish off his hockey career in Quebec. Following 13 seasons in Montreal, where he won five Stanley Cups, including four straight, Lafleur retired early in the 1984–85 campaign. After he took one last lap around the ice at the Forum on February 17, 1985, when the Canadiens sent his number 10 to the rafters, Lafleur hung up his skates. The New York Rangers, however, lured him out of retirement in September 1988, not long after he was inducted into the Hockey Hall of Fame. In his first season in New York, the 37-year-old, who hadn't played in the NHL in nearly four years, scored 18 goals and 45 points. Following his successful comeback campaign, Lafleur wanted to continue playing hockey. There were rumours he was going to return to New York and there were even whispers he was going to sign with the Los Angeles Kings so he could play with Wayne Gretzky, but more than anything else, Lafleur wanted to play in Quebec again.

So on July 14, 1989, he signed a one-year contract with the Quebec Nordiques, which included unlimited option years and the opportunity to join the club's front office for two years after he retired again. While some Canadiens fans were disappointed to see Lafleur join their provincial rival, they were happy to have him back in *La belle province*. Following two seasons with the Nordiques in which he scored 24 goals and 62 points in 98 games, Lafleur retired a final time in 1991. After announcing his retirement once more, Lafleur was set to accept a front-office job with the Nordiques, but by the time the 1991 Expansion Draft commenced, his paperwork hadn't been officially filed yet and the Minnesota North Stars took him with the final pick. Unable to go to Quebec while Minnesota held his rights, Lafleur was traded back to the Nordiques in exchange for Alan Haworth, who hadn't played an NHL game in three years.

JULY 15

MAPLE LEAFS SIGN CURTIS JOSEPH, 1998

A s Curtis Joseph modelled his new Toronto Maple Leafs jersey and raised both hands into the air in celebration, he marked the beginning of a new era for goaltending in Toronto. On July 15, 1998, Joseph, who had spent the past three seasons in net for the Edmonton Oilers, agreed to a four-year, $24-million deal with the Leafs. Although Felix Potvin, who was slated to become a free agent the next year, had been the Leafs' undisputed goaltender for six seasons and was integral to the club's playoff runs to the conference final in back-to-back years, his play had slipped the past two seasons as the team struggled in front of him. The arrival of Joseph all but signalled the end of Potvin's tenure in Toronto. With plenty of teams still interested in his services, it appeared as though a trade was imminent, but nothing materialized. As the 1998–99 campaign approached, Potvin was still with the Leafs. By December, Potvin had made just five starts and was desperate for an opportunity to play elsewhere. The situation was finally resolved on January 9, 1999, when he was traded to the New York Islanders, along with a sixth-round pick, in exchange for former first overall pick and Calder Trophy–winning defenceman Bryan Berard and a sixth-round pick.

While Potvin's departure was heartbreaking for young Leafs fans such as myself, who had grown up idolizing him and his signature mask, Joseph's stellar play in net helped alleviate some of the pain. In his first season in Toronto, Joseph recorded 35 victories, a franchise record, and was named a finalist for both the Vezina Trophy, as the league's top goaltender, and the Lester B. Pearson (now Ted Lindsay) Award, given annually to the NHL's most valuable player as determined by his peers. In the playoffs, he backstopped the Leafs to a conference final appearance for the first time in five years. The next season, Joseph rewrote the club's record book once again, notching 36 regular-season wins. In the playoffs that year, he was arguably the best goaltender, but Toronto couldn't get past the New Jersey Devils, the eventual Stanley Cup champions.

JULY 16

BLUES SIGN SCOTT STEVENS, 1990

When the Washington Capitals' Scott Stevens signed an offer sheet with the St. Louis Blues, it raised eyebrows around the league. Although he was considered one of the top blueliners, the four-year, $5.1-million contract with St. Louis would make him the highest-paid defenceman in the NHL. Stevens would earn more money than Chris Chelios and Ray Bourque, who was just coming off his third Norris Trophy win. General managers such as the Vancouver Canucks' Pat Quinn worried that such salary inflation would put some teams out of business. After Stevens signed the deal, the Capitals had seven days to consider matching the high-priced salary. A week later, on July 16, 1990, Washington declined and Stevens officially became a Blue. Under the league's compensation system for restricted free agents, the Capitals received $100,000 from St. Louis and two first-round picks in the top seven in 1991 and 1992. If the Blues didn't have a top-seven pick in those years, the Capitals would be awarded three more first-round selections from St. Louis through 1995.

While the Blues expected Stevens to patrol the team's blue line for the next four years, he spent only one season with the club. Following the 1990–91 campaign, St. Louis signed restricted free agent Brendan Shanahan and owed the New Jersey Devils compensation. Since the club was already surrendering first-round picks to the Capitals for prying Stevens out of Washington, they had to come up with a different return. It offered goaltender Curtis Joseph, Rod Brind'Amour, and two draft picks, but the Devils refused. They had their sights set on Stevens. But given the steep price the Blues had already paid for the hard-hitting defenceman, they were unwilling to part with him. With the two clubs unable to agree to terms, the matter went to arbitration. On September 3, 1991, arbitrator Edward Houston ruled against St. Louis, and Stevens became a Devil. Although he initially refused to report to New Jersey, Stevens eventually relented and went on to win three Stanley Cups on the Devils' back end.

JULY 17

BOB GAINEY RETIRES, 1989

After 16 seasons with the Montreal Canadiens, Bob Gainey was going to France to become a Squirrel. On July 17, 1989, following an injury-plagued season that limited the 35-year-old Canadiens captain to 49 games, he announced he was retiring from the NHL to take up a player-coach position with the Écureuils, French for "Squirrels," a second-tier division hockey team located in Épinal, a town in northeastern France on the Moselle River.

Drafted eighth overall by Montreal in 1973, Gainey made an immediate impact with the club, and it didn't take long before he established himself as one of the best two-way players in the game, shutting down opposition and stifling their offence. In 1978, he was the inaugural winner of the Frank J. Selke Trophy, awarded annually to the NHL's best defensive forward. Gainey took home the trophy four straight years, a feat yet to be matched. Long-time opponent Bobby Clarke, captain of the Philadelphia Flyers, later said Gainey could dominate a game without even scoring — that was how good he was on both sides of the puck. Following four straight Stanley Cups with the Canadiens, which he capped off with a Conn Smythe Trophy in 1979 as the most valuable player in the playoffs, Gainey captained the team from 1981 until he retired and added another Cup to his collection in 1986.

Although Gainey's playing days were behind him, he wasn't gone from the NHL very long. After one season in France, he was named head coach of the Minnesota North Stars by former adversary Clarke, who had recently assumed the role of general manager with the team. Following two seasons behind the bench, Gainey added GM to his portfolio and continued coaching the club, which became the Stars after it moved to Dallas in 1993, until he stepped down during the 1995–96 campaign to focus on his management duties. After winning a Stanley Cup with Dallas in 1999, Gainey returned to Montreal in 2003 to become the club's general manager, a position he held until 2010 before resigning.

JULY 18
RANGERS ACQUIRE MIKA ZIBANEJAD, 2016

The Ottawa Senators wanted to add more experience to their lineup. On July 18, 2016, in one of his first moves as general manager, Pierre Dorion accomplished that by trading Mika Zibanejad and a second-round pick to the New York Rangers in exchange for Derick Brassard and a seventh-round pick. While Ottawa added a more seasoned centre down the middle in Brassard, who had 563 regular-season and 59 playoff games under his belt, it gave up a younger and more talented player who, by most accounts, was only scratching the surface of his capabilities. Drafted sixth overall by the Senators in 2011, Zibanejad, who had just turned 23 years old, was just coming off back-to-back 20-goal seasons and a career-high 51 points. Although Brassard had one been one of the best players in New York for the past few seasons, he was turning 29 in September. Ottawa might have been gaining a more proven player, but it appeared to be a move that would cost them farther down the road.

While Brassard was an important part of the Senators' playoff run in 2017, which came one goal short of a berth to the Stanley Cup Final, he wasn't in Ottawa long. On February 23, 2018, he was traded to the Vegas Golden Knights for a third-round pick and then was flipped to the Pittsburgh Penguins in exchange for Ryan Reaves. Meanwhile, in New York, Zibanejad blossomed. Although his first season with the Rangers was limited to 56 games because of a broken fibula, he scored a career-high 27 goals in the 2017–18 campaign. The following season, Zibanejad had a breakout year offensively. He led the team in scoring by a considerable margin, recording 30 goals and 74 points. When the Rangers added superstar Artemi Panarin in free agency in 2019, Zibanejad found instant chemistry with the wizarding winger. Centring a line with Panarin, along with Pavel Buchnevich, Zibanejad racked up 41 goals, the fifth most in the league, and 75 points before the 2019–20 season was grounded to a halt by the Covid-19 pandemic.

JULY 19

OILERS SWAP MILAN LUCIC FOR
JAMES NEAL, 2019

As Milan Lucic headed south on the Queen Elizabeth II Highway in Alberta, James Neal was going in the opposite direction. Both players needed a change of scenery. Three years earlier, Lucic had signed a seven-year, $42-million contract with the Edmonton Oilers. Although he scored 23 goals and 50 points in his first season in Edmonton, his play had declined over the past two seasons, and he was coming off a career-worst six-goal campaign. Meanwhile, in Calgary, Neal was struggling, too. After signing a five-year, $28.75-million deal with the Calgary Flames just a year earlier, Neal recorded only seven goals in the 2018–19 season. Despite logging 10 straight 20-goal seasons since breaking into the league, Neal couldn't put the puck in the back of the net in Calgary and was relegated to the fourth line and some nights even the press box. Both players were big-ticket, free-agent signings, but neither had lived up to their billing. With four years remaining on each of their deals, they were eager for fresh starts elsewhere.

On July 19, 2019, the Oilers sent Lucic to the Flames in exchange for Neal. As part of the deal, the Oilers agreed to retain a portion of Lucic's contract and included a conditional third-round pick contingent on Neal recording at least 21 goals the next season and Lucic scoring at least 10 fewer than him. The move quickly paid off for the Oilers. In Neal's second game with Edmonton, he scored two goals, and three nights later against the New York Islanders, he lit the lamp four times for the first time in his career. After scoring another in his fourth contest, Neal had matched his entire goal output with the Flames in 59 fewer games. In Calgary, Lucic rebounded, as well, and found his game again on the club's hard-hitting third line. When the 2019–20 season was paused by the Covid-19 pandemic, Neal was sitting at 19 goals and Lucic was at eight. While Neal likely would have hit 21, it's impossible to know if Lucic would have closed the gap, so the Oilers were forced to surrender the conditional third-round pick.

JULY 20
NORDIQUES SIGN J.C. TREMBLAY, 1972

U nable to reach a deal with the Montreal Canadiens, veteran defenceman J.C. Tremblay jumped to the rival WHA and signed a lucrative contract with the Quebec Nordiques. Known as "J.C. Superstar" for his slick stickhandling, Tremblay had quarterbacked the Canadiens' power play for more than a decade. During the 1970–71 season, he racked up 63 points, a club record for a defenceman, and in the playoffs, he established a league record for most assists in the post-season by a blueliner with 14 helpers as he won his fifth Stanley Cup with Montreal. While Tremblay dazzled the fans with his puck-handling abilities, he also drew their ire for lapses in his own end. A few months earlier, in the fourth game of the Canadiens' opening-round playoff series against the New York Rangers in 1972, it was tied 4–4 late in the third period. As New York put pressure on Montreal, centre Pete Stemkowski stole the puck from Tremblay, who was behind the Canadiens' net, and put it past goaltender Ken Dryden to score what was the game-winning goal. Head coach Scotty Bowman was incensed. While Montreal staved off elimination on the road in the next game, it was knocked out at home in Game 6.

After Tremblay and Canadiens general manager Sam Pollock couldn't agree on a new contract in the off-season, Tremblay signed a five-year, $1-million contract with the Nordiques on July 20, 1972. In his first season in Quebec, Tremblay was relied upon heavily. He averaged upward of 40 minutes per game and relished every second. In addition to his regular shifts, Tremblay ran the power play and penalty kill. Despite the heavy workload, he was doing what he loved: playing hockey. He finished the campaign with 89 points and was named the WHA's top defenceman. After receiving the award, Tremblay, 34 years old at the time, said he hoped to play until he was 41 or 42. He nearly did so. Tremblay played six more seasons with the Nordiques, leading the club to a WHA championship in 1977, before hanging up his skates in 1979 at the age of 40.

FLAMES CLAIM PHIL HOUSLEY, 1998

Phil Housley was disappointed when he was traded to the Calgary Flames as part of a deal for Al MacInnis in 1994. The veteran defenceman said that he and his family weren't interested in moving back to Canada because of the high taxes he'd faced while playing for the Winnipeg Jets. Originally drafted sixth overall by the Buffalo Sabres in 1982, the U.S.-born defenceman was one of the league's premier high-scoring rearguards. After eight seasons on the Buffalo blue line, Housley was dealt to the Jets as part of a blockbuster deal for Dale Hawerchuk in 1990. Although Housley's bank account might have taken a hit in Winnipeg, he had some of his most productive seasons north of the border. In 1991–92, he was named a finalist for the Norris Trophy, and in the following campaign, he racked up 97 points, the most among defenceman that year. But after three seasons with the Jets, Housley requested a trade. When he failed to report to training camp in 1993, he was sent to the St. Louis Blues in exchange for Nelson Emerson and Stéphane Quintal. His time with the Blues, however, was limited by a back injury that kept him out of the lineup for much of the year.

In the off-season, he was dealt to the Flames. Housley eventually warmed to Calgary and rebounded in the lockout-shortened 1994–95 season. After starting off the next season with 52 points in 59 games, he was traded to the New Jersey Devils on February 26, 1996. Following his brief stopover in New Jersey, Housley became a free agent and signed a lucrative three-year contract with the Washington Capitals, which made him the highest-paid player in franchise history. Housley, however, didn't live up to his billing. In two seasons in Washington, he struggled offensively. During the Capitals' run to the Stanley Cup Final in 1998, he mustered just four assists. A month later, the Capitals placed him on waivers, and on July 21, 1998, he was claimed by the Flames. In his first season back in Calgary, Housley returned to form, recording a team-leading 43 assists.

JULY 22

MARTIN BIRON SIGNS WITH ISLANDERS, 2009

t was the longest three weeks of Martin Biron's life. After playing 133 games for the Philadelphia Flyers over the past few seasons, including backstopping the club to the conference final in 2008, the veteran goaltender figured he'd have a new contract for the next season. Although he knew he wasn't returning to Philadelphia, he was one of the most experienced goaltenders on the market, and there were several teams that needed help in net. But when free agency opened on July 1, 2009, he didn't ink a deal. That day he and his agent expected he might wind up in Edmonton, but when the Oilers signed Nikolai Khabibulin, that threw a wrench into their plans. Colorado seemed like a distinct possibility, as well, but the Avalanche went with a cheaper option in career backup Craig Anderson. As the days turned to weeks, Biron's future remained uncertain. Finally, on July 22, 2009, he signed a one-year contract with the Islanders. Although New York had signed Dwayne Roloson a few weeks earlier, with Rick DiPietro still recuperating from a knee injury, it was expected that Biron would share the crease with Roloson until DiPietro returned.

After losing his first five starts with the Islanders, Biron picked up his initial win on October 31, 2009, against his former team, the Sabres, who had drafted him 16th overall in 1995. Biron stopped all 38 shots he faced, recording his 26th career shutout and 200th career victory. But the wins were few on Long Island. After winning another game on November 13, Biron didn't pick up a subsequent victory until February. While it was expected Biron would be on the move when DiPietro returned in January, the former first overall pick made just seven starts before he reinjured his surgically repaired knee and was shut down for the rest of the season. Biron's playing improved, and at the end of the season, the Islanders gave him permission to talk with clubs in advance of free agency. Unlike the previous year, when free agency opened at noon, Biron reportedly signed a two-year deal with the New York Rangers within minutes.

TERRY FOX MEETS BOBBY ORR, 1980

Although Terry Fox passed away before I was born, he's someone who inspires me every day. A few months before he turned 19 years old, Fox learned he had a malignant tumour in his right leg. Following the diagnosis, his leg was amputated just above the knee. After he read about an amputee runner who had run a marathon, Fox got an idea. He decided to run across Canada to raise money for cancer research and awareness. After training for more than a year, Fox began his Marathon of Hope. He dipped his artificial leg into the Atlantic Ocean in St. John's, Newfoundland, on April 12, 1980, and began his incredible quest. By the end of June, Fox had already run more than 1,864 miles and arrived in Ontario. As word of Fox's courageous journey spread, he was welcomed by supporters at every stopover. He even had the chance to meet some of his hockey heroes.

After meeting Darryl Sittler when he arrived in Toronto, Fox met with Bobby Orr on July 23, 1980. Orr, whose brilliant career on the blue line had been cut short by knee injuries, presented Fox with a cheque for $25,000 from Planters Nuts, which represented $10 for every mile he'd run so far. During their encounter, Fox told reporters that if he could give Orr his good knee, he would. That's the type of person he was. Even with another artificial knee, Fox said he would still find a way to make it across Canada. But after 143 days and 3,339 miles, Fox was forced to halt his Marathon of Hope near Thunder Bay, Ontario, when the cancer invaded his lungs. During that span, he had averaged a marathon per day on one good leg, a remarkable athletic achievement. Whenever I'm out for a run and considering calling it quits, I honestly think about what Terry endured and push on. More than four decades after his Marathon of Hope began, cancer research and awareness continues in his name. Fox's legacy reminds us that a courageous person has the power to change the world.

JULY 24

PREDATORS MATCH OFFER SHEET FOR SHEA WEBER, 2012

L ess than a week after the Philadelphia Flyers signed Shea Weber to one of the most lucrative contracts in NHL history, the Nashville Predators matched the offer sheet to keep their captain. Although many in the hockey world believed the small-market Predators wouldn't be able to match the 14-year, $110-million deal, they didn't have much choice. The club had already lost Ryan Suter, a key piece of its defence corps, earlier that month in free agency. Surrendering Weber, who had a cannon of a shot and had averaged more than 29 minutes of ice time the previous season, would have been disastrous for Nashville's blue line. Wanting to send a message to the Predators' fan base that the club was committed to building a Stanley Cup contender, they matched the contract offer on July 24, 2012.

While the Flyers were banking on the Predators not matching, there were some who believed that by threatening to meet the contract demands, Nashville hoped to persuade Philadelphia to sweeten the pot to avoid losing Weber altogether. According to future NHL insider Frank Seravalli, who was a reporter at the *Philadelphia Daily News* at the time, prior to the offer sheet, the two teams had actually been in trade talks for the restricted free agent. Desperate to replace the injured Chris Pronger, the Flyers had set their sights on Weber. Seravalli reported that Nashville GM David Poile and Philadelphia GM Paul Holmgren spent hours on the phone trying to hammer out a deal, but after the discussions seemingly went nowhere, the Flyers submitted the offer. If Nashville didn't match, they would have received four first-round picks, but with Suter and Weber gone, they would have taken a significant step back on the ice. Draft picks would have been a tough consolation-prize sell to the fans. The Predators did the math. With the Flyers unlikely to swap some of the picks they would have owed with players such as Brayden Schenn or Sean Couturier, who could have helped the Predators remain competitive in the near term, Nashville matched and retained their captain.

PENGUINS SIGN MARK RECCHI, 2006

After winning the Stanley Cup with the Carolina Hurricanes in 2006, Mark Recchi said it made him appreciate things more and realize he still wanted to play hockey in the hope of winning another championship. Recchi could think of no better place to do that than with the Pittsburgh Penguins. Recchi had won his first Stanley Cup with Pittsburgh 15 years earlier and hoped to do it again. After starting the 2005–06 campaign with the Penguins, Recchi was dealt to Carolina. Although he won the Stanley Cup during his brief stretch with the Hurricanes, he felt he had unfinished business with Pittsburgh. Returning for his third stint with the club, Recchi signed a one-year, $2.28-million contract on July 25, 2006.

Despite heading into his 18th NHL campaign as a 38-year-old, Recchi didn't show signs of wear. He recorded 24 goals and 68 points. Although he had only scored two goals in Pittsburgh's final 23 regular-season games and none in the playoffs, he was the team's third-leading scorer, behind only stars Sidney Crosby and Evgeni Malkin. In the off-season, the Penguins brought him back for a fourth time when they signed him to a one-year deal on June 22, 2007. Although Recchi scored a goal in the season opener, he struggled offensively, and by mid-November, the veteran winger found himself as a healthy scratch. Even when the Penguins recognized his 500th career goal and gave away bobbleheads in his likeness to mark the occasion on December 3, 2007, Recchi wasn't even in the lineup. Instead, he was in the press box, unceremoniously scratched for the sixth straight game. The next day, Pittsburgh put Recchi on waivers and assigned him to its AHL affiliate in Wilkes-Barre, Pennsylvania. When placed on re-entry waivers a few days later, he was claimed by the Atlanta Thrashers, and his time with the Penguins came to an end. While Recchi didn't get his third championship in Pittsburgh, he did eventually get it in 2011 as a 43-year-old with the Boston Bruins.

JULY 26

KINGS SIGN LARRY ROBINSON, 1989

After nearly two decades with the Montreal Canadiens, Larry Robinson became a Los Angeles King. On July 26, 1989, the six-time All-Star defenceman who had won six Stanley Cups with Montreal, including four straight, signed a three-year contract with Los Angeles reportedly worth $1.6 million. Although the Kings scored the most goals in the NHL during the 1988–89 season, they also allowed the sixth-most goals against. The club hoped that Robinson, who had won the Norris Trophy twice with the Canadiens as the league's top defenceman, would bolster its blue line. In his first season with the Kings, Robinson scored 39 points, but the team still had trouble keeping the puck out of the net, finishing with the fourth-most goals against in 1989-90. After two more seasons in Los Angeles, Robinson hung up his skates a few months before turning 41.

Not long after Robinson retired, former teammate Jacques Lemaire, who was an assistant coach with the Canadiens and general manager of their AHL affiliate, tried to get the storied defenceman behind the bench with the organization. The timing wasn't right for Robinson, though, who was enjoying his time away from the rink, but when Lemaire called again the next year as the head coach of the New Jersey Devils, Robinson accepted the offer to join his staff. After two seasons in New Jersey as an assistant coach, the Kings once again looked to Robinson to strengthen their defence. Exactly six years after they signed him as a player, Los Angeles named him head coach. The Devils had just won the Stanley Cup and were regarded as one of the stingiest teams in the league for a defensive system derisively known as "The Trap." When Robinson returned to the Kings, he was asked about the trap and if he'd bring that style of play to Los Angeles. Robinson, who had grown up in rural Ontario, simply smiled and said, "A trap is what I used to catch muskrats with. We played good defensive hockey." But despite Robinson's defensive acumen, the Kings remained a porous team for the next few seasons.

JULY 27
WHALERS ACQUIRE BRENDAN SHANAHAN, 1995

When the St. Louis Blues signed Brendan Shanahan in 1991, *St. Louis Post-Dispatch* writer Jeff Gordon was so confident the power forward would "blossom into a steady 40-goal scorer with the Blues" that he encouraged readers to cut out his article and stick it on their refrigerator doors. Although Shanahan, who had reached the 30-goal mark in his third NHL season, didn't hit 40 in his first campaign in St. Louis, Gordon's words proved prophetic. In the 1992–93 season, Shanahan recorded 51 goals and 94 points, and the next year, he followed that up with another 50-goal performance, along with 102 points, the eighth most in the league. But after the lockout-shortened 1994–95 season, Shanahan's time with the Blues came to an end. Despite his penchant for finding the back of the net, Shanahan increasingly found himself at odds with head coach and general manager Mike Keenan. The situation became untenable, and on July 27, 1995, he was traded to the Hartford Whalers in exchange for Chris Pronger.

The fans in St. Louis were furious. Shanahan was a prolific scorer just coming into his prime, and after giving up Scott Stevens after one campaign to get him, the club was disheartened to see him leave after four promising seasons. Although Pronger developed into the Hall of Fame defenceman the Blues had hoped for when they signed Stevens in 1990, there was little consolation at the time. In Hartford, it was hoped that Shanahan's offensive prowess would boost the anemic Whalers, who had scored the seventh-fewest goals in the league the previous season. Not long after his arrival, Shanahan was named captain and went on to score a team-leading 44 goals and 78 points. Although he made an immediate impact, it was short-lived. With the team's future uncertain, Shanahan requested a trade to a more stable franchise. On October 9, 1996, in a blockbuster trade with the Detroit Red Wings, the Whalers sent Shanahan, along with Brian Glynn, to Detroit in exchange for Paul Coffey, Keith Primeau, and a first-round pick.

JULY 28
PENGUINS ACQUIRE NICK BONINO, 2015

Although Nick Bonino was only in Pittsburgh for two seasons, he'll always be a Penguin for me. Originally drafted 173rd overall by the San Jose Sharks in 2007, Bonino played three seasons at Boston University before his rights were traded to the Anaheim Ducks. Following a breakout campaign with that club in 2013–14, he was dealt to the Vancouver Canucks, along with Luca Sbisa and a pair of draft picks, in exchange for Ryan Kesler and a third-round pick. But after just one season with the Canucks, Bonino was on the move again. On July 28, 2015, he was sent to Pittsburgh, along with Adam Clendening and a second-round pick, for Brandon Sutter and a third-round pick. Since the Penguins were already set up in the middle with superstars Sidney Crosby and Evgeni Malkin, Bonino was brought in to fill a third-line centre role.

During the Penguins' 2016 playoff run, Bonino clicked with goal-scoring right winger Phil Kessel and speedy left winger Carl Hagelin. They had different skill sets but complemented one another perfectly. Kessel had one of the best releases in the league, there were few who could skate faster than Hagelin, and Bonino got them the puck with dogged determination. The trio formed an effective unit, and it wasn't long before they were dubbed The HBK Line. Although the name was drawn from the first letter of each of their surnames, it caught on because it also evoked memories of former pro wrestler Shawn Michaels, who was known as "The Heartbreak Kid." While Michaels had never attended an NHL match before, the Penguins invited him to Game 5 of the conference final against the Tampa Bay Lightning. Prior to dropping the puck, he was given a jersey with HBK and number 156 on the back, the total of the line's three numbers. Bonino finished the playoffs with a team-leading 14 assists as the Penguins went on to win their first of back-to-back championships. And, of course, who could forget his game-winning goal in Game 1 of the Stanley Cup Final against the Sharks that inspired Harnarayan Singh's memorable call.

JULY 29

RANGERS SIGN "KING HENRIK" TO ENTRY-LEVEL CONTRACT, 2005

After establishing himself as the top goaltender in Sweden, Henrik Lundqvist was ready to prove he could play in the NHL. Five years after the New York Rangers drafted him 205th overall, the 23-year-old netminder signed an entry-level contract with the club on July 29, 2005. Although Lundqvist was coming off a record-setting campaign in the Swedish Hockey League in which he established new benchmarks for highest save percentage and the most shutouts, he was expected to serve as Kevin Weekes's backup. Lundqvist, however, was quickly thrust into the starting role. After Weekes injured his groin during practice on October 12, 2005, Lundqvist was given the nod for the team's home game against the New Jersey Devils the next day. Squaring off against Martin Brodeur, Lundqvist made 20 saves in a 4–1 win to record his first career NHL victory. Following his second straight win in a game against the Atlanta Thrashers, *New York Post* writer Larry Brooks referred to Lundqvist as "King Henrik of Sweden" in his coverage of the contest.

Although it was early to bestow such a monarchic moniker, Lundqvist's arrival certainly appeared to be a coronation. A few nights later, he picked up his first shutout, stopping all 23 shots he faced from the Florida Panthers. Weekes returned to the crease after missing four games but aggravated his injury in a loss to the New York Islanders, so Lundqvist once again took over starting duties. As Weekes continued to battle injuries that season, Lundqvist became the undisputed starter in New York. He finished the season with 30 wins, the most by a rookie in the Rangers' history, and had one of the best save percentages in the league. For his efforts, he was named a finalist for the Vezina Trophy as the league's top goaltender. In the ensuing years, Lundqvist lived up to his sobriquet and established himself as one of the greatest goaltenders in NHL history. Although Lundqvist's reign with the Blueshirts ended when the Rangers bought out the final year of his contract on September 30, 2020, he will forever be known as "King Henrik."

JULY 30
KELLY HRUDEY SWAPS CREASE
FOR STUDIO, 1998

After stopping pucks in the NHL for 15 seasons, Kelly Hrudey hung up his goalie pads on July 30, 1998. But the netminder wasn't out of work long. Shortly after announcing his retirement, Hrudey, who had worked for CBC's *Hockey Night in Canada* as an analyst during the 1998 Stanley Cup Playoffs, signed with the broadcaster to become a full-time analyst. Drafted 38th overall by the New York Islanders in 1980, Hrudey spent parts of six seasons on Long Island before he was traded to the Los Angeles Kings on February 22, 1989, in exchange for Mark Fitzpatrick, Wayne McBean, and future considerations. By the time the netminder arrived in Tinseltown, he already knew he wanted to get into broadcasting when his playing days were finished. During his tenure with the Islanders, Hrudey became fascinated with the process and often went out of his way to make his interviews more entertaining for viewers.

Hrudey continued honing his skills after joining the Kings but caught a break one night during a game against the Minnesota North Stars. The goaltender wasn't playing that evening, so he ended up doing a lengthy intermission interview with legendary Los Angeles sportscaster Stu Nahan. Hrudey remembers they hit it off and he ended up staying on with Nahan for a few minutes. It turned out that *Hockey Night in Canada*'s Ron MacLean and John Shannon caught the segment, which left a lasting impression on them. Hrudey found out years later that they both decided then and there that if they ever had the chance, they'd give the goaltender a shot on the show. While Hrudey continued playing for the Kings, and later, the San Jose Sharks, he never stopped thinking about broadcasting after hockey. Following San Jose's first-round playoff exit in 1998, his final stint with the club, Hrudey joined the CBC and served as an analyst for the remainder of the post-season, making the most of the opportunity. Over the past two decades, he's been a fixture on *Hockey Night in Canada*.

JULY 31
RED WINGS SIGN DOMINIK HAŠEK, 2006

Dominik Hašek could finally retire. After winning the Stanley Cup with the Detroit Red Wings in 2002, the Czech goaltender was ready to hang up his goalie pads. Although he had won six Vezina and two Hart Trophies, as well as an Olympic gold medal, over his illustrious career, Lord Stanley's mug had eluded him. But after finally hoisting the trophy with Detroit, Hašek believed he had accomplished everything he could on the ice and was ready to step away. When he retired, he said he never wanted to put on goalie pads again and joked that if he was ever going to play hockey again, it would be as a forward. But less than a year later, on July 8, 2003, Hašek announced he would be coming back to the NHL. His return, however, was ill-fated. Just 14 games into the campaign, he injured his groin and didn't suit up for the Red Wings again that season. In the off-season, he signed with the Ottawa Senators as a free agent. Following the 2004–05 lockout, he got off to a great start in Canada's capital but injured his groin again representing the Czech Republic at the 2006 Winter Olympics in Torino, Italy, and never played another game for the Senators.

Although his past two seasons had been cut short by groin injuries, Hašek still felt he could contribute to a championship. After the Red Wings were unable to sign Ed Belfour in the 2006 off-season, they called up "The Dominator." Hašek said his groin felt fine and that he was willing to take a low base salary in order to make another run with the Red Wings. So, on July 31, 2006, Hašek returned for his third stint in Detroit. After playing 56 games in the 2006–07, The Dominator came back the following year and split the starting duties with Chris Osgood. Although Hašek was named the starter going into the 2008 post-season, he was replaced by Osgood, but the Red Wings won the championship and Hašek was able to cap his career with a second Stanley Cup.

AUGUST 1
NHL RETURNS DESPITE COVID, 2020

t had been nearly five months since the NHL had played meaningful games. Following the outbreak of the Covid-19 pandemic, the league suspended the regular season on March 12, 2020, with roughly a dozen games remaining for most teams. Although much of the world had ground to a halt, the NHL hadn't ruled out plans to finish the campaign and compete for the Stanley Cup. But as the days turned to weeks and the weeks turned to months, it seemed unlikely hockey would return. It wouldn't be the first time the NHL was unable to complete a season. The entire 2004–05 campaign was wiped out due to a lockout, and when the Seattle Metropolitans and Montreal Canadiens squared off for the Stanley Cup in 1919, the deciding game of the series was cancelled because of the Spanish flu pandemic. No champion was declared. It was hard not to see the parallels. I had even gone as far as to suggest the NHL should engrave every team's name on the Stanley Cup and etch the words "Season not completed," a nod to the "Series not completed" carved into the trophy to acknowledge the outcome of the 1919 Stanley Cup Final. Sure, it would have gotten the Toronto Maple Leafs on the Cup for the first time in more than five decades, but it had more to do with my belief that hockey wasn't coming back.

There was a sense of optimism, however, on May 26, 2020, when the NHL unveiled its "Return to Play Plan." Instead of attempting to complete the regular season, the league would expand the playoffs to 24 teams. The top four teams from each conference would receive a bye to the first round of the playoffs, while the remaining 16 teams would battle it out in a best-of-five series. While there was still a long way to go, it seemed as if maybe, just maybe, hockey would return. Two months later, it actually happened. Following a series of exhibition games at the end of July, the 2020 Stanley Cup Playoffs officially began on August 1.

AUGUST 2

SABRES ACQUIRE JEFF SKINNER, 2018

By the time Jeff Skinner turned 26 years old, he already had eight NHL seasons under his belt. For me, he had always been one of those players who seemed older than he was because even at that age, he was already a veteran player. Drafted seventh overall by the Carolina Hurricanes in 2010, Skinner broke into the league as an 18-year-old, scoring 31 goals and winning the Calder Trophy as the top rookie that year. The following season, Skinner appeared to avoid the sophomore slump, scoring 12 goals in his first 30 games, but after he sustained a concussion in a game against the Edmonton Oilers on December 7, 2011, he missed more than a month. Concussions, however, continued to plague Skinner's early years in Carolina. He missed six games in the lockout-shortened 2012–13 season due to a concussion, and although he rebounded the following year, scoring 33 goals in 71 games, Skinner missed the start of the 2014–15 season after sustaining another concussion in a pre-season game. The next year, however, Skinner turned a corner and played a full campaign for the first time since his rookie debut. Things continued to improve the following season as Skinner racked up 37 goals, a career high, in 2016–17.

But as Skinner was slated to become a free agent in 2019, it seemed unlikely he'd re-sign with the Hurricanes. Despite staying healthy and putting the puck in the back of the net, Skinner's ice time was curtailed during the 2017–18 season under head coach Bill Peters. At the end of the season, the club explored trading Skinner. Although Carolina was reportedly holding out for a package that included a first-round draft pick for the former Calder Trophy winner, the club sent him to the Buffalo Sabres on August 2, 2018, in exchange for Cliff Pu, a second-round pick in 2019, and both a third- and sixth-round pick in 2020. Flanking star centre Jack Eichel, Skinner racked up 40 goals in his first season with Buffalo, then cashed in on an eight-year, $72-million contract extension.

FLYERS SIGN PETER FORSBERG, 2005

t only took 14 years, but Peter Forsberg was finally going to be a Flyer. Originally drafted sixth overall by Philadelphia in 1991, the Swedish centre never actually suited up for the club. A year later, he was part of the bounty the Nordiques received when they sent disgruntled prospect Eric Lindros to the City of Brotherly Love. Following the trade, Forsberg spent three more seasons in the Swedish Elite League before he joined the NHL for the 1994–95 lockout-shortened season. In his first and only season in Quebec, Forsberg scored 15 goals and 50 points and won the Calder Trophy as the league's top rookie. When the Nordiques moved to Denver the next year, Forsberg had a breakout season for the Avalanche, racking up 116 points in the regular season and 21 more in the playoffs, including a hat trick in the first period of Game 2 of the Stanley Cup Final, as the team won its first championship in franchise history.

Over the next eight seasons in Colorado, Forsberg established himself as one of the league's most dominant all-round players. Although there were few NHL players who could rival Forsberg's playmaking abilities and physicality, his career was often curtailed by injuries. After he had surgery to remove a ruptured spleen during the 2001 playoffs in which the Avalanche won a second Stanley Cup, Forsberg sat out the next season. While he recuperated from his injury, Forsberg also underwent a procedure that year to repair damaged tendons in his left foot. He returned in time for the playoffs, and incredibly, led the league in scoring with 27 points. Although Forsberg's foot plagued him for the rest of his career, he returned to dominance the next season. In 2002–03, he scored 106 points, his most productive campaign since his first season in Denver, to win the Art Ross and Hart Trophies. But after another injury-riddled season and the 2004–05 lockout, Forsberg opted not to re-sign with the Avalanche. Instead, on August 3, 2005, he signed a two-year, $11.5-million contract with the Philadelphia Flyers.

AUGUST 4
NICK POLANO NAMED RED WINGS COACH, 1982

Nick Polano had his work cut out for him. After being named head coach of the Detroit Red Wings on August 4, 1982, it was his job to turn the team from perennial losers into contenders. It wouldn't be easy. In the past 16 years, the club had qualified for the post-season just twice, a run of ineffectiveness that led many to dub the team the "Dead Wings." As part of his duties behind the bench, Polano was also named assistant general manager. The additional title was reportedly Polano's idea, and he hoped to work closely with Red Wings GM Jim Devellano during the off-season. Following his first campaign as head coach, with the Red Wings out of the playoffs for the fourth straight year, Polano headed to the 1983 World Championship in West Germany to search for talent. When he returned to Detroit, Polano raved about a Czechoslovakian defenceman he'd spotted named František Musil. At the time, drafting players from behind the Iron Curtain carried significant risk, but Polano urged Detroit to select Musil at the upcoming Entry Draft. But when the Minnesota North Stars nabbed him in the second round, Polano suggested the Red Wings take Petr Klíma, another promising young Czech player he'd scouted, and they did.

Although Polano eventually led the Red Wings to back-to-back playoff appearances for the first time in two decades, he was fired after the 1984–85 campaign. However, he stayed with the club as assistant GM for player development. His top priority in his new role was to help Klíma defect and bring him back to Detroit. The club had tried before, but the mission had failed. According to Tal Pinchevsky, author of *Breakaway*, this time, after meeting Klíma in a hotel in West Germany, where the Czech national team was staying for a tournament, Polano snuck him out under cover of darkness. They spent the next five weeks eluding Czech agents and shuffling around West Germany until Klíma's paperwork came through. Finally, they arrived back in Detroit on September 21, 1985, in time for the start of the NHL season.

RED WINGS SIGN MIKE MODANO, 2010

After wearing a Dallas Stars jersey for the better part of two decades, Mike Modano would have to put on a different NHL uniform. Following the 2009–10 season, the Stars' captain was informed that the team wouldn't be re-signing him. Drafted first overall by the Minnesota North Stars in 1988, Modano went on to become the highest-scoring American-born player in NHL history during his career with Minnesota and Dallas, where the club relocated to in 1993. While Modano's role with the Stars had diminished over the past few seasons, he believed he could still play in the NHL. Although it was difficult to picture himself playing for another team, the 40-year-old veteran wanted to give it a shot. Modano drew interest from the San Jose Sharks and Minnesota Wild, but was aggressively pursued by the Detroit Red Wings. After Modano became a free agent for the first time in his 20-year career, Detroit general manager Ken Holland met with the centre to pitch him on the idea of coming home. Modano had grown up just outside Detroit in Livonia, and the Red Wings seemed like the perfect fit. After thinking it over for a few weeks, Modano decided to go to Detroit. On August 5, 2010, he signed a one-year, $1.25-million contract with the team.

Modano's homecoming, however, didn't go as planned. Just 20 games into the season, he broke his wrist in a contest against the Columbus Blue Jackets and missed the next 41 games while he recuperated from surgery. After returning, Modano struggled to find his fit in the lineup but recorded six points in March, nearly matching his output before the injury. As the regular season was coming to a close, Modano was approaching the 1,500-career-game mark. Sitting at 1,496 games, and with four matchups left on the schedule, the milestone was within reach. But head coach Mike Babcock had other plans. He scratched Modano for a game against Minnesota on April 3, 2011. Modano then played in Detroit's final three games to finish his NHL career at 1,499 games. The following September, he signed a one-day contract with Dallas to retire as a Star.

AUGUST 6

SHARKS ACQUIRE SERGEI MAKAROV, 1993

The San Jose Sharks finally landed Sergei Makarov. More than a year after signing the veteran Calgary Flames winger to an offer sheet, the team completed an earlier trade with the Hartford Whalers on August 6, 1993, to bring Makarov to San Jose. After the Flames matched the offer sheet in July 1992, Makarov played another season in Calgary before he was dealt to Hartford on June 26, 1993, in exchange for future considerations. The Whalers then sent him to the Sharks as part of a swap of first-round draft picks. Makarov was excited about going to San Jose, especially after the team had recently signed Igor Larionov, his long-time linemate in the Soviet Union. Before the two had joined the NHL, they had played together for the Soviet Union's Red Army team, and along with Vladimir Krutov, had formed The KLM Line, one of the most dominant units in hockey. But since Makarov had signed an offer sheet with the Sharks the previous July, he had to wait until a year had passed before he could officially join the team.

By the time Makarov was given permission to play for the Flames in 1989, he was already one of the most decorated players in Soviet hockey history. He had played 11 seasons for the Red Army, and on the international stage had won two Olympic gold medals and seven World Championships. Given his credentials, before Makarov had hit the ice for Calgary, some NHL general managers suggested he shouldn't be eligible for the Calder Trophy as the league's top rookie. In addition to his world-class résumé, Makarov was 31 years old and more than a decade older than some of the league's other players making their NHL debuts. After scoring 86 points, the most among all rookies, in his first season with the Flames, Makarov was awarded the Calder just before he turned 32. Two weeks later, in what became known as "The Makarov Rule," the NHL's Board of Governors changed the eligibility requirements so that players couldn't win the trophy after the age of 26.

AUGUST 7
MAPLE LEAFS MOUNT COMEBACK, 2020

There was still a period to go, but I turned the game off. The Toronto Maple Leafs were down 3–0 and facing elimination. I figured I knew how this one would end. Like many Leafs fans, I thought there wasn't much chance that this team, which had a well-earned reputation for coughing up leads, particularly in critical games, would mount a comeback. Just the night before, I'd watched them squander a 3–1 lead to the Columbus Blue Jackets in the third period only to lose in overtime. Given their track record, I assumed I'd be better off watching something else.

So, instead, my wife and I turned on a reality TV show about high-end real estate in Los Angeles to get my mind off hockey. As we watched, I couldn't help but notice my phone, which was now out of reach, light up. It was probably just a score update informing me that the Blue Jackets had added to their lead. But when the flickering continued, I had to pick up my phone to see what was happening. I couldn't believe my eyes. After finally scoring with less than four minutes left, the Maple Leafs added two more goals to force overtime. I was still in disbelief. While I didn't have the heart to watch the third period, there was no way I was missing overtime. More than halfway through the extra frame, Auston Matthews scored the game-winner on a power play. The Maple Leafs actually made a comeback in the post-season. It felt like a historic moment, and it was. The victory marked the first time in NHL history that a team on the brink of elimination came back to win after trailing by three goals with less than four minutes remaining. Even though I missed the rally in the third period, it was still an incredible feeling. But two nights later, after failing to score a single goal, they were bounced from the post-season, and I was reminded of what it was actually like to be a Leafs fan.

AUGUST 8
DARRYL SITTLER RETURNS TO MAPLE LEAFS, 1991

D arryl Sittler was a Toronto Maple Leaf again. He wasn't returning to the ice but had come back to the organization.
On August 8, 1991, at a team press conference, it was announced that Sittler had signed a one-year deal to serve as a consultant
to general manager Cliff Fletcher in the fields of public and alumni
relations, marketing, and player evaluation. Although Sittler was one
of the greatest players ever to wear the Maple Leaf, his tenure with
the franchise ended rather tumultuously. Prior the 1979–80 season,
Sittler's fifth as captain, owner Harold Ballard brought Punch Imlach
back as general manager. Before long, Sittler had drawn the ire of the
cantankerous Imlach, who detested his influence on the team, as well
as his agent, Alan Eagleson. As the two continued to quarrel, Imlach
was keen to trade Sittler, but because the captain had no-trade-clause
protection, Imlach instead targeted his close friend and linemate
Lanny McDonald, sending him to the Colorado Rockies. In response,
Sittler cut off the *C* from his jersey and told the club the situation with
Imlach had become untenable and he could no longer serve as captain.

During the off-season, with Imlach in poor health, Sittler and
Ballard reportedly patched things up, but Sittler's relationship with
the owner remained strained. Although Sittler returned the next
season with the *C* back on his sweater, things actually worsened in
Imlach's absence. By the 1981–82 campaign, Sittler was willing to
waive his no-trade clause to facilitate a move out of Toronto. Finally,
on January 20, 1982, he was dealt to the Philadelphia Flyers for the
rights to Rich Costello, a second-round pick, and future considerations. Sittler played three seasons in Philadelphia and another with
the Detroit Red Wings before hanging up his skates in 1985. After
Ballard passed away in 1990, Sittler agreed to return to the organization to work with Fletcher. On the same day that he returned, in his
first duty in the new role, Sittler, fittingly, introduced Wendel Clark as
the club's newest captain, the 16th in franchise history.

AUGUST 9
RANGERS NAME COLIN CAMPBELL
HEAD COACH, 1994

J ust a month after winning the Stanley Cup for the first time in more than five decades, the New York Rangers were without a coach. On July 15, 1994, bench boss Mike Keenan resigned from his position. He argued that the club had breached his contract and declared himself a free agent. Two days later, Keenan was named head coach and general manager of the St. Louis Blues. With four years still remaining on his deal, the Rangers implored commissioner Gary Bettman to investigate the matter. After enlisting the help of the league's top brass, however, the Rangers also filed a lawsuit against Keenan to bind him to the contract he had signed with the team a year earlier. Before the matter went to litigation, Bettman resolved the dispute. He agreed to let Keenan assume his post in St. Louis but fined him $100,000 and suspended him from his duties for 60 days. Bettman also ordered the Rangers to pay Keenan a $608,000 bonus, of which he'd return $400,000 to the team, and also fined them $25,000 for pursuing legal action.

The matter might have been settled, but the Rangers still needed a head coach. They looked no further than Colin Campbell, who had been an assistant coach in New York since 1990. Campbell was the perfect fit to take over behind the bench for the defending Stanley Cup champions. Although he'd never been an NHL head coach before, he'd been a steadying influence under Keenan's brief but tumultuous tenure and was admired by the players for his attention to detail. While Campbell didn't have Keenan's tyrannical temperament, he was no pushover. When he was an assistant coach with the Detroit Red Wings years earlier, one of his assignments was to take troubled enforcer Bob Probert under his wing. The story goes that one day when Probert was supposed to be training in the gym, Campbell caught him smoking. After exchanging words, the assistant coach challenged him to a fight in a boxing ring. Although Campbell walked away with a pair of shiners, he had earned Probert's respect.

AUGUST 10
ROB SCHREMP SIGNS WITH MODO, 2011

R ob Schremp seemed destined for stardom in the NHL. He was a talented sniper and playmaker with silky-smooth hands who could do incredible things with the puck that hadn't really been seen before. After being selected 25th overall by the Edmonton Oilers in 2004, Schremp returned to junior hockey and set the Ontario Hockey League ablaze. In his first full season with the London Knights, he scored 41 goals and 90 points in the regular season, then added 29 more points in the playoffs as London went on to win its first Memorial Cup in franchise history. Schremp started the following season by attending the Oilers' training camp but was sent back to the Knights to work on his skating and gain more experience. Back in London, Schremp recorded a junior campaign for the books. In 57 regular-season games, he scored 57 goals and 145 points, the fourth most in franchise history. In the post-season, as the Knights looked to defend their Memorial Cup title, Schremp racked up an astonishing 47 points in 17 games.

Following his prolific final season in London, Schremp turned pro but spent the 2006–07 campaign with Edmonton's AHL affiliate, the Wilkes-Barre/Scranton Penguins. After debuting in the NHL at the end of the year, Schremp started the following season with the Oilers but was sent to the minors after a pair of games. Schremp continued struggling with Edmonton and was eventually waived in 2009. After he was claimed by the New York Islanders, Schremp found a regular spot in an NHL lineup and scored 25 points in 44 games. Despite recording his most productive season in the league, Schremp played just another 45 contests for New York before he was waived again. This time he was scooped up by the Atlanta Thrashers, but at the end of the 2010–11 season, Schremp signed a contract with MODO of the Swedish Elite League on August 10, 2011. He played four seasons overseas before returning to North America in 2015 to play in the AHL, but after one season in Portland, he returned to Europe to play for two more seasons before hanging up his skates.

AUGUST 11
ERIC LINDROS SIGNS WITH
MAPLE LEAFS, 2005

When Eric Lindros dreamed of playing in the NHL, it was in a Toronto Maple Leafs sweater. As a youngster, Lindros grew up idolizing Darryl Sittler on *Hockey Night in Canada* and hoped that one day he could swap out his Leafs pajamas for a jersey. Thirteen years after breaking into the league with the Philadelphia Flyers, his dream finally came true. On August 11, 2005, Lindros signed a one-year, $1.55-million deal with the Leafs. Although he was no longer the dominant player he once was, it was the first time in three years that he was healthy, so he was excited about the future. While Lindros was heralded as "The Next One" for his brilliant skills and physical presence, his career had been derailed by a series of concussions that often kept him out of the lineup.

As his time in Philadelphia was coming to a close, Lindros was actually supposed to be dealt to Toronto, but the trade fell through and he ended up with the New York Rangers. Lindros played well in his first two seasons with the Blueshirts, but a shoulder injury in the 2003–04 campaign limited him to just 39 games. After recuperating during the 2004–05 lockout, which wiped out the entire NHL season, Lindros was ready to get back onto the ice. He scored a goal in his debut with the Leafs and recorded 22 points in his first 30 games before he tore a ligament in his right wrist during a game against the Dallas Stars. Lindros sat out the next 11 weeks while he recovered from the injury. In his first game back on February 28, 2006, he fired a slapshot past Washington Capitals goaltender Brent Johnson, but the goal was disallowed. Less than a week later, in his third contest since returning, Lindros hurt his wrist again attempting another slapshot. Following the game, Lindros choked back tears when he told reporters he would need surgery to repair his injured wrist. He missed the rest of the season and never played another game for the Leafs.

AUGUST 12
PENGUINS SIGN WARREN YOUNG, 1983

After spending most of his professional hockey career riding the bus in the minor leagues, Warren Young got another chance to prove he could play in the NHL. On August 12, 1983, he signed a contract with the Pittsburgh Penguins. Although he had been selected by the California Golden Seals in the 1976 Amateur Draft, Young had been unable to crack an NHL roster. He had played a handful of games for the Minnesota North Stars over the past couple of seasons but spent most of his time in the Central Hockey League. While playing in Oklahoma and Nashville, Young was coached by former Pittsburgh winger Gene Ubriaco. When Ubriaco later joined the Penguins organization in 1983 as the head coach for their AHL affiliate in Baltimore, he suggested the club sign Young. Although Young was considered a lumbering winger, he had a scoring touch, and Ubriaco believed he could play at a higher level. While he spent most of the 1983–84 season in the minors with Ubriaco and the Skipjacks, Young played 15 games on the fourth line with the Penguins.

When he attended training camp the following year, he impressed head coach Bob Berry with his work ethic and made the team to start the campaign. During the pre-season, Young flanked phenom Mario Lemieux, but Berry broke up the line. Prior to the 1984–85 regular season, however, Lemieux asked the bench boss to reunite them. Lemieux believed that Young's doggedness on the puck and finishing abilities would complement his skills. His intuition was right and it paid off for Young. In the first 29 games of the season, Young scored 21 goals. Although he was turning 29 in January, he was a leading candidate for the Calder Trophy. Young finished the campaign with 40 goals and 72 points, second among rookie scorers. He lost the Calder to Lemieux, who finished with 100 points, but his productive season on Mario's wing earned him a lucrative contract with the Detroit Red Wings.

AUGUST 13
COLORADO MATCHES OFFER SHEET FOR JOE SAKIC, 1997

Joe Sakic probably would have become a New York Ranger if it wasn't for Harrison Ford. Seriously. After New York signed the Colorado Avalanche captain to a whopping three-year, $21-million offer sheet, it seemed unlikely that the cash-strapped Avalanche would match. In fact, the Rangers deliberately front-loaded the contract with a $15-million signing bonus, with the hope it would dissuade the Avalanche from matching. Colorado, however, was determined to keep its star player. A year earlier, after scoring 120 points in the regular season, Sakic racked up 34 points in the playoffs and led the team to its first Stanley Cup. The Avalanche had a week to make a decision, but as the days ticked by, there was still no confirmation that the club was going to match.

A day before the deadline, though, a breakthrough occurred. Ascent Entertainment Group, parent company of the Avalanche and the Nuggets of the National Basketball Association, reached a deal with the city of Denver that would allow the organization to build a new state-of-the-art arena downtown. The facility, which would be known as the Pepsi Center, would let the company make up the losses it was incurring at McNichols Arena and bring in new revenue through the sale of exclusive TV rights for Avalanche and Nuggets games. The deal couldn't have come at a better time. With Colorado's financial future secure, it matched the offer for Sakic on August 13, 1997. Although the prospect of a new arena gave the Avalanche a boost, the team also had some help from a Hollywood blockbuster. Earlier in the summer, *Air Force One* starring Harrison Ford, a thriller about terrorists hijacking the U.S. president's plane, debuted at the box office. In its first three weeks of release, it earned $110 million and it just so happened that it was produced and co-financed by Beacon Communications, part of Ascent. Had the film been a flop, it's possible Sakic might have ended up with the Blueshirts on Broadway.

PHIL KESSEL'S DAY WITH THE CUP AND HOT DOGS, 2017

was happy when the Toronto Maple Leafs traded Phil Kessel to the Pittsburgh Penguins on July 1, 2015. Not because I didn't like Kessel but because it got him out of Toronto, where many, myself included, felt he was unfairly maligned. It also gave him a bona fide opportunity to win a Stanley Cup. Although Kessel scored no fewer than 30 goals in four of his five full seasons in Toronto, he was the subject of intense scrutiny throughout his tenure with the Leafs. Toronto is known as a market notoriously tough on its players, and Kessel endured more than his fair share of criticism. Despite having one of the best puck releases in the league, he was the subject of scornful write-ups on everything from his fitness levels and work ethic to his attitude and how he dealt with the media.

Even after Kessel was traded, reporters such as Steve Simmons, a columnist for the *Toronto Sun*, couldn't resist giving him a parting shot. In a piece published the day after Kessel was sent to the Penguins, Simmons wrote that the Leafs had grown tired of Kessel. The columnist also added that during Kessel's time in Toronto, he had a fondness for grabbing a hot dog every day as an afternoon snack. It shouldn't have mattered. Kessel rarely missed a game as a member of the Leafs and was one of the best goal-scorers in the league. If he wanted to indulge in a frankfurter every afternoon, so be it. The problem was that Simmons made the whole thing up. Kessel might have had a penchant for hot dogs, but the daily routine described wasn't true. Once in Pittsburgh, the fake hot dog story became a running joke. Two years later, however, Kessel got the last laugh. On August 14, 2017, he celebrated his day with the Stanley Cup for the second straight year by bringing the trophy to a golf course and filling it with hot dogs. Standing next to Lord Stanley's mug, the two-time champion held a hot dog and grinned for the camera.

AUGUST 15
SHARKS SIGN TONY GRANATO, 1996

Tony Granato thought he might never play hockey again. Not long after crashing into the boards in a game against the Hartford Whalers on January 25, 1996, the Los Angeles Kings winger developed a headache he couldn't shake. At the time, he shrugged it off and suited up for his club's matchup against the Mighty Ducks of Anaheim two days later. The following day, however, Granato didn't feel like himself. During a Super Bowl party at Wayne Gretzky's house, a severe headache set in and he started to forget things. By the time he returned home later that evening, his symptoms had worsened. His balance was off, his head was still pounding, and his memory was continuing to slip. Granato's wife, Linda, realized something was seriously wrong and rushed him to the hospital. Doctors initially thought it might be a brain tumour or an aneurysm, but following a battery of tests, they discovered it was a blood clot. Granato was prescribed medication with the hope it would dissolve the buildup, but when his headaches worsened, doctors suspected the clot was getting bigger and booked him for surgery. He underwent a procedure to remove a clot and an abnormal cluster of blood vessels on his left temporal lobe. Without the operation, Granato could have suffered paralysis and even died.

After recovering from his brain surgery, Granato began thinking about playing hockey again. Although he felt ready to return the following season, the Kings chose not to re-sign him because they were unsure he'd be medically cleared to play. Instead, Granato inked a one-year deal with the San Jose Sharks on August 15, 1996. Even though doctors said he could return to the ice, Granato wore a helmet with extra padding as a precaution. In his first game against the Kings on October 6, 1996, Granato scored a hat trick and added an assist in a 7–6 overtime victory. Overcoming what many thought could have been a career-ending brain injury, Granato finished the season with 25 goals and was awarded the Bill Masterton Memorial Trophy, awarded annually for perseverance, sportsmanship, and dedication to hockey.

AUGUST 16

OILERS SIGN DRAISAITL TO EIGHT MORE YEARS, 2017

Following the 2016–17 season, Leon Draisaitl believed he was just scratching the surface of what he was capable of in the NHL. The Edmonton Oilers thought so, too. After scoring 77 points in the regular season, the German forward elevated his game in the playoffs, taking on tough assignments against some of the game's premier centres such as the Anaheim Ducks' Ryan Getzlaf. Although Draisaitl had spent most of his time in Edmonton flanking Connor McDavid, seeing him match up against Getzlaf with aplomb gave the Oilers a glimpse of what the future could hold. They felt that Draisaitl, who was taken third overall in 2014, could give the club the one-two punch it needed up the middle to become a bona fide Stanley Cup contender. Banking on that possibility, Edmonton inked the Cologne native to an eight-year, $68-million extension on August 16, 2017.

In the first season under his new deal, Draisaitl continued riding shotgun with McDavid, but his production dipped. The following year, however, Draisaitl had a breakout season. On April 6, 2019, he scored his 50th goal of the season, becoming the first Oiler in more than three decades to reach that milestone. Draisaitl finished the campaign with 105 points, the fourth most in the league. Building off that successful season, Draisaitl took his game to the next level in 2019–20, developing into the type of centre the club had hoped he'd become when he signed his extension. Moving off McDavid's wing, Draisaitl found success driving his own line with Ryan Nugent-Hopkins and Kailer Yamamoto, which soon became known as "The Dynamite Line." Up until the pandemic halted the regular season in March 2020, the explosive trio was one of the most dominant units at even strength. Draisaitl led the league with 110 points, becoming the first German player to win the Art Ross Trophy as the NHL's leading scorer. For his efforts, he also won the Hart Trophy as the league's most valuable player and the Ted Lindsay Award, given to the most outstanding player as deemed by the NHL Players' Association.

AUGUST 17

MARC BERGEVIN TRADED TO RED WINGS, 1995

arc Bergevin's teammates had to keep their heads on swivels when he was around. The stay-at-home defenceman was a notorious prankster always looking for unsuspecting victims. Bergevin was so dedicated to pulling off practical jokes that when he was on road trips he brought along an extra hockey bag packed full of props. Bergevin supposedly even kept a wig handy so he could sneak up on his teammates in disguise. While Bergevin relished getting laughs out of his fellow players, he took his role on the ice seriously and was known as a hard-nosed blueliner who did just about anything to keep the puck out of his net.

So when the Tampa Bay Lightning prepared for their inaugural season in 1992–93, Bergevin was exactly the type of player they were looking for. They signed the veteran rearguard hoping he'd bring leadership and experience to the fledgling team. Although Tampa struggled in its first campaign, Bergevin brought consistency to the back end and was the club's most effective defenceman. As part of his duties on the blue line, Bergevin also mentored young defenceman Roman Hamrlík, who was drafted first overall in 1992. But with the victories few and far between for the expansion Lightning, Bergevin's lightheartedness helped keep things loose. He once took a dozen doughnuts, dipped them in the team's hot wax machine, and left them out for his teammates. Winger Rob Zamuner supposedly ate two before he realized he'd been tricked. But Bergevin's favourite gag was sneaking up to the baggage carousel at the airport, tying up all of his teammates' luggage, and chuckling as they attempted to untangle them. Despite the laughs, after three seasons, Bergevin grew weary of the struggling team. He felt some of his teammates didn't show up to play every night, and following the 1994–95 season, he requested a trade. On August 17, 1995, the disenchanted defenceman was dealt to the Detroit Red Wings, along with Ben Hankinson, in exchange for Shawn Burr and a third-round pick.

AUGUST 18
ROBIN LEHNER DEFEATS FORMER TEAM, 2020

With Robin Lehner slated to become an unrestricted free agent in the off-season, the Chicago Blackhawks traded the goaltender to the Vegas Golden Knights just before the 2020 trade deadline as part of a three-team deal. Lehner initially went to the Toronto Maple Leafs in exchange for Mārtiņš Dzierkals, and then Toronto, which agreed to retain a portion of Lehner's salary, traded him to Vegas for a fifth-round pick. Meanwhile, Chicago sent Dzierkals to the Golden Knights for goaltender Malcolm Subban, Slava Demin, and a second-round pick. Although Vegas already had veteran netminder Marc-André Fleury between the pipes, Lehner gave them a solid one-two punch in net as it prepared to make a deep playoff run. Lehner made his Golden Knights debut a few days later, stopping 32 shots in a 4–2 victory against the Buffalo Sabres. He picked up two more wins with his new squad before the regular season was halted by the Covid-19 pandemic.

When the Stanley Cup Playoffs began five months later, Lehner got the nod from head coach Peter DeBoer and started Vegas's opening-round series against his former team, the Blackhawks. He stopped 19 shots in a 4–1 win in the first game and appeared to be DeBoer's goaltender of choice. When the Golden Knights had the chance to close out the series in the fifth game on August 18, 2020, Lehner earned the start again. He made 23 saves in a 4–3 victory, becoming the first NHL goaltender since Hal Winkler in 1927 to earn a series-clinching victory against a team he played for that same season. Although Fleury had played the third game against Chicago, it was clear he had lost the starting job to Lehner. Before Vegas opened its next series against the Vancouver Canucks, Fleury's agent, Allan Walsh, addressed the issue by unwisely tweeting a picture of Fleury with a sword through his back and DeBoer's name on the blade. While it was an unwelcomed distraction for the team, there were no hard feelings between the goaltenders, and Lehner recorded a shutout in the first game against the Canucks.

AUGUST 19

BRUINS SIGN JIM SCHOENFELD, 1983

After he was waived by the Detroit Red Wings at the end of the 1982–83 season, Jim Schoenfeld considered hanging up his skates. Drafted fifth overall by the Buffalo Sabres in 1972, Schoenfeld was a hulking defenceman who was never afraid to get in front of a slapshot to block the puck. He patrolled the Buffalo blue line for nine seasons until he was sent to the Detroit Red Wings, along with Danny Gare and Derek Smith, in exchange for Dale McCourt, Mike Foligno, and Brent Peterson on December 2, 1981. In his only full season with the Red Wings, Schoenfeld suffered a shoulder injury early in the campaign and only suited up for 57 games. Although Schoenfeld had appeared in two All-Star Games during his tenure with the Sabres, his career had been curtailed by injuries. Before arriving in Detroit, he had broken both of his feet, strained his knee, and ruptured a spinal disc. While those were some of the occupational hazards of being a hard-nosed defenceman, Schoenfeld had also dealt with mononucleosis and viral pneumonia, which also kept him out of the lineup.

After contemplating retirement following his release from the Red Wings, Schoenfeld signed a one-year contract with the Boston Bruins on August 19, 1983. Following one season in Boston in which he appeared in 39 contests, Schoenfeld hoped to return to the Bruins, but when he wasn't guaranteed a roster spot he explored other opportunities. His former Sabres coach, Scotty Bowman, invited him to come back to Buffalo as a part-time defenceman, but Schoenfeld held out and eventually took him up on another offer to coach the team's AHL affiliate in Rochester. But after getting off to a record-tying 11–0 start with the Americans, Bowman recalled Schoenfeld to join the Sabres' blue line. After spending the next two weeks getting back into game shape, Schoenfeld played his first game on December 19, 1984, which proved to be a milestone night for his coach. The Sabres defeated the Black Hawks 6–3 and Bowman earned his 691st career victory, tying Dick Irvin for the most in NHL history.

AUGUST 20
TORONTO NAMES PYRAMID-POWER RED KELLY HEAD COACH, 1973

After Toronto Maple Leafs coach John McLellan resigned at the end of the 1972–73 campaign to become the club's assistant general manager, rumours swirled that Red Kelly, who had been fired earlier that season by the Pittsburgh Penguins, would take over behind the bench. Kelly was beloved in Toronto. He had spent seven seasons there as a player, winning four Stanley Cups. Although Kelly had started his career as a defenceman with the Detroit Red Wings, after being traded to the Leafs in 1960, he was shifted up front to centre. Kelly, who was already highly regarded for his playmaking abilities on the back end, embraced his new role. In his first full season in Toronto, Kelly dished out a team-leading 50 assists. After he won his fourth Stanley Cup with the Leafs in 1967, he hung up his skates to start coaching. Following two seasons behind the bench with the Los Angeles Kings, Kelly was named head coach of the Penguins in 1969. Despite guiding that club to its first-ever post-season appearances, Kelly was dismissed in 1973.

Over the off-season, Kelly considered several options but decided to return to Toronto, signing a four-year agreement on August 20, 1973. Although Kelly led the Leafs to the playoffs in each of his first two seasons, they failed to advance beyond the quarter-finals. In 1976, he tried something different. Before the third game in their series against the Philadelphia Flyers, Kelly placed small pyramids under the Leafs' bench. He believed pyramids had supernatural powers that could be leveraged by the team. After the Leafs won the game, he brought his club in on his secret. Prior to the next contest in Toronto, Kelly hung a large pyramid from the ceiling in the dressing room and encouraged his players to harness its power. Darryl Sittler placed six of his sticks below and stood beneath it before hitting the ice. He ended up scoring five goals that night, tying a playoff record, as the Leafs forced a decisive Game 7. Kelly's pyramid power, however, was fleeting. Toronto was eliminated a few nights later in Philadelphia.

BLUE JACKETS SIGN MICHAEL PECA, 2007

Michael Peca was supposed to become a New York Ranger. Following the 2006–07 season with the Toronto Maple Leafs in which he was limited to just 35 games with a broken leg, Peca was poised to become the third-line centre with the Blueshirts after New York had already signed coveted free agents Scott Gomez and Chris Drury. The Columbus Blue Jackets were also vying for the two-time Selke Award winner's services, but they appeared to be out of the running late in the off-season when it was announced that Peca's deal with the Rangers was imminent. Despite the reports, Columbus remained determined to land the veteran centre. General manager Scott Howson, who was the assistant GM of the Edmonton Oilers when the club acquired Peca in 2006, knew what he could bring to the club. Peca had been an integral part of Edmonton's run to the Stanley Cup Final in 2006, scoring six goals and 11 points.

But when Peca's contract with the Rangers never materialized, the Blue Jackets seized the opportunity. On August 21, 2007, the club signed Peca to a one-year agreement. Peca later told the *Columbus Dispatch* that he and the Rangers apparently had a deal in place for three weeks but lamented that there wasn't enough commitment on the team's side to get it done. Nevertheless, after spending much of the previous campaign on the sidelines recovering from injury, Peca was eager to get back on the ice. In his fourth game with the Blue Jackets, Peca scored against the Buffalo Sabres, notching his first goal in nearly a year. Although Peca missed some games with a groin injury and concussion, he proved to be a solid contributor for the Blue Jackets, finishing the campaign with eight goals and 34 points, the third-most points on the team that season. After signing another one-year deal in the off-season, Peca rejoined the Blue Jackets. His return to Columbus, however, didn't go as planned. Early in the season, Peca received a 10-game suspension for abuse of an official, but following an appeal, it was reduced to five games.

AUGUST 22
KINGS ACQUIRE TERRY HARPER, 1972

Doctors thought Terry Harper might never walk again. As a youngster growing up in Regina, Saskatchewan, Harper suffered third-degree burns to his arms, chest, stomach, and legs in a fire. Despite going through years of procedures and skin grafts, Harper was determined to defy his physician's expectations and even get back onto the ice to play hockey. Although his doctors didn't initially think hockey was a good idea, they relented, believing the sport could actually help rebuild muscles in his legs. Through hard work and fierce determination on and off the ice, Harper recovered from his injuries and eventually made his hometown Pats in 1957. A few years later, he made the jump to the NHL with the Montreal Canadiens. Patrolling the blue line in Montreal for the next 10 seasons, Harper established himself as one of the league's most hard-nosed defencemen, winning five Stanley Cups along the way.

But after more than a decade with the Canadiens, Harper wanted a change. After he started thinking about moving to the rival WHA, former teammate Rogie Vachon, who was traded to the Los Angeles Kings a year earlier, invited him to California to check things out. Not long after, on August 22, 1972, Montreal sent Harper to the Kings in exchange for cash and future draft picks. He was eventually named captain, and under head coach Bob Berry was an integral part of a defensive turnaround in Los Angeles. Following three strong seasons with the Kings, Harper was sent to the Detroit Red Wings as part of a blockbuster trade for Marcel Dionne. Harper, however, refused to report to the Motor City. Less than two weeks earlier, he had signed an extension with the Kings and alleged he'd been misrepresented. Harper subsequently sued the Kings for breach of contract and filed an antitrust lawsuit against the NHL. Even after he eventually joined the Red Wings in October 1975, he still planned to go forward with litigation. But after Detroit agreed to renegotiate his contract, he dropped the lawsuits a month later.

AUGUST 23
SENATORS ACQUIRE DANY HEATLEY, 2005

Dany Heatley needed a fresh start. Drafted second overall by the Atlanta Thrashers in 2000, Heatley broke into the NHL the next season and scored 26 goals in his rookie campaign. The following year, he racked up 41 goals and dazzled fans, even veteran players such as Jeremy Roenick, with a four-goal performance at the 2003 NHL All-Star Game. Prior to the 2003–04 season, however, his life changed forever. On September 29, 2003, while driving his Ferrari at high speed with teammate Dan Snyder, Heatley lost control and crashed into a brick-and-wrought-iron fence. While Heatley sustained a broken jaw and tore ligaments in his right knee, Snyder was thrown from the sports car and fell into a coma. He died six days later. Heatley missed most of the 2003–04 campaign while he recovered from his injuries but returned in February, scoring 13 goals and 25 points in 31 games.

During the off-season, Heatley was indicted on six charges related to the fatal crash, including vehicular homicide in the first degree and vehicular homicide in the second degree. If Heatley was convicted on all counts, he faced up to 20 years behind bars. Although Snyder's family could never forget what happened, they forgave Heatley for what had transpired that fateful day and didn't want him to go to jail. After Heatley pleaded guilty to second-degree vehicular homicide, along with three other charges, the judge took the family's wishes into consideration at sentencing and gave the winger three years' probation instead of sending him to prison. Heatley, however, remained besieged with guilt. When he returned from playing overseas during the 2004–05 NHL lockout, he asked for a trade. He felt he couldn't move on if he remained in Atlanta, since it would always remind him of the accident. The Thrashers granted his request, and on August 23, 2005, they traded him to the Ottawa Senators in exchange for Marián Hossa and Greg de Vries. In his first season in Ottawa, Heatley scored 50 goals and 103 points.

AUGUST 24
ŠŤASTNÝ BROTHERS DEFECT, 1980

Gilles Leger had been trying to figure out a way to bring the Šťastný brothers to North America for a while. Ever since he'd been the coach and general manager of the Birmingham Bulls of the WHA, he'd attempted to sign them. The three skillful brothers — Marián, Peter, and Anton — all played for the Czechoslovakian team Slovan Bratislava, but they had appeared on Leger's radar after he spotted them while scouting international tournaments. After the Bulls were disbanded following the WHA's merger with the NHL in 1979, Leger was hired by the Quebec Nordiques, one of the four surviving teams from the defunct league, to serve as director of player development. In his new role with Quebec, Leger continued his efforts to land the Šťastnýs and found a receptive ear with team president Marcel Aubut.

After the Nordiques took the youngest Šťastný, Anton, with the 83rd overall pick in the 1979 NHL Entry Draft, Leger and Aubut began hatching a plan to bring the brothers to Quebec City. They both attended the 1980 Winter Olympics in Lake Placid, where the brothers had a starring role on the Czechoslovakian team. While the Nordiques' executives hoped that with the Šťastnýs already in North America, they would be able to abscond with them north of the border, their plans were dashed. The brothers knew they would never get past the watchful eyes of Czechoslovakian agents on high alert for potential defections. And so they bided their time. According to Tal Pinchevsky, author of *Breakaway*, later that August, when Bratislava was playing in Innsbruck, Austria, Peter and Anton contacted the Nordiques. Leger and Aubut quickly hopped on a plane. Once they met with the brothers, along with Peter's pregnant wife, Darina, they fled to the Canadian embassy in Vienna. Marián, however, didn't make the escape. Peter and Anton felt it was too risky for their older brother, who would be leaving behind a family. Two days after defecting, on August 26, 1980, Peter and Anton were introduced as the newest members of the Nordiques.

AUGUST 25
DEVILS REACQUIRE CHRIS TERRERI, 1998

When the New Jersey Devils were eager to bring in an experienced backup goaltender for Martin Brodeur, they went with the Devil they knew. On August 25, 1998, they reacquired Chris Terreri from the Chicago Blackhawks in exchange for a conditional pick in the 1999 NHL Entry Draft. Fifteen years earlier, Terreri had been drafted in the fifth round by New Jersey. After finishing his collegiate career at Providence College, which included a Hockey East championship in 1985, Terreri turned pro with the Devils in 1986. He got his first taste of NHL action on October 18, 1986, when he entered the final period in relief in a game in which the Pittsburgh Penguins had already shelled the Devils for eight goals. Three days later, he made his first start, making 40 saves in a 6–3 loss to the New York Islanders.

After further development in the AHL over parts of the next three seasons, Terreri established himself as the team's starting goaltender in the 1990–91 campaign. He maintained that position for the next three seasons until the emergence of Martin Brodeur in 1993. Following New Jersey's Stanley Cup victory in 1995, he was traded to the San Jose Sharks for a second-round pick. After a few seasons in San Jose and Chicago, Terreri returned to the Devils. Although Brodeur was the undisputed starter in New Jersey, Terreri embraced the opportunity to serve as the veteran backup. On October 24, 1998, Terreri made his first appearance for the Devils since November 11, 1995, stopping 20 shots in a 3–1 win over the Boston Bruins. During the next couple of seasons, Terreri played solidly as Brodeur's understudy and won his second Stanley Cup with the club in 2000. Not long after the championship, he was selected by the Minnesota Wild in the expansion draft but was sent back to New Jersey, along with a ninth-round pick, for Brad Bombardir. Terreri made 10 more appearances for the Devils before he was traded to the New York Islanders, along with a ninth-round draft pick, in exchange for John Vanbiesbrouck.

AUGUST 26
EDDIE O RETURNS TO BLACKHAWKS, 1998

After breaking into the NHL in 1984 with the Chicago Blackhawks, Eddie Olczyk was returning to play for his hometown team. Growing up in Chicago, it had always been his dream to play for the Blackhawks. After the team took him third overall in the NHL Entry Draft, it became a reality. But Olczyk's time with the Blackhawks was fleeting. Despite scoring 79 points as a 19-year-old in his second season in Chicago, Olczyk spent just one more season with the Blackhawks before he was traded to the Toronto Maple Leafs. Following a few seasons in Toronto, which included a 90-point campaign in 1988–89, Olczyk had stopovers in Winnipeg, New York, Los Angeles, and Pittsburgh before he had the opportunity to bookend his career in Chicago. On August 26, 1998, the veteran forward signed a one-year discounted deal to become a Blackhawk again.

Although Olczyk was excited about the homecoming, things didn't start off as planned. Early in the season, he was put on waivers and assigned to the club's International Hockey League affiliate, the Chicago Wolves. After playing seven games with the Wolves, Olczyk was recalled on November 23, 1998. When he returned to the Blackhawks, he was given an opportunity on the top line with Tony Amonte and Alexei Zhamnov. Olczyk clicked with his new linemates, who both happened to be former teammates, and finished the season with 10 goals and 25 points in 61 games. The next year, Olczyk was invited to come to training camp without a contract. After a solid camp and with the support of head coach Lorne Molleken, Olczyk signed another one-year contract on October 1, 1999. A week later in a contest against the Phoenix Coyotes, Olczyk suited up for his 1,000th career NHL game. Not long after his milestone night, Olcyzk had to get surgery to repair a herniated disc in his back. The procedure sidelined him for two months, and even once he returned, he was in and out of the lineup. Olczyk played his final NHL game at home before the Chicago faithful on April 9, 2000.

AUGUST 27
KINGS TRADE MARTY MCSORLEY, 1993

There was no replacing Marty McSorley. He had been one of the
most popular Los Angeles Kings players since arriving in 1988
as part of the trade for Wayne Gretzky. During his time with
the Edmonton Oilers, the hulking McSorley had established himself
as Gretzky's bodyguard and continued to embrace that role with the
Kings while chipping in offensively. Following the team's run to the
Stanley Cup Final in 1993 in which McSorley scored 10 points in 24
games, the hard-nosed defenceman was tabled a five-year, $4-million
offer sheet, which included a $5-million signing bonus, from the St.
Louis Blues. It was considerably more than what the Kings were offering, but since McSorley was classified as a group three free agent, the
team wouldn't have received any compensation if they didn't match it.
And so on August 27, 1993, the Kings matched the contract, but less
than an hour later, they traded McSorley to the Pittsburgh Penguins
in exchange for Shawn McEachern.

When Gretzky learned the news that his long-time friend and
teammate had been traded, he was crestfallen. McSorley, however,
wasn't gone long. After just 47 games in Pittsburgh in which he scored
21 points and racked up 139 penalty minutes, the Kings reacquired
him, along with Jim Paek, in exchange for McEachern and Tomas
Sandström on February 16, 1994. Owner Bruce McNall felt he owed
it to the fans to bring McSorley back, and after hearing his star player
as well as head coach Barry Melrose lament the defenceman's absence
throughout the season, he pulled the trigger on the deal. McSorley
made an immediate impact upon his return to Los Angeles. Two days
later, in a game at home against the Philadelphia Flyers, McSorley
opened the scoring less than 30 seconds after the puck was dropped.
Although the Kings lost the game 4–3, Marty was back. Just over a
month later, when the club hosted the Vancouver Canucks, McSorley
assisted on Gretzky's 802nd career goal to surpass his boyhood idol,
Gordie Howe, for the most goals in NHL history.

AUGUST 28
KINGS REACQUIRE LUC ROBITAILLE, 1997

Luc Robitaille was back with the Los Angeles Kings. Three years after trading him to the Pittsburgh Penguins in exchange for Rick Tocchet and a second-round pick in 1994, Los Angeles reacquired him from the Rangers on August 28, 1997, in exchange for Kevin Stevens. Although Robitaille had scored no fewer than 40 goals in each of his first eight seasons with the Kings, the team originally traded him away just a season after he had racked up 63 goals. Despite his prolific production, there was a perceived rift between him and superstar Wayne Gretzky. Following the deal, Robitaille had hinted that it was Gretzky's influence within the organization that got him shipped out: "My feeling is, players should play, managers should manage." Although he didn't name Gretzky explicitly, he told reporters to draw their own conclusions. But after just one season in Pittsburgh, Robitaille was traded to the New York Rangers, where he was eventually reunited with The Great One.

While the Rangers brought Robitaille in to score goals, he mustered just 23 tallies in his first season with the Blueshirts and finished the campaign with more penalty minutes than points. He opened the following season on a line with Gretzky, but after another slow start to the year, Robitaille requested more ice time in November. It wasn't long before he became the subject of trade speculation. While it was thought the premier left winger would have been a perfect fit with the Montreal Canadiens, Robitaille shot down those rumours, stating that he wasn't interested in suiting up for his hometown. He played out the season in New York, and then in the off-season, he made his way back to Los Angeles. Although Robitaille's return provided the rebuilding Kings with a silver lining, he struggled in his season back, scoring just 16 goals and contending with an abdominal injury that kept him out of the lineup for 25 games. The following season, however, Robitaille returned to his scoring ways. He notched 39 goals, his best output since the 1993–94 campaign with the Kings.

MAPLE LEAFS NAME JOHN FERGUSON, JR., GM, 2003

J ohn Ferguson, Jr., had his work cut out for him taking on a Toronto Maple Leafs team with an aging core and a weak blue line. But before he could begin retooling the club, he already had to contend with criticisms from the media. When he was officially named general manager of the Leafs on August 29, 2003, many pundits had already panned the decision, citing he was too inexperienced to take on the role. Although he had his detractors, there were some who felt he was ready to assume the high-profile position in Toronto. Ferguson had grown up in the hockey world. His father, John Sr., had been a hard-nosed winger for the Montreal Canadiens who, after his playing career, went on to serve as general manager of the New York Rangers and Winnipeg Jets. John Jr. followed in his father's footsteps. After being selected in the final round of the 1985 NHL Entry Draft, he played professionally for four seasons in the AHL before hanging up his skates in 1993. After retiring, he joined the Ottawa Senators, where his father was the director of player personnel, and worked as a scout for three seasons. In 1997, he joined the St. Louis Blues organization as the assistant GM and president of the Worcester IceCats, the club's AHL affiliate, and then four years later, was named vice-president and director of hockey operations for the big club in St. Louis.

When Ferguson joined the Leafs in 2003, he took over the GM duties from Pat Quinn, who remained with the club as head coach. Although the Leafs advanced to the conference finals in Ferguson's first season at the helm in Toronto, it proved to be the only bright spot in his tenure. Following the 2004–05 NHL lockout, the club missed the playoffs for the next two years. While Ferguson is best remembered for trading Tuukka Rask to the Boston Bruins for Andrew Raycroft, he also dismissed Quinn, who was beloved and only missed the playoffs once in his seven seasons behind the Toronto bench. Ferguson was eventually dismissed on January 22, 2008, closing a chapter in the Leafs' history most fans would like to forget.

AUGUST 30
SELÄNNE RETURNS FOR ONE
LAST SEASON, 2013

After spending the summer contemplating his future, Teemu Selänne decided he was coming back for one final NHL season. On August 30, 2013, he signed a one-year, $2-million contract to return to the Anaheim Ducks. Instead of simply issuing a press release to announce the news, Selänne and the team had some fun and released a humorous video on the Ducks' YouTube page. The short film begins with Selänne on a golf course, but as things unfold, it becomes clear the 43-year-old winger is having a rough day on the links. He can't get out of a sand trap, loses his ball, and still can't get out of the sand trap. As his frustration builds, he chips the ball into a water hazard. Reaching the breaking point, Selänne pitches his club and then tosses his bag into the pond. But once he realizes his cellphone is in his bag, he jumps into the water to fish it out. Swimming the bag back to shore, a soaking Selänne retrieves his phone and punches up Anaheim GM Bob Murray's number. "I'm coming back," he says with exasperation. "Yeah, but this is it, this is my final one."

After taking the league by storm in his debut season with the Winnipeg Jets in 1992 and scoring 76 goals, a rookie record likely to stand the test of time, Selänne spent most of his career with the Ducks in two separate stints. In 2007, two years after returning to Anaheim as a free agent, Selänne was an integral part of the club's first Stanley Cup victory. In the years that followed, he remained a key contributor and even racked up 80 points in the 2010–11 campaign as a 40-year-old. Although his role had diminished over the past two seasons, he still showed flashes of the speed and goal-scoring prowess he was renowned for. In his final NHL season, Selänne picked up 27 points in 64 games. Not long after retiring, the Ducks announced they would send Selänne's number 8 jersey to the rafters in a ceremony on January 11, 2015.

STARS SIGN PAT VERBEEK, 2001

P at Verbeek didn't reel in any big ones, but he caught plenty of fish. While still waiting for a contract for the upcoming season, the feisty undersized winger, affectionately known as "The Little Ball of Hate" for his ferocious play on the ice, took part in a Bassmasters fishing tournament at Lake St. Clair in Michigan. Verbeek first got into fishing during his time with the Hartford Whalers and then participated in bass fishing tournaments in Dallas when he was with the Stars. After joining the Detroit Red Wings in 1999, Verbeek continued fishing in the cool waters Michigan had to offer. For him, the two sports paired perfectly because once hockey season ended, fishing began. In the 2001 off-season, however, Verbeek had more time for angling than expected. Following two seasons in Detroit, the 37-year-old wasn't extended an offer and became a free agent. It wasn't that long ago that he'd been one of the most coveted players available. Five years earlier, he'd signed a three-year deal with the Stars at the beginning of free agency that made him the highest-paid player on the team. Verbeek's fierce play and relentlessness proved to be a catalyst for Dallas, and he was an integral part of the club's Stanley Cup victory in 1999.

Although Verbeek was a few years older now, he still felt he could contribute to a team. While he waited for a contract, he tossed his line into the water. Less than a week after the fishing tournament in Michigan, he got a nibble. On August 31, 2001, he officially signed a one-year deal to return to Dallas. While his offensive production wasn't what it had been, Verbeek remained a driving force for the club and an important voice in the dressing room. Following his stint with the Stars, Verbeek had hoped to play at least one more season in the league, but after sitting out the 2002–03 campaign, he officially retired on April 23, 2003. He hung up his skates as the only player in NHL history to score 500 career goals and rack up 2,500 penalty minutes, as well.

SEPTEMBER 1
CANUCKS SIGN THOMAS VANEK, 2017

Although Thomas Vanek was nearly a decade removed from his last 40-goal campaign, he was still a proven goal-scorer and a power play specialist. On September 1, 2017, the Vancouver Canucks signed the Austrian winger to a one-year, $2-million contract. Splitting time with the Detroit Red Wings and Florida Panthers the previous season, Vanek combined for 17 goals and 48 points. If the Canucks could squeeze that type of production out of the 33-year-old winger, he'd be a valuable asset for the club in future trades. While Vanek didn't get on the score sheet in his debut with the Canucks, he netted a goal in the club's second game of the season and soon found chemistry with rookie Brock Boeser and fellow veteran Sam Gagner. On December 28, 2017, in a game against the Chicago Blackhawks, the trio combined for 12 points. Vanek finished the contest with two goals and three assists but could have easily had more. Early in the game, he fired a shot at a wide-open net, but Chicago goaltender Anton Forsberg got his paddle on it and prevented a certain goal.

With the NHL trade deadline approaching and the Canucks in the basement of the Pacific Division, it appeared as though Vanek would be on the move. Sitting second in team scoring with 41 points, Vanek would bring a scoring touch to any team that wanted to add depth for a playoff run. After he was kept out of the lineup for Vancouver's game against the Arizona Coyotes on February 25, 2018, he was dealt to the Columbus Blue Jackets the next day in exchange for Jussi Jokinen and Tyler Motte. Although some felt the rebuilding Canucks should have gotten more out of the deal, Motte has performed admirably in the club's bottom six. In his first full season in Vancouver, Motte scored nine goals and 16 points on the fourth line. The following year during the 2020 playoffs, Motte elevated his game, scoring four goals in two straight games to help the Canucks knock off the St. Louis Blues, the defending Stanley Cup champions.

SEPTEMBER 2
SHARKS SIGN ANTTI NIEMI, 2010

Despite backstopping the Chicago Blackhawks to their first Stanley Cup in nearly five decades, Antti Niemi wouldn't be returning to the club. After signing with the team in 2008 as an undrafted free agent, the Finnish netminder spent the 2008–09 campaign with the Rockford IceHogs, the Blackhawks' AHL affiliate. The following season, Niemi shared the crease in Chicago with Cristobal Huet but earned the starting job heading into the 2010 Stanley Cup Playoffs. In the team's opening-round series against the Nashville Predators, Niemi posted two shutouts, becoming the first Blackhawks goaltender since Tony Esposito in 1974 to record two in one playoff series. Niemi continued to play well throughout the post-season and was an integral part of the club's championship victory against the Philadelphia Flyers.

Following the celebrations, however, the Blackhawks had to make several difficult decisions. They were hard up against the salary cap heading into the next season and had to jettison a number of key players. After an arbitrator awarded Niemi $2.75 million for one season on July 31, 2010, the goaltender became the club's latest salary cap casualty. Rather than try to make room for Niemi's contract, general manager Stan Bowman left the arbitrator's award on the table. Two days later, he signed veteran netminder Marty Turco, and Niemi became an unrestricted free agent. Niemi, however, wasn't out of work long. On September 2, 2010, he inked a one-year, $2-million contract with the San Jose Sharks, the team the Blackhawks swept in the conference final to advance to the Stanley Cup Final. Although Niemi struggled early in San Jose, winning just one game in his first five starts, his play improved significantly. In the month of February alone, he picked up 10 victories and recorded a sterling .934 save percentage that helped the Sharks rise to the top of the Pacific Division. For his efforts, the team rewarded him by signing him to a four-year, $15.2-million contract extension on March 1, 2011.

SEPTEMBER 3
BOBBY ORR SIGNS FIRST NHL
CONTRACT, 1966

t was supposedly the most lucrative contract ever offered to a
player coming out of junior hockey. On September 3, 1966,
the Boston Bruins signed Bobby Orr to his first NHL contract.
Reportedly worth up to $50,000, the agreement was the culmina-
tion of two months of negotiations between the club and Orr's agent,
Alan Eagleson, and Orr's father, Douglas. It was a considerable raise
from the last contract he'd signed with the Bruins. A few years earlier,
Boston had signed Orr to a professional services contract. The club
had been hoping to ink the young blueliner ever since a contingent
of Bruins, including long-time coach Milt Schmidt and scout Wren
Blair, spotted him playing in Gananoque, Ontario, as a 13-year-
old. The pair were supposedly interested in a pair of players on the
other team but were soon captivated by Orr. Blair spent the next year
convincing Orr's parents that their son should play for the Oshawa
Generals, a junior club sponsored by the Bruins. Just before Orr's
14th birthday, the family agreed to put pen to paper. As part of the
agreement, in exchange for committing their son to developing in the
Bruins' farm system, the Orrs received a cash bonus, a new car, and an
assurance that the team would pay to stucco the family home.

Heading into the 1963–64 season with the Generals, Orr was
heralded "the hottest hockey prospect in a decade." It didn't take
long for him to live up to his billing. Following three seasons in
Oshawa in the Ontario Hockey Association, Orr was ready to make
the jump to the Bruins. After picking up an assist in his NHL debut,
Orr scored his first goal in a matchup against the Montreal Canadiens
at home on October 23, 1966. Following the goal, a slapshot from
more than 50 feet out, the Boston faithful rose to their feet and gave
Orr a standing ovation that lasted nearly a minute. Although the
Bruins ended up losing the game, it was the first of many goals Orr
would score in the Garden.

SEPTEMBER 4
JOEL KIVIRANTA SCORES HAT TRICK, 2020

Joel Kiviranta was only in the lineup because Andrew Cogliano was unfit to play. The Dallas Stars winger was suiting up for just his third game of the 2020 post-season, and the stakes couldn't have been higher. It was Game 7 against the Colorado Avalanche with a berth to the Western Conference Final on the line. An undrafted free agent, Kiviranta signed a two-year entry-level contract with Dallas in May 2019 and spent most of the following season with the club's AHL affiliate, the Texas Stars. Kiviranta made his NHL debut on January 3, 2020, in a game against the Detroit Red Wings, but after seven games with the Stars, he was reassigned to the minors. It wasn't long, however, before he was called up again. In his first game back on February 1, he scored his first NHL goal against the New Jersey Devils. It would be the only goal he'd score during the regular season. After just a few more games with Dallas, Kiviranta was sent back to the AHL, where he continued playing in Cedar Park, Texas, until the Covid-19 pandemic halted the season.

When the NHL resumed later that summer, Kiviranta joined the Stars in the Western Conference bubble in Edmonton. Although he played a round-robin matchup and another game in the Stars' first-round series against the Calgary Flames, Kiviranta spent most of August on the sidelines. But when Kiviranta replaced Cogliano in the lineup on September 4, he became the unlikeliest playoff hero. Early in the second period, he scored his first career post-season goal to tie the game 2–2. After the Stars fell behind 4–3 in the final frame, Kiviranta scored the tying goal in the last few minutes to force overtime. Less than eight minutes into the extra frame, Kiviranta took a pass from defenceman Andrej Sekera and roofed it past Michael Hutchinson to complete the hat trick and send the Stars to the conference final. It was just the seventh Game 7 hat trick in NHL history and the first since Wayne Gretzky accomplished the feat against the Toronto Maple Leafs in 1993.

SEPTEMBER 5
BOB ESSENSA SIGNS WITH COYOTES, 1999

With Nikolai Khabibulin holding out for a better deal, the Phoenix Coyotes needed to shore up their goaltending. On September 5, 1999, they signed veteran netminder Bob Essensa to a one-year deal. Essensa was no stranger to the organization. He was originally drafted 69th overall by the Winnipeg Jets in 1983, and after playing four years at Michigan State, he made his NHL debut on February 13, 1988. After spending most of his time in the minors for the next two seasons, Essensa became a full-time NHL starter in 1990. Over the next four seasons in Winnipeg, Essensa picked up 92 wins until he was traded to the Detroit Red Wings on March 8, 1994, as part of a four-player deal. After finishing the 1993–94 campaign with the Red Wings, Essensa spent the next two seasons with the club's minor league affiliates in the AHL and IHL. By the time Essensa made his way back to the NHL in 1996 with the Edmonton Oilers, the Jets had relocated to Phoenix, where they became the Coyotes.

Following a few seasons in Edmonton as a backup, Essensa returned to where he began his NHL career. On October 11, 1999, he made his first start for the franchise in more than five years. Essensa made 22 saves in a 2–2 tie with the Buffalo Sabres. While Khabibulin and the Coyotes remained at an impasse, Essensa split the starting duties that season with Sean Burke. In the off-season, Essensa signed with the Vancouver Canucks, and following a year there, he played nine games for the Sabres before hanging up his goalie pads in 2002. Not long after retiring, Essensa joined the Boston Bruins as a goaltending coach. After spending more than a decade working with Boston's netminders, Essensa was nearly called back to the crease. On March 28, 2015, he found himself in a Bruins uniform. After Tuukka Rask left the game against the New York Rangers just 10 seconds into the second period, the 50-year-old Essensa had to gear up and serve as the backup for Niklas Svedberg, who made 16 saves and allowed two goals in relief.

SEPTEMBER 6
CANADA STUNNED IN SUMMIT SERIES, 1972

B efore the 1972 Summit Series began, one of the Soviet trainers declared that after the first three games, he believed Canada and the Soviet Union would be tied. It was a bold prediction. Many believed the eight-game exhibition tournament, which featured the top Canadian players from the NHL squaring off against the best players from the Soviet Union, would be an easy victory for Team Canada. Dick Beddoes, a *Globe and Mail* columnist, even went as far as suggesting the Canadians would finish the tournament undefeated. "If the Russians win one game, I will eat this column shredded at high noon in a bowl of borscht on the front steps of the Russian embassy," he wrote just days before the tournament began. But after the first game, Beddoes and much of the hockey world were forced to eat their words. The Soviets outplayed their opponents, controlling the game from the outset with creative passing and trouncing Canada 7–3 before a stunned crowd at the Montreal Forum. After regrouping from the defeat, the Canadians took the second game in Toronto by grinding the Russians down with the style of play they were more accustomed to in the NHL.

When the series shifted to Winnipeg for the third contest on September 6, 1972, it appeared as though the Soviet trainer might have been onto something. Although J.P. Parise opened the scoring for Canada less than two minutes into the game, the Russians knotted it up just over a minute later with a short-handed goal. Despite having a two-goal lead in the second period, Canada's defensive miscues allowed the Soviets to even the score 4–4 in the final minutes of the frame. While Canada outshot the Soviet Union for most of the game, it mustered just six shots in the final period. Had it not been for the superb play of goaltender Tony Esposito, who was only overshadowed by his counterpart Vladislav Tretiak, the Russians might have broken the deadlock. And so, after three games, the series was tied, just as the Soviet trainer had predicted.

SEPTEMBER 7
MUZZ PATRICK TAKES OVER BEHIND BENCH, 1962

Muzz Patrick would be pulling double duty for the New York Rangers. A month before the 1962–63 season began, the New York general manager announced he would be stepping behind the bench. During the off-season, Doug Harvey, just coming off his first campaign with the Blueshirts as a player-coach, resigned from his coaching duties to focus on patrolling the blue line. In the meantime, Patrick added to his portfolio. It wasn't the first time he'd coached the Rangers. Prior to becoming general manager of the team in 1955, Patrick, who had won a Stanley Cup with the club in 1940 as a player, coached the Rangers for the better part of two seasons. Even during his time as GM, Patrick had some experience behind the bench. In November 1959, the team transitioned from head coach Phil Watson, a severe taskmaster who reportedly wouldn't even let his players drink water during games, to Alf Pike, a former Rangers winger known as "The Embalmer" because he once worked as a mortician in the off-season. During Pike's tenure, Patrick filled in as coach for a pair of games.

Although Patrick wasn't the only general manager in the league serving as coach, as well, joining colleagues Sid Abel and Punch Imlach who did both jobs with the Detroit Red Wings and Toronto Maple Leafs, respectively, it proved to be challenging for the veteran executive. After 34 games, Patrick resigned from his coaching duties, citing that his role wasn't meant to be permanent and that the team had always wanted a full-time bench boss. Patrick named Red Sullivan, a fiery redhead currently serving as a player-coach with the club's AHL affiliate in Baltimore, as his replacement. Although the Rangers hoped Sullivan's arrival would turn the team's season around, the club missed the playoffs. Sullivan coached New York for two full campaigns before he was dismissed early in the 1965–66 season and replaced by Emile Francis, who had succeeded Patrick as GM a year earlier.

SEPTEMBER 8

BLACK HAWKS ACQUIRE FRANK BRIMSEK, 1949

Called up to replace an injured Tiny Thompson in 1938, goaltender Frank Brimsek had an immediate and long-lasting impact with the Boston Bruins. In his first 10 games, he recorded six shutouts and was soon known as "Mr. Zero" for his uncanny ability to keep the puck out of his net. Brimsek finished the regular season with 33 victories, including 10 shutouts, and received both the Calder and the Vezina Trophies, becoming the first goaltender in NHL history to earn both awards. Brimsek's sterling play continued in the post-season as he backstopped the Bruins to the club's first Stanley Cup in a decade. Proving that his rookie season was no fluke, Brimsek continued to be one of the league's top goaltenders, guiding the Bruins to another championship title in 1941 and winning his second Vezina a year later. After the 1942–43 season, however, Brimsek put his country ahead of hockey and joined the United States Coast Guard to support the war effort. Following the end of the Second World War, Brimsek returned to Boston. In his first season back, Brimsek guided the Bruins back to the Stanley Cup Final for the first time since he'd enlisted, but the club came up short against the Montreal Canadiens.

Despite a two-year absence, Brimsek continued to be the most valuable player on the Bruins and finished the 1947–48 season as the runner-up for the Hart Trophy. But in 1949, tragedy struck Brimsek and his family off the ice. In January, his infant son, Frank Jr., succumbed to complications from pneumonia. Brimsek was heartbroken. Although he finished the season in Boston, he requested a trade so that he could be closer to his family in Eveleth, Minnesota. On September 8, 1949, Brimsek was dealt to the Chicago Black Hawks in exchange for cash. In what would prove to be his final season, Brimsek recorded 22 victories, including five shutouts. When he hung up his goalie pads in 1950, Brimsek was the NHL's all-time leader in wins and shutouts by an American goaltender, records that stood for decades.

SEPTEMBER 9
MARIO LEMIEUX CALLED TO THE HALL, 1997

t was a call that came too early. When Mario Lemieux answered the phone on September 9, 1997, it was the Hockey Hall of Fame on the other line. It was letting the former superstar centre know it would be waiving the three-year waiting period and that he'd be inducted into hockey's pantheon of greatness in November. Lemieux was overwhelmed by the honour, joining the likes of Dit Clapper, Maurice Richard, Ted Lindsay, Red Kelly, Terry Sawchuk, Jean Béliveau, Gordie Howe, and Bobby Orr as the only players in NHL history to bypass the typical waiting period. But Lemieux, only turning 32 in less than a month, should have been getting ready for another season.

Drafted first overall by the Pittsburgh Penguins in 1984, Lemieux made an immediate impact in the NHL, scoring a goal on his first shot on his first shift in his first game. While he soon established himself as one of the greatest players ever to lace up skates, Lemieux's career was curtailed by Hodgkin's lymphoma and chronic back problems. After sitting out the 1994–95 season to recuperate from his radiation treatments, Lemieux returned and scored 69 goals and 161 points the following season, earning his fifth Art Ross and third Hart Trophies. Although he followed that up with another great performance the next year, Lemieux stunned the hockey world when he announced he'd be retiring following the 1997 playoffs. A few months after getting the call, Lemieux was officially inducted into the Hockey Hall of Fame on November 17, 1997. Two nights later, Lemieux was honoured again in Pittsburgh when the Penguins raised his number 66 jersey to the rafters at Civic Arena. While most fans thought it would be the last time they'd see Lemieux on the ice, he came out of retirement a few years later. In his first game back on December 27, 2000, Lemieux set up Jaromír Jágr just 33 seconds into the contest. Despite more than a three-year absence, Lemieux finished the season with 76 points in 43 games.

SEPTEMBER 10
DEVILS SIGN IGOR LARIONOV, 2003

gor Larionov wasn't ready to retire yet. Although he'd thought about hanging up his skates at the end of the 2002–03 season, he changed his mind after the Detroit Red Wings, the defending champions, were unceremoniously swept in the opening round of the playoffs. Larionov wanted to play one more year to have another chance to hoist the Stanley Cup. While Detroit had extended him a contract reportedly worth $1 million to return for one final season, Larionov waited all summer to see if the team would improve its offer. But after Joe Nieuwendyk left the New Jersey Devils and signed a deal with the Toronto Maple Leafs on September 9, 2003, the Devils suddenly had a hole in the middle of their lineup. Looking to address their need at centre, they signed the 42-year-old Larionov to a one-year, $1.5-million contract the very next day.

Known as "The Professor" for his cerebral play, Larionov made his NHL debut in 1989 with the Vancouver Canucks after leaving the Soviet Union. Following three seasons with that club and two more with the San Jose Sharks, Larionov was acquired by the Red Wings in 1995, where he formed the Russian Five with Slava Fetisov, Slava Kozlov, Vladimir Konstantinov, and Sergei Fedorov. After winning back-to-back titles in Detroit, Larionov left for the Florida Panthers as a free agent in 2000 but was traded back to the Red Wings not long into the 2000–01 campaign and won his third Stanley Cup in Detroit the next season. While Larionov hoped the Devils would give him an opportunity to win another championship before he hung up his skates, he soon clashed with head coach Pat Burns. Larionov's preference to hold on to the puck didn't fit with New Jersey's defensive dump-and-chase approach to the game. Although he recorded four points in his first three contests for the Devils, Larionov quickly cooled off and was in and out of the press box. On March 30, 2004, following nine consecutive games as a healthy scratch, Larionov scored his first goal of the season in what would prove to be his final NHL regular-season appearance.

SEPTEMBER 11

LEAFS AND RANGERS SQUARE OFF AT WEMBLEY, 1993

After opening the 1992–93 season with a pair of exhibition games between the Montreal Canadiens and Chicago Blackhawks in England, the NHL returned again the following year. Looking to take a page out of the National Football League's book, which had been playing its American Bowl exhibition series at Wembley Stadium in London for nearly a decade, the league hoped to grow the game in Europe. As part of another two-game series at Wembley Arena, the Toronto Maple Leafs and New York Rangers squared off in the first matchup on September 11, 1993. Although it wasn't a sold-out crowd, the players were still treated as royalty. The benches at Wembley were too short to accommodate the entire team, so the arena staff appropriated some cushioned, velvet-covered chairs for the players. Not a bad way to wait for your next shift.

Following a slow start to the game, things picked up when Mike Gartner got the Rangers on the board with a power play goal with less than eight minutes remaining in the first period. The lead, however, was short-lived. Toronto's Doug Gilmour responded 22 seconds later with a short-handed goal to knot up the score. After Wendel Clark and Esa Tikkanen scored early in the second period, the Maple Leafs and Rangers went into the final frame tied 2–2. Tikkanen struck again in less than four minutes to give New York the lead. Although Kent Manderville tied it up at the halfway mark, the Rangers took the lead for good when Sergei Nemchinov scored with just over six minutes to play. With one second remaining, Alexei Kovalev potted an empty-netter to seal a 5–3 victory for the Rangers. While more fans turned up for the second game the next day, which saw the Rangers sweep the two-game series with a 3–1 win, the exhibition didn't earn the NHL much fanfare in London. In between games, the league even had Wendel Clark and Mike Krushelnyski put on hockey demonstrations in bustling Covent Garden, but few turned out for those showcases. The league didn't schedule any games in England again until 2007.

SEPTEMBER 12

ISLANDERS SIGN RICK DIPIETRO, 2006

Rick DiPietro was set to be a New York Islander for the rest of his career. On September 12, 2006, the club signed the goaltender to a massive 15-year, $67.5-million deal, topping the record-setting 10-year pact it had made with centre Alexei Yashin five years earlier. Although DiPietro had been drafted first overall by the Islanders in 2000, at the time of the deal, he had only played two full seasons in the NHL. Despite an unproven track record, the Islanders, at the direction of owner Charles Wang, signed the goaltender to a contract that many felt would hamstring the franchise. When asked about the deal by the Canadian Press, NHL Deputy Commissioner Bill Daly simply said, "Some decisions turn out well, others not so well. Time will tell whether this will be a good decision or a bad one for the Islanders." It didn't take long for it to become one of the worst deals in league history.

Although DiPietro had a solid start to the 2006–07 season, he sustained a series of concussions toward the end of the campaign that kept him out of the lineup until the playoffs. While DiPietro would return and play 63 games the following regular season, he was soon plagued by hip and knee injuries that limited his time in the crease. By the end of the 2012–13 lockout-shortened season, DiPietro had managed to suit up for just 50 games for the Islanders over the past five years. Under the new collective bargaining agreement, teams could rid themselves of up to two onerous contracts by paying out two-thirds of their value in what were known as compliance buyouts. Before the free agency period opened on July 5, 2013, the Islanders announced they were placing DiPietro on unconditional waivers for the purpose of buying out the final eight years of his contract. While the buyout prevented DiPietro's deal from counting against the team's salary, it would pay him $1.5 million per year for the next 16 years. By the time the Islanders stop cutting DiPietro cheques, he'll be 47 years old.

SEPTEMBER 13
BLUE JACKETS SIGN ANSON CARTER, 2006

Anson Carter didn't want to leave the Vancouver Canucks. He had found a home playing on a line with Daniel and Henrik Sedin. The trio clicked during the 2005–06 campaign, with Carter scoring 33 goals, a career high, and the twins having breakout seasons. Carter, who joined the Canucks in 2005 as a free agent, was coming off a season that saw him suit up for three different NHL clubs. He figured his resurgence in Vancouver and contribution to the Sedins' career years would ensure his return. But as the off-season dragged on, Carter remained unsigned. While he was reportedly seeking a multi-year deal, it was believed that despite leading the team in goals, the Canucks had only offered him another one-year contract for slightly more money than the agreement he'd signed a year earlier.

As training camps approached, and with the Canucks unwilling to improve their offer, Carter signed a one-year, $2.5-million deal with the Columbus Blue Jackets on September 13, 2006. After playing 54 games with that team, Carter was dealt to the Carolina Hurricanes on February 23, 2007, in exchange for a draft pick in 2008. In 10 games with the Hurricanes, Carter recorded one goal. The following season, he was invited to the Edmonton Oilers' training camp but couldn't crack the roster and ended up playing 15 games in Switzerland for HC Lugano before retiring.

Since hanging up his skates and becoming an analyst, Carter, who was one of the NHL's few Black players, has had the chance to reflect on his hockey career and thinks that race played a factor, particularly in his contract negotiations. "I really believe if I was a different colour hockey player, and I'm going to say it, I really believe I would've been looked at a lot differently," he said in an interview on Sportsnet's *Hockey Central* on June 9, 2020. Given the natural chemistry Carter had with the Sedins that season, his departure from Vancouver was always curious, but in the context of his later remarks, one has to think that race might have impacted the club's decision.

SEPTEMBER 14
CANUCKS SIGN GARY LUPUL, 1979

What Gary Lupul lacked in size, he made up for in heart. A native of Powell River, British Columbia, Lupul was an undersized but feisty player. Although he was a fast skater and lit the lamp 53 times with the Victoria Cougars of the Western Hockey League in 1978–79, at five foot eight, he was diminutive by hockey standards and went undrafted to the NHL. The Vancouver Canucks, however, invited him to training camp in 1979 and offered him a contract on September 14. Lupul started the campaign with the Dallas Black Hawks of the Central Hockey League but was called up to Vancouver a few months later. He made his NHL debut on December 8, 1979, against the Detroit Red Wings and scored on his very first shot of the game. Lupul found the back of the net again in the next two games but was then held off the score sheet for the next 10 contests. He stayed with the Canucks for the rest of the season, recording nine goals and 20 points in 51 games.

Over the next five seasons in Vancouver, Lupul endeared himself to the fans and was beloved on and off the ice. While he recorded a career high 44-point season in the 1983–84 campaign, Lupul is probably best remembered for what happened in a game the following year. On October 17, 1984, the Canucks took on the Penguins in Pittsburgh, where superstar rookie Mario Lemieux was making his home debut. Just over two minutes into the game, Lupul and Lemieux dropped the gloves. It was a physical mismatch. As the much larger Lemieux connected with a series of undercut punches, Canucks goaltender John Garrett jumped into the brawl to defend Lupul. Following the altercation, Garrett was given a game misconduct for joining the fight and Richard Brodeur had to finish the game. While Lemieux might have gotten the better of Lupul, the scrappy forward had some words of advice for the rookie when speaking to reporters after the game: "If he ever takes on someone who knows how to fight, he'll get his ass kicked."

SEPTEMBER 15

HAWERCHUK TO LEMIEUX TO GRETZKY TO LEMIEUX, 1987

When Dale Hawerchuk went onto the ice for a faceoff in his own end with just over a minute remaining in the decisive game of the Canada Cup, he thought to himself, *There's no damn way in the world I'm going to lose that draw.* Two nights earlier, Hawerchuk assisted on the opening goal less than a minute into the game to give the Canadians an early lead against the Soviet Union. The Soviets took the first game in the best-of-three championship series and the Canadians were looking to even things up. Following the early goal, Canada went on to win the game 6–5 in double overtime, in what many have referred to as the greatest hockey game ever played, to force a do-or-die contest. But in the pivotal game, the Russians jumped out to an early 3–0 lead that quieted the home crowd. The Canadians, however, fought back. After Hawerchuk assisted on Brent Sutter's goal to make it 4–4, he scored in the final minutes of the second period to take the lead.

Not long after Alexander Semak tied the game with eight minutes remaining in regulation time, Hawerchuk drew his faceoff assignment. The 17,026 fans at Copps Coliseum in Hamilton were on their feet. Lining up against Soviet centre Slava Bykov, Hawerchuk won the draw. Mario Lemieux managed to pick up the loose puck while Bykov tripped over Valeri Kamensky in his pursuit. Getting the puck around Igor Kravchuk, Lemieux passed it up to Wayne Gretzky, who raced into the Soviet end with Larry Murphy. With Murphy open on the far side, Soviet defenceman Igor Stelinov slid in an attempt to block a cross-ice dish, but Gretzky passed it back to Lemieux, who fired the puck over the glove of goaltender Sergei Mylnikov to give Canada a 6–5 lead with 1:26 remaining on the clock. The Soviets were unable to muster a response, and Canada won the championship. While the game-winning drive is best remembered for Gretzky's shrewd pass to Lemieux, it wouldn't have happened without Hawerchuk winning that draw.

SEPTEMBER 16
CANADA WINS CANADA CUP AGAIN, 1991

The hockey gods don't forget. In the third period of the second game in the best-of-three championship series for the 1991 Canada Cup, the United States was on a power play against Canada. The score was knotted at two goals apiece. Having dropped the first matchup 4–1 to the Canadians two nights earlier, the Americans needed a victory to force a decisive third game. With 10 seconds remaining in the penalty, the United States tried to regroup in Canada's end for one last drive with the man advantage. Moments earlier, Brett Hull had a great opportunity with a one-timer, but it was turned away by Bill Ranford, who had once again been brilliant in net for the Canadians. As the Americans set up once more, Hull dished the puck across the ice to defenceman Gary Suter, who was on the far point. The pass landed on Suter's stick, but he had trouble corralling it before he made the next pass.

As Suter went to shovel it away, he was picked off by Steve Larmer, who raced down the ice on a short-handed breakaway and put the puck between the legs of goaltender Mike Richter to give the Canadians a 3–2 lead. Copps Coliseum erupted in a raucous celebration. Canada was less than eight minutes away from winning its third straight Canada Cup. In the final seconds of regulation time, the Americans pulled Richter for an extra attacker in a last-ditch effort to force overtime, but Dirk Graham put the puck into the empty net with 42 seconds remaining to seal the victory. Two nights earlier, before coughing up the game-winner to Larmer, Suter had nailed Wayne Gretzky from behind, sending him crashing into the boards midway through the second period in the first game of the series. Gretzky, leading the tournament in scoring with four goals and eight assists, left the ice and headed to the dressing room with back spasms. He didn't play again for the rest of the championship. Although Suter wasn't penalized for the hit, he paid the price two days later. The hockey gods don't forget.

SEPTEMBER 17

PANTHERS NAME ALEKSANDER BARKOV CAPTAIN, 2018

Derek MacKenzie always knew the day would come. When the Florida Panthers named him captain before the start of the 2016–17 season, there was an understanding that he would eventually have to relinquish the title when Aleksander Barkov was ready to embrace the role. Drafted second overall by Florida in 2013, Barkov was the future of the franchise. He was undisputedly the Panthers' best player and was well on his way to becoming one of the league's top all-round forwards. Although he was a quiet player, he led by example with his play on the ice and the extra time he spent working on his skills. While Barkov continued to develop, MacKenzie, a long-time veteran, took on the captain's duties for the Panthers. Following the 2017–18 campaign in which Barkov racked up 51 assists and 78 points, both career highs, to lead the team in scoring, he was approached about taking the next step in his leadership development with the club.

On September 17, 2018, before the start of the pre-season, the Panthers named Barkov captain. At the press conference, MacKenzie ceremoniously gave Barkov the captaincy, proudly handing him a jersey with the captain's *C* stitched onto it. Although Barkov had just turned 23 years old, making him the youngest captain in franchise history, he was ready to take on the greater responsibilities. In his first season as captain, Barkov took his game to the next level. He finished the campaign with 35 goals and 96 points, the 10th most in the NHL that year. Despite playing in nearly every situation and matching up against the toughest opponents, Barkov earned just four penalties that year and earned the Lady Byng Memorial Trophy, bestowed annually on the player who best exemplifies a combination of sportsmanship and skill. While Barkov appears to be a perennial candidate for that award as he continues to become one of the league's premier two-way forwards, it seems only a matter of time before he wins the Frank J. Selke Trophy, awarded every year to the forward who displays the most skill defensively.

SEPTEMBER 18

TEAM NORTH AMERICA PLAYS FIRST GAME, 2016

t was the most fun hockey team ever assembled. For the reincarnation of the World Cup of Hockey in 2016, the NHL assembled two new clubs for the tournament: Team Europe, a collection of players from eight different European countries, and Team North America, comprised of the most talented players aged 23 and under from Canada and the United States. While some had suggested both teams were gimmicky, Team North America was just what the league needed. With the game getting faster and more skilled, it gave the NHL the perfect opportunity to showcase its brightest young players. Led by phenom Connor McDavid, the team also featured Nathan MacKinnon, Jack Eichel, Johnny Gaudreau, and Auston Matthews, recently drafted first overall by the Toronto Maple Leafs.

Although Team North America had generated a buzz before the tournament even began, it surpassed those expectations when it played its first group stage game against Finland on September 18, 2016. Colloquially known as "The Young Guns" for its blinding combination of speed and skill, Team North America proved to be too much for the Finnish squad. After taking a 1–0 lead early in the game, the hotshot squad outshot its opponent 18–6 in the second period and added three more goals to take a 4–0 lead. Valtteri Filpulla scored Finland's lone goal late in the final frame, but it was too little, too late and North America secured a 4–1 win. The Young Guns dropped their next match to the Russians but picked up a 4–3 overtime victory against Sweden in their final qualifying game. Although they failed to qualify for the knockout stage, Team North America provided fans a glimpse into the future of the NHL. That season, Matthews made his electrifying debut with the Leafs and finished the campaign with 40 goals to win the Calder Trophy. Meanwhile, McDavid, playing in his first full season since breaking his clavicle in his rookie year, racked up 100 points to earn his first Art Ross and Hart Trophies as well as the Ted Lindsay Award.

MAPLE LEAFS ACQUIRE GRANT FUHR, 1991

F
ollowing an exhibition game against the Toronto Maple Leafs, Edmonton Oilers goaltender Grant Fuhr told reporters he didn't expect to be in Edmonton much longer. That didn't come as a surprise. Fuhr had been the subject of trade rumours ever since he returned from a 60-game suspension for substance abuse issues. In his first game back on February 18, 1991, his first contest in nearly a year, Fuhr turned away all 27 shots he faced in a 4–0 victory against the New Jersey Devils. Although it appeared as though he might be moved before the trade deadline, Fuhr wound up earning the starting job for the playoffs from head coach John Muckler and ended up backstopping the Oilers all the way to the conference final. In the off-season, however, speculation picked back up again. While Fuhr was revered in Edmonton for his role in the club's string of championships, he still had three years remaining on his deal, and with the emergence of Bill Ranford, who won the Conn Smythe Trophy when the team nabbed its fifth Stanley Cup in 1990, it seemed unlikely Fuhr would be back for another campaign with the Oilers.

Just a few days after the pre-season contest against Toronto in which Fuhr made 36 saves in a 4–4 tie, he was dealt to the Leafs. General manager Cliff Fletcher, watching from the stands that game, had wanted to add a goaltender of Fuhr's calibre for quite some time. On September 19, 1991, he acquired Fuhr, along with Glenn Anderson and Craig Berube, in exchange for Vincent Damphousse, Peter Ing, Scott Thornton, and Luke Richardson. A few weeks later, on October 3, Fuhr made his debut with the Leafs. He made 17 saves in a 4–3 loss against the Montreal Canadiens. Fuhr finished the season with 25 victories, but Toronto failed to qualify for the playoffs. The next season, Fuhr played 29 games before he was sent to the Buffalo Sabres, along with a fifth-round pick in 1995, in exchange for Dave Andreychuk, Daren Puppa, and a first-round pick in 1993.

SEPTEMBER 20
DEVILS TRADE KIRK MULLER, 1991

Dissatisfied with the way his salary negotiations were going, Kirk Muller walked out of the New Jersey Devils' training camp. Muller, who had been the club's captain since 1987 and was the franchise's all-time leading scorer, was entering the option year of a four-year deal with the Devils and was eager to sign a long-term extension to stay in New Jersey. While Muller was reportedly seeking $800,000 per season, it was believed the Devils had instead offered him a contract with a much lower annual salary and less term. Muller was disappointed. Although his production had dropped the past season when he was shifted from centre to the wing, during his tenure as captain, he recorded three straight 30-goal campaigns. But just a few days after leaving camp to hold out for a better deal, the Devils sent Muller packing.

On September 20, 1991, he was traded to the Montreal Canadiens, along with Roland Melanson, in exchange for Stéphane Richer and Tom Chorske. In his first game against his former team, Muller scored the opening goal in a 3–2 overtime victory over the Devils. Just over a month later, he signed a four-year contract extension with the Canadiens. In his first season in Montreal, Muller's production rebounded and he finished the year with 36 goals and 77 points to lead the team in both offensive categories. Meanwhile, in New Jersey, Richer, who had fallen out of favour in Montreal, found his fit with the Devils. A two-time 50-goal scorer with the Canadiens, Richer had one of the hardest shots in the league. Legend has it that during his time in New Jersey, he once fired a slapshot at Martin Brodeur during warm-up that was so hard it shattered the goaltender's jock. Richer scored 29 goals in his first season with the Devils and then recorded back-to-back 30-goal campaigns. In the end, the trade worked out well for both clubs. Muller played an integral role in Montreal's championship in 1993, and Richer scored two goals in the Stanley Cup Final in 1995 as the Devils secured their first title in franchise history.

SEPTEMBER 21

NHL SHOWCASES HOCKEY IN CHINA WITH DRAGONS, 2017

Keen to expand hockey's reach and develop a foothold in a country home to more than a billion people, the NHL announced on March 29, 2017, that it would play a pair of pre-season games between the Vancouver Canucks and Los Angeles Kings in China the following September. At the time, the NHL hadn't even committed to sending players to the 2018 Olympics in neighbouring South Korea, but the league was eager to make inroads in China before the 2022 Winter Olympics in Beijing. However, the NHL was also determined to grow the game in the country at the grassroots level. The pre-season matchups in what was being called the China Games would just be the start of what the league hoped would be a long-term relationship to develop more interest in hockey in the nation.

And so on September 21, 2017, the Kings and Canucks squared off in Shanghai, marking the first time the NHL played a game in China. As the two teams skated onto the ice at Mercedes-Benz Arena, they were joined by a golden dragon held up on poles by a group of skaters snaking its way around the playing surface in front of the crowd of 10,088 spectators. After the dragon retreated to its lair, the puck was dropped. Just over seven minutes into the game, Adrian Kempe notched the opening goal on a power play to put Los Angeles on the board. With less than five minutes remaining in the first period and the Kings on a penalty kill, Tanner Pearson picked up a loose puck in the neutral zone and raced into the Canucks' end on a breakaway to score short-handed. He added another in the final minutes of regulation time as the Kings picked up a 5–2 victory. Two nights later, they played again in Beijing, with Los Angeles sweeping the series in a 4–3 shootout victory. The following year, the NHL returned to China, with the Boston Bruins and Calgary Flames playing another set of pre-season games in Shenzhen and Beijing.

SEPTEMBER 22

SHANNON SZABADOS PLAYS IN WESTERN HOCKEY LEAGUE, 2002

Early into the third period, Tri-City Americans goaltender Tyler Weiman headed to the bench to change his stick. Forced to stay there until the next stoppage in play, 16-year-old Shannon Szabados made her way to the crease, becoming the first woman to appear in a regular-season game in the Western Hockey League (WHL). Szabados remained in the net for 20 seconds but didn't face any shots. Although the moment was fleeting, it wasn't the first time Szabados had made history in the WHL. The Americans had invited her to training camp, and after a strong showing, she cracked the roster. On September 4, 2002, she was on the bench for an exhibition game against the Vancouver Giants, becoming the first woman to suit up for a WHL game. Three days later, she got her first start, joining Manon Rhéaume and Charline Labonté as the only women to play in a Canadian major junior hockey game. Rhéaume was the first to break the barrier when she played for the Trois-Rivières Draveurs of the Quebec Major Junior Hockey League (QMJHL) during the 1991–92 season, and Labonté played 26 games with the QMJHL's Acadie-Bathurst Titan a few years earlier.

In her Tri-City debut, Szabados made 28 saves in a 6–4 victory against the Spokane Chiefs. Following her strong showing at camp and in the pre-season, Szabados stayed with the team for the opening of the 2002–03 campaign. But just over a week after making her regular-season cameo, she was assigned to the Sherwood Park Crusaders of the Alberta Junior Hockey League. The Americans felt it was the best move to further her development and keep her on the team's 50-player protected list. Szabados had signed with the Crusaders a year earlier, becoming the first girl in the province to make the junior league. In her first game with Sherwood Park on October 2, 2002, Szabados stopped all 13 shots she faced in an 8–0 victory against the Bonnyville Pontiacs. That contest also featured another female goaltender, Maghan Grahn, who took over midway through the second period after the Pontiacs fell behind 4–0.

SEPTEMBER 23
STEVE STAMKOS RETURNS, 2020

I t had been nearly seven months since Steve Stamkos played his last NHL game. A few days after appearing in the Tampa Bay Lightning's game against the Toronto Maple Leafs on February 25, 2020, the Lightning captain underwent surgery to repair a core muscle. As Stamkos recuperated from the procedure, the NHL season was halted due to Covid-19. During the summer waiting for hockey to return, he aggravated the injury working out. Although he wasn't ready to play when the playoffs began in August, Stamkos hunkered down with the team in the Eastern Conference bubble in Toronto with the hope he'd be able to suit up in the post-season. But as Tampa Bay knocked off opponent after opponent, Stamkos still hadn't returned to the lineup. With the Lightning inching ever closer to the Stanley Cup, it was hard not to feel for Stamkos.

Over the past few years, his team had seemed poised to win a championship, but Stamkos couldn't catch a break. In 2015, he led the Lightning to the Stanley Cup Final, but the club came up short against the Chicago Blackhawks. The following year, after missing most of the playoffs following surgery to remove a blood clot, Stamkos returned for Game 7 of the Eastern Conference Final against the Pittsburgh Penguins, but Tampa lost 2–1. A few years later, after winning a record-tying 62 games, the Lightning were the odds-on favourite to win the Cup but were unceremoniously swept in the first round by the Columbus Blue Jackets. And now, with the Lightning back in the final, it seemed as if the team would actually pull it off this time, but Stamkos was stuck on the sidelines. However, on September 23, 2020, he returned for Game 3. In just his third shift back, he broke into the Dallas Stars' zone and fired the puck into the far-side top corner of the net to give the Lightning a 2–0 lead. You couldn't have scripted a better return. Although Stamkos didn't play again after the first period, he left a lasting impression. Five days later, he finally got the chance to hoist the Cup.

SEPTEMBER 24
SABRES ACQUIRE JASON WOOLLEY, 1997

As an assistant coach in Florida, Lindy Ruff had seen what Jason Woolley could bring to the Panthers' defence corps. Following the club's run to the Stanley Cup Final in 1996, however, Woolley was dealt to the Pittsburgh Penguins, along with Stu Barnes, in exchange for Chris Wells. After Woolley finished the 1996–97 in Pittsburgh, recording 36 points in 57 games, he became a restricted free agent. By September, he still hadn't reached a deal with the team and didn't attend the Penguins' training camp. Meanwhile, Ruff, named the Buffalo Sabres' head coach just a few months earlier, advocated for Woolley. Although the defenceman was often regarded more for his play in the offensive zone than in his own end, Ruff knew there was more to his game and thought he'd be a great fit.

On September 24, 1997, heeding the advice of their coach, the Sabres agreed to terms with Woolley and acquired him from the Penguins in exchange for a fifth-round pick in 1998. He made his Sabres debut a week later when the club opened the season on the road against the St. Louis Blues. In his first season in Buffalo, Woolley scored nine goals, a career high, and 35 points, the second most among Sabres defencemen. The next year, Woolley took his game up a notch. After racking up 43 points in the regular season, he was integral to the club's deep playoff run. By the time the Sabres made it to the Stanley Cup Final, Woolley was the team's leading scorer. In the opening game of the series against the Dallas Stars, he scored one of the biggest goals in franchise history. With less than five minutes remaining in the first overtime period, Woolley fired the puck past goaltender Ed Belfour to give Buffalo its first victory in a Stanley Cup Final game in more than two decades. On the broadcast, the Sabres' colourful play-by-play announcer Rick Jeanneret referred to it as "the shot heard round the world." Woolley picked up one more point that series, but the Sabres couldn't overcome the Stars.

SEPTEMBER 25
GEORGE MCPHEE PUNCHES LORNE MOLLEKEN, 1999

George McPhee was incensed. Following a penalty-filled exhibition game in Columbus, the Washington Capitals' general manager stormed down to the Chicago Blackhawks' dressing room to talk to coach Lorne Molleken. Although Washington won the game 3–1, McPhee was upset with Chicago's tactics. A few days before the contest, McPhee had reportedly called up his colleague, Bob Murray, the Blackhawks' GM, and told him to bring his most talented players and leave the tough guys behind. The league was looking to market the game to Columbus, where the Blue Jackets would be hitting the ice next year for their inaugural season, and McPhee wanted to ensure they showcased their top talent. But it seemed Murray never got the memo. When they squared off on September 25, 1999, the Blackhawks had Bob Probert, Dave Manson, and Reid Simpson in the lineup, the type of players McPhee was hoping would stay in Chicago. Things played out exactly as McPhee anticipated. After Manson was tossed from the game for attempting to injure Steve Konowalchuk in the second period, the two teams ended up combining for 113 penalty minutes. Following the game, Washington head coach Ron Wilson told the media that Chicago "didn't come here to play hockey."

When McPhee confronted Molleken, tempers boiled over. He grabbed the Blackhawks' bench boss and punched him in the face. As the players came to the defence of their coach, a skirmish ensued just outside the dressing room. When it was finally broken up by police and security guards, McPhee emerged from the brawl with a cut on his face and had one of the sleeves torn from his suit jacket. Following the altercation, McPhee faced disciplinary action from the league. After an investigation, he was suspended from his duties with the Capitals for one month and fined $20,000. While he supposedly wanted to set a good example for Columbus, McPhee ended up becoming arguably the first GM in NHL history to be suspended for fighting.

NORMAND LÉVEILLÉ RETURNS TO BOSTON FOR FAREWELL, 1995

Normand Léveillé had a promising career with the Boston Bruins. After the Montreal native racked up 55 goals and 101 points with the Chicoutimi Saguenéens of the Quebec Major Junior Hockey League in the 1980–81 season, he was taken 14th overall by Boston in the NHL Entry Draft. He made his debut with the Bruins the next year, scoring 14 goals and 33 points. But early into his second NHL campaign, Léveillé was fighting for his life. During the first period in a game against the Vancouver Canucks on October 23, 1982, Léveillé took a hit from Marc Crawford but continued playing. As the frame drew to a close, Bruins assistant coach Jean Ratelle was concerned that something was wrong with Léveillé and summoned the Canucks' team doctor, Ross Davidson. After Dr. Davidson examined Léveillé during intermission, he was rushed to Vancouver General Hospital, where further testing and a CT scan revealed that the 19-year-old winger had suffered an acute intracerebral hemorrhage as a result of an undiagnosed congenital condition. To relieve the pressure and stop the bleeding in his brain, he underwent emergency surgery that left him in critical condition. Léveillé spent the next month in a coma before he was transferred home to Montreal, where he began his lengthy recovery process. While he was initially confined to a wheelchair and couldn't speak, Léveillé eventually learned to walk again and regained some of his speech, but the right side of his body remained paralyzed.

Although Léveillé was never able to play hockey again, he did return to the ice. On September 26, 1995, when the Bruins played their final game at Boston Garden, a pre-season matchup against the Montreal Canadiens, Léveillé was invited to be part of the closing ceremonies. Putting on skates for the first time in more than a decade, Léveillé stepped onto the ice with his cane and received a heartwarming ovation from the crowd. With some help from captain Ray Bourque, his former teammate, Léveillé went for one last skate at the Garden.

SEPTEMBER 27
KEN KLEE SIGNS WITH MAPLE LEAFS, 2003

As another NHL season approached, blueliner Ken Klee was sitting in his house in Morrison, Colorado, waiting for the phone to ring. The stay-at-home defenceman had spent the last nine seasons with the Washington Capitals but became an unrestricted free agent in the off-season. Although Klee was coming off another solid campaign in Washington, where he was a team-leading plus 22, he was still without a contract. While Klee had drawn significant interest from several teams, including the Toronto Maple Leafs, he was holding out for a multi-year pact. As training camp neared in September, Klee and the Leafs were supposedly close to an agreement, but talks broke down when he refused to uproot his family for a one-year contract. While Klee was adamant about not settling for a short-term deal, he still expressed interest in going to Toronto and was optimistic the club and he could come to terms. He even went as far as saying he was sitting on a contract offer from another team but hoped he could make a deal with the Leafs instead.

Still without a job at the end of September, Klee acquiesced. On September 27, 2003, he signed a one-year pact with Toronto. Although he missed 16 games in the 2003–04 campaign due to abdominal and shoulder injuries, Klee proved to be a workhorse for the Leafs. The hard-nosed defenceman played the fourth most minutes on the team that year and even racked up 25 assists, a career high. Following his promising year with the Leafs, Klee didn't have to wait long for his next contract. On June 18, 2004, he signed a two-year extension to stay in Toronto, finally getting the multi-year deal he was looking for. The 2004–05 lockout, however, interfered with those plans. When the NHL resumed in 2005, Klee played 56 more games with the Leafs before he was traded to the New Jersey Devils in exchange for Aleksander Suglobov. In the off-season, Klee then signed a one-year contract with the Colorado Avalanche.

SEPTEMBER 28
SUMMIT SERIES ENDS, 1972

The nation was at a standstill. On the afternoon of September 28, 1972, Canada and the Soviet Union squared off in the eighth and decisive contest of the Summit Series. Everyone was engrossed and practically dropped what they were doing to tune in. Although the games were aired in the afternoon because of the time difference, the outcome of the series took priority over just about everything else. It wasn't simply another game. It was a battle for hockey supremacy and the collision of two competing political ideologies at the height of the Cold War. Canada was transfixed.

In British Columbia, Premier Dave Barrett raced to the legislature press gallery as soon as the morning cabinet meeting concluded so he could watch the final period of the contest. At schools across Canada, classes were interrupted for the broadcast of the final four games in Russia. My father distinctly remembers that at his high school in Levack, Ontario, the hometown of future Los Angeles Kings legend Dave Taylor, televisions were set up in the cafeteria and library, something many students across the country could attest to. There are even stories of how students refused to leave school at dismissal because the game was still going on. Instead of catching their buses home, they huddled around the TVs in their classrooms to finish watching the game.

In Stratford, Ontario, classical actor William Hutt was onstage as part of a production of *King Lear*. As he looked into the audience, filled largely with high school students, he got the distinct impression they were preoccupied with the match. As he finished one of his scenes, he proclaimed that Canada had triumphed over the Soviets. The crowd erupted into a raucous ovation. Hutt later told the Canadian Broadcasting Corporation that he'd never heard such loud applause before. With 34 seconds remaining in regulation time, Paul Henderson scored his third straight game-winning goal to take the series. In that moment, it felt as if the entire nation was on its feet.

SEPTEMBER 29
CANADA WINS WORLD CUP OF HOCKEY, 2016

watched the first game of the best-of-three 2016 World Cup of Hockey between Canada and Team Europe, a contingent of NHL players representing eight different European countries, but all I can say is that Canada won. Earlier that day, my wife, Chantal, found out she was going to be induced the next day to give birth to our first daughter. She wasn't supposed to be due for another two weeks, so, needless to say, our minds were preoccupied with that. After the game finished, we went to bed but didn't expect to get much sleep that night. Of course, as it turned out, I fell asleep while Chantal barely caught a wink. When we woke up the next morning, we headed to the hospital, where my daughter, Zoe, was born early the following morning on September 29, 2016. It was the best day of our lives and we were so happy.

Although we were eager to head home with our new bundle of joy, we had to stay in the hospital for the next 24 hours. By that evening, I was running on a few hours of sleep and hockey was the farthest thing from my mind. But as I walked by the family lounge, I noticed the TV was on and playing the second game of the World Cup of Hockey Final. I remember thinking that wouldn't it be great if I brought Zoe in there so we could watch our first hockey game together. It seemed like such a nice idea until I remembered that you weren't allowed to leave the room with your baby. The last thing I needed on my first night as a father was a hospital alarm to blare because a baby was missing from the maternity ward. So, using my better judgment, I left Zoe in her bassinet and snuck out occasionally to catch peeks at the game. I thought maybe she and I could watch the final game of the series at home, but Brad Marchand scored the game-winning goal with 44 seconds remaining in regulation to clinch the championship for Canada.

SEPTEMBER 30

COYOTES CLAIM PAUL BISSONNETTE OFF WAIVERS, 2009

They say timing is everything. After the Pittsburgh Penguins selected Paul Bissonnette in the fourth round of the star-studded 2003 NHL Entry Draft as a defenceman, he soon found himself mired in the minors after getting off on the wrong foot with the team brass. Working his way back to the AHL from the East Coast Hockey League, two rungs below the NHL, in the 2007–08 season, Bissonnette was shifted from patrolling the blue line to serving as an enforcer on the left wing. Embracing the pugilistic role, Bissonnette found a new lease on life with the franchise. The following year, he made the Penguins roster out of camp and suited up for 15 NHL games that season but spent most of the campaign with Wilkes-Barre/Scranton, Pittsburgh's AHL affiliate, where he established a club record by collecting a fighting major in seven consecutive games. After the Penguins won the Stanley Cup in 2009, however, Bissonnette knew it would be difficult to crack the reigning champions' roster and figured he'd be sent to the minors to await a call-up.

But after the club put him on waivers in advance of the 2009–10 season, GM Ray Shero informed him that three teams, the Minnesota Wild, Toronto Maple Leafs, and Phoenix Coyotes, had put in claims for him. Bissonnette never thought he'd be picked up, but to his surprise on September 30, 2009, the Coyotes plucked him from the wire. As Bissonnette later told me, going to the desert changed his career. "I landed in the perfect place at the perfect time. I had an instant connection with the team and probably spent more time in the NHL than I should have, and I think it was just because of that right situation," he recounted. In Phoenix, Bissonnette's hard-nosed play quickly endeared him to the Coyotes' faithful, and he became a fan favourite for the next six seasons. Off the ice, he also garnered attention for his Twitter presence, which he later leveraged to launch himself into a career in hockey media after he hung up his skates.

OCTOBER 1
OILERS RE-SIGN MARTY MCSORLEY, 1998

With the 1998–99 season approaching, Edmonton Oilers general manager Glen Sather was still tinkering with his roster and wanted to add some muscle to his lineup. On October 1, 1998, he signed Marty McSorley to a one-year, $1-million deal. Although McSorley was 35 years old and heading into his 16th NHL campaign, he was still regarded as one of the league's more formidable enforcers. He might not have been the same player who patrolled the ice for the Oilers in the 1980s and protected Wayne Gretzky, but McSorley still provided the team with a heavyweight punch. Playing in a limited role, he suited up for 46 games that season and finished with just five points and 101 penalty minutes. While the veteran rearguard was looking to play one more year, when the 1999–2000 season commenced, he was still unsigned. By November, there was speculation that he was going to journey across the Atlantic to play for the London Knights in Britain's elite hockey league, where his brother, Chris, was the coach.

Just when it seemed he might be heading overseas, McSorley signed a contract with the Boston Bruins on December 7, 1999. Looking back, McSorley probably should have just gone to England instead. On February 21, 2000, in a game against the Vancouver Canucks, McSorley and fellow enforcer Donald Brashear squared off in the first period. Late in the game, with the Canucks leading, McSorley challenged Brashear to a rematch, but when he refused, McSorley attacked him. With less than three seconds remaining in the contest, McSorley viciously slashed him across the right side of his head. Brashear fell backward and hit his head on the ice, popping his helmet off. After the incident, McSorley was suspended indefinitely and charged with assault with a weapon. Following a trial, on October 6, 2000, Vancouver provincial court judge Bill Kitchen found McSorley guilty and sentenced him to a conditional discharge. McSorley's NHL suspension ended on February 21, 2001, but he, rightly, never played another game in the league.

OCTOBER 2
KEVIN WEEKES GETS FIRST WIN, 1999

Goaltender Kevin Weekes had been waiting a long time to notch his first NHL victory. After making his first career start with the Florida Panthers on October 23, 1997, Weekes started six more times that season but went winless in all of his outings. He began the following campaign in the minors with Florida's IHL affiliate, the Detroit Vipers, before he was dealt to the Vancouver Canucks as part of the blockbuster trade for Pavel Bure. Weekes made his first start for Vancouver on March 3, 1999, but allowed four goals in a 4–3 loss to the San Jose Sharks. He made seven more starts to close out the regular season but lost each of those contests. His first career win remained elusive. When the Canucks opened the 1999–2000 season, their 30th in the league, starter Garth Snow was out with a groin injury, so Weekes got the nod. Making his 16th career start, Weekes turned aside 32 shots in a 2–1 victory against the New York Rangers, finally picking up his first NHL win.

Following the game, Weekes beamed in the dressing room as he fielded questions from reporters. He knew he'd never have to answer another question about when he'd get his first win. Although he was happy to get the first victory under his belt, Weekes didn't want to make a big deal out of it: "You always need a starting point and you need all kinds of experiences to grow. But it's our first win of the season and not the Stanley Cup." Four nights later, with Snow still unavailable to play, Weekes picked up his second straight win as the Canucks defeated the Chicago Blackhawks 5–4. Weekes recorded four more triumphs with Vancouver before he was traded to the New York Islanders, along with Dave Scatchard and Bill Muckalt, in exchange for goaltender Felix Potvin and two draft picks on December 19, 1999. In his first game on Long Island four days later, Weekes made 36 saves in a 4–2 win over the Rangers.

OCTOBER 3
PENGUINS CLAIM CHRIS THORBURN, 2006

The Pittsburgh Penguins had their eye on Chris Thorburn. Even prior to squaring off against the Buffalo Sabres in a few exhibition games before the 2006–07 season began, the hard-nosed winger had been on their radar. Drafted 50th overall by Buffalo in the 2001 NHL Entry Draft, Thorburn had spent the past three seasons with the club's AHL affiliate, the Rochester Americans. Growing up in Sault Ste. Marie, Ontario, a steel mill town on the St. Marys River, Thorburn brought that same kind of blue-collar spirit to the ice. Although he had developed a reputation as a player who wasn't afraid to drop the gloves, Thorburn had some skill.

In the 2005–06 campaign with the Americans, he scored 23 goals, the most he'd notched in a single season since playing bantam in the Soo. While he might have been coming off an exceptional year offensively, the Penguins coveted him because of the physical presence he brought to the lineup. They knew he was battling Jiří Novotný and Dan Paille for the final two spots on Buffalo's opening-night roster, and after watching him close up in the pre-season, were ready to put a claim in for him if he was reassigned to Rochester.

Sure enough, on October 3, 2006, a day after the Sabres sent him to the minors, the Penguins picked him up on waivers. Although Thorburn was primarily used in Pittsburgh in a checking role, head coach Michel Therrien gave him a few opportunities to earn additional ice time. On November 6, 2006, in a game against the Anaheim Ducks, Thorburn skated on the top line with Sidney Crosby and Evgeni Malkin. After picking up an assist on a tying-goal in the opening period, later that frame, Thorburn scored his first career NHL goal with helpers from the two Penguins superstars. Despite his offensive outburst, Thorburn spent the rest of the season relegated to the fourth line and was in and out of the press box. The next year, however, after he was traded to the Atlanta Thrashers, Thorburn established himself as an NHL regular.

OCTOBER 4

BRUINS RETIRE RAY BOURQUE'S JERSEY, 2001

After finishing his career with the Colorado Avalanche and winning a Stanley Cup, Ray Bourque returned to Boston for a fitting tribute. On October 4, 2001, the Bruins raised his number 77 jersey to the top of FleetCenter (now TD Garden). Bourque had played two decades in Boston and held franchise records in games played, assists, and points. After finally getting his hands on Lord Stanley's mug with the Avalanche just a few months earlier, Bourque hung up his skates. As he stepped back onto the ice in Boston, he received a thunderous ovation from the Bruins' faithful. Following an impassioned speech to the sold-out crowd, Bourque and his family grabbed a rope and carefully raised his number 77 to the rafters, where it joined the digits of legends such as Milt Schmidt, Bobby Orr, Johnny Bucyk, and Phil Esposito, who all proudly looked on in person during the ceremony.

Although Bourque was just in his rookie year when Bucyk's jersey was retired on March 13, 1980, he had a starring role when the team bestowed the honour on Esposito seven years later. By then, Bourque had established himself as one of the league's top defencemen and had been wearing number 7, the same number Esposito wore during his time with the Bruins, since breaking into the league in 1979. While Esposito said that it wasn't necessary for Bourque to relinquish the number, the Bruins' captain had something up his sleeve. On December 3, 1987, when Bourque skated onto the ice at Boston Garden to present Esposito with his sweater, he pulled his own jersey up and over his head, revealing another one underneath. As Esposito looked on, Bourque revealed that he would, in fact, be switching to number 77 out of admiration and respect for the Bruins Hall of Famer. It came as a surprise to Esposito, and the sentiment wasn't lost on him. As the two embraced, the crowd roared with approval. Bourque would sport number 77 for the rest of his tenure in Boston until it, too, was ceremoniously retired by the club.

MATT DUMBA MAKES NHL DEBUT, 2013

Matt Dumba almost made the NHL as an 18-year-old. No easy task for any player, let alone a defenceman. Dumba, a mobile blueliner with a booming shot, was taken seventh overall by the Minnesota Wild in the 2012 draft. Although he made Minnesota's roster out of training camp following the 2012–13 lockout, he didn't suit up for any games, and a week later was sent back to junior hockey. The following season, however, Dumba returned to Minnesota and made the opening-night lineup. But this time he stuck around. On October 5, 2013, Dumba made his long-awaited Wild debut. He played just over 10 minutes in a 4–3 overtime loss to the Anaheim Ducks, but a week later he scored his first career NHL goal in a 5–1 victory against the Dallas Stars. While Dumba was eventually loaned to Team Canada for the World Junior Championship that year and finished the rest of the campaign back in junior hockey with the Portland Winterhawks, he had proven he could play at the NHL level.

In the ensuing years as Dumba became a key part of Minnesota's back end, he also established himself as a leader off the ice. Following the death of George Floyd, a Black man killed while in police custody in Minneapolis, Dumba, a Filipino Canadian, helped found the Hockey Diversity Alliance, formed to eradicate systemic racism and intolerance in hockey. As the fight against racial injustice continued throughout the summer, Dumba brought the struggle to the ice. Before the puck was dropped for a game between the Edmonton Oilers and Chicago Blackhawks on August 1, 2020, Dumba stood at centre ice and delivered an impassioned speech. "Racism is everywhere, and we need to fight against it," he said. "Hockey is a great game, but it could be a whole lot greater, and it starts with us." Following his address, Dumba knelt for the U.S. national anthem while Malcolm Subban and Darnell Nurse, two of the league's few Black players, put their hands on his shoulders in a show of solidarity.

OCTOBER 6

KINGS DRAFT QUINTON BYFIELD SECOND OVERALL, 2020

Huddled with his family in his home in Newmarket, Ontario, Quinton Byfield sported a dapper white suit jacket and bowtie. Ever since he could remember having to dress up to go to the rink for hockey games, Byfield has worn a bowtie. He didn't like the feel of neckties, so he adopted the bowtie for comfort but also to stand out. Even without the bowtie, Byfield didn't have a hard time standing out. When I saw him play his first game for the Sudbury Wolves of the Ontario Hockey League, I was blown away. Sudbury hadn't had a player like Byfield in a long time, perhaps forever. He is just such a dynamic and talented player. Every time he's on the ice, you gravitate toward what he's doing. Simply put, he leaves a lasting impression on you.

As he developed into one of the most highly touted prospects in hockey, the bowtie has stayed with him. So when it came time to pick something to wear for the biggest night of his young career, there wasn't much to think about. Byfield was going to be wearing a bowtie. On October 6, 2020, Byfield and his family were brimming with anticipation to find out which NHL team was going to select the strapping centre in the NHL Entry Draft. The event should have been held months earlier at the Bell Centre in Montreal, but after the Covid-19 pandemic halted the hockey season, the draft was pushed back and held virtually in the fall following the conclusion of the Stanley Cup Playoffs. After the New York Rangers took Alexis Lafrenière with the top pick, the Los Angeles Kings were on the clock next. From Los Angeles, Rob Blake, the Kings' general manager, who was selected by the club 70th overall in 1988, announced that the team was taking Byfield second overall, making him the highest-drafted Black player in NHL history. As confetti floated to the floor in his family's home, Byfield traded in his blazer for a black-and-silver jersey. Quinton had just become a King.

CHRIS KONTOS SCORES FOUR GOALS IN LIGHTNING DEBUT, 1992

When left winger Chris Kontos signed with the expansion Tampa Bay Lightning in the 1992 off-season, he knew it was his last kick at the can in the league. Drafted 15th overall by the New York Rangers in 1982, Kontos had spent the past decade bouncing between the NHL and the minors. When he agreed to terms with the Lightning, he actually hadn't played in the league for more than two years. After playing six games for the Kings at the tail end of the 1989–90 campaign, Kontos spent the next season in the International Hockey League. The following season, he joined the Canadian national team but was cut from the squad before the 1992 Winter Olympics in Albertville, France. Although the upstart Lightning needed some veteran experience in their inaugural season, the 28-year-old journeyman wasn't even expected to make the team. Heading into training camp, he had already been pencilled in for a spot on Tampa's farm team in Atlanta, but after impressing general manager Phil Esposito with a strong showing at camp, Kontos made the opening-night roster.

When the Lightning headed onto the ice at the Florida State Fairground's Expo Hall to take on the Chicago Blackhawks on October 7, 1992, Kontos was in the starting lineup. Less than five minutes into the game, he scored the first goal in team history. Fifty-eight seconds later he did it again. After the first period, the Lightning were up 5–1, but Kontos wasn't done just yet. He notched two more goals in the middle frame as the team cruised to a 7–3 victory. Kontos had never scored more than eight goals in a single NHL season, and yet he potted four in Tampa Bay's first game, establishing a club record that still stands as of the end of the 2020–21 season. He added 23 more goals that season and finished with 27 goals and 51 points. Although he established career highs in both categories by significant margins, he never played another game in the NHL.

OCTOBER 8
GORDIE HOWE SIGNS WITH RED WINGS, 1946

When Gordie Howe signed his first contract with the Detroit Red Wings, all he wanted was a team jacket. After attending Detroit's training camp in 1944, Howe was sent to the club's junior hockey affiliate in Galt, Ontario. Before leaving, he asked Red Wings coach and general manager Jack Adams for a team jacket because he wanted to feel like part of the organization. Adams told him he'd get him one. Although Howe wasn't able to play any regular-season games for Galt because he couldn't arrange a transfer from Saskatchewan to the Ontario Hockey Association, he stuck around and practised with the team all season instead of returning home to Saskatoon. But by the time the campaign finished, Howe still hadn't received a jacket.

When he returned to Windsor the following year for another Red Wings training camp, Howe was still thinking about the jacket. After a strong showing at camp, he signed a professional contract that sent him to Nebraska to play in the U.S. Hockey League. But before heading for Omaha, Howe reminded Adams about the jacket. While Adams told him once again he'd get him one, Howe was still empty-handed at the end of the 1945–46 season. After his next training camp with Detroit, Howe was ready to take the next step in his career. On October 8, 1946, he signed an NHL contract with the Red Wings. Although Howe didn't press Adams on the terms of the deal, he recounted in his autobiography *Mr. Hockey* that he was adamant that the GM had to deliver on the jacket. This time, however, Adams came through. After Howe put pen to paper, Adams sent him to a store in downtown Detroit so he could finally pick up his coat. Putting on the jacket, Howe truly felt he was a member of the Red Wings. Even as he came to personify the franchise over the next decades, Howe held on to that jacket tightly. When the Red Wings gave him a new one for his 80th birthday in 2008, he said he'd kept the original and that it still fitted.

OCTOBER 9
ARIANA GRANDE GETS HIT BY PUCK, 1998

Ariana Grande rarely missed a Florida Panthers home game. Ever since she was two years old, the Boca Raton native had been going to matchups with her parents, Ed and Joan. During a January game in the 1997–98 season, four-year-old Grande was taking in the action when Florida defenceman Gord Murphy ripped a shot that deflected off the glass. There was no "safety net" and the puck struck her in the right wrist. Although she was shaken up by the incident, she would "be alright." Following the game, when Murphy learned he'd hit the tiny fan, he and other Panthers gave her some of their equipment as a "sweetener." The next season when the Panthers took on the Tampa Bay Lightning in their first game at their new arena in Sunrise on October 9, 1998, Grande was in attendance. At some point during the first period, Grande, who had just turned five a few months earlier, was hit by a puck again.

"Imagine" the odds. There was no way to explain it. It was "obvious" it was "just like magic." But this time the puck had changed "positions" and smacked her in the left wrist. Her parents rushed her to a first-aid station that was "right there." The medics held out her arm and examined it from "side to side," but it was only bruised. After she had "no tears left to cry," she was sent back to her seat with an ice pack to ease the swelling. Although she might have been "better off" to leave, she stayed for the rest of the game. During the first intermission, her parents bought her a Zamboni ride at an auction to make up for the "problem." Although her wrist was a little sore, she proudly waved to the fans as she made her way across the ice. A few years later, Grande returned to the arena "one last time," but she wasn't there to watch a hockey game; she was singing the national anthem. It turns out she was quite the singer and grew up to become one of the most "successful" pop artists on the planet. "Thank u, next."

OCTOBER 10

DANNY GARE SCORES FIRST GOAL, 1974

D anny Gare wasted no time in his NHL debut. On October 10, 1974, 18 seconds into his first game with the Buffalo Sabres, he scored his first goal. It was the second-fastest goal by a rookie in league history, a few seconds off the record held by Gus Bodnar, who had scored 15 seconds into his first game with the Toronto Maple Leafs on October 30, 1943. After etching his name in the record book with his tally, Gare added an assist in the second period as the Sabres went on to defeat the Boston Bruins 9–5. Gare's quick goal was no fluke. Finding a home on the right side of Buffalo's second line with Craig Ramsay and Don Luce, he finished the regular season with 31 goals and 62 points. Although he qualified as a finalist for the Calder Trophy as the league's top rookie, he lost to Atlanta's Eric Vail, who potted 39 goals with the Flames. During the playoffs, Gare recorded seven goals to lead the team in goal scoring, along with star Rick Martin, as the Sabres advanced to the Stanley Cup Final for the first time in franchise history.

The following season, after scoring in the Sabres' home opener against the Detroit Red Wings, he began racking up goals. Despite not getting much time on the power play, Gare still found ways to find the back of the net. Following a game against the California Seals on November 28, 1975, in which he recorded a pair of goals, Gare was atop the league in goals with 18 in his first 22 games of the campaign. Heading into the last game of the regular season, he was sitting at 47 goals but managed to notch a hat trick against the Maple Leafs on April 4, 1976, to hit the 50-goal mark, becoming just the second player in Sabres history to reach that milestone. Although Gare was sidelined for most of the 1976–77 campaign due to recurring back problems from an injury, he reached the 50-goal mark again with Buffalo a few years later, racking up 56 in 1979–80.

OCTOBER 11

GORDIE HOWE RETURNS TO NHL, 1979

Gordie Howe hadn't lost his passion for hockey. Although he was 51 years old and heading into his 33rd professional season, he still had a desire to lace them up. After initially hanging up his skates in 1971 and taking a front-office job with the Detroit Red Wings, Howe was lured out of retirement a couple of years later by the prospect of playing with his sons, Mark and Marty, for the Houston Aeros of the upstart WHA. Although he hadn't played for two years, Howe felt reinvigorated to be on the ice again with his sons. In his first season in Houston, he scored 31 goals and 69 assists and earned the Gary L. Davidson Award as the WHA's most valuable player. Howe stayed with the Aeros for four seasons, including back-to-back championships, before he and his sons packed their bags for New England in 1977. After playing two seasons for the Whalers, Howe found himself back in the NHL. In 1979, four of the WHA's teams — the Whalers, Winnipeg Jets, Edmonton Oilers, and Quebec Nordiques — were part of a merger with the NHL.

Although Howe had nothing left to prove, he came back for the club's inaugural season in the NHL. When his newly renamed Hartford Whalers were in Minnesota to open the 1979–80 season, following practice, Howe was asked what made him want to return for another season at his age. "I'll tell you when I decided to play this season," he told John Gilbert, a staff writer for Minneapolis's *Star Tribune*. "My dad, who is 86, was being interviewed on television in Edmonton. The guy interviewing him asked, 'At what age does a man lose his sexual desires? My dad said, 'You'll have to ask someone older than me.'" While Howe was the oldest player in the league by a significant margin, it didn't feel that way to him. He just loved the game. Although Howe didn't get on the score sheet in his first NHL game in more than eight years, he played every game that season and finished the campaign with 41 points as a 52-year-old.

OCTOBER 12
DON MURDOCH SCORES FIVE GOALS, 1976

D
on Murdoch scored 88 goals during his final season in junior hockey but never scored more than four in a single game. But the next year, after graduating to the NHL on October 12, 1976, Murdoch scored five goals against the Minnesota North Stars, matching a record for most goals in a game by a rookie. Although it was just his fourth game with the New York Rangers, Murdoch had already done well against Minnesota. He had made his NHL debut less than a week earlier against the North Stars, putting two goals past netminder Gary Smith. After picking up a goal in his second game against the Cleveland Barons, Murdoch, nicknamed "Murder" because he was so lethal on the ice, squared off against Smith and the North Stars again a few nights later in his fourth contest. The Rangers went into the second period up 4–2 when Murdoch scored to extend the lead just before the halfway mark of the middle frame. The North Stars scored a pair of goals to close the gap, but Murdoch potted another one to make it 6–4. And with 10 seconds remaining in the period, the Rangers rookie found the back of the net once more to complete the hat trick, his first in the NHL.

After Rod Gilbert made it 8–4 more than midway through the final period, Murdoch scored his fourth and fifth goals in the last three minutes to lead the Rangers to a 10–4 victory. Although it was his only hat trick that season, he scored two more goals on Smith on December 4 in another lopsided affair. At the end of the season, Smith told Murdoch he owed him a new suit because of all the goals he'd scored on him that year. Although Murdoch's pace cooled, he picked up 32 goals that season but probably would have had more if he hadn't injured his left ankle in practice on February 16, 1977. He finished runner-up for the Calder Trophy to the Atlanta Flames' Willi Plett, who had the same number of points but one more goal.

OCTOBER 13

DARREN HAYDAR SCORES FIRST AND ONLY NHL GOAL, 2007

D arren Haydar might only have one NHL goal to his name, but he was one of the best AHL players of all time. Drafted 248th overall by the Nashville Predators in 1999, Haydar turned pro with the Milwaukee Admirals, Nashville's AHL affiliate, in 2002–03. Although he was called up to the Predators for two games early in the campaign, Haydar spent the rest of the season in Milwaukee, recording 75 points in 75 games to earn the Dudley (Red) Garrett Memorial Award as the league's most outstanding rookie. The following year, after notching 59 points in the regular season, Haydar led the playoffs in scoring to guide the Admirals to a Calder Cup in 2004. After returning to the Calder Cup Final two years later, Haydar signed with the Atlanta Thrashers in the off-season but found himself back in the minors with the Chicago Wolves.

His first season in Chicago, however, was one for the books. On December 23, 2006, Haydar recorded a point in his 32nd straight game, establishing a new AHL record. He ended up extending his streak to 39 games, recording 79 points over that span. Haydar was called up to Atlanta for a handful of games that February but finished the season in the AHL, racking up 122 points to earn the Les Cunningham Award as the league's most valuable player. After leading the playoffs in scoring for the third time in the past four years, Haydar started the 2007–08 campaign in the minors but was recalled by the Thrashers early in the season. On October 13, 2007, in a game against the New Jersey Devils, Haydar scored his first NHL goal. Although Haydar played 16 games for Atlanta that season, it proved to be his only goal in the big leagues. After being sent back down to Chicago in December, Haydar led the Wolves to a Calder Cup that spring. He made one more appearance in the NHL in 2010 with the Colorado Avalanche and spent five more seasons in the AHL. Haydar was inducted into the AHL Hall of Fame in 2020.

OCTOBER 14

TED LINDSAY COMES OUT OF RETIREMENT, 1964

The Detroit Red Wings had lured Ted Lindsay out of retirement. Four years after he'd hung up his skates with the Chicago Black Hawks, the 39-year-old Lindsay, the highest-scoring left winger in NHL history, was ready to lace up his skates again. After contemplating a comeback in the off-season with Red Wings manager and coach Sid Abel, who was his former centre on Detroit's famed Production Line, Lindsay announced on October 14, 1964, that he was returning to the NHL. Although it had been in the works for a while and Lindsay had been practising with the club since training camp, he waited to share the news until he felt he was truly able to compete again. The following evening, he was back on the ice at the Olympia when the Red Wings hosted the Toronto Maple Leafs for their season opener. During the pre-game introductions, Lindsay, who had played more than a decade for Detroit before he was banished to Chicago for his role in trying to establish the first players' union, received a rousing standing ovation from the Red Wings' faithful.

Although Lindsay didn't get on the score sheet in his first game back, he did factor into the scoring. After Toronto goaltender Johnny Bower took a slashing penalty near the end of the first period for giving Lindsay a whack in his crease, Detroit's Ron Murphy scored on the ensuing power play to tie the game. In addition, near the end of the middle frame, Lindsay, nicknamed "Terrible Ted" for his toughness and fiery temper, took a holding penalty but also earned a 10-minute misconduct and a $25 fine for calling referee Vern Buffey a nasty name. He might have picked it up from teammate Gordie Howe, who Lindsay once said spoke two languages: English and profanity. Lindsay finished the season with 28 points in 69 games. Although he considered returning for another year, he retired before the 1965–66 campaign and was honoured by the team on October 12.

OCTOBER 15
MARIO LEMIEUX RACKS UP
EIGHT POINTS, 1988

Mario Lemieux racked up two goals and six assists as the Pittsburgh Penguins trounced the St. Louis Blues 9–2 at Civic Arena in Pittsburgh on October 15, 1988. Brian Sutter, the Blues' head coach, couldn't help but think about the previous season when his team limited the future winner of the Art Ross and Hart Trophies to a pair of points over three contests. "He got us back," Sutter told reporters. And then some. Lemieux's offensive outburst established a new Penguins club record, and he became only the 10th player in NHL history to score eight or more points in a game. Although Lemieux had surpassed his previous career high of six points in a game, the 23-year-old star was pretty nonchalant about his record-setting performance. "There were a lot of power play goals and a lot of loose pucks tonight," he said following the game. "I was just fortunate to put a couple in."

The couple of goals he put in were both on breakaways, and the six assists were just one helper shy from tying the league record for most assists in a game. Three of those assists help set up Rob Brown's first career NHL hat trick. Brown, who was Lemieux's right winger, was equally casual about his setup man's evening. "You expect it," he said. "If he only gets three or four points, you think he has a broken leg." Lemieux's productive night was a preview of things to come that season. He picked up 26 points in his next eight straight games to give him 41 points in just the first 12 games of the season. After starting another gaudy point streak on November 30, which spanned 15 games and 44 points, Lemieux concluded it on New Year's Eve with one of the most memorable individual efforts in NHL history. On December 31, in a matchup against the New Jersey Devils, Lemieux got eight points again, but he scored five goals in five different ways, making the achievement truly unforgettable. Lemieux finished the campaign with 85 goals and 199 points to earn his second straight Art Ross.

OCTOBER 16
JERRY TOPPAZZINI TENDS THE TWINE, 1960

With time winding down in a game between the Boston Bruins and Chicago Black Hawks on October 16, 1960, Boston goaltender Don Simmons took a shot to his face from Eric Nesterenko. Bleeding from his nose, Simmons left the net with 33 seconds remaining on the clock. Although the game was well out of reach for the Bruins, who were trailing 5–2, instead of waiting for Simmons to get bandaged up, hard-nosed winger Jerry Toppazzini stepped into the crease. Despite not wearing any protective goalie equipment, Toppazzini was prepared to stop whatever Chicago threw at him. Although Black Hawks coach Rudy Pilous dispatched his top scorers, including burgeoning sniper Bobby Hull, onto the ice for one last onslaught, Toppazzini faced no shots in his brief appearance between the pipes, becoming the last position player to replace a goaltender during an NHL game.

Even if Hull had managed to rifle off a shot, Toppazzini would have found a way to block it. Born and raised in Copper Cliff, Ontario, a mining town just west of Sudbury, Toppazzini was as hard as a coffin nail. Even after he hung up his skates, he remained a tough customer. Following his hockey career, Toppazzini returned home and established a tavern known as the Beef 'n' Bird. With the spoked *B* on the marquee and the walls adorned with pictures of Bobby Orr and Gerry Cheevers, it was a veritable Bruins shrine and an ode to Toppazzini's playing days in Boston. Before Toppazzini, who was colloquially known as "Topper," passed away in 2012, my father-in-law, Moe, a diehard Habs fan, once told me a story about how he went to the "Beef" wearing a Montreal Canadiens jacket. Moe ordered a beer from Toppazzini, who was frequently behind the bar, but when the grizzled bartender returned with the bottle, he had begrudgingly stuck his finger in it. When my father-in-law came back with the same jacket again, he was asked by one of Toppazzini's sons to leave it at home next time. You don't wear Habs gear in Topper's bar.

OCTOBER 17
FLAMES MOUNT COMEBACK AGAINST NORDIQUES, 1989

The Quebec Nordiques had it in the bag. With just over eight minutes remaining in a game against the Calgary Flames on October 17, 1989, Quebec was leading 8–3. It should have been an easy two points, but instead, the Nordiques walked away with only one point after Calgary scored five unanswered goals to tie it 8–8. After jumping out to an early lead in the first period, the Nordiques bolstered their advantage when the Flames' Jiří Hrdina drew a game misconduct on a high-sticking penalty. On the ensuing five-minute major power play, the Nordiques scored two goals to extend their edge. While the score was 4–3 in favour of Quebec at the midway point of the second period, another game misconduct by Theo Fleury sent the Nordiques on another five-minute power play. After Guy Lafleur and Peter Šťastný, who was closing in on the 1,000-point mark, each scored, Quebec went into the third period with a 6–3 lead. Following two more Nordiques goals in the final frame, the game seemed out of reach for Calgary.

The Flames, however, weren't ready to throw in the towel just yet. After Gary Roberts scored with less than seven minutes remaining in regulation time, he did it again 16 seconds later. And 11 seconds after that, Jim Peplinski potted one to cut the deficit to two goals. Calgary's three goals in 27 seconds was the fifth-fastest three goals by one team in NHL history. It was a good start, but the club still needed two more goals if it hoped to force overtime. With less than one minute remaining and the Nordiques on the power play, the Flames pulled goaltender Mike Vernon for the extra attacker and scored two quick short-handed goals in four seconds to tie the game. When overtime solved nothing, the game was declared an 8–8 tie. While it was an incredible comeback by the Flames, Quebec head coach Michel Bergeron was furious that his team had squandered the lead. "This is worse than a loss," he told reporters. Hey, at least they got a point.

OCTOBER 18
WILD RECORD FIRST VICTORY, 2000

ive games into their inaugural season, the Minnesota Wild were still searching for their first victory. After dropping their initial two games on the road, they tied their home opener 3–3 against the Philadelphia Flyers. Following a quick trip to St. Louis, where they were shut out by the Blues, the Wild returned to the Xcel Energy Center for a four-game home stand. But after losing 5–3 to the Edmonton Oilers in their first game back, the wait continued. A few days later, on October 18, 2000, the Wild had another opportunity when they hosted Tampa Bay. Despite falling behind 1–0 to the Lightning in the first period, the Wild's special teams went to work in the middle frame, scoring two goals on power plays and another short-handed, along with one at even strength, to head into the final period with a 4–2 lead. Although there was still 20 minutes to play, it was the first time the Wild had gone into the third with a two-goal advantage, and things looked promising. The Lightning, however, scored early in the period to cut the deficit, and after they tied the game with less than six minutes to go, it seemed as though Minnesota might have to wait for another match to get that elusive first triumph.

But with less than three minutes remaining, rookie Marián Gáborík, who had been benched for most of the game because of poor play in the earlier periods, scored his third goal of the season to break the tie and take the lead. With less than a minute remaining, Gáborík scored again, putting the puck into the empty net, all but sealing the victory. Although Tampa Bay's Fredrik Modin scored with 12 seconds left, Wild fans were able to breathe a sigh of relief when the final buzzer sounded. After five tries, Minnesota was victorious in their sixth attempt. While there was still a long way to go, it was an important franchise milestone. The Wild picked up 24 more victories in their debut season, but finished last in their division and missed the playoffs.

BOBBY ORR'S FIRST AND LAST ASSISTS, 1966 AND 1978

One of the most anticipated debuts in NHL history happened on October 19, 1966, when Bobby Orr played his first game for the Boston Bruins. Taking on the Detroit Red Wings in the Boston Garden, the phenom rearguard was heralded by the Bruins' faithful nearly every time he was on the ice. Although there were concerns that the 18-year-old defenceman would be overmatched by his big-league opponents, Orr played beyond his years and looked like a veteran. Early in the second period, he assisted on Wayne Connelly's goal to give the Bruins a 2–0 lead. While newspaper coverage praised his play that game, Orr was harder on himself. Following the matchup, he poked fun at his assist: "I looked terrible." While it might not have been the play he'd envisioned, the puck still went in the net and Orr skated away with his first career assist.

And though it seemed as if he'd continue piling up assists for years to come, exactly 12 years after making his NHL debut and notching that first assist, Orr recorded his final one in the league. On October 19, 1978, in a game against the Minnesota North Stars, Orr, who was then with the Chicago Black Hawks, recorded a helper on John Marks's first-period goal. Orr also added a goal, his first in nearly two years, late in the middle frame as Chicago cruised to a 6–2 victory. By the time Orr had signed with the Black Hawks in 1976, he'd already undergone several surgeries on his left knee. In his first season in Chicago, he played only 20 games before his troublesome knee gave him problems again. Following another procedure in April 1977, Orr sat out the entire 1977–78 campaign to recover, hoping to make a comeback the next year. But early in 1978–79, his knee had betrayed him again. While he played three more games for the Black Hawks, picking up his last point in a game against the Red Wings on October 28, 1978, just over a week later at the age of 30, an emotional Orr announced his retirement.

OCTOBER 20
BRUINS ACQUIRE DAN PAILLE FROM SABRES, 2009

The Buffalo Sabres and Boston Bruins took their divisional rivalry seriously. Ever since Buffalo had joined the league in 1970, the two teams had never traded players. But, readers might ask, what about Peter McNab and André Savard? During the 1976 off-season, McNab, who was taken 85th overall by the Sabres in the 1972 amateur draft, and Savard, who was selected sixth overall by the Bruins a year later, were both in need of new contracts. Although the teams still held their rights, neither player was able to come to terms with their respective clubs, and so on June 11, 1976, they switched sides: Savard went to the Sabres, McNab went to the Bruins. While McNab, who was fresh off a trip to the Stanley Cup Final with Buffalo, immediately signed with his new team, Savard didn't reach a deal with the Sabres for almost another week.

And while it was most certainly a trade between the two teams, the fact that neither player was under contract gives it an interesting wrinkle. It took more than three decades before the Sabres and Bruins finally made a transaction involving a player on an active roster. On October 20, 2009, Buffalo traded winger Dan Paille to Boston in exchange for a third-round draft pick in 2010. Paille, who was drafted in the first round by the Sabres in 2002, was in the last year of a two-year deal he'd signed with the club in 2008. Paille had scored 19 goals and 35 points in his second full season in Buffalo, but the Bruins wanted to shore up their bottom six and bring more sandpaper to the lineup. Once in Boston, Paille clicked with Shawn Thornton and Gregory Campbell, forming one of the most effective fourth lines in NHL history. While they preferred to be known as "The Merlot Line" because of the burgundy colour of their practice jerseys, the trio was more than simply a fourth line and were an integral part of the team's Stanley Cup victory in 2011.

OCTOBER 21
GUY LAFLEUR AND MARCEL DIONNE, 1975, 1984, 1988

G uy Lafleur and Marcel Dionne are forever linked. In the 1971 NHL Amateur Draft, Lafleur went first overall to the Montreal Canadiens while Dionne was drafted right after him by the Detroit Red Wings. Although they were always connected because of their draft class, they also had a special connection to this day. On October 21, 1975, Lafleur scored two goals and added three assists in a 7–1 win over the Pittsburgh Penguins. Lafleur, who started off the season at a torrid scoring pace, was just coming off a 53-goal campaign, and many believed he'd push for 60 that year. Although he fell four goals shy of that mark, Lafleur eventually reached that milestone with the Canadiens. Exactly nine years later, Dionne, beginning his 10th season with the Los Angeles Kings, squared off against the Black Hawks in Chicago. While the Kings lost 5–2, Dionne assisted on Charlie Simmer's third-period goal to give him 800 career assists, making him the seventh player in NHL history to accomplish that feat.

Dionne played one more full season with the Kings before he was traded to the New York Rangers, along with Jeff Crossman and a third-round pick, on March 10, 1987, in exchange for Bob Carpenter and Tom Laidlaw. By that point, Lafleur had already retired, but the two connected again a year later when Lafleur made his return to hockey with the Rangers. After more than a decade playing against each other, Dionne and Lafleur were finally on the same bench, and on October 21, 1988, they scored as teammates for the first time. Taking on the Washington Capitals at the Capital Center in Landover, Maryland, Dionne scored a goal and added two assists, while Lafleur chipped in with a goal in a 4–1 victory. Their time together, however, was fleeting. Dionne was used sparingly that season by the Rangers and appeared in only 37 games before he retired in 1989 after he was unable to find another job in the league. Meanwhile, following his comeback with the Blueshirts, Lafleur returned to Quebec and played two seasons for the Nordiques before hanging up his skates for good.

OCTOBER 22
MARIO LEMIEUX SCORES HAT TRICK, 1992

Mario Lemieux was playing as if possessed. After leading the Pittsburgh Penguins to back-to-back Stanley Cups and earning his second straight Conn Smythe Trophy as the most valuable player of the playoffs, Lemieux started the 1992–93 regular-season as if he were shot out of a cannon. Following a match-up against the Detroit Red Wings on October 22, 1992, in which Lemieux recorded his 28th career hat trick and picked up two assists, his third five-point performance of the year, the superstar centre was sitting at 27 points in just eight games. While it was early in the season, it seemed as though Lemieux would easily challenge Wayne Gretzky's records for the most goals (92) and points (215) in an NHL season. A big reason for his jaw-dropping pace was because, for the first time in years, Lemieux entered the 1992–93 campaign without back problems. Although Lemieux had still been one of the best players in the league, he acknowledged he wasn't able to give a complete effort on the ice while he contended with back injuries. But with the Penguins' captain now seemingly unencumbered by those recurring issues, he appeared poised to set the league ablaze.

After 40 games, Lemieux had 39 goals and 104 points and was within striking distance of the records when he stunned the hockey world by announcing he'd been diagnosed with Hodgkin's lymphoma. Despite missing the next 23 games to undergo cancer treatments, Lemieux returned on March 2, 1993, and picked up right where he'd left off. Although he trailed Pat LaFontaine by 12 points in the scoring race, Lemieux recorded a blistering 56 points in Pittsburgh's final 20 games to finish the season with 69 goals and 160 points, beating LaFontaine by 12 points to earn his fourth Art Ross Trophy. We'll never know what Lemieux could have accomplished if he'd remained healthy that season, but if he had maintained that torrid pace over a full 82-game season, he might have finished with 94 goals and 218 points.

OCTOBER 23
BLACKHAWKS CLAIM STEVE SULLIVAN, 1999

When I lived in Timmins, Ontario, my claim to fame was that I lived on the same street as Steve Sullivan, who grew up in the small gold mining town and was drafted by the New Jersey Devils in 1994. But by the time my family and I moved to Timmins, Sullivan had been traded to the Toronto Maple Leafs as part of the Doug Gilmour trade. This wasn't just any NHL player living on our street. Sullivan was a Maple Leaf! And for my mother, the biggest Toronto fan I know, that was a big deal. I remember during the summers when he returned to Timmins, my mom would drive us past his house just to try to get a glimpse of him before turning around and heading home.

Despite scoring a career high 20 goals and 40 points in just 63 appearances in the 1998–99 season, Sullivan never really fitted in with Toronto. Prior to the 1999–2000 campaign, he had asked GM and head coach Pat Quinn to be moved somewhere else to get more opportunities to play. And so on October 21, 1999, the Maple Leafs placed Sullivan on waivers to make room for a new signing. Two days later, he was claimed by the Chicago Blackhawks. In his first season with that club, Sullivan scored 22 goals and 64 points. By the time he suited up for his second year with Chicago, my family had moved to Sudbury, but we still followed his career closely. Sullivan scored 75 points that year, but what I'll always remember was when he was heckled by a fan in the first row after getting high-sticked in a game against the Colorado Avalanche on January 26, 2001. As the second period came to a close, Patrick Roy attempted to clear the puck off the glass and it went into the stands, nailing the same fan who had been taunting Sullivan. After teammate Tony Amonte pointed out who it was, Sullivan skated over to the glass, and after a few choice words, got the last laugh.

OCTOBER 24
MIKE BOSSY SCORES 250TH
CAREER GOAL, 1981

After winning his second straight Stanley Cup with the New York Islanders, Mike Bossy went into the 1981–82 season in the option year of his contract. After scoring eight goals to open the campaign, the right winger appeared close to inking a new deal. Coming off a 68-goal season, the sniper had plenty of reasons to stay in New York. Playing alongside centre Bryan Trottier and Clarke Gillies, forming what was known as the formidable "Trio Grande Line," Bossy found early success with the Islanders, becoming the first player in NHL history to score 50 goals in each of his first four seasons. While Bossy and the club sorted out the details of his next contract, the Islanders hosted the Washington Capitals on October 24, 1981. Late in the second period, Bossy caught a pass from Trottier just over the red line and skated in on a breakaway. Bossy, who had scored two goals against Washington the night before, fired a shot past goaltender Dave Parro to give the Islanders a 4–3 lead. It was Bossy's 250th career goal, a feat he managed to accomplish in just his 315th game.

A few days later before New York took on the Edmonton Oilers, Bossy signed a five-year extension with the Islanders. Although Bossy was only 24 years old then, he figured it would be his final NHL contract. "I've always maintained that I wanted to retire around 31 or 32, and now I can say that I'm 99 percent sure this will be it for me," Bossy said after the deal was announced. While Bossy hoped to end his career on his own terms, his words proved prophetic. Exactly seven years after scoring his milestone goal against the Capitals, Bossy choked back tears at an emotional press conference as he announced his retirement due to back injuries. After suiting up for just 63 games in the 1986–87 campaign and missing the 50-goal mark for the first time in his career, Bossy sat out the entire 1987–88 season before making the difficult decision to hang up his skates on October 24, 1988.

OCTOBER 25
PAT LAFONTAINE TRADED TO SABRES, 1991

P at LaFontaine wanted out of Long Island. Heading into the option year of his contract with the New York Islanders, the star centre had requested a trade because he didn't see eye to eye with club owner John Pickett. Although New York had offered him a four-year, $6-million deal to stay, LaFontaine had rejected the offer, reportedly stating that he would never play for the team again as long as Pickett was the owner. When the 1991–92 season opened, LaFontaine stuck to his word and refused to report to the team. After missing the club's first eight games of the season, on October 25, 1991, LaFontaine was sent to the Buffalo Sabres, along with Randy Wood, Randy Hillier, and future considerations, in exchange for Pierre Turgeon, Benoît Hogue, Dave McLlwain, and Uwe Krupp. That same day, the Islanders also dispatched captain Brent Sutter and Brad Lauer to the Chicago Blackhawks for Adam Creighton and Steve Thomas. With Sutter's departure, the team had severed its last link to the Stanley Cup–winning squads in the 1980s.

While LaFontaine still needed a new contract, he looked forward to a fresh start in Buffalo and began skating with his new teammates the next day. Two days after the trade, before the Sabres hosted the Hartford Whalers, LaFontaine inked a multi-year deal estimated to be worth roughly the same amount as the contract he'd turned down to stay in New York. In his first game with the Sabres, LaFontaine scored a goal and picked up two assists in a 5–1 victory against Hartford. Following his goal late in the first period, LaFontaine received a warm welcome from the Sabres' faithful, who rose to their feet and gave him a standing ovation. Despite missing nearly the first month of the campaign and another month while he recovered from a broken jaw, LaFontaine finished the season with 46 goals and 93 points in just 57 games. The following season, playing with Alexander Mogilny, LaFontaine racked up 148 points, the most in one season by a U.S.-born player.

OCTOBER | 323

OCTOBER 26

GRETZKY REACHES 2,000-POINT MARK, 1990

When I think about Wayne Gretzky scoring his 2,000th career point, the first thing that comes to mind is the Pro Set hockey card I had as a kid. The image on the front of the card has Gretzky with his arms raised in celebration after reaching the landmark. While it's not necessarily a noteworthy snapshot, what always registered with me was that, to his right, 2,000 was inscribed vertically. Although I was probably only six years old when I first got my hands on that card, and even though I didn't understand the numeral value of the number, I knew it was significant. As I got older and learned more about the game, I always went back to that card. It was a staggering amount of points. I don't have all the cards from my collection, but I have held on to that one. Every time I pick it up, it always reminds me of the time when I first realized just how special Gretzky was as a player. The idea that he could rack up that many points, whether you're six years old or thirty-five, seems unfathomable.

But somehow he did it. With just over five minutes remaining in the first period in a game against the Winnipeg Jets on October 26, 1990, Gretzky cleared the puck out of the Los Angeles Kings' zone by passing it up to Tony Granato, who was at centre ice. Granato quickly flipped it to Tomas Sandström, who took off on a breakaway and put the puck through the pads of Winnipeg goaltender Bob Essensa. Gretzky's assist gave him 2,000 career points, making him the only player in NHL history to reach that incredible plateau. As Gretzky's teammates poured out onto the ice to congratulate him, the Jets' fans at Winnipeg Arena rose to their feet to give him a well-earned standing ovation. The most confounding part of the milestone is that was just his regular-season point total. It didn't even include the 110 points he scored in the WHA as an 18-year-old or his 284 career points from the Stanley Cup Playoffs.

OCTOBER 27
RANGERS STAGE COMEBACK AGAINST THE WILD, 2014

T he New York Rangers probably should have lost the game. Hosting the Minnesota Wild on October 27, 2014, New York went into the final frame trailing 3–0. The Rangers had been woefully outplayed by Minnesota through 40 minutes of regulation time. Although neither team had scored in the first period, the Wild outshot the Rangers 11–3 in the second and took a commanding three-goal lead. By the time the third period commenced, the Rangers had been outshot 28–8 and a comeback seemed out of the question. It didn't help that New York was also down a couple of players. Winger Chris Kreider had been ejected early in the first period for boarding, and defenceman John Moore got the gate less than halfway through the second period.

But then the Rangers got on the board. Defenceman Kevin Klein fired a shot from just within the blue line, cutting the deficit to two. Less than two minutes later, Rick Nash shovelled in a loose puck in front of the Minnesota crease to make it 3–2. Although Wild winger Jason Zucker scored 47 seconds later to restore his team's two-goal lead, the Rangers had some life. Just over two minutes later, New York winger Carl Hagelin nearly scored when he wired a shot off the crossbar. As the puck dropped behind goaltender Darcy Kuemper, Derick Brassard swooped in and put it into the back of the net. The Rangers were within one. As time wound down, New York continued searching for the equalizer. With less than four minutes remaining, rookie Anthony Duclair scored his first career goal to tie the game. Thirty-seven seconds later, Mats Zuccarello potted his first of the season to give the Rangers a 5–4 lead, capping off a five-goal outburst in the third period. The Wild were stunned. When the final buzzer sounded, it marked the first time the Rangers had come back to win a game after trailing 3–0 in the third period since they accomplished that feat against the Detroit Red Wings on January 4, 1956.

OCTOBER 28

TYLER TOFFOLI SCORES INSANE BUZZER BEATER, 2017

With less than a second remaining in overtime in a game between the Los Angeles Kings and Boston Bruins on October 28, 2017, the Kings got ready to take a faceoff deep in the Bruins' end. Boston had just iced the puck, so it was unable to make a line change, leaving faceoff specialist Patrice Bergeron on the bench to watch the draw. Although there was only 0.9 seconds left on the clock, the Kings approached the faceoff as one final opportunity to win the game before heading to a shootout. With the faceoff in the right circle, head coach John Stevens sent out perennial Selke Trophy candidate Anže Kopitar, who had won 52.7 percent of his faceoffs the previous season, along with right-handed shooters Drew Doughty and Tyler Toffoli, who both positioned themselves behind the Kings' captain. If Kopitar could win the faceoff cleanly and get it back to either of them, there still might be enough time to fire off a one-timer.

In anticipation of the draw, both Doughty and Toffoli took practice swings with their sticks in case the puck came their way. Kopitar lined up against winger David Pastrňák and readied himself. The referee dropped the puck, and just as they had planned, Kopitar won the draw and sent it to Toffoli, who rifled a one-timer past goaltender Tuukka Rask to win the game with an improbable buzzer beater. While the Bruins and the TD Garden crowd tried to make sense of what had just happened, the Kings mobbed Toffoli on the ice. Although it certainly appeared as though he had beat the clock, the team had to wait for a replay to make it official. Upon video review, the officials confirmed that it was indeed a good goal. The puck had crossed the line with 0.4 seconds remaining, giving Toffoli his second of the night and netting the Kings a 2–1 victory. Before the faceoff, the officials had actually added 0.5 seconds back on the clock following the Bruins' icing. That half a second was all Toffoli needed to score one of the quickest goals in NHL history.

OCTOBER 29
CANADIENS HOST RANGERS AND ROYAL COUPLE, 1951

Floyd Curry put on a performance fit for a king. On October 29, 1951, the Montreal Canadiens winger scored three straight goals in the second period against the New York Rangers to notch his first and only career hat trick, with Princess Elizabeth and Prince Philip among the patrons at the Montreal Forum. The royal couple were in Canada on a five-week tour, and as part of their engagements, they took in a hockey game. In preparation for their arrival, a special viewing box decorated with flags and buntings had been prepared behind the Canadiens' bench in the arena. Guarded by a contingent of Mounties, the princess and her husband took in their first NHL game. According to newspaper reports, the couple enjoyed the action, particularly Prince Philip, who got a kick out of the hard-hitting body checks. Following Curry's three-goal outburst in the middle frame, Maurice Richard added two tallies to move within one goal of the 300 career mark in the final frame as Montreal cruised to a 6–1 victory.

While the matchup of the Canadiens and Rangers was the first full-length NHL game the royals had taken in, it wasn't their first brush with the league. A few weeks earlier, not long after arriving in Canada, Princess Elizabeth and Prince Philip were at Maple Leaf Gardens for an exhibition game between the Toronto Maple Leafs and the Chicago Black Hawks as part of a fundraiser for disabled and underprivileged children. Following the game, which consisted of three 10-minute periods, the royals headed to Sunnybrook Hospital. That evening, while the couple attended an official dinner hosted by Ontario lieutenant governor Ray Lawson, the Maple Leafs, the league's reigning champions, took on the Black Hawks for real. Missing a key member in the lineup, Toronto lost 3–1. Bill Barilko, who had scored the Stanley Cup–winning goal against the Canadiens that past spring, was still missing after going on a fishing trip in Northern Ontario in the summer with Dr. Henry Hudson. The Leafs wouldn't win another Cup until 1962, the year Barilko's body was discovered.

OCTOBER 30
SUTTER BROTHERS SQUARE OFF, 1983

The City of Brotherly Love was the perfect backdrop for a game between the Philadelphia Flyers and the New York Islanders on October 30, 1983. Although the two teams had squared off two weeks earlier in New York, this time it was unique. Eight days after that initial meeting, the Flyers acquired Rich Sutter from the Pittsburgh Penguins, reuniting him with his identical twin brother, Ron. The pair had played junior hockey together in Lethbridge, Alberta, but after going six spots apart in the first round of the 1982 draft, they started their NHL careers on different teams. With the twins joining the league for the 1983–84 season, it truly became a family affair for the Sutters, who had now graduated six brothers to the NHL ranks. Older brother Brian, who played for the St. Louis Blues, was the first, followed by Darryl with the Chicago Black Hawks, and Duane and Brent, both playing with the Islanders.

So with the twins now back together in Philadelphia, the upcoming game against New York held special significance. With Rich and Ron taking on Brent and Duane on the Islanders, it would mark the first time in NHL history that four brothers played together in the same game. Prior to the puck being dropped at the Spectrum, the brothers got together to take in the moment. While Duane and Brent got the better of their younger brothers, with both of them picking up two points in a 6–2 victory, they appreciated how special the game was. "I think having four brothers in the same league is good for the game of hockey," Brent told reporters after the match. "I'm very happy to see the twins together." Rich and Ron played in Philadelphia for parts of the next three seasons before Rich was traded to the Vancouver Canucks in 1986. The pair, however, were reunited again for the 1991–92 season when Ron was dealt to the Blues. During their first season together in St. Louis, Rich and Ron found another familiar face behind the bench: they were coached by older brother Brian.

OCTOBER 31
CANUCKS AND DUCKS IN MARATHON
SHOOTOUT, 2008

The Vancouver Canucks and Anaheim Ducks had no problem scoring during regulation time in a game on October 31, 2008. After going into the second period trailing 2–1, Vancouver scored four goals in a span of just over seven minutes to take a 5–2 lead but then squandered that lead in less than two minutes after giving up three quick goals to Anaheim. The Canucks went ahead 6–5 just over eight minutes into the final frame and held on to the lead until Corey Perry scored with less than a minute remaining to pick up his fifth point of the night. While the goals were plentiful through 60 minutes, particularly in the second frame, the same couldn't be said for overtime, and eventually, the shootout. When extra time solved nothing, the Canucks and Ducks went to the shootout.

First, Anaheim's Teemu Selänne was stopped. He had scored two goals in regulation time earlier to bring his career total to 560 to match Guy Lafleur for 20th on the NHL's all-time list. Then Kyle Wellwood and Ryan Getzlaf each scored for their respective teams. After that the goals were few and far between. Alex Burrows and Corey Perry were each stopped, then Mason Raymond had a chance to win it for the Canucks but was denied on the backhand by goaltender Jonas Hiller. Next up was Anaheim's Brendan Morrison, a former long-time Canuck, but he was stymied by Roberto Luongo. Ryan Kesler had another chance to win for Vancouver, but Hiller got a piece of the puck and the shootout continued. Following eight more unsuccessful attempts, Anaheim's François Beauchemin tried to break the deadlock with a slapshot, but it, too, was turned aside by Luongo. When Kevin Bieksa went up next for Vancouver, he tried to fake a slapshot but had the puck roll off his stick, deking to his backhand. After seven more misses, Canucks defenceman Mattias Öhlund, the 26th shooter, fired a shot that went off Hiller's elbow and then off the post and in to mercifully bring the exhibition to a close in the 13th round.

NOVEMBER 1
VAL JAMES BECOMES FIRST BLACK AMERICAN NHLER, 1981

When Val James stepped onto the ice at the Buffalo Auditorium, he knew he had made history. Late in the third period of a game against the Philadelphia Flyers on November 1, 1981, James took his initial shift in the NHL, becoming the first Black American player in the league. Born in Ocala, Florida, James grew up on Long Island, New York, where he began playing hockey. After learning how to skate, he quickly established himself as a tough, formidable player not afraid to drop his gloves. Following two seasons of junior hockey with the Quebec Remparts, James turned pro with the Erie Blades, where he was part of three straight league championships under head coach Nick Polano. When Polano became an assistant coach with the Buffalo Sabres, he urged head coach Scotty Bowman to give James a shot.

After attending training camp in 1981, James earned a contract with the organization. Following his first NHL appearance, he was sent down to Buffalo's AHL affiliate, the Rochester Americans. He was recalled later in the season for a handful of games, but one incident after a matchup in Boston illustrates the struggles James faced as a Black player in the NHL. In his memoir, *Black Ice*, James recalls that after a game against the Boston Bruins, a group of belligerent fans threw a beer bottle at the Sabres' bus and shouted racist slurs. "Those drunks had taken away the joy and pride I felt at achieving a lifelong dream," James writes. Despite the ugliness of that moment and the racism he experienced throughout his career, James was determined to pursue his hockey dreams. He spent the next year in Rochester and scored the championship-winning goal in the Calder Cup Final against the Maine Mariners. James returned to the NHL in 1986 as a member of the Toronto Maple Leafs, becoming the first Black player to suit up for that club. Following four appearances with Toronto, James played parts of three more seasons in the minors, capping off nearly a decade of professional hockey.

NOVEMBER 2
WAYNE GRETZKY TRADED TO OILERS, 1978

Wayne Gretzky, Peter Driscoll, and Eddie Mio didn't know where they were going when they stepped onto the chartered jet; they just knew they were no longer members of the Indianapolis Racers of the WHA. Although Gretzky had just signed a seven-year, $1.7-million personal services contract with team owner Nelson Skalbania before the season began, the Racers were hemorrhaging cash. While Gretzky was a rising star, he didn't have the draw in Indianapolis that Skalbania had expected and the owner wanted to sell off the wunderkind, along with Driscoll and Mio, to keep the franchise afloat. Skalbania gave Gretzky the option of either going to the Edmonton Oilers or the Winnipeg Jets but still had to iron out the details. When the trio boarded the plane on November 2, 1978, their final destination was still up in the air. The legend goes that while the players were still flying, Skalbania challenged Jets co-owner Michael Gobuty to a game of high-stakes backgammon. If Gobuty won, Gretzky, Driscoll, and Mio would go to the Jets.

That tale, however, is more fiction than fact; the truth is that the Winnipeg ownership simply turned down the trade proposal and the three players ended up in Edmonton after Skalbania reached a deal with Oilers owner Peter Pocklington, who reportedly paid $850,000. The next night, Gretzky suited up in his first game for the Oilers as the team, fittingly, took on the Jets. He scored a goal in a 4–3 overtime victory. Gretzky finished the season in Edmonton with 43 goals and 104 points in 72 games. When the WHA's Oilers, Jets, Quebec Nordiques, and New England Whalers merged with the NHL during the off-season, Gretzky made the jump to the NHL the following year. The rest, as they say, is history. Gretzky went on to win four Stanley Cups in Edmonton and establish himself as one of the greatest players ever to lace them up. Imagine how different hockey history might have been if that plane had landed in Winnipeg.

PEKKA RINNE SIGNS SEVEN-YEAR DEAL, 2011

Just hours before taking on the Phoenix Coyotes on November 3, 2011, goaltender Pekka Rinne signed a seven-year, $49-million contract extension with the Nashville Predators. At the time, it was the biggest deal in team history and sent a clear message to the fans that the ownership group was committed to building a contender on the ice. Since becoming Nashville's starting goaltender in 2008–09, Rinne had established himself as one of the NHL's top netminders. Over the past three seasons, he had recorded 20 shutouts, tying Martin Brodeur for the most in the league over that span. During the 2010–11 campaign, Rinne recorded a sterling .930 save percentage and finished as runner-up for the Vezina Trophy and was in contention for the Hart Trophy. He was Nashville's most valuable player, and the team was keen to lock him up for the future.

Just a few days after making 20 saves against the Anaheim Ducks to pick up his 22nd career shutout and establish a new franchise record, Rinne signed on to stay with the Predators for the next seven years. Playing later that same day against Phoenix, Rinne made 35 saves in a 3–0 victory. A new lucrative contract and a shutout — not a bad way for the Finnish netminder to celebrate his 29th birthday. Although the new deal didn't kick in until 2012–13, the Predators certainly got their money's worth that season. From January 7 to February 4, Rinne strung together 11 straight victories, establishing a new franchise record for most consecutive wins by a goaltender. He finished the campaign with a league-leading 73 games played and 43 wins and was named a finalist for the Vezina Trophy for the second straight year. Exactly seven years later, playing in the final year of his seven-year agreement, Rinne signed a two-year, $10-million contract extension with Nashville. Later that same day, on his 36th birthday, the Predators hosted the Boston Bruins, and just like the last time he put pen to paper, Rinne turned aside every shot he faced to record his 53rd career shutout. Happy birthday, Pekka!

NOVEMBER 4

BLUE JACKETS TROUNCE CANADIENS 10–0, 2016

As a dyed-in-the-wool Toronto Maple Leafs fan, I find no satisfaction telling this next story. The last thing I'd want to write about is how on November 4, 2016, the Columbus Blue Jackets scored 10 unanswered goals against the Montreal Canadiens. There's not much I'd personally gain by rehashing a double-digit blowout in which Montreal failed to score a single goal. And it certainly doesn't matter to me that it was the fifth time in the Canadiens' history that they lost by 10 goals and the first since an 11–1 drubbing by the Detroit Red Wings on December 2, 1995, which just so happened to be Patrick Roy's last game as a member of the Canadiens. He went on to earn two more Stanley Cups with the Colorado Avalanche while Montreal hasn't won anything since 1993, but that's beside the point.

It certainly doesn't matter that the Blue Jackets set a franchise record for most goals in a game and that the cannon at Nationwide Arena was fired so many times that it ran out of gunpowder. Actually, that last part might not be true, but you get my point. I'm not writing this story simply to humiliate Habs fans. I might be an unabashed Toronto supporter, but it's not as if I'd go through every single Columbus goal beginning with Cam Atkinson, who opened the scoring more than halfway through the first period. Forget that Seth Jones made it 2–0 less than a minute later or that David Savard extended the lead just over two minutes after that. Don't think I'm going to tell you about the Blue Jackets' three straight power play goals in the second period or how captain Nick Foligno got his second of the game to make it 7–0. I'm not interested in how Josh Anderson made it 8–0 or how Scott Hartnell tipped the puck through Al Montoya's legs to make it 9–0. And it certainly doesn't mean anything to me that Columbus's 10th goal was scored by Anderson, who now plays for the Canadiens. That's definitely not this type of story.

NOVEMBER 5
PAVEL BURE MAKES NHL DEBUT, 1991

Pavel Bure was so eager to start the next chapter of his hockey journey that he was willing to pay for the privilege out of his own pocket. After reaching a four-year, $2.7-million deal with the Vancouver Canucks, Bure and the team still had to reach a settlement with the Central Red Army team over his rights before he could make his NHL debut. Drafted in the sixth round of the 1989 Entry Draft, Bure was one of the brightest prospects playing in the Soviet Union. Some of the league's other general managers, however, launched a complaint against Vancouver, arguing that Bure hadn't played enough games for the Soviet national team to make him eligible for the draft that year. It was only once Igor Larionov, who had recently joined the Canucks, dug up records nearly a year later that proved Bure had enough games under his belt in Russia to have been included in the draft, that NHL President John Ziegler ruled in favour of the Canucks.

While the matter was settled with the league, the club still had to negotiate Bure's release from the Soviets. After going back and forth with the Red Army team, the Canucks offered $200,000, with Bure kicking in $50,000 of his own money just to close the discussion. Less than a week later, on November 5, 1991, Bure made his debut with the Canucks. Although he didn't get on the score sheet in a 2–2 tie against the Winnipeg Jets, he dazzled Vancouver's faithful with his blistering speed and electrifying end-to-end rushes. In his coverage of the game, *Vancouver Sun* columnist Iain MacIntyre referred to Bure as "the fastest Soviet creation since *Sputnik*," and given his impressive speed, suggested that perhaps he should be colloquially known as "The Rocket." A week later, Bure recorded his first two NHL goals in a matchup against the Los Angeles Kings. He finished the season with 34 goals and 60 points to win the Calder Trophy as the league's top rookie. MacIntyre was definitely onto something. Over the course of his NHL career, Bure became known as "The Russian Rocket."

NOVEMBER 6
WHALERS NAME PAUL MAURICE HEAD COACH, 1995

Paul Maurice didn't plan to get into coaching. Following his junior career with the Windsor Spitfires, he was going to finish his degree at the University of Windsor and then enroll in law school. But partway through the 1987–88 season, his plans were thrown for a loop. After overcoming a career-threatening eye injury with the Spitfires during his rookie season, Maurice went on to captain the team and become one of the most reliable defensive defencemen in the Ontario Hockey League. When the club, however, opted to give one of the two overage spots it had been using for Maurice to veteran goaltender Pat Jablonski, who returned to Windsor in December 1987 after starting the season in the professional ranks, the Spitfires' captain was left on the sidelines. A week after getting cut, though, Maurice returned to the team as an assistant coach on January 11, 1988.

While he continued his education, Maurice embraced his new role behind the bench. After spending parts of three seasons working with the Spitfires while juggling his studies, Maurice became a full-time assistant coach with the OHL's expansion team, the Detroit Compuware Ambassadors, in 1990. Following three years as an assistant in Detroit, later renamed the Junior Red Wings, Maurice was appointed head coach by GM Jim Rutherford following the dismissal of Tom Webster. After guiding the team to a J. Ross Robertson Cup and berth in the Memorial Cup in 1995, Maurice joined the Hartford Whalers, reuniting with Rutherford, as an assistant coach for the 1995–96 season. Not long into the campaign, however, Maurice was promoted to head coach on November 6, 1995. Just a couple of months shy of his 29th birthday, Maurice became the youngest coach in North America's four major professional leagues at the time. Although Maurice might not have planned for a career in coaching, he has gone on to become just one of nine coaches in NHL history to reach the 700-win milestone.

NOVEMBER 7
PHIL ESPOSITO TRADED TO RANGERS, 1975

The way Phil Esposito remembers it, Boston Bruins head coach Don Cherry knocked on the door of his Vancouver hotel room on November 7, 1975. The Bruins were in town to play the Canucks the following evening. In advance of the game, Cherry delivered some urgent news to the five-time Art Ross Trophy winner. In some accounts, it's just Cherry, but in other versions, teammate Bobby Orr also joined the bench boss in Esposito's room. In any case, Cherry was there to tell his star winger, who was just coming off his fifth-straight 50-goal season with the Bruins, that he was being traded. A stunned Esposito reportedly said something to the effect of "Please don't tell me it's New York, because if you do, I'm going to jump out the window." In the version with Orr, Cherry turned to the defenceman, who was standing near the window, and simply said, "Close the window." Esposito, along with Carol Vadnais, was headed to the Blueshirts in exchange for Brad Park, Jean Ratelle, and Joe Zanussi.

While Esposito likely never made a dash for the window, he was surprised and angry. When Bruins general manager Harry Sinden later called his former player to deliver the news himself by telephone, Esposito demanded to know why. Sinden wasn't able to assuage his concerns other than to tell him it was a tough decision but in the best interests of the Bruins. Although both clubs were coming off premature exits in the 1975 playoffs and had sluggish starts to the 1975–76 regular season, the trade still shocked the hockey world. Esposito had won the scoring title in five of the past seven seasons. The two times he didn't win it he finished runner-up to Orr, while Park and Ratelle had been cornerstones in New York. Nevertheless, both teams believed it was the shakeup they needed. Later that same evening, Esposito made his Rangers debut, scoring two goals and adding an assist in a 7–5 loss to the California Golden Seals. The next night, Ratelle and Park both picked up assists in a Bruins defeat.

MAURICE RICHARD'S FIRST AND RECORD-SETTING GOALS, 1942 AND 1952

Near the halfway mark of the second period in a game against the New York Rangers on November 8, 1942, Montreal Canadiens rookie Maurice Richard picked up the puck in his own end, raced all the way down the ice, and fired a shot past New York goaltender Steve Buzinski to record his first career NHL goal. It held up as the game-winner and was a preview of what the Montreal faithful could expect from the fiery winger. Exactly 10 years after his first tally, Richard was playing against the Chicago Black Hawks and hunting for his 325th goal to move him past Nels Stewart, known as "Old Poison" for his lethal shot, who had held the league record for most career goals since retiring in 1940. Halfway through the second period, Richard netted a backhander past Chicago goaltender Al Rollins to surpass Stewart and establish a new milestone.

Following the game, Montreal general manager Frank Selke told the press that Richard's record-setting puck would be gold-plated and sent to Queen Elizabeth II, who as princess had taken in a Canadiens game a year earlier with her husband, Prince Philip, as a gift. Selke described how one side of the puck would feature the likenesses of the queen and Prince Philip, while the other side would be engraved with Richard's image.

I couldn't help but laugh when I first learned about the puck being shipped to her royal majesty. My dear father-in-law, also named Maurice but goes by Moe, is an ardent Habs fan, and as I've learned over the years, not a supporter of British royalty. Moe and I have also had plenty of conversations about how Richard didn't receive his proper due in English Canada, which I don't necessarily disagree with, because of the Rocket's French-Canadian heritage, so I can't help but chuckle as I think about Moe learning that rather than letting Richard keep his record-setting puck, it was sent to Queen Elizabeth and is probably mothballed somewhere in Buckingham Palace.

NOVEMBER 9

ERIK COLE AWARDED TWO PENALTY SHOTS, 2005

E rik Cole was on a short-handed breakaway when he was hauled down by the Buffalo Sabres' Jochen Hecht just before the half-way mark of the third period in a game between the Carolina Hurricanes and the Sabres on November 9, 2005. Cole was awarded a penalty shot and subsequently scored on goaltender Martin Biron to give the Hurricanes a 4–1 lead. Seven minutes later, after Thomas Vanek scored two for the Sabres to cut the deficit to one, Cole was awarded another penalty shot when hooked by Dmitri Kalinin. This time, however, Cole was stopped by Biron. Although Cole wasn't able to convert on the second opportunity, he'd made history by becoming the first NHL player to be awarded two penalty shots in the same game. Well, that's what we believed to be true at the time.

More than a decade later, it turned out that Cole wasn't actually the first. In 2017, when the league was still in the process of digitizing all its game sheets to make them available online, hockey historian and author Bob Duff, who assisted in those efforts, happened to notice that the official game report for a game between the Chicago Black Hawks and the Detroit Red Wings on November 24, 1938, noted that two penalty shots had been issued to Mud Bruneteau, who nearly three years earlier had scored the overtime winner to end the longest game in NHL history. That statistic had seemingly been lost to history, but after further investigation, Duff corroborated that Bruneteau had indeed taken two penalty shots that game but was unsuccessful on both. While the discovery didn't diminish the significance of Cole's accomplishment in 2005, it put it in the proper historical context and brought Bruneteau back into the narrative, where he belonged. One of the greatest things about hockey history is that it isn't static; rather, our understanding of it is constantly evolving. As we continue to dig deeper into this game we all love, we learn more about it and uncover new facts that help us tell better and more informed stories.

NOVEMBER 10

CANUCKS REACQUIRE TREVOR LINDEN, 2001

Trevor Linden was a Canuck again. On November 10, 2001, Vancouver reacquired their former captain from the Washington Capitals, along with a second-round draft pick, in exchange for first-round and third-round draft picks. Drafted second overall by the Canucks in 1988, Linden eventually established himself as the heart and soul of the team and became a beloved fan favourite on and off the ice. But after nearly a decade with the club, Linden found himself at odds with the organization following the arrival of coach Mike Keenan in 1997. Before the regular season even began, Linden relinquished the captaincy to newly arrived free agent Mark Messier, a move that didn't sit well with the Vancouver faithful. The situation worsened early in the campaign, however, when the team dismissed head coach Tom Renney and Keenan took over behind the bench. It quickly became apparent that under the Keenan regime there wasn't a fit for Linden. While Linden might not have been the player he once was, particularly after struggling with injuries over the past season, Keenan had no qualms about calling out his play publicly, which only further strained their relationship. It wasn't a matter of if Linden would be traded but when. Finally, on February 6, 1998, Linden was traded to the New York Islanders in exchange for Bryan McCabe, Todd Bertuzzi, and a third-round pick.

But after parts of two seasons on Long Island and stopovers with the Montreal Canadiens and Washington Capitals, Linden returned to Vancouver. As he approached his 1,000th career game later in the season, Linden, the consummate team player, told the Canucks he didn't want any fanfare to mark the occasion in order to keep the focus on the team's battle for a playoff spot. On March 26, 2002, he suited up for the milestone game and received a standing ovation during a video tribute early in the first period. The Canucks shut out the Los Angeles Kings that night 4–0 and went undefeated in their final eight games to clinch a post-season berth.

NOVEMBER 11
RED WINGS CLAIM DREW MILLER OFF WAIVERS, 2009

Early in the 2008–09 regular season, the Detroit Red Wings just couldn't catch a break. In the third game of the season, Detroit lost Johan Franzén, who scored 34 goals the previous season, to a torn knee ligament. He was expected to be out for at least four months while he recovered from surgery. A few weeks after that in a matchup against the Edmonton Oilers, Valtteri Filppula, who had been centring a key line with Todd Bertuzzi and Dan Cleary, broke his wrist. The injuries continued to pile up when a few games later, winger Jason Williams fractured his right fibula early in the second period in a game against the Toronto Maple Leafs. While head coach Mike Babcock told the media the team couldn't worry about players who weren't available to the club, the Red Wings needed some reinforcements. On November 11, 2009, a day after the Tampa Bay Lightning placed left winger Drew Miller on waivers, Detroit claimed him. For Miller, who was raised in East Lansing and played three seasons at Michigan State before starting his NHL career with the Mighty Ducks of Anaheim, it was a bit of a homecoming.

While he wasn't expected to come in and replace Franzén's goal output, Miller quickly established himself as a valuable role player who could compete on both sides of the puck. Although Miller had been drafted by Anaheim in 2003, he had never found a fit with the big club and spent most of his time in the AHL before he was traded to Tampa Bay in 2009. But with Detroit devastated by injuries, Miller finally proved he could play at the NHL level. He finished the 2009–10 season with 10 goals and 19 points in 66 games and re-signed with the Red Wings in the off-season. Following another solid campaign in which he recorded another 10 goals while serving as a valuable penalty killer, Miller signed a two-year, $1.65-million extension. While Miller might have been brought in to shore up Detroit's forward corps, he went on to play more than 500 games for the Red Wings.

NOVEMBER 12

FIRST GAME AT MAPLE LEAF GARDENS, 1931

Conn Smythe wanted a new arena for his team. He believed that a modern, large-capacity facility would help attract more fans for his Toronto Maple Leafs and famously said he wanted a rink "people can be proud to take their wives or girlfriends to." Determined to make his dream a reality, even in the depths of the Great Depression, Smythe got shovels into the ground on June 1, 1931, at the corner of Church and Carlton Streets. To keep costs down on the project, he partially paid construction workers in future stock in Maple Leaf Gardens. While the labourers might have preferred more cash in their pocket at the time, it turned out to be a fortuitous move, since it wasn't long before the arena became known as "The Carlton Street Cashbox." Just five and a half months after first ground was broken, Maple Leaf Gardens was completed — an incredible feat of engineering and construction.

The Leafs played their first game in their new home on November 12, 1931, when they hosted the Chicago Black Hawks. Following the opening ceremonies, Chicago's Harold "Mush" March scored the first goal in the building just over two minutes after the inaugural drop of the puck. Although Charlie Conacher got the Leafs on the board to tie the game in the second period, Vic Ripley notched another goal for the Black Hawks early in the final frame to spoil the party. While it wasn't the outcome Toronto had hoped for, Leafs captain Hap Day said the team would do their best to bring the Stanley Cup to the new arena. Fans didn't have to wait long for Day's pledge to come true. In Toronto's debut season at the Gardens, they went on to sweep the New York Rangers in the best-of-five final to clinch the club's first Stanley Cup on Carlton. Over the next three and half decades, Toronto won seven more Cups on home ice. The Maple Leafs called the Gardens home for nearly seven decades before moving to the Air Canada Centre (now Scotiabank Arena) more than halfway through the 1998–99 campaign.

NOVEMBER 13
BLUES USE THREE GOALTENDERS IN ONE GAME, 1968

Thirty-nine-year-old Jacques Plante had recently come out of retirement for the St. Louis Blues, and with the team alternating between him and fellow veteran netminder Glenn Hall, rookie Robbie Irons was usually dressed on the bench to serve as backup. So when Hall got the nod to take on the New York Rangers on November 13, 1968, Plante took a seat in Madison Square Garden, where he had played for two seasons before initially hanging up his goalie pads. But just over two minutes into the game, Hall was tossed from the game after he got into a heated argument with referee Vern Buffey. Hall, who was wearing a mask in a game for the first time in his long career, was upset after he let in a goal from 60 feet just over a minute into the contest. When teammate Noel Picard was assessed a delay-of-game penalty not long after that, Hall, still fuming from his mistake, lost it with Buffey. After exchanging words with the official, Hall reportedly lunged at him and was subsequently tossed from the game, the first time he'd been ejected in his 16 seasons in the NHL.

As Irons hopped onto the ice to replace Hall, Plante raced down from the stands to suit up. But during Irons's warm-up, he injured his right knee. Although he stayed in the crease, Irons was forced to leave the game less than three minutes later. Suddenly, Plante was the last man standing. With the Blues trailing 1–0, he took up his post between the pipes at the five-minute mark of the first period. Plante stopped all 21 shots he faced, and St. Louis notched three goals to take a 3–1 victory. Although Plante was perfect in relief, he joked with reporters about how he should have been credited with a shutout. Two games later, though, Plante made 44 saves in a 1–0 victory against the Chicago Black Hawks to earn his 66th career shutout. Plante and Hall went on to share the Vezina Trophy that season as the league's top goaltenders.

DYLAN FERGUSON APPEARS FOR GOLDEN KNIGHTS, 2017

G oaltender Dylan Ferguson was sitting in a Boston Pizza with a couple of his Kamloops Blazers teammates. Their food had just arrived when one of his friends looked up at the television and then turned to back to him to explain what he'd seen on the screen. The Golden Knights' third-string goalie Oscar Dansk had just sustained an injury in a game against the New York Islanders. Vegas was in its inaugural NHL season and was already on its third netminder following injuries to starter Marc-André Fleury and backup Malcolm Subban. Ferguson was in disbelief. Within 30 seconds, his phone started to ring. He picked it up. On the other end of the line was Golden Knights assistant general manager Kelly MacCrimmon. Ferguson was getting recalled to Vegas on an emergency basis. After taking care of the bill for his table, Ferguson left the restaurant to get himself organized. Later that evening, he caught a red-eye flight to New York City to join the team. The next night, the 19-year-old goaltender found himself sitting on the bench in Madison Square Garden.

Originally selected in the seventh round by the Dallas Stars in the 2017 Entry Draft, Ferguson was traded to the Golden Knights just a few days later. After attending the team's first training camp in September, Ferguson signed an entry-level contract with the club before being sent back to junior hockey in Kamloops. But following Dansk's injury, Vegas was running out of goaltenders and that was when Ferguson got the call. After spending the next six games as Maxime Lagacé's backup, Ferguson saw duty on November 14, 2017, against the Edmonton Oilers. Late in the third period, with Vegas trailing 7–2, Ferguson got the nod from head coach Gerard Gallant to relieve Lagacé, who was struggling after tweaking his back early in the final frame. Stepping onto the ice, Ferguson was overcome with excitement. He allowed one power play goal and stopped another shot in just over nine minutes of relief. Although it might not have been how he envisioned making his first big-league appearance, it didn't matter — he was in the NHL.

NOVEMBER 15
BLUE JACKETS ACQUIRE
SERGEI FEDOROV, 2005

Following the 2004–05 lockout and the introduction of a salary cap, the Mighty Ducks of Anaheim found themselves in a pinch. To avoid what general manager Brian Burke referred to as a crisis, the team was forced to unload Sergei Fedorov and his $6-million contract. On November 15, 2005, Anaheim sent Fedorov and a fifth-round pick to the Columbus Blue Jackets in exchange for Tyler Wright and rookie defenceman François Beauchemin. While the Ducks got out of a financial jam, Burke later divulged in his book *Burke's Law* that Fedorov had become a problem for the club and was keen to get rid of him. Fedorov, who had spent his entire NHL career with the Detroit Red Wings, had signed a five-year contract with the Ducks in 2003 following a contentious departure from Detroit. In his first and only full season in Anaheim, the former Hart Trophy winner potted 31 goals and 65 points to lead the team in scoring. After the NHL lockout, Fedorov played three games for the Ducks before he injured his groin, sidelining him for more than a month. He returned to action for a pair of games and then was dealt to the Blue Jackets a few days later.

Not long after arriving in Columbus, Fedorov made league history. On November 30, 2005, in a game against the Minnesota Wild, Fedorov became the first Russian-born player to appear in 1,000 career games, picking up an assist in a 3–2 shootout victory. Following parts of two more seasons with the Blue Jackets, Fedorov was traded to the Washington Capitals on February 26, 2008, in exchange for prospect Ted Ruth. After finishing the season with the Capitals, the 38-year-old signed a one-year deal with the club for the opportunity to continue playing alongside fellow Russian sniper Alex Ovechkin. Not long into the 2008–09 season in a game against the Dallas Stars, Fedorov notched his 474th and 475th career goals to surpass Alexander Mogilny for the most goals by a Russian-born player. He finished his career with 483 tallies, but his record was surpassed by Ovechkin on November 19, 2015.

NOVEMBER 16
THREE RED WINGS MILESTONES, 2001

t was a hat trick of milestones for the Detroit Red Wings. On November 16, 2001, when the team hosted the Minnesota Wild, three players from Detroit's star-studded team each etched their names into the league's record book. Just 36 seconds into the middle frame, with the Red Wings leading 1–0 and on a power play, Brendan Shanahan got the puck to captain Steve Yzerman, who fired it past goaltender Dwayne Roloson to notch his 650th career goal, moving him past Mario Lemieux into eighth place on the NHL's all-time list. Nine minutes later, after Nicklas Lidström made it 3–0, Yzerman notched a short-handed tally to extend the team's lead. With time winding down in the second period, Yzerman and Brett Hull, who had joined the team as a free agent in the off-season, set up Luc Robitaille, another big free-agent signing, for his 601st career goal, tying him with Jari Kurri, who was inducted into the Hockey Hall of Fame a few days earlier, for the 12th most in NHL history.

A few minutes after Minnesota scored three goals in the first half of the third period to cut the deficit to two, Robitaille scored again to move past Kurri to take sole possession of 12th on the list. After Shanahan scored less than 30 seconds later to make it 7–3, Hull assisted on Detroit's final goal that evening, which gave him 1,200 career points; making him the 33rd player in NHL history to reach that plateau. The three milestones that night were just a few of the benchmarks that trio accomplished that season. Later in the campaign, Robitaille picked up his 611th career goal, surpassing Bobby Hull for the most in league history by a left winger. During that same contest, with Bobby in the stands, Brett scored the game-winning goal to move past his father for the third-most game-winning tallies in NHL history. A few days later, Yzerman recorded his 1,000th career assist, becoming the ninth player in league history to accomplish that feat. And, of course, by season's end, all three players hoisted the Stanley Cup.

NOVEMBER 17
COYOTES CLAIM ILYA BRYZGALOV, 2007

t was a whirlwind day for Ilya Bryzgalov. After being placed on waivers by the Anaheim Ducks on November 16, 2007, the Russian netminder was claimed by the Phoenix Coyotes the following day. Just hours after being plucked from the waiver wire, Bryzgalov made his first appearance with his new team. Luckily, the Coyotes were already in Los Angeles to take on the Kings and it was just a short drive from Anaheim to the STAPLES Center. Nevertheless, by the time all the paperwork was processed, Bryzgalov arrived at the rink as the team was sitting down for its pre-game meeting. Despite not having much time to prepare, Bryzgalov made some big saves in the first period to keep the game knotted at zero. After Coyotes captain Shane Doan scored to put Phoenix on the board just after the halfway mark of the second period, Bryzgalov remained perfect through 40 minutes of play. He was tested in the final frame, but the Kings couldn't solve him. Bryzgalov stopped all 28 shots he faced in a 1–0 victory, becoming the first goaltender in franchise history to record a shutout in his first game with the team.

A few days later, the Coyotes hosted the Kings at Jobing.com Arena (now Gila River Arena) and Bryzgalov proved to be lights-out once again, making 28 saves in a 4–1 win. It didn't take long for Bryzgalov to take on his former team. Two nights after picking up his second straight win with Phoenix, the Coyotes travelled to Anaheim to take on the Ducks. Squaring off against Jonas Hiller, who replaced him as backup to Jean-Sébastien Giguère, Bryzgalov made 23 saves in a 4–3 shootout victory. Following his first three starts with the Coyotes, Bryzgalov had stopped 79 of 83 shots and was undefeated. His hot start proved to be no fluke, and after compiling a 16–10–2 record to begin his tenure with the club, the Coyotes signed him to a three-year, $12.75-million contract extension on January 22, 2008. Bryzgalov finished the season with 26 victories, including three shutouts, in 55 appearances.

NOVEMBER 18
VÁCLAV NEDOMANSKÝ MAKES NHL DEBUT, 1977

Václav Nedomanský had spent more than a decade starring on the Czech national team before he defected to Canada in 1974 to join the Toronto Toros of the upstart WHA, becoming the first player to escape from behind the Iron Curtain and suit up for a North American squad. In his first season with the Toros, Nedomanský, who quickly became known as "Big Ned" because of his stature, recorded 41 goals and established himself as a fierce competitor on both sides of the puck. The following campaign, Nedomanský picked up 56 goals, the third most in the league that year. After the club relocated to Birmingham, Alabama, for the 1976–77 campaign and became known as the Bulls, Nedomanský notched another 36 goals in his first season playing in the United States. But early in his second season in Birmingham, on November 15, 1977, the big Czech centre was sent to the NHL's Detroit Red Wings, along with Tim Sheehy, in exchange for Steve Durbano and Dave Hanson, who played one of the Hanson brothers, Jack, in the film *Slap Shot*. It was the first time the Red Wings had executed a trade with a team from the rival league.

A few nights later, Nedomanský made his NHL debut, picking up assists on all three of Detroit's goals in a 5–3 loss to the Atlanta Flames. Not long into his tenure with the Red Wings, Nedomanský had the chance to take on some of his former countrymen when Detroit hosted the Czech team Pardubice in an exhibition game on January 2, 1978. The team reportedly tried to get Nedomanský scratched from the contest for defecting a few years earlier, but the Red Wings were adamant about him remaining in the lineup. Although he was still recovering from tonsillitis and the flu, Nedomanský suited up for the game, potted a goal, and added an assist in a 5–4 victory. Nedomanský played in Detroit for four more years before rounding out his NHL career with stops with the St. Louis Blues and New York Rangers. He was inducted into the Hockey Hall of Fame in 2019.

NOVEMBER 19
GRETZKY CHIRPS DEVILS, 1983

Wayne Gretzky didn't mince his words. After the Edmonton Oilers trounced the New Jersey Devils 13–4 on November 19, 1983, a game in which he recorded a hat trick and added five assists, Gretzky was very candid in his thoughts about New Jersey. "It got to the point it wasn't even funny," he told the *Edmonton Sun*'s Dick Chubey following the game. "How long has it been for them? Three years? Five? Seven? Probably closer to nine. Well, it's about time they got their act together. They're ruining the whole league. They better stop running a Mickey Mouse organization and put somebody on the ice. I feel damn sorry for Ron Low and Chico Resch." Gretzky's comments, particularly the line about the Devils being a Mickey Mouse organization, quickly made the rounds throughout the hockey community. Gretzky immediately regretted what he'd said. While he might have intended that his remarks were to highlight some of the problems the league's weaker teams such the Devils faced, it was out of line.

Within a few days, Gretzky had publicly apologized for what he'd said. He had reportedly already spoken to New Jersey chairman John McMullen, president Robert Butera, and general manager and coach Billy MacMillan in private, but the damage had already been done. Before the Oilers had even released their official statement, MacMillan had been dismissed by the Devils. While MacMillan's job was already in jeopardy — the Devils had just two victories through the first 20 games of the season — Gretzky's comments didn't help. When the Great One speaks, the hockey world listens. Gretzky tried to put his comments behind him, but when the Devils hosted the Oilers on January 15, 1984, fans showed up at the Meadowlands Arena wearing Mickey Mouse ears. Whenever Gretzky was on the ice, the New Jersey faithful booed him relentlessly. Following the Oilers' 5–4 victory that evening, Gretzky addressed his welcome from the fans and stated, "I've been booed worse than that."

NOVEMBER 20
FRED SASAKAMOOSE MAKES NHL DEBUT, 1953

When Fred Sasakamoose was just seven years old, he and his brother, Frank, were forcibly taken from their family on the Sandy Lake Reserve in Saskatchewan and brought to a residential school. Sadly, this was the same fate that befell many Indigenous children across Canada in the 20th century. Beginning in the late 1880s, the federal government, in collaboration with churches and religious orders, established a system of residential schools from coast to coast that sought to assimilate Indigenous children into Canadian society by removing them from their families. While in attendance at these schools, which were often overcrowded and substandard, students were forbidden from speaking their first language and practising their culture, and many were victims of emotional, physical, and sexual abuse. Many children never even made it home, succumbing to the conditions at the schools or dying while they tried to escape back to their families.

During Sasakamoose's time at St. Michael's School in Duck Lake, one of the priests noticed he had talent on the ice and eventually brought him to Moose Jaw to hone his skills. Following a few seasons of junior hockey, Sasakamoose was called up to the Chicago Black Hawks early in the 1953–54 campaign. On November 20, 1953, in a game against the Boston Bruins, Sasakamoose made his NHL debut, becoming one of the first Indigenous hockey players to make it to the big league. Sasakamoose played 10 more games with the Black Hawks that season before he returned to Moose Jaw. Sasakamoose didn't make another appearance in the NHL, but he continued playing hockey until 1966. Although his time in the league was brief, his impact was immeasurable for the Indigenous players who followed in his footsteps. After Sasakamoose's death in 2020, former 60-goal scorer Reggie Leach told the CBC that "a lot of people say he only played 11 games. But those 11 games were everything to our First Nations people."

NOVEMBER 21
RANGERS TROUNCE GOLDEN SEALS 12-1, 1971

t was one of the most lopsided defeats in NHL history. On November 21, 1971, the New York Rangers trounced the visiting California Golden Seals 12–1. The game didn't start off as bad as it ended; the Blueshirts inflicted most of their damage in the final frame. Following the first period, the Rangers had taken a 2–0 lead off goals by Jean Ratelle and Vic Hadfield, and the game was still within reach for the woeful Golden Seals. Ted Irvine and Ratelle extended their team's lead with two more markers through the first half of the second period, but the Golden Seals cut the deficit to three when they got on the board with less than three minutes remaining in the stanza. It proved to be California's only goal that game, and it was vehemently protested by the Rangers. After the Golden Seals' Norm Ferguson scored, the goal light didn't go off, prompting New York to launch an appeal with referee Art Skov about whether the puck had actually gone into the net. Following a lengthy consultation with his linesmen, Skov ruled that it was, in fact, a good goal.

Although the Rangers were incensed at the time, once the puck dropped for the third period, California's lone goal didn't matter. Just 41 seconds into the period, Ratelle scored his third of the night to complete the hat trick, and within a span of three minutes, Irvine and Ratelle each added another tally to make it 7–1. But the Rangers weren't done. Rookie Gene Carr got on the board a few minutes later, and fellow newcomer Pierre Jarry potted two quick goals in eight seconds before Carr added another on a power play to make it 11–1. Finally, with just 36 seconds remaining, Bill Fairbairn scored to cap off an eight-goal period, matching the NHL record for most goals in a single frame. On those eight goals, the Rangers accumulated 23 points, surpassing the mark established by the Detroit Red Wings on January 23, 1944, for the most points in a period.

NOVEMBER 22
GRETZKY REACHES 500-GOAL
MILESTONE, 1986

Heading into a matchup against the Vancouver Canucks on November 22, 1986, Wayne Gretzky was just three goals away from reaching the vaunted 500-career-goal mark. If anyone could notch a hat trick to reach that milestone, it was Gretzky, who already had 38 to his name, the most in NHL history. But when Gretzky learned on the morning of the game that 19-year-old goalie Troy Gamble, who had been called up from junior hockey to replace the injured Richard Brodeur, was making his first career start for Vancouver, he knew his odds had increased. Following the game, Gretzky later said, "This morning I knew they were playing the young goalie … and I knew it would be a good night for Wayne Gretzky." I'm using that quote as a bit of foreshadowing, but also to highlight the fact that in this instance, Gretzky referred to himself in the third person. I've combed through plenty of Gretzky quotes over the years, and even interviewed him by telephone, and never once found an example of the Great One using the third person.

It didn't take long for Gretzky to start making good on his prediction. Less than two minutes into the game, Gretzky came around from behind the Canucks' net and put it past Gamble to move within two of the plateau. Early in the second period, Gretzky entered the Vancouver zone with Glenn Anderson and unleashed a slapshot from just above the left faceoff circle to notch career goal number 499. As the Canucks trailed 4–2 late in the third period, they pulled Gamble for the extra attacker. With just 18 seconds remaining on the clock, Gretzky fired the puck from centre ice and into the empty net, completing the hat trick to become the 13th player in NHL history to reach the 500-goal mark. Playing in just his 575th career game, Gretzky became the fastest player to accomplish that feat, beating out New York Islanders sniper Mike Bossy, who had reached the plateau in 647 games less than a year earlier.

NOVEMBER 23
JETS CLAIM MARKO DAŇO ON WAIVERS, 2018

After starting the season as a healthy scratch, the Winnipeg Jets placed Marko Daňo on waivers on October 14, 2018. Originally acquired by Winnipeg a couple of years earlier as part of a trade that sent captain Andrew Ladd to the Chicago Blackhawks, Daňo had spent much of the past season in the press box as a scratch. Wanting to give him a fresh start and make room for centre Nic Petan, who was coming back to the lineup following the death of his father, the Jets put Daňo on waivers just five games into the 2018–19 campaign. To accommodate Petan's return, the club could have reassigned other players to its AHL affiliate, the Manitoba Moose, without putting Daňo on waivers, but head coach Paul Maurice was adamant about giving the Slovak winger a chance to play elsewhere. "Marko had been an outstanding professional last year," he told reporters. "He went through the entire year kind of dealing with this, not being in. And we want to give him an opportunity to play."

The next day, Daňo was claimed by the Colorado Avalanche. But after going eight games without a point and spending a few match-ups as a scratch, Colorado put Daňo on waivers on November 22, 2018. Although the Jets had waived him just over a month earlier, they plucked Daňo off the waiver wire the next day and assigned him to the Moose. Daňo finished the season in the AHL, recording 12 goals and 30 points in 51 games. In the off-season, the Jets opted not to extend a qualifying offer to Daňo, so he became an unrestricted free agent and eventually signed a one-year, two-way contract with the Columbus Blue Jackets, the team that had originally drafted him 27th overall in 2013. While Daňo was called up for a few games in Columbus, he spent most of the 2019–20 season in the minors with the Cleveland Monsters. Daňo returned to the Jets organization when he signed a one-year, two-way contract on November 5, 2020, but early in training camp, Daňo was once again placed on waivers by the club.

NOVEMBER 24
PATRIK LAINE SCORES FIVE GOALS, 2018

Patrik Laine might have been a goaltender. When the Tampere, Finland, native starting playing hockey at the age of four, he took turns at every position, and when it was his turn to be goalie, he embraced the opportunity. Laine soon discovered he was pretty good at keeping pucks out of the net. He remained in the crease for quite a few years until his father, Harri, convinced him he should hang up his pads and play forward. It proved to be sage advice. After joining Tappara, his hometown team in Liiga, Finland's top professional league, for a handful of games in 2014–15, Laine helped the club win a league championship and was named MVP of the playoffs the following year. On the heels of his title with Tappara, Laine was taken second overall by the Winnipeg Jets in the 2016 NHL Entry Draft. In his first season with Winnipeg, Laine scored 36 goals to lead the team in goal scoring. The next season, he followed up his rookie performance with a 44-goal campaign, trailing only Alex Ovechkin, his boyhood idol, for the most in the league that year.

A few months into his third NHL season, Laine racked up goals at a prolific rate. By the time the Jets took on the St. Louis Blues on November 24, 2018, the Finnish sniper had already recorded 11 goals that month, including two hat tricks. Near the end of the first period, Laine fired a one-timer to break a 1–1 tie. Less than two minutes into the middle frame, he rifled a shot from the left faceoff circle to give Winnipeg a 3–2 lead. Just over 10 minutes later, he completed the hat trick, and before the period ended, added another. Early in the final frame, he scored his fifth of the game, becoming the first player since the Detroit Red Wings' Johan Franzén in 2011 to accomplish that feat. The offensive outburst against the Blues gave him 19 goals for the season, vaulting him into sole possession of the NHL goal-scoring lead, but Laine cooled off and finished the campaign with 30.

NOVEMBER 25
HARRY NEALE SWINGS STICK AT BULLS FANS, 1976

With time winding down in a game against the Birmingham Bulls of the WHA, New England Whalers head coach Harry Neale stood on the bench and boisterously celebrated an empty-net goal that gave his team a 5–3 lead, sealing their 13th consecutive victory over the Bulls franchise, which had relocated from Toronto prior to the start of the regular season. The Birmingham faithful didn't take kindly to Neale's jubilation and proceeded to hurl cups, popcorn, programs, and any other debris they could find at the New England coach. As unruly fans inched closer to the glass behind the bench, Neale grabbed a hockey stick and swung it in their direction, injuring three of them. Following the incident, Neale was questioned by police in the visitors' dressing room, but no charges were filed. Two days later, however, a warrant was issued for his arrest when one of the spectators he struck, an elderly woman, pressed charges.

When the Whalers returned to Alabama for a game on February 1, 1977, the matter still hadn't been resolved. It was supposed to be settled the morning before the matchup, but the complainant had failed to show up at court, pushing it onto the docket the following day. With Neale still considered public enemy number one in Birmingham, the police stepped up their presence at the arena in case any fans in attendance that evening wanted to even the score. Officials doled out 120 penalty minutes in a fight-filled first period, but unlike the last matchup, all of the conflict was confined to the ice. The next day, Neale was cleared of all charges. But it wasn't the last time the fiery coach was involved in an altercation with fans. On March 20, 1982, as head coach of the NHL's Vancouver Canucks, Neale and some of his players went into the stands of the Quebec Coliseum to square off with some Nordiques fans. Neale was later suspended 10 games by the league for his involvement in that incident.

NOVEMBER 26
MAREK MALIK SCORES MEMORABLE SHOOTOUT GOAL, 2005

The New York Rangers were running out of shooters. With only two available skaters remaining on the bench for a shootout against the Washington Capitals on November 26, 2005, the team turned to defenceman Marek Malik. The lumbering Czech blue-liner wasn't exactly known for his scoring prowess. Originally selected in the third round of the 1993 NHL Entry Draft by the Hartford Whalers, Malik had scored 27 regular-season goals over nearly the next decade in the league. After the Capitals' Matt Bradley, the first shooter in the 15th round, was stopped by Henrik Lundqvist, Malik was up for the Rangers. It was the defenceman's first shootout attempt in the league — the tiebreaker format had just been implemented that year following the lockout — so no one was sure what kind of tricks, if any, Malik had up his sleeve.

As he moved in on Washington netminder Olaf Kölzig, he brought the puck back through his skates, and with his stick still between his legs, roofed the puck into the top of the net, popping up Kölzig's water bottle and ending the shootout. It was a circus trick shot from the most unlikely shooter, which is why it's gone down as one of the most memorable shootout moments in NHL history. But for me, Malik's reaction is just as indelible as the goal. As he skated away from the net, he acknowledged the crowd by simply nodding and raising his left arm. He had just scored an incredible goal, ending the longest shootout in league history up to that point, and yet he celebrated with a nonchalance that suggested it was a move he'd pulled off hundreds of times before. Following the game, Malik divulged that he'd worked on the technique in practice and figured that, with Kölzig stopping nearly every attempt so far in the shootout, he had nothing to lose by trying it out. He was right. Malik finished his NHL career with 33 goals, but none were as unforgettable as that between-the-legs move. It has been immortalized on countless highlight reels and has been imitated by players everywhere.

COACH DIT CLAPPER SUITS UP FOR BRUINS, 1946

With the Boston Bruins down a defenceman for an up-coming game against the New York Rangers, head coach Dit Clapper suited up and joined the blue line. It wasn't unfamiliar territory for the 39-year-old Clapper, who had served as a player-coach for Boston the past season before becoming a full-time bench boss after hanging up his skates in 1946. Although Clapper was only filling in for Johnny Crawford, who was out with a bruised right calf, he ended up making NHL history. When Clapper stepped onto the ice for the Bruins' game against the Rangers on November 27, 1946, he became the first player in league history to appear in 20 seasons. Clapper had originally joined the Bruins for the 1927–28 season as a defenceman, but general manager and coach Art Ross switched him to right wing. Two years later, Clapper racked up 41 goals, the second most in the league that year behind only linemate Cooney Wieland, who potted 43 that season. After playing up front with the Bruins for nearly a decade, Clapper was moved back to defence. Paired with Eddie Shore, Clapper quickly picked up where he'd left off as a rearguard and was named to the NHL First All-Star Team for three consecutive years.

During the 1944–45 campaign, Clapper got his taste of coaching, filling in for Ross when he was unable to travel with the team. At the end of the season, Ross stepped aside from his coaching duties and Clapper took over as bench boss while continuing to patrol the blue line. After making his historic appearance as a substitute for Crawford, Clapper played five more games for the Bruins that season before returning to the bench full-time. Less than a month after playing his final game for the club, Clapper was inducted into the Hockey Hall of Fame, becoming the first living player to receive that distinction. A week after being called to the hall, the Bruins also honoured Clapper by raising his number 5 to the rafters of Boston Garden on February 12, 1947. Clapper coached two more seasons for the Bruins before retiring in 1949.

NOVEMBER 28
ROBERTO LUONGO MAKES NHL DEBUT, 1999

Two years after becoming the highest-drafted goaltender in NHL history, Robert Luongo made his much-anticipated debut for the New York Islanders. Taken fourth overall by New York in the 1997 Entry Draft, following two more seasons of junior hockey, Luongo started the 1999–2000 campaign in the minors. After backup netminder Wade Flaherty went down with a shoulder injury, Luongo was recalled, and on November 28, 1999, the young goaltender got the nod and made his first NHL start in a game against the Boston Bruins. Although the woeful Islanders were outshot more than two to one, Luongo put on a stellar performance that night, making 43 saves in a 2–1 victory and demonstrating why the team was right to select him so high. With Luongo believed to be the franchise's goaltender of the future, a few weeks later, the Islanders traded regular starter Felix Potvin and two draft picks to the Vancouver Canucks in exchange for goaltender Kevin Weekes, Dave Scatchard, and Bill Muckalt. Luongo spent the rest of the season splitting starting duties with Weekes until he was sent back down to the AHL in early March.

Although Luongo was backstopping a dreadful Islanders team that finished with the second-fewest goals that year behind only the ex-pansionist Atlanta Thrashers, he managed to pick up seven victories in his rookie campaign. It seemed as if Luongo would be on Long Island for quite a while, but not long after the club took goaltend-er Rick DiPietro first overall at the 2000 NHL Entry Draft, general manager Mike Milbury sent Luongo and former third-overall pick Olli Jokinen to the Florida Panthers in exchange for Mark Parrish and Oleg Kvasha. Following the trade, Milbury told reporters he was "rolling the dice here a bit," while Panthers GM Bryan Murray boast-ed that Luongo "will be one of the best goaltenders in the NHL." I'm sure you can guess who turned out to be right. In Florida, Luongo established himself as a full-time starter and went on to become one of the best goaltenders in league history, racking up the third-most career wins by the time he retired in 2019.

NOVEMBER 29
PETERS LEE AND MAHOVLICH TRADED FOR PIERRE LAROUCHE, 1977

've included the following story for none of the reasons you might expect. See if you can figure it out before getting to the end. After a disappointing season, Peter Mahovlich knew his days were numbered with the Montreal Canadiens. Although Mahovlich scored 34 goals and 105 points in the 1975–76 season playing with wingers Guy Lafleur and Steve Shutt, head coach Scotty Bowman bumped him off that line in favour of Jacques Lemaire the following year. The hulking centre struggled offensively and finished the campaign with just 15 goals and 62 points. Even though Mahovlich picked up his fourth Stanley Cup with the Canadiens in 1977, he had a sluggish start to the 1977–78 regular season. After scoring only three goals in 17 games, Mahovlich was dealt to the Pittsburgh Penguins, along with minor-leaguer Peter Lee, on November 29, 1977, in exchange for Pierre Larouche and future considerations. Mahovlich rebounded in Pittsburgh, finished the year with 25 goals and 61 points in 57 games, and quickly established himself as a fan favourite.

The trade also worked out for Lee, who was starting his second straight season with Montreal's AHL affiliate, the Nova Scotia Voyageurs. Drafted 12th overall by the Canadiens in 1976, Lee had been unable to crack the big club's deep roster, but the move to Pittsburgh provided the young right winger with the chance to prove himself at the NHL level. In his first full season with the Penguins, Lee scored 32 goals, a benchmark he reached again with the club two years later. Meanwhile, in Montreal, Larouche, who had scored 53 goals for the Penguins in 1975–76, eventually hit the 50-goal mark with the Canadiens, becoming the first player in NHL history to accomplish that feat with two different teams. So what's the reason I included this story? The trade was a rare three-peat. Peter and Peter to Pittsburgh for Pierre, which is French for Peter. You can groan now.

NOVEMBER 30
STRIKE OF OFFICIALS COMES TO END, 1993

The NHL's referees and linesmen started the 1993–94 season without a contract. The league and the officials' association had been trying to reach a new agreement since the season began, but they had been unable to hammer out a deal. The officials were hoping for a new contract that would include an increase in salaries and a more robust benefits package, but the two sides remained far apart during talks. On November 12, 1993, the officials' association unanimously rejected what was reportedly the league's final offer. Although the two sides continued to negotiate over the weekend, they reached an impasse on Sunday evening, and the following day, November 15, the NHL's referees and linesmen staged the first full walkout by officials in league history. With three games on the docket that evening, the league had to move quickly, hiring replacement officials from the junior, professional, and college ranks. With very little time to prepare, the substitute officials hit the ice that evening with radio headsets in their helmets so they could be in constant contact with their supervisors in the arenas.

Over the next 16 days, NHL games were overseen by replacement officials, inciting criticism from some of the players about the calibre of the officiating. Finally, on November 30, following a marathon bargaining session in a hotel in Dorval, Quebec, the officials and the league reached a four-year deal. The agreement was ratified the next day, and the NHL's regular officials were back on the ice on December 2 for a slate of six games. It came as a relief to the players. While New York Rangers captain Mark Messier was diplomatic and suggested the replacements had tried their best, St. Louis Blues sniper Brett Hull, who had been a vocal critic throughout the walkout, didn't hold back when he heard the news: "Since they are officially not refs anymore, can I say how bad they really are? If they [the NHL] thought even one of those fellows could be a real ref, they are out of their minds."

DECEMBER 1
BERNIE NICHOLLS SCORES
EIGHT POINTS, 1988

Not long into the 1988–89 season, Bernie Nicholls recalled that Wayne Gretzky, who had recently joined the Los Angeles Kings a few months earlier as part of a blockbuster deal that had rocked the hockey world, gave him a tip while the team was on a road trip to Winnipeg. Gretzky told him that teammate Jari Kurri used to take his hockey stick home for good luck. At the time, Nicholls was using a new stick every game but thought maybe Gretzky was onto something. After the morning skate, Nicholls took his stick back to the hotel with him. Later that day, he bagged a hat trick against the Winnipeg Jets, and from then on, the goal-scoring centre was usually never far from his twig on game days. Even in Los Angeles, Nicholls wasn't shy about carting his stick around with him even if it meant lugging it into a restaurant for a pre-game meal. Although he might have spotted a few raised eyebrows, Nicholls wasn't about to deviate from his new routine, especially as he continued to light the lamp.

So, when the Kings hosted the Toronto Maple Leafs on December 1, 1988, Nicholls stuck to his plan. Since he lived far from the Great Western Forum at the time, he typically spent game days at the Airport Park Hotel across from the arena and walked later that day, stick in hand, to the game. When the first period came to a close, Nicholls already had three assists. Early in the middle frame, he assisted on a goal by Dave Taylor and added two goals of his own as the Kings went into the third period with a commanding 6–1 lead. Nicholls added two more assists in the final 20 minutes to bring his total to eight points, establishing a new club record for most points in a game and bringing his season total up to 30 goals and 63 points through 26 games. Nicholls finished the campaign with 70 goals, a club record, and 150 points, all with his stick by his side on and off the ice.

DECEMBER 2
MARTIN BRODEUR SIGNS WITH BLUES, 2014

Martin Brodeur wasn't ready to hang up his goalie equipment yet. Although the 42-year-old goaltender wasn't re-signed by the New Jersey Devils following the 2013–14 season, his 20th campaign with the club, he wanted to continue playing. Originally drafted 20th overall by New Jersey in 1990, Brodeur broke into the league three years later, winning the Calder Trophy in his first season as the league's most outstanding rookie. Over the course of his tenure with the Devils, Brodeur backstopped the club to three Stanley Cup championships, earned four Vezina Trophies, and rewrote the league's records book, establishing new benchmarks for the most victories and shutouts by a goaltender. When the 2014–15 season began, Brodeur still hadn't signed elsewhere, but he was determined to stay in the crease.

Following an injury to St. Louis Blues goaltender Brian Elliott, who went down with a sprained knee in late November, there looked to be an opening on the team. Brodeur began practising with the club on a tryout basis, and on December 2, 2014, he signed a one-year, $700,000-deal. The bonus-laden contract would net Brodeur $10,000 for every point the Blues earned with him between the pipes, but he didn't care about the money; he just wanted to keep playing. "Hockey's fun," he told reporters. "I just couldn't see myself stopping right now." Two days after putting pen to paper, Brodeur donned a different uniform for the first time in his career, allowing four goals in a 4–3 loss to the Nashville Predators. But it didn't take long for the veteran goaltender to record a win with his new team. On December 6, after relieving rookie Jake Allen in a matchup against the New York Islanders, Brodeur made 14 saves to secure the victory, earning a $20,000 bonus for 40 minutes in the crease. Not a bad night's work. The future Hall of Famer made five more appearances for the Blues, including his final career shutout on December 29 against the Colorado Avalanche, before he officially announced his retirement on January 29, 2015.

DECEMBER 3
JOE THORNTON SCORES FIRST NHL POINT, 1997

The wait was finally over for Joe Thornton. On December 3, 1997, in a game against the Philadelphia Flyers, the Boston Bruins' six-foot-four centre finally notched his first career NHL point. Selected first overall by Boston nearly six months earlier in the NHL Entry Draft, Thornton, coming off a 122-point campaign with the Soo Greyhounds of the Ontario Hockey League, was expected to make a big impact on a Bruins team that had finished the previous season at the bottom of the standings. His anticipated debut, however, had to wait. During a pre-season game against the Pittsburgh Penguins on September 23, 1997, Thornton fractured his left arm in the first period and was expected to be sidelined for six to eight weeks. He missed the first three games of the regular season, but just over three weeks after breaking his arm, he made his NHL debut on October 8 against the Phoenix Coyotes.

After playing the next six games on the road and registering no points, Thornton was scratched for the team's next home game. Thornton eventually made his first appearance in front of the Boston faithful two nights later, recording a penalty but no points in a 5–4 loss to the Florida Panthers. As Thornton adjusted to the NHL, he was relegated to the fourth line and continued to spend more time in the press box as a scratch. Finally, after going 21 games without a point, the hulking rookie got on the score sheet. Just over six minutes into the third period of Boston's matchup against the Flyers, Thornton caught a drop pass from P.J. Axelsson just above the blue line in the attacking zone. He continued driving toward the net and backhanded the puck past goaltender Garth Snow to give the Bruins a 2–0 lead. It took a little longer than he expected, but Thornton finally recorded his first NHL point. As of this writing, 41-year-old Thornton, now with the Toronto Maple Leafs, finished the 2020–21 campaign with 20 points, bringing his career total to 1,529, the 14th most in league history.

DECEMBER 4
MAPLE LEAFS ACQUIRE JIM RUTHERFORD, 1980

Looking for help in goal, the Toronto Maple Leafs acquired veteran netminder Jim Rutherford from the Detroit Red Wings on December 4, 1980, in exchange for rookie centre Mark Kirton. Drafted 10th overall by Detroit in 1969, Rutherford made his NHL debut a year later, but after playing 29 games for the Red Wings in 1970–71, he was claimed by the Pittsburgh Penguins in the 1971 intraleague draft. Following a few years in Pittsburgh, the Red Wings got Rutherford back in 1974 when they reacquired him, along with Jack Lynch, in exchange for Ron Stackhouse. For the next four years, Rutherford served as the club's starting goaltender until the arrival of Rogie Vachon from the Los Angeles Kings in 1978.

Although the Leafs were just as porous as the Detroit teams Rutherford had backstopped, he hoped he could make a difference in Toronto, where the club had given up 101 goals through its first 23 games of the season. In his first appearance for the Leafs, on December 6, 1980, Rutherford made 29 saves in a 5–2 victory against the Quebec Nordiques, snapping the club's seven-game winless streak. Despite Rutherford's solid start with his new team, he didn't win another game for more than two months. After racking up seven losses and two ties, Rutherford finally got his second win with Toronto on February 12, 1981, the first of three straight victories. Those wins, however, would be his last with the club. On March 10, 1981, the Leafs traded Rutherford to the Los Angeles Kings for future considerations. Rutherford, originally destined for Los Angeles when the Red Wings signed Vachon a few years earlier, played 10 games for the Kings over the next two seasons before finishing his NHL career in Detroit. After hanging up his goalie pads, Rutherford eventually went on to a Hall of Fame career as an executive, serving as the architect of a Stanley Cup with the Carolina Hurricanes and back-to-back championships in Pittsburgh.

DECEMBER 5
JACOB MARKSTRÖM GETS FIRST CAREER NHL SHUTOUT, 2017

After 129 games, Jacob Markström finally recorded his first career NHL shutout. On December 5, 2017, in a contest against the Carolina Hurricanes, the Vancouver Canucks goaltender stopped all 30 shots in a 3–0 victory. Early in his career, when he was still with the Florida Panthers, Markström had actually come close on a couple of occasions. On March 19, 2013, while facing Carolina, Markström had been working on a shutout until Jordan Staal spoiled his bid with less than three minutes remaining in the game. In the very next matchup, Markström was perfect again through most of regulation time but gave up a goal to the New York Rangers' Marián Gáborík with just over four minutes on the clock. Markström picked up victories in both games, but his first NHL shutout remained elusive. Nearly four years later, Markström finally reached the milestone against the Hurricanes, but he had come pretty close to matching an unofficial league record for the most games played without a shutout.

Prior to the Canucks' game that night, Markström was just four games shy of Eldon "Pokey" Reddick's mark. Reddick, who played 132 games over parts of six seasons in the NHL, had finished his big-league career without a shutout. Reddick racked up more than 30 shutouts playing nearly two decades in the minors and overseas, but for whatever reason, he just couldn't accomplish the feat in the NHL. The only reason I know this is because Sean McIndoe, a.k.a Down Goes Brown, someone who I've long admired for his uncanny ability to bring some of the most obscure moments in hockey history to life, wrote an article about it for Sportsnet that was published the morning before Markström suited up against the Hurricanes. After explaining how unlikely Markström's streak had been, McIndoe's final line in the story was actually "Congratulations in advance on the shutout tonight, Jacob." And sure enough, later that evening, after McIndoe seemingly conjured up the hockey gods, Markström did, in fact, get his long-overdue shutout.

DECEMBER 6
PATRICK ROY TRADED TO AVALANCHE, 1995

There was no coming back for the Montreal Canadiens' Patrick Roy. After being left in net for nine goals in a game against the Detroit Red Wings on December 2, 1995, Roy was finally relieved midway through the second period. The veteran goaltender was incensed and felt as though he'd been hung out to dry. As he made his way down the Canadiens' bench, he brushed by head coach Mario Tremblay before turning back toward the seat of team president Ronald Corey. Roy supposedly told Corey that he would never play in Montreal again and then calmly took a seat at the end of the bench. The next day, general manager Réjean Houle met with Roy to try to salvage the relationship with the club, but the fiery goaltender had made up his mind: he had played his last game for the Canadiens. While Houle tried to keep the three-time Vezina Trophy winner in the fold, Corey didn't exactly help the situation. According to the *Montreal Gazette*, the president called Roy and initially told him to come to the Forum to grab his equipment and never return. Not long after delivering that icy message, however, Corey called him back and explained that he would be welcomed back to the organization. But it was too late, Roy was done.

Following days of speculation as to where Roy would land, in the early morning hours of December 6, 1995, the Canadiens traded him, along with captain Mike Keane, to the Colorado Avalanche in exchange for Jocelyn Thibault, Andrei Kovalenko, and Martin Rucinsky. The Avalanche already had a strong core of players that included Joe Sakic and Peter Forsberg, but the addition of Roy really put them over the top and made them instant Stanley Cup favourites. After finishing the regular season in Denver with 22 victories, Roy backstopped the Avalanche to their first Stanley Cup in franchise history. Five years later, Roy won his second title with Colorado and picked up his third Conn Smythe Trophy, becoming the first and still the only player in NHL history to win the playoff MVP award three times.

DECEMBER 7
ISLANDERS FIRE TERRY SIMPSON, 1988

Following a sluggish start to the 1988–89 regular season, the New York Islanders decided to make a coaching change behind the bench. On December 7, 1988, the club dismissed Terry Simpson. Although Simpson had guided the team to its sixth division title the year before, the Islanders had only won seven games to start the campaign and were sitting well outside a playoff spot. General manager Bill Torrey figured that if there was anyone who could turn the team's fortunes around it would be former coach Al Arbour. Arbour, who had been behind the Islanders' bench for 13 years and guided the team to four consecutive Stanley Cup championships, had retired a few years earlier and was in the middle of this third season as the club's vice-president of player personnel. While Arbour hadn't thought about returning to coaching, he was ready to take on the role again. Torrey was confident that Arbour could pull the club out from the depths of the Patrick Division, but it was no easy task.

Although the players might have liked Arbour more — one of the chief complaints in the dressing room was that Simpson had a tough exterior they just couldn't crack — the team continued to struggle. Under Arbour's direction, the club posted a 21–29–3 record and missed the post-season for the first time in 15 years. But Arbour returned the following season and led the team back into the playoffs. After missing the post-season for the next two years, in 1993, Arbour and the Islanders knocked off the defending back-to-back champions, the Pittsburgh Penguins, in overtime in Game 7 to advance to the conference final, their furthest run since 1984. Following one more season behind the bench, Arbour retired for the second and final time after the 1993–94 campaign. Over the course of his career, he coached 1,499 games for the Islanders. More than a decade later, at the behest of head coach Ted Nolan, the club brought Arbour back for one game so he could reach the 1,500-game milestone with the franchise.

DECEMBER 8
SUBBAN BROTHERS SQUARE OFF, 2017

For the first time in their NHL careers, brothers P.K. and Malcolm Subban, one a defenceman, the other a goaltender, squared off in a regular-season game, becoming just the 10th set of brothers in league history to play against each other in which one is a skater and the other is in net. On December 8, 2017, the Nashville Predators hosted the Vegas Golden Knights at Bridgestone Arena in a family affair. P.K. patrolled the blue line for Nashville, Malcolm tended the twine for Vegas, and their father, Karl, who was in attendance as part of the Golden Knights' fathers' trip, was in the stands. P.K. got a shot off on his younger brother, but Malcolm stopped it and earned bragging rights that night as he went on to earn the victory in a shootout. Following the game, Malcolm told reporters, "It's pretty cool. Obviously, it's a great experience, like I said, being out there with my dad and my brother."

Due to the four-year age gap between them, growing up, the Subban brothers had never played against each other except on an outdoor rink or in games of road hockey, but four years before their matchup in Nashville, they actually had their first NHL encounter. On September 16, 2013, when P.K. was still with the Montreal Canadiens and Malcolm was still with the Boston Bruins, they played against each other in a pre-season game in Montreal. Malcolm, who was drafted 24th overall by Boston a year earlier, was making his first appearance in the NHL. After Chad Johnson started the game, Malcolm took over midway through the second period, not long after P.K. had fired a slapshot past Johnson for his lone goal of the game. P.K. got one more shot on his brother, but Malcolm turned that aside, along with 11 others, in a flawless performance to secure a 6–3 win for Boston. Since their first regular-season matchup, P.K. and Malcolm have faced each other three more times, including one game in which the elder Subban rifled four shots on his younger brother, but as of this writing, P.K. has yet to put a puck past Malcolm in the NHL.

DECEMBER 9
MARKUS NÄSLUND SCORES FOUR GOALS AGAINST PENGUINS, 2003

t had been nearly a decade since the Pittsburgh Penguins traded Markus Näslund to the Vancouver Canucks, but he still relished the opportunity to suit up against his former team. Drafted 16th overall by Pittsburgh in 1991, Näslund played parts of a few seasons with the club before he was traded to Vancouver on March 20, 1996, in exchange for Alek Stojanov, a deal covered earlier in this book and one the Penguins would have liked to take back. Stojanov played just 45 games with Pittsburgh and then went on to play five seasons in the minors before hanging up his skates in 2002. Meanwhile, at that same time in Vancouver, Näslund was just coming off his second straight 40-goal season with the Canucks and finished the 2002–03 campaign as the runner-up for the Hart Trophy. Näslund didn't need any further vindication, but he always looked forward to the opportunity to elevate his game against the team that drafted and traded him away.

When the Canucks hosted Pittsburgh on December 9, 2003, Näslund had a little extra motivation. His parents, Sture and Ulla, were visiting from Sweden and were in the crowd at GM Place. Although Näslund was just coming off a groin injury that had kept him out of the lineup for one game, he wasn't going to miss taking on his former team in front of his family. He certainly didn't disappoint that night. Early in the second period, while falling to his knees, he backhanded the puck past Penguins goaltender Marc-André Fleury to tie the game 1–1. After Pittsburgh took the lead again later that frame, Näslund responded on a power play to knot it up again. Just over six minutes into the third period, Näslund completed the hat trick, his 10th career three-goal performance, to put Vancouver up 3–2. But after the Penguins tied it to force overtime, Näslund played the hero 24 seconds into the extra frame, putting the puck through Fleury's legs to secure the victory.

DECEMBER 10
JOHNNY BUCYK SCORES SIX POINTS, 1970

Johnny Bucyk certainly earned his money that night. On December 10, 1970, in a pre-game ceremony at Boston Garden, Bruins president Weston Adams, Jr., presented Bucyk with a $1,000 bill to commemorate his 1,000th NHL game. Bucyk originally broke into the league with the Detroit Red Wings in 1955 but was traded to Boston after just his second season in Detroit. Over the next decade with the Bruins, Bucyk established himself as an integral part of the club and led the team in scoring four times before the arrival of stars Phil Esposito and Bobby Orr. Following the ceremony, as the Bruins prepared to take on the Buffalo Sabres, Bucyk later admitted that he was feeling nervous about the matchup. "A lot of times when they have special ceremonies for a guy he falls flat on his face that night, and I was scared of something like that happening," he told reporters.

Perhaps it was the crisp $1,000 bill in his wallet, but the 35-year-old left winger put on one of the best performances of his career. After picking up assists on goals by Orr and Fred Stanfield in each of the first two periods, Bucyk set up Stanfield again early in the final frame before he scored two goals in just over five minutes to match his career high. After two more goals by the Bruins, Bucyk earned his fourth assist on the final goal that evening as Boston cruised to an 8–2 victory. Following the game, when asked about how he would spend the rare banknote, in between puffs on a cigar, Bucyk said he was going to keep it. "I'll never be broke with that in my pocket," he explained. While Bucyk's outing against the Sabres was one for the books, he did it again on February 25, 1971, scoring three goals and adding three helpers in a game against the Vancouver Canucks. He finished the season with 51 goals and 116 points. Bucyk played seven more years for the Bruins, and at the time of his retirement, was the franchise's all-time leader in games played, goals, assists, and points.

DECEMBER 11
BLADON SETS SINGLE-GAME POINTS RECORD FOR DEFENCEMEN, 1977

Among his Philadelphia Flyers teammates, defenceman Tom Bladon was known as "Sparky," but on December 11, 1977, they called him "Bobby," as in Bobby Orr. Although Bladon bristled at the comparison, they had good reason. That night, in a game against the Cleveland Barons, Bladon picked up eight points, surpassing Orr's record and establishing a new NHL benchmark for the most points in a game by a defenceman. Early in his tenure with the Flyers, Bladon had scored four points in a matchup against the Vancouver Canucks but had never had an offensive outburst like the one against Cleveland. Despite being an important part of the Flyers' back end, Bladon was regularly the subject of trade rumours and often drew the ire of the Philadelphia faithful. Flyers head coach Fred Shero once joked that he was considering putting earmuffs on the blueliner to drown out the taunts at the Spectrum. But on that evening in December, Bladon silenced his critics with the performance of his career.

After Bladon scored Philadelphia's second goal of the game, with just over two minutes remaining in the opening period, he assisted on two others as the Flyers went into intermission with a 4–0 lead. Following a goal by Rick MacLeish, Bladon scored two straight goals in the middle frame to complete the hat trick, the first of his NHL career. But he wasn't done yet. Less than three minutes into the third, Bladon scored again and then set up two more goals, capping off an 11–1 rout over the Barons. Although reporters wanted to make the comparison to Orr, Bladon insisted that no parallel could be drawn. In a telephone interview with the *Edmonton Journal*'s Terry Jones, Bladon, an Edmonton native, chalked it up to luck. "It's just a freak thing," he said. "A freak thing that happened to me…. Every time I shot the puck at the net, it seemed to go in the net." Bladon undoubtedly had some good fortune that night, but his record has stood the test of time. Although Paul Coffey matched it eight years later, it has yet to be surpassed.

DECEMBER 12

BOBBY RYAN SCORES GOAL WITH MIKKO KOIVU'S STICK, 2010

No stick, no problem. After losing his stick in the corner of his own end, Minnesota Wild captain Mikko Koivu grabbed Bobby Ryan's stick right out of his hands. As Koivu skated away with Ryan's stick, the Anaheim Ducks forward threw his hands in the air, incredulous that a penalty hadn't been called. But with no whistle forthcoming, Ryan chased the puck. As play continued along the boards, Minnesota forward Antti Miettinen, who wasn't involved in the scrum along the wall, kept nudging his captain's stick closer to the action, thinking that perhaps Koivu might drop Ryan's stick in favour of his own. After all, Koivu, a left-handed shooter, was using a wrong-handed stick. Ryan was a righty and it would have made sense for him to pick up his own stick if he could.

But as Koivu continued playing with his opponent's twig, Ryan figured he might as well scoop up the discarded stick. Even if it was the wrong hand, it was still better than nothing. Just a few seconds after Ryan picked up the stick, Anaheim defenceman Toni Lydman rifled a shot from the far right side. Goaltender Niklas Bäckström initially made the save, but the rebound bounced to Ryan standing on the opposite side of the crease. As Bäckström tried to slide back over, Ryan shot the puck into the wide-open cage. Even with a wrong-handed stick, there was no way he was missing from that angle. As Koivu skated through the top of the crease following the goal, Ryan boastfully lifted "his" stick in the air with both hands to show him the result of his handiwork. Koivu actually argued with the officials that the goal shouldn't count because Ryan wasn't using the proper stick, but Ryan reminded the Minnesota captain that he wouldn't have even been in that situation if Koivu hadn't yanked his stick out of his hands. It happened to be Ryan's first goal in nearly two weeks, and following the game, he joked with reporters that maybe he should go out and pick up a few left-handed sticks.

DECEMBER 13
MANON RHÉAUME PLAYS REGULAR-SEASON PRO GAME, 1992

A few months after becoming the first woman to play in the NHL, Manon Rhéaume continued to break down barriers later that season. On December 13, 1992, she entered the crease for part of the second period of the Atlanta Knights' game against the Salt Lake Golden Eagles of the International Hockey League, becoming the first woman ever to play in a regular-season professional hockey game. Following her appearance in the Tampa Bay Lightning's pre-season match against the St. Louis Blues, Rhéaume signed a contract with Atlanta, the IHL affiliate of the Lightning. As Rhéaume skated onto the ice at the Omni Coliseum in Atlanta, she drew a standing ovation from the crowd. While Knights goaltender David Littman played the first period, Rhéaume went in to start the middle frame. In just under six minutes of action, she allowed one goal and made three saves. After Littman returned to the net and gave up two more goals, one fan reportedly stood and shrieked at head coach Gene Ubriaco to put Rhéaume back in.

Following her brief but historic appearance, Rhéaume earned her first professional start later in the season when the Knights hosted the Cincinnati Cyclones on April 10, 1993. Although she gave up six goals in an 8–6 loss to the Cyclones, Rhéaume said it was important to get a full pro game under her belt. "I needed to play in this kind of situation," she told reporters. "Now that the first game is down, I'm going to feel better for the next one." The following year, Rhéaume started the season with the Knoxville Cherokees of the East Coast Hockey League (ECHL). On November 6, 1993, she made 32 saves in a 9–6 win over the Johnstown Chiefs, earning her first professional victory. A week earlier in the ECHL, Erin Whitten of the Toledo Storm entered a game against the Dayton Bombers in relief of injured netminder Alain Harvey. Whitten went on to secure a 6–5 victory, becoming the first woman to win a professional hockey game.

DECEMBER 14
MIKE GARTNER HITS 700, 1997

The Phoenix Coyotes were taking a calculated risk. To clear a roster spot for newly signed defenceman Michel Petit, they had to put a player on waivers. General manager Bobby Smith decided to roll the dice by putting 38-year-old Mike Gartner on waivers. At the time, Gartner was still recovering from torn knee ligaments, and Smith figured the injury, along with his age and $1.1-million salary, would make teams shy away from putting in a claim on the veteran sniper. Smith turned out to be right. Gartner cleared waivers and remained with the Coyotes. Although Gartner was initially dismayed when he learned he'd been placed on waivers, he and his teammates were happy when they found out he'd be staying in Phoenix. Gartner was zeroing in on a rare NHL milestone and didn't want to accomplish it anywhere else. Before he injured his knee, Gartner was two goals away from the 700-goal mark. He'd come close the season before, but after finishing with just one goal in his past 16 games, Gartner remained four away from the plateau.

When the 1997–98 regular season began, the goals remained few and far between for Gartner. But after going scoreless in his first nine games, he got on the board in his 10th contest and then picked up another tally two games later before injuring his knee in a matchup against the Calgary Flames on November 2, 1997. In his fourth game back from injury, Gartner potted a goal against the Pittsburgh Penguins to move within one. Then, finally, on December 14, 1997, in the first period against the Detroit Red Wings, Gartner put the puck past goaltender Chris Osgood to become just the fifth player in NHL history to score 700 career goals. As he was mobbed by his teammates, the Coyotes' fans gave him a roaring ovation. Never before had the feat been accomplished in front of a home crowd, making it all the more special. Just a few weeks earlier, Gartner was placed on waivers and laid up with a knee injury, but now he was in the illustrious 700-goal club.

DECEMBER 15
WINNIPEG JETS HOST TUXEDO NIGHT, 1979

n their first season in the NHL after joining as part of the merger with the WHA, the Winnipeg Jets organized a Tuxedo Night on December 15, 1979, when they took on the reigning Stanley Cup champions, the Montreal Canadiens. Since the game was going to be nationally televised on *Hockey Night in Canada*, Winnipeg wanted to look its best. The idea came from the Jets Booster Club, which then worked with a local tuxedo rental firm that agreed to offer the suits at half the normal rental price. It's estimated that 1,000 fans showed up at the Winnipeg Arena that evening wearing tuxedos. In addition to the finely dressed patrons, everyone from the usherettes to the Zamboni driver wore tuxedos. Even Jets head coach Tom McVie sported one behind the bench. Although Montreal tried to spoil the party by scoring less than a minute into the game, the Jets quickly took over the contest. They scored six straight goals, capped off by a Willy Lindström hat trick, to take a 6–2 victory against the defending champions.

While Tuxedo Night proved to be a hit, it also marked the end of Bobby Hull's era with the organization. Hull, who had been struggling, scoring just four goals and 10 points through the first 18 games of the season, turned up late for the games against the Canadiens and was scratched by McVie. "The rule is that if you show up late for a game, you don't play," the bench boss told reporters. "It's the same rule for everybody." Rather than sticking around to watch his team play, Hull went home. The next day, when the Jets were supposed to depart to play the Edmonton Oilers, the veteran sniper was a no-show. Hull never played another game for the Jets. After sitting out the next few months with an ailing shoulder, he was traded to the New England Whalers on February 27, 1980, in exchange for future considerations. Hull played his last NHL regular-season game on April 6, along with Gordie Howe, before hanging up his skates.

DECEMBER 16

PATRICK BROTHERS GO HEAD-TO-HEAD, 1934

As veteran New York Rangers coach Lester Patrick looked out at the ice, he spotted a familiar face on the opposing bench, his younger brother, Frank. The elder Patrick had been coaching the Blueshirts since they joined the NHL in 1926, but Frank, who had spent the past two decades playing and coaching in the Pacific Coast Hockey Association, was in his first season behind the bench with the Boston Bruins. On December 16, 1934, when the Rangers hosted the Bruins, the Patricks squared off for the first time in the NHL, marking the first time that two brothers opposed each other as coaches. While the Patrick brothers might have been the first full-time coaches to go head-to-head in the league, it actually wasn't the first instance in which brothers coached against each other.

Toward the end of the 1927–28 campaign, Bruins coach and general manager Art Ross became ill and had to take some time away from the club. Defenceman Sprague Cleghorn, who had earned a reputation as one of the dirtiest players in the league, was tapped to take on the additional coaching duties in Ross's absence. On February 21, 1928, Cleghorn and the Bruins took on the Pittsburgh Pirates, who were coached by younger brother, Odie. Sprague got the better of his younger sibling as Boston shut out the Pirates 2–0. Ross eventually returned to close out the season, and the Bruins went on to face the Rangers, led by second-year coach Lester Patrick, in the playoffs. New York defeated Boston and advanced to the Stanley Cup Final where it overcame the Montreal Maroons to secure its first championship in franchise history. Patrick brought another title back to the Blueshirts in 1933 before he took on his brother more than a year later. In that brotherly matchup between the Rangers and Bruins in December 1934, it just so happened that New York's first goal was scored by Bun Cook with an assist from his older brother, Bill. The Blueshirts added another in the third to give Lester a victory over Frank.

DECEMBER 17
A PAIR OF GRETZKY MILESTONES, 1983 AND 1986

Heading into a game against the Quebec Nordiques on December 17, 1983, Wayne Gretzky was working on a record-setting 32-game point streak. He'd already surpassed Guy Lafleur's league benchmark of 28 the previous season when he made it to 30 games, but now the Edmonton Oiler wanted to see how far he could push it. At just over the halfway mark of the first period, Gretzky set up Willy Lindström to tie the game at one goal apiece. The assist not only kept Gretzky's streak going but also gave him his 500th career NHL assist and 800th career point in just his 352nd career game. Let those numbers sink in for a moment. Gretzky needed just 352 games to collect 800 points. That's a pace of more than two points per game. But Gretzky's night wasn't over yet. He picked up another assist two minutes later and then got three more helpers and added a goal in the third period to finish with six points in an 8–1 rout of the Nordiques.

The six-point performance pushed Gretzky's consecutive point streak to 33 games, three more than the previous season, but the end proved to be nowhere in sight. Gretzky's streak was finally halted at 51 games on January 28, 1984, when he failed to register a point in a 4–2 loss to the Los Angeles Kings. Over the course of that run, he scored 61 goals and racked up 153 points. Even if he'd stopped playing that campaign after those 51 games, he still would have finished with one of the best single-season performances in NHL history. Other than Gretzky, only Mario Lemieux and Steve Yzerman ever finished a regular season with more than 153 points. Exactly three years later, Gretzky scored four goals for the eighth time in his career in another victory over the Nordiques. The four goals gave Gretzky his 41st hat trick, already an NHL record at the time. Over the rest of his illustrious career, Gretzky added nine more hat tricks to finish with 50 games with three or more goals, a mark that will likely stand the test of time.

DECEMBER 18
MATS SUNDIN SIGNS WITH CANUCKS, 2008

The Toronto Maple Leafs were on pace to miss the playoffs for the third straight year, but Mats Sundin refused to waive his no-trade clause in advance of the 2008 deadline to be dealt to a club bound for the post-season. The 37-year-old Swede, who had been with Toronto since he was acquired in a blockbuster deal with the Quebec Nordiques in 1994, felt that to fully appreciate winning a Stanley Cup, you had to be with a team for the entire year. While Sundin was one of the greatest players in franchise history, he was on an expiring contract, and many fans hoped he'd accept a trade, if only so they could get some assets for their captain, who appeared to be playing his final campaign in Toronto. After the season, as free agency approached, the Leafs gave the Montreal Canadiens permission to talk with Sundin. But no deal materialized, and on July 1, 2008, Sundin, the highest-scoring Swedish player in NHL history, officially became an unrestricted free agent.

While Sundin received a number of enticing offers from teams that included the Vancouver Canucks, New York Rangers, Canadiens, and even the Leafs, he still hadn't made a decision by late summer. As the regular season approached, he continued to train, but when he still hadn't signed by the start of the campaign, he returned home to Sweden while he contemplated his future in the NHL. Finally, after months of speculation and rumours tying him to teams from the Anaheim Ducks to the Ottawa Senators, Sundin signed a one-year contract with the Canucks on December 18, 2008. When the deal was announced, he was still back home in Sweden for Christmas and was expected to join the club after the holidays. Sundin made his debut with Vancouver on January 7, 2009, against the Edmonton Oilers, his first NHL game in more than nine months. He finished the season with nine goals and 28 points in 41 games and then hung up his skates. At the time of his retirement, Sundin had the 25th most points in NHL history with 1,349.

DECEMBER 19
HARRY LUMLEY MAKES NHL DEBUT, 1943

The Detroit Red Wings were about to embark on a three-game road trip, but there was one problem. Their starting goaltender, Normie Smith, was unwilling to travel for out-of-town games because of his commitment to his job at Ford Motor Company in Detroit. Smith had tended goal for the Red Wings in back-to-back championships in 1936 and 1937, but early in the 1938–39 campaign, he missed the team train from New York to Montreal and was suspended indefinitely by coach and general manager Jack Adams. When Adams tried to send Smith to the club's International-American Hockey League (renamed the AHL in 1940) affiliate in Pittsburgh, the goaltender refused to report, stating he wasn't going to take away someone's job in the minors. Instead, he abruptly announced he was hanging up his goalie pads and began working at Ford full-time. While Adams was able to coax him out of retirement five years later, Smith still refused to accompany the team on road trips because of his job.

So when the Red Wings took on the New York Rangers on December 19, 1943, 17-year-old Harry Lumley, who was starting his first pro season in the AHL with the Indianapolis Capitals, made the start. Despite allowing six goals in a 6–2 loss to New York, Lumley had made NHL history by becoming the youngest goaltender to appear in the league, a record that still stands. Less than a week after his historic debut, Lumley actually found himself facing off against his own team. During a home game against the Rangers on December 23, New York goaltender Kevin McCauley stopped a puck with his face and didn't return for the third period. Detroit loaned Lumley to the Rangers, and he stopped all 10 shots he faced in the final frame, the last time he suited up for an NHL game that season. Following his brief indoctrination to the league, Lumley eventually returned and led the Red Wings to a Stanley Cup in 1950 before finishing his career in Chicago, Toronto, where he won the Vezina Trophy in 1954, and Boston.

DECEMBER 20
KINGS MOUNT LATE THIRD-PERIOD COMEBACK AGAINST OILERS, 1986

"A rather bizarre evening, wasn't it?" is how the Los Angeles Kings' head coach explained it when he spoke with reporters following the club's game against the Edmonton Oilers on December 20, 1986. Edmonton's Wayne Gretzky put it another way: "We were trying to get the ninth goal and gave up the fifth, sixth, seventh, and eighth instead." With less than 10 minutes in regulation time, the Oilers were sitting on a 8–4 lead, poised to collect their seventh straight victory. Although the Kings had jumped out to a 2–1 advantage early in the game, they squandered their lead, giving up four goals to Edmonton in the first period. Marcel Dionne closed the gap to one in the second stanza, but after the Oilers scored two more and added another early in the final frame, it appeared as though the game was out of reach for the Kings.

But just over the halfway mark in the third, Bernie Nicholls scored to make it 8–5. Four minutes later, Morris Lukowich, who had already picked up an assist in the first period, scored to cut the lead to two. While time wasn't on their side, the Kings hoped to force overtime. Just 44 seconds after Lukowich's goal, Dionne scored his second of the night, and suddenly they were within one with plenty of time still on the clock. As the third period drew to a close, the Kings pulled goaltender Darren Eliot for the extra attacker. With 34 seconds remaining in the game, Nicholls, who initiated the comeback earlier in the frame, put the puck past Grant Fuhr in a goalmouth scrum to knot it at 8–8, capping off a late third-period rally of four straight goals. Although overtime solved nothing and the game ended in a tie, it felt like a victory for Los Angeles, which had been pretty much down and out. Following the game, rookie Luc Robitaille, who thought the Oilers were mocking them earlier in the game, felt as if the Kings got the last laugh. "Now we're laughing," he said.

DECEMBER 21

MIKE SULLIVAN PICKS UP FIRST VICTORY WITH PENGUINS, 2015

The last time the Pittsburgh Penguins promoted their AHL coach in the middle of the season, they went on to win the Stanley Cup. In 2009, with 25 games remaining in the regular season, Dan Bylsma replaced head coach Michel Therrien and went on to guide the team to its first title in nearly two decades. That thought probably hadn't crossed general manager Jim Rutherford's mind when he fired Mike Johnston on December 12, 2015, and named AHL bench boss Mike Sullivan as his replacement; he just needed to make a coaching change. Pittsburgh had struggled out of the gate and was sitting outside a playoff spot. Meanwhile, in Wilkes-Barre/Scranton, Sullivan and the "Baby Penguins," as they are affectionately known, began the season with a sterling 18–5–0 record.

Although Sullivan had a number of stints as an assistant coach throughout the league before joining Wilkes-Barre/Scranton in 2015, it was his first head-coaching gig in the NHL since 2006. In 2003, not long after hanging up his skates as a player, Sullivan was named head coach of the Boston Bruins. But after two seasons behind the bench in Boston, Sullivan was dismissed when the club failed to qualify for the playoffs in 2006, then spent nearly the next decade working in an assistant capacity. While Rutherford hoped Sullivan's red-hot start in the AHL would rub off on the Penguins, it took some time to get his first win under his belt. After losing his first four games, Sullivan got his first victory with Pittsburgh on December 21, 2015, when it defeated the Columbus Blue Jackets 5–2. Under Sullivan's leadership, the Penguins went 33–16–5, which included 12 victories in March, and entered the post-season as a favourite to win the Stanley Cup. Two months later, after knocking off the San Jose Sharks in six games in the final, Sullivan hoisted Lord Stanley's mug, becoming just the sixth head coach in NHL history to win the trophy after being hired mid-season.

DECEMBER 22
BRETT HULL SCORES 500, 1996

Christmas came early for Brett Hull. On December 19, 1996, the St. Louis Blues fired head coach and general manager Mike Keenan. Ever since Keenan had joined St. Louis in 1994 following his tumultuous and abrupt departure from the New York Rangers, he had clashed with the Blues' superstar sniper. Early in his first full season behind the bench in St. Louis, Keenan stripped Hull of the captaincy, and over the next year, the two continued to outwardly despise each other. While there were rumours that Keenan was going to put the *C* back on Hull's sweater, he never got the chance. The feud finally came to an end when the Blues sent Keenan packing just before the holiday break. A few days later, when the Blues hosted the Los Angeles Kings on December 22, Hull received another gift, well, technically three.

With 19 seconds remaining in the first period, Hull fired a shot from the slot to record his first goal since December 8, giving the Blues a 2–1 lead. Early in the middle stanza, he scored again. Although the Kings scored a pair of quick goals to tie the game just before the midway point of the second period, St. Louis added two more and went into the final frame with a 5–3 lead. After Hull assisted on Stéphane Matteau's goal just 20 seconds into the third, he completed the hat trick, his 26th career three-goal performance, just over 10 minutes into the frame to reach the 500-goal mark. Hull became the 24th player in league history to accomplish that feat, but it also gave him and his father, Bobby, who had scored 610 career goals, a unique distinction. They became the first father-son duo to each score 500 or more goals in the NHL. Although Bobby wasn't able to attend that night, it was a special moment for Brett, who was elated to notch the milestone in front of the Blues' fans. While Hull registered 12 goals under Keenan to start the season, he scored 30 more under interim coach Jimmy Roberts to finish the campaign with 42.

DECEMBER 23
ISLANDERS MIX IT UP IN SANTA BRAWL, 2003

t seemed like a good idea at the time. In the spirit of the season, the New York Islanders ran a promotion for the team's last game before the holiday break. Anyone who showed up at Nassau Coliseum on December 23, 2003, dressed like Santa Claus would be admitted free for the matchup against the Philadelphia Flyers. The team had been struggling to fill the stands and hoped the festive promotion would put more butts in seats. While the Islanders expected the initiative might draw 250 people, it reportedly attracted upward of 1,000 Santa Clauses. During the first intermission, the Santas were invited onto the ice to participate in a parade. The club had only budgeted a few minutes for the activity, but with so many more Santa-clad Islanders fans in attendance than anticipated, things didn't go according to plan. At some point during the procession, a few of the Santas ripped open their jackets to reveal they were actually wearing rival New York Rangers jerseys, much to the chagrin of the Long Island crowd.

The Islanders Santas, however, quickly sprang into action. After one of the interlopers sporting a white Lady Liberty jersey that the Rangers debuted in the 1998–99 season was decked into the glass, they set their sights on another Rangers fan sporting a Pavel Bure sweater and taunting the Islanders faithful. When he, too, was knocked into the boards and then pushed onto the ice, he tried to remove the offending tunic to ward off his Christmas attackers, but they were relentless. As he was mobbed, they tried to seize his jersey. Even a youngster dressed in a tiny Santa suit joined the fracas and attempted to remove the trespasser's sweater. It was only after an official intervened that the helpless Rangers fan was able to take off his jersey and safely leave the ice. There were probably more penalties in the Santa brawl than in the game, since there were only three infractions called, all in the third period, as the Islanders defeated the Flyers 4–2. Needless to say, that was the last time the Islanders offered that holiday promotion.

DECEMBER 24
JOHNNY BOWER RECORDS 30TH CAREER SHUTOUT, 1966

After missing the last three games with a shoulder injury, Johnny Bower returned to the net on December 24, 1966, when the Toronto Maple Leafs hosted the Boston Bruins. The 42-year-old goaltender, who had been sharing the crease that year with Terry Sawchuk and Bruce Gamble, turned in his best effort so far that season. After captain George Armstrong got Toronto on the board more than halfway through the second period, Bower did the rest. He turned aside all 29 shots he faced that evening to record his first shutout of the campaign, and the 30th of his NHL career, as the Leafs picked up a 3–0 victory over Boston. When the club took on the Bruins again the next day in a Christmas rematch at Boston Garden, Bower got the nod once more. In another sterling performance, he made 35 saves in a 4–2 win.

But no holiday story about Johnny Bower would be complete without mentioning "Honky the Christmas Goose." Two years earlier, the Leafs were approached by Chip Young, a CBC producer hoping to enlist one of the club's players to sing vocals on a Christmas song he was putting together for a forthcoming album. Bower, who revelled in dressing up as Santa Claus at the team's Christmas parties, seemed the perfect fit. With all proceeds going to charity, Bower was in. And so, in November 1964, he and his son, John Jr., who was brought in to sing backup vocals with a chorus of youngsters, recorded a song about a plump goose named Honky who could no longer fly but managed to save Christmas by helping Santa navigate the skies by honking from the sleigh. Bower could actually carry a tune, and the song quickly became a holiday classic in Canada. According to Dan Robson, author of *Bower: A Legendary Life*, the record sold 21,000 copies in its first week of release and went on to sell upward of 40,000 units that holiday season, making it the best-selling Canadian record ever at the time. It even hit number 29 on the CHUM Radio charts in Toronto.

SETH MARTIN GETS FIRST AND ONLY CAREER SHUTOUT, 1967

O ver the years, Seth Martin had received a number of offers to play in the NHL, but he kept turning them down. While Martin was widely regarded as the top amateur goaltender in the world, hockey remained a secondary consideration for him. He was happy with his family in Trail, British Columbia, where he worked as a firefighter for a smelter, and wasn't interested in giving that up for a life in the big league. In 1953, Martin started backstopping the Trail Smoke Eaters of the Western International Hockey League (WIHL) and quickly established himself as one of the league's best goaltenders. In 1961, when the Smoke Eaters were selected to represent Canada at the World Championships, Martin led the Canadians to gold. As Martin continued to make a name for himself in the WIHL, winning the Allan Cup, the championship for Canada's top senior amateur team, with Trail in 1962, he was invited to join the country's burgeoning national development program in 1964, representing Canada at the Winter Olympics that year in Innsbruck, Austria. Martin returned to the World Championships again in 1966 and 1967, where he cemented his strong reputation among his European counterparts.

Although Martin had previously spurned offers from the NHL, in June 1967, he agreed to join the expansion St. Louis Blues and was between the pipes for the club's first-ever regular season game, a 2–2 tie against the Minnesota North Stars. Later that campaign, on Christmas Day, Martin stopped all 23 shots he faced in a 1–0 victory against the North Stars to record his first and only NHL shutout. Despite forming a solid tandem with Glenn Hall that year, Martin left the NHL at the end of the season to return home, where he continued playing in the WIHL. Years later, before the Summit Series began, a Russian official reportedly asked Montreal sportswriter Red Fisher if Canada's goaltender, Ken Dryden, was as good as Seth Martin, a testament to the impact the Trail netminder had made internationally.

DECEMBER 26
MAPLE LEAFS BLOWN OUT ON BOXING DAY, 1991

Following a lopsided defeat at the hands of the Pittsburgh Penguins on December 26, 1991, Toronto Maple Leafs head coach Tom Watt tried to make sense of the loss when speaking with reporters. "All I could think of was Murphy's law," he said. "Everything that could go wrong did go wrong." But Watt had a better musing to describe his reaction to the rout. He explained that as he kept glancing up at the clock and wishing time would tick down faster, he was reminded of a line by Democrat Adlai Stevenson, former governor of Illinois. It's actually a quote attributed to Abraham Lincoln that Stevenson referenced in his concession speech when he lost the presidential race to Republican Dwight Eisenhower in 1952, but the sentiment is the same: "I'm too old to cry, but it hurts too much to laugh." I think that's a quote that resonates with a lot of Leaf fans of a certain vintage today, but certainly on that night, you didn't have to be a politician to understand what Watt was getting at.

After Pittsburgh's Joe Mullen scored the opening tally less than three minutes into the game, Toronto's Kevin Maguire quickly tied it up, but that proved to be the extent of their scoring that evening. It also happened to be the only goal Maguire scored that season and was his last in the NHL. The Penguins went on to score 11 unanswered goals to secure a 12–1 win, matching the team record for the largest margin of victory. Mullen, who finished the contest with four goals, also set a club record by becoming the first Pittsburgh player to record back-to-back four-goal games. The New York City native lit the lamp four times against the New York Islanders before the holiday break. Superstar captain Mario Lemieux managed two goals and five assists and between him, Mullen, and Kevin Stevens, the trio combined for 19 points against the Leafs. The only silver lining for Toronto fans was that Pittsburgh's output was still two goals fewer than the record-setting 14 Buffalo put past the club on March 19, 1981.

DEAN PRENTICE BREAKS BACK AND STILL MAKES PENALTY SHOT, 1964

E arly in the second period in a game between the Chicago Black Hawks and Boston Bruins on December 27, 1964, the latter's Dean Prentice broke into the Chicago end on a short-handed breakaway. But as Prentice approached the goal, he was tripped from behind by Stan Mikita and slammed into the boards. While still lying on the ice, Prentice was awarded a penalty shot. Although he was badly hurt, the veteran winger pulled himself up and took the shot. He moved in slowly on goaltender Denis DeJordy and beat him to tie the game 2–2. Prentice returned to the bench but was forced to leave the game and was taken to a hospital in Chicago. Initial X-rays reportedly revealed bruising but no broken bones, so Prentice returned home with the team. Once back in Boston, Prentice underwent further examination, and new X-rays revealed he had a compression of vertebrae in his lower back. Prentice was ordered to stay in bed for a week and then undergo additional testing.

After missing the club's first three games to start the new year, it was learned that Prentice had actually suffered hairline fractures to two of the vertebrae in his lower back, which meant that when he took that penalty shot against the Black Hawks, he did it with a broken back. Prentice missed the rest of the season and was in a body cast for months while he recovered from the injury. Although it was unclear if he'd return to the ice, by the summer, he was out of the cast and working in a brewery warehouse. He told the *Boston Globe*'s Tom Fitzgerald that he'd spent two months hauling kegs and cases of beer and felt better than ever. In his first game back, Prentice picked up an assist in a 6–2 loss to the Black Hawks. That season he recorded seven goals and 29 points in 50 games with the Bruins before he was traded to the Detroit Red Wings on February 16, 1966. In the playoffs, Prentice scored the game-winning goal to eliminate Chicago and punch Detroit's ticket to the Stanley Cup Final.

DECEMBER 28
MAURICE RICHARD'S EIGHT-POINT NIGHT, 1944

Moving sucks. No one willingly wants to carry a refrigerator up a flight of stairs or lug a couch down a hallway. By the end of the day, your body is probably aching, and even once you've gotten through the big stuff, you probably still have dozens of boxes to unpack. When it's all over, I couldn't imagine going into the office, but that's exactly what Maurice Richard did on December 28, 1944. Before the Montreal Canadiens hosted the Detroit Red Wings at the Forum, the fiery winger spent the day moving his family to a new home in Montreal. Although Richard was exhausted after hauling furniture all afternoon, he didn't want to let his teammates down, so he suited up for the game that evening. While Richard had doubts about how well he'd play under the circumstances, he turned in a performance for the ages. Just over a minute after the opening faceoff, Richard scored his 20th goal of the season to give the Canadiens an early lead. He racked up four more goals and added three assists to finish the matchup with eight points, establishing a new NHL record for most points in a game.

Richard's feat has become legendary. It has even been immortalized in a *Heritage Minute*, which depicts a tired Richard dragging a sofa up a staircase. It makes for a great yarn, but it didn't unfold the way we'd like to think. Not long ago, Dave Stubbs, a columnist for NHL.com, stumbled upon comments Richard made to the French-language newspaper *La Presse* nearly 15 years after that fabled night. In his remarks to columnist Gerald Champagne, Richard divulged that he actually made the move across town the day before the game and not the day of. The discovery doesn't diminish Richard's achievement in any way, since five goals and eight points in a game is still an incredible feat no matter what he did that day. And at least now you don't have to feel bad if, after your move, all you did was crack open a cold beer in a room surrounded by boxes.

DECEMBER 29
LEFTY WILSON SUBS FOR
DON SIMMONS, 1957

Not long into a game against the Detroit Red Wings on December 29, 1957, Boston Bruins goaltender Don Simmons dislocated his shoulder in a scrum. The game was tied 1–1 and there was still more than two full periods to play. But with no Boston substitute available, 38-year-old Ross "Lefty" Wilson, Detroit's assistant trainer and practice goalie, suited up and entered the crease for the Bruins. Wilson had tended the twine for the Red Wings' AHL affiliate, the Indianapolis Capitals, for a few seasons, but hung up his goalie pads in 1950 and joined the big club as a trainer. Although Wilson gave up a goal late in the first period to Jack McIntyre, he stopped everything else that came his way. After Boston's Bronco Horvath knotted up the game at two goals apiece in the middle frame, there were no more goals scored that evening. Wilson was credited with 23 saves and earned the tie.

While it was the most Wilson had ever played in the NHL, it wasn't his first appearance in the league. A few years earlier, in a matchup against the Montreal Canadiens, Detroit goaltender Terry Sawchuk left the game in the third period after he cut his right knee following a collision with Maurice Richard. Although it was reported that Claude Evans, one of Montreal's minor-league goaltenders, was supposed to replace Sawchuk, it was actually Wilson who took up the position between the pipes, making his first big-league appearance. Wilson faced no shots in the final 16 minutes of regulation time and Detroit lost 4–1. Two years later, on January 22, 1956, when the Red Wings hosted the Toronto Maple Leafs, Wilson took over for Harry Lumley, who was then with Toronto, after he pulled a muscle in his thigh in the final frame. Wilson was perfect in relief, stopping all nine shots he faced as the Red Wings closed out the game with a 4–1 victory. Although Wilson had never played beyond the minor professional ranks, he still made three appearances for three different teams in the NHL.

DECEMBER 30
FRANK UDVARI PUTS ON STRIPES AGAIN, 1978

With time winding down in the first period in a game between the Atlanta Flames and New York Islanders on December 30, 1978, referee Dave Newell was struck by a puck and collapsed to the ice. He suffered a fractured jaw and was unable to continue officiating the rest of the match. Usually when a starting referee is incapacitated, one of the linesmen takes over refereeing duties for the rest of the game, but it just so happened that there was as a Hall of Fame referee in the stands willing to take his place. Frank Udvari, the supervisor of the NHL's officials, was watching from the press box. Although it had been more than a decade since he officiated his last game and was turning 55 years old in a few days, he rushed down to the officials' room to take his injured referee's place. Udvari began officiating in the AHL in 1951 and then made the jump to the big league in the 1951–52 campaign. During the course of his NHL career, Udvari officiated 718 regular-season games, including the contest that led to Maurice Richard's infamous suspension, along with 70 games in the playoffs, including 11 straight Stanley Cup Final matchups.

While Newell was taken to the Nassau County Medical Center of Long Island, Udvari quickly changed to get onto the ice. Although he kept on his grey slacks from the suit he wore to the game, he donned Newell's striped jersey and borrowed a pair of skates from Islanders star Bryan Trottier. Udvari finished the game, issuing nine penalties in a 4–2 victory for New York and even disallowed an apparent goal by Trottier while laced up in an extra pair of the centre's skates. Udvari performed admirably as Newell's replacement but wasn't tempted to make a comeback. It was his final NHL appearance on the ice, though he stayed on as the league's supervisor of officials until 1983. Meanwhile, Newell recovered from his injury and continued refereeing in the league until hanging up his stripes in 1990.

DECEMBER 31
MARIO LEMIEUX'S NEW YEAR'S EVE MILESTONES

New Year's Eve is probably the most overrated day of the year. I won't lie, when I was younger, I used to look forward to it, but I think as you get older you realize it's just another day. Sure, it's fun to get together with friends and family and ring in the New Year, but it's certainly not the magical evening some people make it out to be and hardly anything special happens. But try telling that to Mario Lemieux. Some of his most memorable NHL performances happened in games on New Year's Eve. During his second season with the Pittsburgh Penguins, Lemieux went into the club's final game of 1985 feeling under the weather. David Fink of the *Pittsburgh Post-Gazette* reported that the burgeoning superstar was still recovering from a three-day cold and felt drowsy from the medication he'd been taking. Well, he certainly didn't show any symptoms on the ice. Lemieux picked up four goals and added two assists to finish with six points, a new career high, in an 8–4 victory over the St. Louis Blues.

Exactly three years later in a New Year's Eve matchup against the New Jersey Devils, Lemieux turned in what is perhaps the single greatest individual effort in NHL history. The Penguins superstar scored five goals, five different ways, against New Jersey. He scored at even strength, short-handed, on a power play, on a penalty shot, and finally, into an empty net. It was simply an incredible performance. Oh, and he also added three assists to finish with eight points, matching his career high for most points in a game. Although there was no topping that New Year's Eve show, four years later, Lemieux recorded a goal and an assist in a game against the Toronto Maple Leafs to give him 101 points in just 38 games that season, marking just the fourth time in league history that a player reached the 100-point mark in fewer than 40 games. Wayne Gretzky did it twice and Lemieux had already accomplished the feat three years earlier in 1988–89 when he reached the plateau in 36 contests.

ASSISTS

P utting a book together is a lot like playing hockey: you need to have a good team if you're going to be successful. A stick tap to Dundurn for having me back again. Thanks to Scott Fraser, Kathryn Lane, and Elena Radic for getting us back on the ice for *Hockey 365, The Second Period.*

Perhaps even more important than a good goalie is a good editor, so thank you to Michael Carroll for getting the most out of my words.

Chances are you picked up this book not because of me but because Ron Beltrame did such a fantastic job on the cover art. Thanks again, Ron.

While I was able to put together most of *Hockey 365* from primary and secondary sources, I was fortunate enough to get some of the people involved in these stories to share their time with me. Thanks to Craig Simpson, Martin Biron, Sarah Ayres, Dylan Ferguson, and Paul Bissonnette for reflecting on some of these moments with me.

Hockey 365 is meant to be a fun read, but I took great care to make sure I got my facts straight. Sometimes that involved bugging people like Wyatt Arndt and Rob Taub to confirm Vancouver Canucks and New York Islanders facts respectively. I also leaned on the Society of International Hockey Research for some fact-checking. They're a great organization and well worth the annual fee to become a member. Thanks in particular to Bob Duff from that group for taking some additional time to answer some of my questions. That being said, any errors I made are mine exclusively.

If you've been following my writing for the Los Angeles Kings over the past few seasons, you'll recognize some of these yarns. Thanks to Robyn Dutton for letting me rework some of the stories I wrote for her and the team to include in this book.

A special thanks to Ashley Craig and Waubgeshig Rice for reviewing some earlier drafts of a few of the stories. I appreciated the insightful feedback they graciously provided.

As always, my mom, Patti, saw most of the Toronto Maple Leafs and Doug Gilmour stories in advance. She's my longest-tenured editor, and I know she wouldn't have it any other way. Thanks to my dad, Tony, for taking a stroll down memory lane and providing details about what he remembers from the 1972 Summit Series. And, of course, thanks to both of them for their continued unwavering support and encouragement.

Thanks to my in-laws, Sue and Moe, but particularly my father-in-law for providing some of the material for these stories, even if he wasn't aware of it at the time.

To my sister Kyleigh, brother-in-law Sam, and nephew Wesley, along with my brother-in-law André, sister-in-law Ashley, and nephew Leo. You guys have what they call "intangibles" in hockey. You didn't necessarily help directly with the development of the book, but you're part of my team, and through your actions and support, you make the final product on the ice that much better.

Finally, to my wife, Chantal, and my girls, Zoe and Sophia — I'm the luckiest husband and father to have you all on my team. You make every day brighter. Zoe, this is your second *Hockey 365*, and I can't help but smile while I think about you reading Papa's books to Sophia. Chants, we did it! Once again, I literally couldn't have done it without you, so thank you for being so understanding and supportive of me throughout this process. And unlike the last book, I managed to write most of this during normal hours, so at least you didn't have to go to bed alone every night. I love you.

And last but not least, you. Yes, you, the reader. Thank you for spending your precious time reading my words and looking back on some of the game's greatest moments.

ABOUT THE AUTHOR

Mike Commito is the director of applied research and innovation at Cambrian College. Not long after completing his Ph.D. in history from McMaster University in 2015, Mike started writing about hockey history for places that included VICE Sports and Sportsnet. In 2018, he earned the Paul Kitchen Award from the Society for International Hockey Research, which recognizes the best hockey history research project of that year, for his Sportsnet article about the 1954 Kenora Thistles. In 2018, he published his first book, *Hockey 365: Daily Stories from the Ice*. That same year, he became the team historian for the Sudbury Wolves of the Ontario Hockey League and began contributing regularly to the LA Kings' website. Mike lives in Sudbury, Ontario, with his wife, Chantal, and two daughters, Zoe and Sophia.